THE LISTENER'S
HISTORY OF
MUSIC

BY
PERCY A. SCHOLES

LONDON
OXFORD UNIVERSITY PRESS
NEW YORK   TORONTO

Oxford University Press, Ely House, London W. 1

GLASGOW   NEW YORK   TORONTO   MELBOURNE   WELLINGTON
CAPE TOWN   IBADAN   NAIROBI   DAR ES SALAAM   LUSAKA   ADDIS ABABA
DELHI   BOMBAY   CALCUTTA   MADRAS   KARACHI   LAHORE   DACCA
KUALA LUMPUR   SINGAPORE   HONG KONG   TOKYO

ISBN. 0 19 316106 0

PRINTED IN GREAT BRITAIN

NOTE

THIS Complete Edition of *The Listener's History of Music* comprises the three volumes as follows:

    I. TO BEETHOVEN.

    II. THE ROMANTIC AND NATIONALIST SCHOOLS OF THE NINETEENTH CENTURY.

    III. TO THE COMPOSERS OF TO-DAY.

THE LISTENER'S
HISTORY OF MUSIC

VOLUME I. TO BEETHOVEN

BEETHOVEN

After the drawing by Louis Letronne

The Listener's History of Music

A BOOK FOR ANY CONCERT-GOER
GRAMOPHONIST OR RADIO LISTENER
PROVIDING ALSO A COURSE OF STUDY FOR
ADULT CLASSES IN
THE APPRECIATION OF MUSIC

by

PERCY A. SCHOLES

With incidental comments by
SIR W. HENRY HADOW · SIR RICHARD R. TERRY
DR. ERNEST WALKER · EDWIN EVANS

———————

IN THREE VOLUMES

Volume I. To Beethoven

SEVENTH EDITION

LONDON
OXFORD UNIVERSITY PRESS
NEW YORK   TORONTO

Oxford University Press, Ely House, London W. 1

GLASGOW NEW YORK TORONTO MELBOURNE WELLINGTON
CAPE TOWN IBADAN NAIROBI DAR ES SALAAM LUSAKA ADDIS ABABA
DELHI BOMBAY CALCUTTA MADRAS KARACHI LAHORE DACCA
KUALA LUMPUR SINGAPORE HONG KONG TOKYO

First Edition 1923
Second Edition 1925
Third Edition 1929
Fourth Edition 1933
Fifth Edition 1941
Sixth Edition 1943
Seventh Edition 1954
Reprinted 1956, 1960, 1963,
1967, and 1974

Printed in Great Britain
at the University Press, Oxford
by Vivian Ridler
Printer to the University

THE AUTHOR'S INTRODUCTION

SOME time ago I wrote a little book called *The Listener's Guide to Music*. It surprised me by running through four large editions in its first three years (and many others since then), so that I am led to suppose that it is looked upon as being of some service to the people for whom it was written—those who love music, but 'do not know much about it'.

Yet that book is in one way incomplete. Whilst it tells what a Symphony is like, a Sonata, a Fugue, a Nocturne, or a March, it does not tell how these things came into being. And whilst it tells what are the instruments of the modern Orchestra, and gives pictures of them so that they may be recognized, it does not tell where the modern Orchestra and modern Orchestration came from. To be sure there is one chapter on the evolution of music. It comes at the end of the book and is called 'The Chain of Composers'. But this chapter is necessarily short, and, indeed, it is in but a mere eight pages that it brings its reader down from far-away Palestrina to the music of to-day.

Of these eight pages this present volume and those which follow it are an expansion. These three volumes attempt to tell the story of the development of music from the sixteenth century to the twentieth, and to tell it simply. They do not go behind the sixteenth century, because the man for whom they are written has, in the ordinary way of his musical life, little chance of hearing anything earlier than the work of sixteenth-century writers. Indeed, apart from Folk-Song and Plainsong, we may consider the sixteenth century, for practical purposes, as the beginning of Music, as the ordinary music-lover understands the word, and the whole idea of the book is to enable this untrained music-lover to understand *the music that he is accustomed to hear*. There is nothing 'antiquarian' anywhere in the book, since it is based entirely upon such types of music as we of to-day actually enjoy in Concerts and Recitals, or at Church, or at home from our Gramophones or Pianos, and such as we ourselves sing or play if we are ourselves singers or players. (Opera, I may say in parentheses, is largely left over for treatment in the second volume.)

This book is, then, an attempt to 'tidy-up' the mind of the music-lover. He hears Holst's *Planets*, a Fugue of Bach, a Sonata of Beethoven, Stravinsky's *Rite of Spring*, an Elizabethan Madrigal, and a Vaughan Williams symphony. He recognizes that in these pieces are represented different periods, different schools, different ideals, different styles and the expression of different personalities, and as he reads this book I hope to show him how those periods succeeded one another, how those schools and styles grew out of one another, how those varying personalities expressed themselves in varied types of music, and influenced one another. This, I hope, is a contribution to 'Appreciation', which without an historical background can hardly be complete.

The present volume brings the subject down to Beethoven, and the succeeding ones carry it from Beethoven to our own day. After study of the three volumes the reader's view of the subject will necessarily be rather 'sketchy', but most people find it best to make a rough sketch before they attempt a finished picture, and having made your outline sketch by reading me, you may, with my blessing, go on to read writers who will help you to fill in the abundant detail.

The main part of each volume is that in larger type. The thought of this runs on continuously, showing, under a division into periods, the evolution out of lesser things of ever bigger (and often greater) ones. Interpolated are notices in smaller type of LEADING COMPOSERS OF THE PERIOD. Under this heading short notices are given of the lives and work of typical composers of each of the periods discussed.

During the general reading of the book these notices should be at least skimmed, if only as offering incidental views of the musical life and conditions of each period. This done, the notes concerning any particular composer may be read with greater attention at the time when any of his works are to be actually heard or performed. Partly, then, these notes are given for reading and partly for reference.

In considering this book I suggest that the main criterion is not what is put in but what is left out. Have I left out enough to make easy reading for the reader I have in mind ? Have I left out the right things ? Have I, after all my omissions, presented in what remains a simple, connected generalization of the subject ? I hope I have! The United States Government has, I am told, issued a work of about 135 volumes, each of 1,000 pages, upon the Civil War, a subject which H. G. Wells in his *History of the World* treated in thirteen lines. Necessarily mine is more like the method of Mr. Wells, and in another matter I have followed him:

I have submitted my generalization to the close scrutiny of several authorities upon the subject in its various branches, and have, where it seemed desirable, by means of footnotes or appendixes, given and commented upon their remarks. The initials attached will be readily recognized as those of Sir W. Henry Hadow, late Vice-Chancellor of Sheffield University, editor of the Oxford History of Music, and author of its volume upon *The Viennese Period*; Sir Richard R. Terry, long our recognized leading authority upon Modes, Plainsong, the Sacred Choral Music of the fifteenth and sixteenth centuries, and cognate subjects; and Dr. Ernest Walker, of Balliol College, author of *A History of Music in England* and of an admirable little critical volume on Beethoven, and a very close student of the development of Piano Music and Chamber Music. I am greatly indebted to these gentlemen, both for their general approval and their suggestions, as also to Mr. W. R. Anderson for his very careful general reading of the proofs.   I have to thank Messrs. Augener, Ltd., for permission to use their edition (No. 8006ᵃ) of Beethoven's Fifth Symphony; Messrs. J. & W. Chester, Ltd., 11 Great Marlborough Street, London, W.1, for permission to quote from their edition of Purcell's Harpsichord Music; Messrs. Maurice Piéna and Messrs. Litolff, for permission to use their edition of Mozart's Overture to *Figaro*.   The late Mr. Cecil J. Sharp kindly gave me permission to quote from his collections of Folk-Songs and Folk-Dances.   Further, I am under obligation to Mr. Frederick Page, of the Oxford University Press, for much general assistance.

NOTE

The other volumes of the *Listener's History* are published as follows:

Vol. II.   The Romantic and Nationalist Schools of the Nineteenth Century.

Vol. III.   To the Composers of To-day.

CONTENTS

PERIOD II—TO BACH AND HANDEL

PERIOD III—TO BEETHOVEN

Contents

LIST OF ILLUSTRATIONS

PERIOD I

To Byrd and Palestrina

I

THE BASIS OF THE ART

THERE are two musical races in the world—the birds and the humans. The humans are the more musical—they sing all the year round. Love is one great impulse behind music, witness the nightingale in June and Schumann's hundred songs in the year of his marriage. If you want to know what else lies behind it read Herbert Spencer, Jules Combarieu and the philosophers and psychologists generally, and then compare their guesses with any of your own.

Most birds are but simple-minded musicians, having nothing but 'folk-songs', handed down from father to son, in some cases varied a little with the season, but passing from generation to generation little changed or none. Man proudly boasts 'composers', actual professionals, but he has not had them long.

Melody, Harmony, Rhythm, Form

The birds have but melody; no 'feathered choir' yet produced 'the harmony of the grove' in any but the poets' sense. Man has harmony, but he has apparently only had it for a little over a thousand years. The bird's rhythmic sense is not always very acute, though it decidedly has one. Man's rhythmic sense is perhaps stronger than his melodic, so that marching short-trousered through the streets in youth he can take pleasure in a piece compounded of the mere tap of a drum.

The bird has little idea of 'form' in music, though in some cases it admits the principle underlying all form (variety plus repetition), alternating one tiny phrase, several times repeated, with another similarly repeated.[1] With man form early became a very important element in music.

Instruments

And with the idea of rhythm and form well developed in his subconsciousness man began to feel the need of other means of sound production than his own throat. So came 'instruments'—first, probably, purely rhythmic (the Drum), then melodic also (the Pipe and the Viol), and at last (when some of the possibilities of vocal combination had been discovered and shown him the way) harmonic also (the Lute, and the Keyboard instruments).

Ars longa

Then man began to take more notice of qualities of tone, or 'colours', produced by different kinds of strings and tubes, and various methods of using them, and gradually he developed the Piano and Organ, the String Quartet and the Orchestra. Meantime, as singers and players became more skilful, voices better trained and instruments more complex, and as the infinite varieties of rhythm, the principles of form, and the effects of harmonic combinations became better understood, pieces of music became longer and longer, until, from the mere repetition of a couple of contrasted strains, each but a few seconds in duration, man arrived at the production and performance of Symphonies lasting an hour apiece. The principles of the one music were the same as those of the other, as the constructional principles of a poultry-shed are the same as those of a Parthenon. But they were applied more elaborately.

The Limitations of the Human Mind

There is no essential mystery about the basis of melodic shape, or harmonic progression, or formal procedure in music.

[1] See Turnbull, *Bird Music* (Faber & Faber, 1943) ; Garstang, *Songs of the Birds* (Lane, 1922) ; Witchell, *The Evolution of Bird Song* (1896); Pratt, *The Lore of the Lyre Bird* (Robertson & Mullens, Melbourne, 1940). And refer to the gramophone companies' catalogues for relevant records.

That basis is psychological. Man needs work varied with play, tension varied with relaxation, rise varied with fall, discord varied with concord, 'quick movement' varied with 'slow movement', serious 'first subject' varied with lighter 'second subject'. It is all a matter of how much the human mind can bear without tiring. Jack must have neither 'all work and no play' nor 'all play and no work', neither all concord nor all discord, neither all quick nor all slow, neither all sad nor all jolly, neither all serious-minded nor all light-hearted. Vary things judiciously and he will accept any scheme of life or of art you choose to lay before him. He is not very particular so long as you allow for the limitations of his capacity. And the history of music is the history of the gradual better understanding of those limitations by the people who make music, and, perhaps (in some smaller measure), the very partial reduction of the limitations in the minds of those who hear it. We are growing up, both sets of us (composers and listeners); but we are perhaps still not fairly out of the schoolboy or flapper stage, and the finest music we hear to-day may conceivably seem but as child's play to the man of A.D. 3000, studying it in the British Museum. Yet the *principles* of that man's music must be the same as those of ours—unless the human mind completely alters.

An Apology for this Chapter

Perhaps all this is a queerish opening for a work of history. Apology for it takes two forms: (*a*) one must begin a book somehow; (*b*) this beginning, at all events, emphasizes a vital truth—*The study of the history of music is not the study of any arbitrary or conventional development, but of a gradual widening of the human understanding.*

But why begin with the birds? Because by so doing I have insinuated subtly into the reader's mind the idea of the essentially simple basis of the art. Music is just the gratification of a natural need. The character of the gratification has varied from age to age, and from composer to composer, yet has developed pretty logically on the whole. And the record of this logical development constitutes The History of Music.

But how would you have had me begin? Would you have thought better of me if I had opened with the gloomy but dignified periods of the staid, four-volumed Burney?

> 'It is with great, and almost hopeless diffidence, that I enter upon this part of my work; as I can hardly animate myself with the expectation of succeeding in enquiries which have foiled the most learned men of the two or three last centuries . . . . The music of the ancients, according to Euclid, Alypius, and Marteanus Capella was ...'

By beginning with the birds I have at least spared you Euclid!

II

THE BEGINNINGS OF MUSIC IN SONG AND DANCE

THE two primitive forms of musical expression are Song and Dance—music used as the medium for the emotional expression of thought, and music used as the foundation for emotional expression through bodily movement. The one is primarily Melodic, the other primarily Rhythmic. You can, if you wish, express emotional thought without any rigidly fixed rhythm at all, as here—

Mag - ní - fi - cat   á - ni - ma   mé - a   Dó - mi - num

Free Rhythms and Fixed Rhythms

There *is* rhythm in that—but it is prose rhythm, not poetic (i. e. metrical) rhythm. It is, roughly speaking, the kind of rhythm you find in—

Make a joyful noise unto the Lord, all ye lands,

not the kind you find in—

All people that on earth do dwell,
Sing to the Lord with cheerful voice.

Song music, of course, quickly tends to become metrically rhythmic, especially if it is taken up by large masses of people for corporate singing. But the rhythmic element is not so pronouncedly essential as the well-ordered rise and fall of the

8   Beginnings of Music in Song and Dance

voice.   In Dance, on the other hand, rhythm is almost every-thing.   In default of a better instrument you could dance to the note of a solo drum, but you would not like to sing, or be sung to, for a quarter of an hour on one note.   Look through Cecil Sharp's collection of folk-songs and you will find a good many with very free rhythms (rhythms still further varied, probably by the same singer on different occasions).

Look through his folk-dances and you will find them all four-square and clean-cut.

To put it fairly—the tendency of Song is to melodic beauty and melodic expression; the tendency of Dance to rhythmic vitality and rhythmic expression.

All Music derives from Song or Dance

Now the influences of Song and Dance, these two primitive means of musical expression, run through all music, even the most modern.   A Bach Suite is a development of the Dance, a Bach Fugue (as will shortly be seen) of the Song, a Beethoven Slow Movement of the Song, a Beethoven Scherzo of the Dance. The opening of Stravinsky's *Rite of Spring* is a development of the Song element—

In a page or two, however, Stravinsky plunges us into a development of Dance—

In much music the elements are to be found combined. They were actually combined in the primitive Carol and the Elizabethan 'Ballet', which were intended to be simultaneously sung and danced, and the combination of their influences is to be found in many a piece of symphonic music.

Amongst different nations (nations ethnologically differently predisposed, and subjected to different conditions of climate and of mode of life) different forms and flavours of Song evolve, and different styles of Dance.

The Harmonic Idea

So far all the music we are considering is Melodic or Rhythmic or a combination of the two. We have not, as yet in this chapter, taken any account of Harmonic Music. European music began to emerge from its purely Melodic-Rhythmic phase only about the year 600, and did not develop the Harmonic in any very artistic way until (say) 1400–1500. Adam and Eve's love-songs were Melodic, so were Antony and Cleopatra's. The troops of Julius Caesar marched to Rhythmic or Rhythmic-Melodic music. So, most likely, did those of William the Conqueror. The Psalms were sung in Solomon's Temple to pure Melody, and nobody ever thought of singing them in even the most rudimentary form of Harmony until almost the time of Charlemagne.

When the idea of Harmony did come into the world it grew out of the difficulties of the churchmen in singing the psalms and hymns of the church in unison, with a body of singers whose voices were of course neither all tenor nor all bass.

In this, apparently, a practical inconvenience at last began to receive attention. The first means of removing the inconvenience that suggested itself was the simplest and most obvious—the voices, divided according to natural range, chanted the Plainsong in parallel lines at two pitches (five notes apart). From this it is apparently a short stage (but in reality it proved a pretty long one) to the more sophisticated idea of leaving the Plainsong to one part (the 'Tenor' = holding part) and allowing the others to circle around it, weaving a polyphonic web of sound. A further stage abandoned the Plainsong altogether, and thus completely *original* harmonized music came into existence—free harmonic settings of the Canticles and the various parts of the Mass, substituted for the former traditional melodic settings. The process was carried over into secular music, and so came into existence the Madrigal. The Masses and Madrigals of

Palestrina in Italy, Byrd and others in England, and Victoria in Spain mark the climax of this period of unaccompanied *woven* choral music.

From the first glimmerings of the idea that a number of differently pitched voices, singing together in a choir, might be provided with different 'parts' to sing, suited to their different natural ranges of voice, to the culmination of the effort to provide for them a music that should be beautiful and expressive, we have a period of roughly one thousand years. Think of this period as running from 600 to 1600 and you will not be greatly out. Obviously an essential for the development of choral music was a practical notation. Unisonous Song could be handed down traditionally and taught by ear ; Choral Song required accurate and detailed written record. A means of providing such record was not easily found, and the slow evolution of notation presumably acted as a brake upon the wheel of progress.

Harmony, you will see, is a product of Song, but you will later find that Dance influenced its development.

A European Art

To this day Harmonic Music is a purely European art; except in Europe and lands colonized from Europe, music is still unisonous. It has never occurred to the Grand Lama of Tibet, or the high priest of the Juju tribe in the Central African jungle, or even to the Muezzins of the Arabs who invented Algebra, or any Sarastros of the Egyptians who raised the Pyramids, that a group of their people, singing together, can be occupied in singing strains that are different from one another and yet blend into a pleasant combination. And before centuries enough have elapsed for them to invent harmony for themselves they will have come under the civilizing influence of some British or American Missionary Society, and will have learnt to revel in Sankey's Sacred Hymns and Solos, in Anglican Chants with harmonium accompaniment, in the alternate austerities and gaieties of the English Hymnal, and in Jazz as reproduced by the Gramophone. Then they will send their most musically gifted youths and maidens to the R. A. M. and the R. C. M., and the great American Schools of Music, and will found their own Academies, Schools, and Conservatories on European lines, and thus the world, if it does not look out, may never see the full natural development of the musical instincts of Africa and Asia.

Melodic Song To-day

Meantime simple melodic song continues even in Europe. Unisonous Plainsong is still to be heard to-day (and very beautiful it can be); and so is unisonous Folksong (than which, at its best, nothing can be more beautiful). But the churchmen have brought in 'Counterpoint' (that *weaving* of voice parts that has been mentioned). It has grown out of Unisonous singing as the elaborate tracery of their cathedrals of the 'Decorated' period (the fourteenth century) grew out of the single lines of the plain round-headed Saxon or Norman arch (of the tenth, eleventh, and twelfth centuries).

The unaccompanied Choral Music of the best period will be discussed in the next chapter, as will also the Instrumental Music—the Church Choral Music, which was developed out of primitive Unisonous Song (but in some of its branches showed the influence of the Dance), and the Instrumental Music, which largely developed out of the Dance (but in some of its branches showed the influence of the Song).

III

THE CLIMAX OF PURE CHORAL MUSIC

THE only way to get a true idea of the nature and value of the music of any period, school or composer, is to hear plenty of it, and then (consciously and subconsciously) to generalize from what one has heard. Fortunately, it is to-day not difficult to find opportunities of hearing the choral music of the sixteenth century. Some Service Music may be heard in churches, Madrigals are often included in the programmes of choral societies, and the Gramophone records a fair number of representative pieces, Choral and Keyboard. Moreover, music of this period is, nowadays, often included in Radio programmes.

An Example Analysed

We will take as a typical example of the choral music of the period the *Missa Aeterna Christi Munera* of Palestrina. We can buy a copy of this for a small sum (Chester). With this in his hands the reader will be able to get a very fair grasp of the principles of sixteenth-century choral music, and even without it, by the help of the description that follows, he will, I hope, get a fair general notion. This Mass was chosen, when preparing the first edition of the book, because it existed as a set of Gramophone Records. The best plan will be to study this chapter and then, if Gramophone Record illustration is desired, to apply what has been learnt to a close aural examination of whatever work of Palestrina the Gramophone Companies have at the time on the market.

The Music of the Mass

The services of the Roman Church were originally sung to unisonous Plainsong. Then, as choral music became common, certain parts of the Mass were set in three, four, or more parts for Choirs, the intervening parts for priest and assistants being left in the traditional Plainsong. The sections here chorally set by Palestrina are as follows:

Kyrie

Gloria

Credo

Sanctus, Benedictus and Hosanna

(The Benedictus and Hosanna are really parts of the Sanctus, but are here set as three separate pieces.)

Agnus Dei

(Set in two portions.)

In accordance with the terms of a reform instituted by the Church at this period, Palestrina has set each piece without verbal repetitions. Roughly speaking, each of his four voices (three in the *Benedictus*, five in the *Agnus*) gives out the words once and once only. There is, then, no undue development of a theme, and consequent repetition of words, for purely musical purposes. The music is to be primarily liturgical, but within these limits Palestrina will naturally wish to make it as expressive as possible.

The Composer's Problem

Artistically the problem before the composer (or one of the problems) is, whilst providing the words with a straightforward musical setting, at the same time to suggest a feeling of musical unity. He achieves this by means of a comparatively small number of musical themes, which are varied in rhythm whilst maintaining (roughly at any rate) their melodic shape. His opening is as follows:

Here is a polyphonic growth from a very simple melodic germ, which, at different pitches, makes its appearance in every one of the four parts—note the tendency to repeat the 'germ' at the interval of the fifth, and recall one practical reason for this (p. 10). As the Mass progresses, we find the germ theme changing in such ways as the following:

And the whole Mass ends, very impressively, with the same theme with which it began—

Now this is merely one of the themes of the Mass, though the chief one.   It binds together the music of the whole service, and so gives unity.   Variety is obtained by the use of other germ themes often rather strikingly contrasted with the first one and with each other ; such are—

(which may, in origin, be, it is true, a descendant of the original germ).

(which appears to be an outgrowth of the original, standing on its head).

Warp and Woof in Music

Out of a comparatively small amount of material, then, Palestrina has woven his fabric ('woven' is the word, surely, for this kind of music, which consists of the intertwining of a fixed number of strands). And as he weaves he is producing a 'woof' as well as a 'warp'. Looked at as warp the composition is a horizontal combination of melodies; looked at as woof it is a perpendicular collection of chords. The composer necessarily has both aspects in mind as he pens his piece, but the horizontal (or 'warp') aspect is probably uppermost with him.

Such music as this we speak of as 'Contrapuntal' or as 'in Counterpoint'. The 'woof' (= perpendicular, i. e. 'Harmonic') element is there, but is less observable than the 'warp' (= horizontal, i. e. 'Contrapuntal'). A moment's thought will show that all Contrapuntal music must be also Harmonic, and a second moment's thought that not all Harmonic music need be Contrapuntal.

Counterpoint, as we find it in Palestrina and Byrd (i. e. after a thousand years of development), is a highly sophisticated form of art, but it has all grown out of the traditional Plainsong, which, in its turn, has grown out of the natural inflections of spoken language.

Choral Rhythm in the Sixteenth Century

Let us now look at a rather longer section of the Mass—

After a little observation a rhythmic peculiarity comes to light. Sing over the various parts in a flexible sort of way. Then regard their combination. It will be felt that the accentuation of the various voices conflicts a good deal, one voice with another. There is no carefully provided simultaneous pressure on the first of the bar ; indeed, the interactions of the voices tend strongly to destroy this effect. A Salvation Army drummer would, indeed, hardly know where to deliver his blow. We cannot say that this is un-rhythmic music, but the rhythm is certainly rendered very complex to the ear by the freedom of accentuation of the parts, and as a matter of fact the bar-lines you see in the music are but a recent addition, designed to keep together modern singers who are used to such guidance.

Now plain rhythm represents the dance element in music, and here that element is banished. The spiritual triumphs over the carnal, if you like, and a feeling of aloofness is conveyed, tending to the awe of mysticism. This is typical of the sacred music of the period (and even of some of the secular). The dance element, as we shall see, was very powerful in music at every period, but from the purer forms of choralism, and especially of sacred choralism, it was banned.

Three Kinds of Madrigal

Here is a secular piece, a Madrigal of the period (Byrd's *Lullaby, my sweet little Baby*), which shows much the same general characteristics, save that, in keeping with its subject, it naturally has a little cradle swing about it—

That is barely distinguishable in style from the sacred music.
It is in Counterpoint, with the Harmony as a secondary
element. Here, however, is a brighter, quicker, more rhythmic
piece (Weelkes' *On the Plains, Fairy Trains*), in which the
Harmonic element naturally comes into more prominence—

On the plains, fai-ry   trains, &c.

Here is another in which the Melodic element (in the soprano
part) triumphs, the Harmonic comes next in importance, and
the Contrapuntal last. This kind of Madrigal is called an
'Ayre'—

Since first I saw your face I re-solv'd to   hon - our and re - nown ye.

And here is a Madrigal which is frankly a choral dance, and
hence called a 'Ballet' (pronounce the 't' in this use of the
word)—

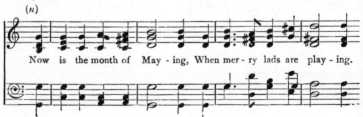

Now   is   the month of   May - ing, When mer - ry lads are   play - ing.

That also is primarily Harmonic and Melodic and only secondarily Contrapuntal, though the Contrapuntal enters more frequently later in the piece, in a *fa-la* refrain.

Much music similar to that mentioned in this chapter can be obtained in the form of Gramophone records, and the reader is advised to take the opportunity of hearing as much of it as possible, training himself to follow the 'parts', and so adding to his understanding—and consequently to his pleasure. There is no real understanding of the history of music without the hearing of much music of the various periods, schools and composers, and one point that will have become abundantly clear from the study of these few examples of sixteenth-century choral music is its variety. Here, within the Madrigal form, are three fairly distinct styles—

(i) The *Madrigal proper*—very 'contrapuntal', and making its effect a good deal by its 'points of imitation' (i. e. one voice taking up some little theme from another voice). It lacks a melody, yet is every bit melody—melody in the alto, the tenor and the bass, as well as melody in the treble. You may hear some ignorant or unthinking person speak of something of Palestrina or of Byrd or of one of their contemporaries as lacking in melody. And, generally speaking, it does lack one quite outstanding song-tune, such as this person would call a 'melody'. But herein is a paradox : this unmelodic music is all-melodic music.

(ii) The *Ayre*, a sort of solo song with choral accompaniment—to exaggerate slightly.

(iii) The *Ballet*, a choral dance.

It should be mentioned that the original intention in these pieces was that they should be performed with one voice to a part (a choral string-quartet or quintet rather than a choral orchestra, so to speak), and so performed they are heard in the many of the gramophonic performances mentioned.

The Spirit of the Music

What is the spirit of the sixteenth-century choral music? The sacred music is often aloof, but not cold. It represents the feeling of an age of faith. There were at that time sceptical coteries, and there were popes and princes of the church who were ' no better than they should be '. But to Palestrina and Byrd and their fellows the spiritual thought they set must surely have been spiritual truth. They meant what they sang. They believed in heaven and saw it—clearly, though very far off. Much of their music is serene, remote, mystical, with all human emotion wiped out save that of rapt devotion. As for the Madrigals, there are some that sing of love, as Dante sang of Beatrice, in almost a religious way, the music in this matter sometimes transcending its words. And there are others that are fanciful and light-hearted, where the music well accords with the ingenious trivialities of the age of euphuism.[1]

Popular Music of the Period

This music so far discussed was music for the performance of churchmen on the one hand, and of the aristocratic cultured laymen on the other. There was another choral music for the man in the street and the man in the lane—the simple contrapuntal amusements, the 'canons' or catches of which one, universally known even to-day, will serve as an example—*Three Blind Mice*. And, when in church, this man (in Protestant England, at any rate, and just as much in Protestant Germany) was delighted to have at last a part in the service—in the metrical psalm-tune (in Germany the hymn also). The age we are discussing was a musical age, and musical culture seems to have been more widespread then than at present. Yet probably to a tradesman of the Rialto or of Gutter Lane a full-blown Madrigal was as a String Quartet to many simple people to-day. His untrained ear would hardly follow its involutions.

---

[1] On the passage. ' They meant what they sang ', &c., E. W. makes the following comment : ' I do not myself think this can be stressed. As a general principle of musical criticism to argue from the work to the man always seems to me a very dangerous proceeding.'

IV

THE BEGINNINGS OF KEYBOARD MUSIC

PROGRESS in any department of musical art takes place along a path running over a series of alternate hills and valleys. Composers climb a hill until its summit is reached and then descend abruptly to climb another. In pure unaccompanied Choral Music, as we have seen, they had been toilsomely climbing for about a thousand years, and they now planted their flag on the first peak they had yet reached. But in Instrumental Music, until the end of this period, little progress had yet been made of which we can take account to-day. Instruments had been invented and improved, and simple music written for them, but it was all rather chaotic at a period when the Choral side of the art was already being reduced to good order.

Instruments of the Sixteenth Century

Amongst the instruments which had become popular were three played by means of a keyboard—the Organ, the Harpsichord, and the Clavichord (see Appendix 4). At first there had been some difficulty in finding suitable music for these, and there was a strong tendency to imitate the music written for voices. Similarly a family of bowed string instruments had grown up, the Viols, precursors of our own Violin family of to-day, and, here again, the music provided was often of a choral character, and so little was the distinction recognized between what can be done effectively by a body of choralists and what can be done effectively by a String Quartet that pieces were published with the easy-going inscription 'Apt for Voyces and Viols'.

First Attempts at a Keyboard Style

Gradually the idea gained ground that Choral style, String style, and Keyboard style were three different things, and it is now universally conceded that the last-named of these styles, the keyboard style, was very much the creation of the English performers who clustered around the courts of Elizabeth and James I—to the everlasting glory of those courts.   It is little exaggeration to say that the technique of keyboard composition, as we find it in Bach, Mozart, Beethoven, Schumann and Chopin, Scriabin, Debussy and Ravel, has been gradually built up upon an English foundation—and we might even almost say a London foundation.

What the Virginals was like

Leaving the Organ aside, as still very undeveloped and of minor musical importance at this period, we may say that the instrument for which these composers chiefly wrote was the Harpsichord, in one of its earlier and simpler forms known as the Virginals. Its peculiarity as compared with the Pianoforte of to-day was that the strings were mechanically plucked instead of being mechanically hammered. This gave it a pleasant, silvery, tinkling quality of tone, but allowed it little range of force, and no power of gradually filling out to loudness, or gradually thinning down to softness. The technical problem before the composer was to discover the kinds of passage that could effectively be performed on such an instrument.

Some Types of Passage

Obviously rapid scaly passages would 'come off', and so we find a good deal of this kind of thing—

(a)   JOHN BULL, *Piper's Galliard.*

Now this is as unchoral as can be, as is also this—

(b)   BULL, *The King's Hunt.*

And so it would be easy to go on, compiling examples of passages from the Virginalists of this period which were strongly differentiated from the choral style of the time, and were, indeed, not merely truly instrumental in style but truly 'keyboard'.

Choral Style on the Keyboard

But, of course, not all choral influence could be (or should be) discarded, and we find something very like a bit of a Palestrina or Byrd Mass in such a passage as the following:

(c)   GIBBONS, *Fantazia of foure Parts.*

A little examination will show that this is written in four parts, just as strictly as if it were written for four human voices, and that it is founded upon a theme given to the voices in turn, just as we saw was the case in many a passage in the Masses and Madrigals of the period.

Folk-Dance Influences

Other keyboard pieces were based upon dance rhythms and forms, as, for example, the Pavans and Galliards, popular at the period, and the 'Almans' and Jigs—

JOHN BULL, *A Gigge: Dr. Bull's My Selfe.*

And Folk-Song Influences

And often the Virginals composer, instead of seeking inspiration in the choral style or the dance rhythm, turned to the popular song of the day and made that his foundation. When he did this he generally evolved an Air with Variations, and so out of a short already existing song tune compiled a long new keyboard piece. Here, as an example, is the opening of a popular tune, taken by Byrd as the theme for a set of variations, with, beneath it, the openings of several of these variations—

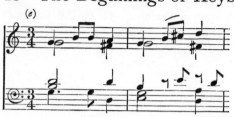

These extracts are all worth the trouble of a little careful study. What, in each case, has the composer done to his original theme? Look into this carefully and then reflect upon the important influence this sort of writing must have had upon the composer's mind in training him to grasp the content and possibilities of 'development' of a musical theme—whether one taken from some tune of the day or an original one, by himself.

Foundations

Let us turn now to general considerations, and so review the subject from a slightly different point of view. Here is a group of talented musicians who can all play the Virginals admirably, and who all wish to please a Queen who also plays that instrument admirably, and to provide interesting practice for their many aristocratic pupils. How are they to go about it? What shape shall their pieces take?

I. Choral 'shape' has already been worked out by themselves and their predecessors, and so they write a certain number of keyboard pieces in this shape. In effect they are then writing voice-music for fingers, and though a certain amount of it is tolerable and even acceptable, something brighter is needed. But in adopting this style these composers, though they do not know it, are laying the foundations of the Bach keyboard fugue.

II. There are the Dance Tunes of the time. Some of these are slow and solemn, others are quick and lively. They have necessarily become codified, for dancing is bound to be carried on according to convention—a certain number of steps one way, a certain number the other way, so many forward, so many back, so many to the right, so many to the left, join hands here and loose them there. All this means exactly-cut lengths of tune, of so many bars apiece, coming to a momentary point of repose at the end of each length.

All Galliards must be pretty much alike in rhythm and in phrasing or people will not be able to join in dancing a Galliard when one is struck up. And all Pavans and all Gigues must conform to their respective prescriptions. So these things all become set, and if a fiddler makes a new dance tune he makes it to a model already prepared for him by previous generations of dancers and of dance-tune makers. And the instrumental composer, basing his piece on a dance style, thus finds his 'form' pretty well settled for him. Most likely his piece falls into two equal parts, with a repose or half-repose of some sort in the middle and a full repose at the end. Here, for instance, is an old dance and song tune alluded to by Shakespeare—

The influence of dance in leading composers to clearly arranged forms will now be readily seen, and, as a matter of fact, just as Choral Song, through the Fantasia, at this period pointed the way to be followed by Bach in the instrumental Fugue, so Dance, at the same period, pointed the way to be followed by Bach in the various separate pieces (or 'movements') which make up his Suites.

III. And as for the Variations of the period, they pointed the way to be followed by Bach in his great 'Goldberg' Variations, by Handel in his (so-called) 'Harmonious Blacksmith', by Haydn in his F minor Piano Variations, by Beethoven in his Diabelli Variations, by Brahms in the finale of his Symphony in E minor, and by Elgar in his 'Enigma' Variations. All this is anticipating, but it is well, sometimes, in studying history to look forward as well as back.[1]

[1] On the reference to the Elgar work E. W. comments: 'The Elgar are hardly Variations *pari passu*, are they? They are a different art-form really; like many other modern so-called *Variations* they are often merely meditations on suggestions from the theme, without any closer

And, still looking forward, we see the principle of the Variation applied in the 'episodes' of Bach's fugues, where he has to fill in a few bars to join one section of the fugue with another, and does so by taking a germ of some kind from a previous passage and developing it by various processes until it grows into a stretch of the required length of interesting material. We see it, too, in the middle portion of a Beethoven sonata-form movement, which is a 'development' of the themes given out in the previous portion of the movement. And we see it in the Symphonic Poem, from Liszt to Strauss, and in the ever-changing treatment of the germ-themes, or 'Motifs,' in the later Wagner Music Dramas.

I reinforce this argument as to the importance of the invention of the Variation form by a quotation from Parry:

'The principle of variation has pervaded all musical art from its earliest days to its latest, and appears to be one of its most characteristic and interesting features. In its early stages it was chiefly a mechanical device, but as the true position of ideas in music has come more and more to be felt and understood, the more obvious has it become that they can be represented in different phases. Thus the interest of the development of instrumental movements in modern symphonies and sonatas is frequently enhanced by the way in which the subjects are varied when they are reintroduced according to the usual principles of structure; in operas and similar works ever since Mozart's time characteristic features are made all the more appropriate by adapting them to different situations; and it is even possible that after all its long history the Variation still affords one of the most favourable opportunities for the exercise of their genius by the composers of the future.'

A Final Thought

In thinking over this chapter and the previous one the

organic connexion of any kind.' This, I think, is a fair criticism, and worthy of quotation; yet I allow the passage to stand, since it is none the less true that the modern meditation-rather-than-variation type is the direct descendant of the simple Elizabethan variation form.—P. A. S.

reader will realize, I hope, that the first slopes of a mountain can be quite as full of interest as the summit. And, of course, the period 1550–1625 (roughly) is, at one and the same time, chorally a summit and instrumentally merely a lower slope.

To use another metaphor, the same set of men were putting the roof on one cathedral and laying the first courses of another. Other men, before their lives opened, had done the greater part of the work of the cathedral they finished, and other men, after their lives closed, were to do the greater part of the work of the cathedral they began. But they finished off the one beautifully, and began the other beautifully, and in looking at their two cathedrals we can feel equally grateful to them for their finishing touches and their foundations.

Do not imagine that because the keyboard music of the sixteenth century is primitive it is therefore uninteresting. Any one with eyes and imagination can get days of pleasure out of Giotto's 'primitive' wall paintings in the Madonna dell' Arena Chapel at Padua, and any one with ears and imagination can get pleasure out of the 'primitive' piano music of, say, Giles Farnaby.

V

A SHORT CHAPTER ABOUT 'MODES' AND 'SCALES'

In listening to any simple piece of music, a good deal of the general impression it makes upon our mind is due to the 'scale' from which its notes are taken. There are many different scales in use, and more are being invented constantly.

The Major Scale

'God save the King' is made out of these notes—

If we sing the tune we feel that the chief of these notes, the central note, as it were, the note to which the ear returns as a point of rest, is G. We therefore re-arrange our notes so that they stand on G—

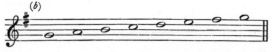

and then say that 'God save the King' is in the key of G. The particular kind of G scale from which this tune is made is the one we call G major. If we cared we could pitch it a little higher, in the key of A major, or lower, in the key of F major. It would then sound exactly the same, except for the difference in pitch, since all the major scales are exactly alike but for higher or lower pitch.

The Minor Scale

Distorting 'God save the King', for the purposes of explanation, here it is, made out of another scale, called G minor—

Again, we could pitch it in a lower key or a higher one, still keeping it in the minor.

The Whole-Tone Scale

So far, then, we have seen two forms of scale—the Major and the Minor. Here is a third form of scale fairly common in modern music—

That is, for obvious reasons, called the 'Whole-Tone Scale'[1] (of course, this scale too can be taken at various pitches). Here is a passage from Debussy's *Afternoon of a Faun*—

---

[1] 'Strictly, I suppose, this is a *chord* rather than a scale.'—E. W.

The scale from which all these notes are taken (until they leave it at the very end) is the Whole-Tone Scale beginning on F—

Modulation and the Lack of it

Now the scales from which the old Plainsongs were made were many. And a piece of Plainsong would be in the same scale throughout, whereas a modern piece may begin in the major, shift to the minor, go back to the major, bring in a bit of the 'whole-tone', and end, as it began, in the major. Moreover, it may begin in C major and go to G major or A flat major or A minor or any other major or minor scale at the fancy of the composer. All this freedom is of comparatively late growth. You do not find it (to anything but a very trifling extent) in the Melodic style of music (i. e. the Plain Song and Folk Song stages), nor in the Early Contrapuntal styles of development.

But in the period we have just been discussing you find it beginning. For instance, if you look at that Palestrina Mass you will see that it is nearly all (as we to-day should say) in the key of F major, but that once or twice it 'modulates' (or changes key) into C major, or B flat major, or G minor. But it is characteristic of the music of the period that little modulation is to be found in it, and often this gives the music of the period (especially the choral music) a peculiar flavour, which until one is used to it might be called 'sameness'. Then again much of it (especially that of the earlier portion of the period) is written not in our modern scales, which were then only just coming in, but in older scales called 'Modes'. This, to us, often gives an archaic flavour.

What the Old 'Modes' were like

Here is one of the old Modes, the 'Dorian'—

(g)

Now if you look back to Byrd's *Lullaby*, on page 19, you will see that it opens in just this scale. From a glance at the key-signature (or lack of such) you might say—'C major or A minor'. Yet, as you play the passage you feel that not C nor A is the central note (or note of repose), but D. Yet the passage is not in D major or it would have F sharps and C sharps, whereas it has F naturals and C naturals. And it is not in D minor, or it would have C sharps and B flats, whereas it has C naturals and B naturals. It is, then, in the Dorian Mode, though by and by accidentals creep in that take it into other Modes and sometimes even suggest our modern keys.

The Decay of the Modes

Here then is an illustration not merely of one of the old Modes, but of what was happening to them. These Modes were very suitable for melodic song, but, when writing in parts became much developed, composers began to feel that they could improve the effect here and there by inflecting (sharpening or flattening) a note. The instinct which pushed them to this was really pushing them to the destruction of all the Modes except two, or rather the gradual alteration of the Modes so that they all came to resemble two of their number which, somehow, were more suitable for harmonic-contrapuntal writing, the Ionian (our modern ' Major Key ') and the Aeolian (practically our modern ' Minor Key ')—

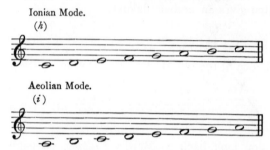

Note that all the Modes could be taken at any pitch just as the present day Major Key or Minor Key can. What defines a mode is not pitch, but order of tones and semitones. And because in a ' modal ' piece of music the tones and semitones fall a little differently from what they do in a piece in a major or minor key, the effect is different and sometimes, to unaccustomed ears, a little disturbing.

LEADING COMPOSERS OF THE PERIOD

PALESTRINA

Born probably 1525; died 1594. The birthplace of Giovanni Pierluigi da Palestrina is indicated in the surname which has attached

Palestrina.

itself to him. Palestrina is a small place about twenty miles from Rome, with a cathedral, of which, after a choir-boy and student life in Rome, Giovanni became organist and choir-master at the age of (probably) eighteen. Six or seven years later his Bishop became Pope, and made him choirmaster of the Julian Chapel in the Vatican. For a couple of centuries or more the Sistine Chapel (the Pope's own private chapel, regarded therefore as, in one way, the chief church in Christendom)

had been largely recruited with Flemings and other foreigners, and the Julian Chapel Choir at St. Peter's had been constituted, shortly before Palestrina's time, with the express intention that it should become a training school for Italian musicians and a means of using their services. Shortly after appointment the new choirmaster brought out a new book of masses, which was the first ever dedicated by an Italian to the reigning Pope. A woodcut, from which our illustration is taken, showed Palestrina on his knees offering the volume to the Pope, and the dedication ran—

'A few days ago, having set to music in a more exquisite manner these Christian praises to the most high God, no other name but yours seemed worthy of the dedication, not only because you alone are next to God on earth, but because you are so disposed by nature to encourage music, that I hope that it will not be un-acceptable to you if I sing your praise after that of God, and that I may be permitted this favour for a long time is my wish and my prayer.   Farewell.'

At the age of about thirty, Palestrina was made a member of the actual Pontifical (i.e. the Sistine) Choir; here, however, his patron made a gift which was not strictly legal, since it violated the rules of the Choir, in that the new member was a married man, was not in orders, and had a poor voice. A new Pope, Marcellus, reigned but three weeks ; the incident of a meeting of his Choir which he called one Good Friday, at which he impressed upon the members the necessity for church music being sincere and suitable to its occasion, and of its not obscuring by its complexity the words set, is probably commemorated in the title of a work of a few years later, Palestrina's *Missa Papae Marcelli*. The next Pope, Paul IV, was legal-minded, and the irregularity of Palestrina's position coming to his notice, dismissal on a pension followed.

Palestrina's reputation, however, was already established, and he did nct wait long for another appointment. In a few months he became choirmaster of the Lateran. Later he occupied a similar post at Santa Maria Maggiore, and at last, at the age of about forty-six, returned to his old post of choirmaster of the Julian Chapel.

A good deal has been made of Palestrina's part in 'saving' church music from destruction by the Council of Trent. The Council had declared that church music should be purified from methods tinged with secularity (as, for example, the use of some popular tune as the basis, or *canto fermo*, upon which the mesh of counterpoint should be woven) ; but it had not taken the drastic decisions sometimes reported of it in histories of music. Two Cardinals (one of them the learned but simple-minded and devoted St. Charles Borromeo) were appointed to see that the reasonable resolutions taken were carried into effect. They called together eight Papal singers, who easily agreed with them on certain reforms, but demurred to the suggestion that contrapuntal music should be verbally intelligible. It is traditional that certain of Palestrina's pieces were brought forward by the two Cardinals as evidence to the contrary, and in any case it is at least probable that his example and his advice had both great influence upon the outcome of the whole proceedings.

Palestrina's life was not embittered by poverty, as has been sometimes suggested. Both he and his wife inherited buildings and vineyards in their native place, and the work he did was not ill-paid, as payments then went. A complaint he made on that score was probably prompted not by inability to meet his domestic needs but by the lack of resources sufficient to publish his works, and indeed, though he brought out various volumes, much remained unpublished at his death. Such trials as came to him arose from the inevitable disappointments and rubs of musical professional life in all places and ages, and from domestic bereavements, which with him were frequent and severe. Yet his life must, on the whole, be counted a prosperous and happy one, and it was enriched with friendships, amongst which is to be numbered that of St. Philip Neri, the founder of the Oratorio. The association of these two noble-minded men was very close, Palestrina acting for some time as musical director of the Oratorians, and doubtless conducting their congregational musical services, both in the church which had been built for Neri and in the open air on the Coelian Hill.

In the year of the Jubilee (1575), when pilgrims of all nations flocked to Rome to obtain the indulgence offered to them, a procession of fifteen thousand Palestrinans, divided into three huge choirs, marched to Rome and entered it, singing their great townsman's music.

ORLANDO DI LASSO

Born *c.* 1530; died 1594. Orlando di Lasso (or Orlandus Lassus) is the greatest representative of the Flemish School. Roughly, the facts as to the parts played by different nations in the development of the pure choral style are these : (i) Everywhere, from the ninth century to the beginning of the fifteenth, church musicians were at work fashioning a choral technique, and no nation had any actual supremacy during this period. (ii) In the first half of the fifteenth century an Englishman, John of Dunstable, showed the way to an enormously more artistic treatment, and his reforms were universally adopted. (iii) Then the Flemings took up the leadership, and became so famous that the chief posts in Rome (and Italy generally) were filled by them, and their compositions spread widely. The last and greatest of the Flemings was Orlando di Lasso. (iv) By that time the Italians had made progress and were already taking up the leadership; two great schools, then, overlap in Lasso and Palestrina, who were born within a few years of one another and died in the same year

Lasso was born at Mons.   He wrote an enormous quantity of music and travelled extensively, visiting France, England, and Italy; he was for a time *maestro* of the Lateran in Rome.   In his late twenties he received an invitation from the cultured Albert V, Duke of Bavaria, to settle at Munich as his director of chamber music. He married a lady of the court.   Later he was promoted—

> 'The Duke seeing that Master Orlando had by this time learnt the language, and gained the good-will and love of all, by the propriety and gentleness of his behaviour, and that his compositions (in number infinite) were universally liked, without loss of time elected him master of the chapel, to the evident pleasure of all. And, indeed, with all his distinguished colleagues, he lived so quietly and peacefully, that all were forced to love him, to respect him in his presence, and to praise him in his absence.'

He was recognized as a great choirmaster—

> 'One great quality was the firmness and genius he evinced when the choir were singing, giving the time with such steadiness and force, that, like warriors taking courage at the sound of the trumpet, the expert singers needed no other orders than the expression of that powerful and vigorous countenance to animate their sweetly sounding voices.'

He soon made fresh travels—

> 'The Duke, seeing his predecessor's chapel was far beneath his own ideal, sent messages and letters, with gifts and promises through all Europe, to select learned musical artists, and singers with fine voices and experience.   And it came to pass in a short time, that he had collected as great a company of virtuosi as he could possibly obtain, chosen from all the musicians in Germany and other countries by his composer, the excellent Orlando di Lasso.'

All this illustrates the condition of music at this period, as an art fostered by the aristocracy and the church, and is here inserted with that in view.

A picturesque incident of Lasso's life was this : On Corpus Christi day, 1563, the weather was so bad that the Duke ordered that the usual procession round the town should be abandoned and the circuit of the aisles of the church alone be made.   Singing a motet of Lasso, the choir and the church dignitaries proceeded, when, on approaching the porch, the storm ceased, they were able to pass out into the open, and the ceremonies were carried through as in other years. This gave Lasso the status, amongst his fellow townsmen, of a divinely favoured being, and his motet that of a valuable storm-stopper, in which capacity it was subsequently used, though with what results history does not record.

The four sons of Lasso all became musicians, and after his death they piously published many of his works. The family musical talent persisted into a third generation.

TOMMASO LUDOVICO DA VICTORIA

Born 1535 or rather later; died 1611. Victoria is considered the greatest Spanish representative of the choral school of the sixteenth century, though he spent most of his active working life in Rome. At thirty-three he was Maestro di Cappella of the Collegium Germanicum in Rome, to which institution he had already for some years been attached in a minor capacity. A year or two later he was choirmaster of St. Apollinaris, a post he held for fourteen years, during which period he published a number of books of church music. He then returned to Spain, taking an appointment at the Chapel Royal, at Madrid, and there publishing other works. Victoria was not only greatly influenced in his work by the Roman School, but, in his turn, exercised influence upon it. Much of his music is of very great beauty, and he ranks very high amongst the musical workers of his period.

(The spelling 'Vittoria' is incorrect.)

WILLIAM BYRD

Born 1543; died 1623. Probably a Lincolnshire man, since he was organist of Lincoln Cathedral at twenty. At twenty-six he

Byrd.

became a Gentleman of the Chapel Royal, and for about thirty years lived at Harlington, ten miles out of London. 'It is thought that he chose this retired village as his residence in order that he might escape difficulties in connexion with his duties created by the fact that he adhered staunchly to the unreformed doctrines . . . yet regular attendance at the Chapel Royal must in these circumstances have taxed Byrd's energies, more particularly because the journey lay across the dangerous Hounslow Heath' (Fellowes). Later he settled near Ongar, in Essex, becoming something of a country gentleman, and securing the right to bear arms.

Byrd's work is nearly all of the finest quality—Church Music, Secular Choral Music, String and Keyboard Music. Byrd was the founder of the English Madrigal School.

A new recognition of the value of Byrd's compositions has lately come about, and some British musicians are now not hesitating to claim for him a status equal to that of Palestrina, formerly considered to stand head and shoulders above every composer of the period. Certainly Byrd's biggest things, like those of Palestrina, have the quality of sublimity that marks the really great mind.

JOHN BULL

Born *c.* 1562; died 1628. Bull was one of the boys in Queen Elizabeth's Chapel Royal. At the age of about twenty he became organist of Hereford Cathedral. A few years later he became a Gentleman of the Chapel Royal, and a Mus. Doc. of both Cambridge and Oxford. At about forty he petitioned Queen Elizabeth for a grant 'to relieve his great poverty, which altogether hinders his studies'; the petition was successful. Later he was appointed by the Queen Professor of Music at Gresham College, in the City, and had to give—

Bull.

'The solemn music lecture twice every week, in manner following, viz. the theoretique part for one half-hour, or thereabouts, and the practique, by concert of voice or instruments, for the rest of the hour, whereof the first lecture should be in the Latin tongue and the second in English; but because at this time Mr. Dr. Bull, who is recommended to the place by the Queen's Most Excellent Majesty, being not able to speak Latin, his lectures are permitted to be altogether in English, so long as he shall continue in the place of music lectyrer there'.

In 1607 when King James I dined at Merchant Taylors' Hall,

'John Bull, Doctor of Musique, one of the organists of His Majesties Chappell-royall, and free of the Merchant-taylors, being in a citizen's gowne, cappe, and hood, played most excellent melodie upon a small payre of Organes,[1] placed there for that purpose onley'.

At the age of about fifty Bull went abroad, 'being possessed of crotchets as many musicians are' or (alternatively) 'through the guilt of a corrupt conscience to escape the punishment which notoriously he had deserved and was designed to have inflicted on him by the hand of justice'. He lived successively at Brussels and Antwerp,

[1] 'Payre' in the same sense as in 'pair of scissors'; cf. the French use, 'les orgues'.

being organist of the cathedral at the latter place. There he died. He was of great fame as Virginalist and Organ player and composer. He also wrote Church Music.

Bull seems to have been on terms of friendship with the great Dutch organist, Sweelinck. Bull wrote a Fantasia on a Fugue of Sweelinck's, and Sweelinck included a canon by Bull in his book on Composition. As a virtuoso performer of the first rank, it is more than probable that Bull's influence on Sweelinck was considerable. It was Sweelinck who founded the great Dutch and North German school of organ playing. His pupil Scheidemann handed the tradition to Reinken, and Reinken greatly influenced Bach, who, as a boy, frequently walked to Hamburg to hear him. So there is a link established between Bull and Bach, and, in fact, Bull stands at the beginning of the period of development of contrapuntal instrumental music which Bach closed.

JOHN BENNET

Born ? ; died ?   His one book of Madrigals was published in 1599 and some songs appeared in 1614. Nothing is known of his life. ' Bennet was essentially a refined and tuneful musician, with a sound technique so far as it went. . . . He was certainly at his best in the gayer moods.' ' He owes his popularity amongst modern madrigal singers almost exclusively to his sparkling *All creatures now are merry minded* and to his *Weep, O mine eyes*. Both of these are quite first-class of their line, but the former is much more homophonic than was usual with this class of work ' (Fellowes).

JOHN DOWLAND

Born 1563 ; died 1626.   His place of birth is disputed (? London or Ireland). At eighteen he went to Paris as a page in the train of Sir Henry Cobham, and during his three years' stay there became a Roman Catholic. At twenty-six he took the Mus. Bac. degree at Oxford, and a few years later went to Italy to study with Marenzio. On his return he became a Protestant again, and resided, as a graduate, at Trinity College, Dublin. At thirty-five he brought out a book of Songs with Lute accompaniment that became very popular and went through five editions. At thirty-six he was appointed Court Lutenist to the King of Denmark. At forty-seven he returned to England. He held various positions here, being Lutenist to Lord Walden, and later one of the Six Lutenists of Charles I. For years he had been making a large income abroad, but he had spent money freely and he died poor and embittered. Dowland's fame as a Lutenist was great, and he received many offers of preferment—

> 'When I came to the Duke of Brunswick he used me kindly and gave me a rich chain of gold, £23 in money, with velvet and satin and gold lace to make me apparell, with promise that if I would serve him he would give me as much as any prince in the world. From thence I went to the Lantgrave of Hessen, who gave me the greatest welcome that might be for one of my quality, who sent a ring into England to my wife, valued at £20 sterling, and gave me a great standing cup with a cover gilt, full of dollars, with many great offers for my service. From thence I had great desire to see Italy and came to Venice and from thence to Florence, where I played before the Duke and got great favours.'

Dowland also boasted that his works had been published at Paris, Antwerp, Cologne, Nuremberg, Frankfort, Leipzig, Amsterdam, and Hamburg.

RICHARD EDWARDS

Born about 1523; died 1566. Note that this composer is much earlier than any of the others here mentioned, with the exception of Taverner. He is included because his choral piece *In going to my naked* (modernized 'lonely') *bed* is likely to be heard at choral concerts. Edwards was educated at Christ Church, Oxford. He became Master of the Children of the Chapel Royal. At Candlemas, 1565, he produced at Lincoln's Inn a play performed by his choir-boys, and next year a play of his was acted before Queen Elizabeth in Christ Church Hall, Oxford, which pleased the Queen, who sent for him and 'gave him promise of reward'. But he died a week or two later.

Edwards' work precedes that of the madrigal school proper and the beautiful part-song mentioned above will be found to be grave and sober, and in style indistinguishable from a piece of church music.

JOHN FARMER

Born *c.* 1565; died *c.* 1605. Farmer was organist at Christ Church Cathedral, Dublin.   He deserted his post and the Chapter issued an order saying that if they did not see him soon they did not wish to see him at all.   So he returned, and shortly after was presented to a country Vicarage.   Not being in orders, Farmer farmed this out, and his vicarial duties were done vicariously.   He lived his last year in London.   He wrote Madrigals and Psalm Tunes, &c., also a text-book of Counterpoint.

GILES FARNABY

Born *c.* 1560 ; died *c.* 1600.   Very little is known of his life.   He published a book of Madrigals and wrote a number of admirable keyboard pieces, many of which are brief but significant and characteristic.   He is, to normal people, the most attractive Keyboard Writer of the period, and his works are now increasingly played.

THOMAS FORD

Born 1580 ; died 1648.   A musician on the staff of the Prince of Wales, and then one of the musicians of Charles I.   He is buried in St. Margaret's, Westminster.   Ford wrote Solo Vocal Music with Lute accompaniment, Madrigals, a little Church Music, &c.

ORLANDO GIBBONS

Born 1583 ; died 1625. He was the son of one of the City Waits of Cambridge—a body of players and singers attached to the Mayor and Corporation. Two of Orlando's brothers became professional musicians. Orlando began life as a choir-boy at King's College (his brother Edward being Master of the Choristers). Then, at twenty-one, he became Organist of the Chapel Royal, and nineteen years later of Westminster Abbey. His death took place at Canterbury, where he was in attendance on Charles I, who had gone there to receive his bride on her arrival from the Continent, and he is buried in the Cathedral there, where a bust of him is to

Gibbons.

be seen. He left a great many pieces of fine Church Music, a smaller number of Madrigals, many 'Fancies' or 'Fantasias' for Viols, and some Virginals Music. His Church Music is of especial importance.

THOMAS MORLEY

Born 1557 ; died *c.* 1603. As a young man, Organist of St. Giles', Cripplegate, later of St. Paul's Cathedral, and also, finally, a Gentleman of the Chapel Royal. As Byrd was in danger as a Roman Catholic, so Morley was in danger as a Protestant. It appears that he went abroad on some secret service. See a letter by one Paget, a Catholic agent in Flanders :

'Ther is one Morley that playeth on the organies in poules that was with me in my house. He seemed here to be a good Catholicke and was reconsiled, but notwith-standing suspecting his behaviour I entercepted letters that Mr. Nowell [presumably the Dean of St. Paul's] wrote to him wherby I discovered enoughe to have hanged him. Neverthelès he shewing with teares great repentaunce and asking on his knees forgivenes, I was content to let him goe. I here since his comming thether he hath played the promotor and apprehendeth Catholickes.'

Morley wrote a large number of Madrigals, in which he frequently showed a gay and light-hearted spirit. He also wrote some Church Music and Keyboard Music. In 1597, being ill and obliged to keep his house, he occupied himself usefully in writing a popular text-book, the *Plaine and Easie Introduction to Practicall Musicke*.

JOHN TAVERNER

Born *c.* 1495; died 1545. Nothing seems to be known of his earlier life, beyond the fact that he was almost certainly of an old Lincolnshire family, and had already made a considerable reputation at Tattershall (Lincolnshire), where most of his music was written, before he became Master of the Children of Cardinal College (now Christ Church), Oxford, in 1526. See Anthony Delaber, in Foxe's *Acts and Monuments*.

'Then went I straight to Friswides,[1] and Evensong was begon, and the Deane and the other Canons were there in their gray Amices: They were almost at *Magnificat* before I came thether, I stoode at the quier doore and heard Master Taverner play, and others of the Chappell there sing, wyth and among whome I my selfe was wont to sing also.'

Taverner and other members of the College were accused of heresy, and thrown by Wolsey into a cellar 'with a deep cave under the ground, of the same Colledge, where their salt fyshe was layde, so that through the fylthe stincke thereof, they were all infected'. The Cardinal pardoned Taverner—saying he was 'but a Musitian'!

For his duties at Oxford he received a salary of £10 per annum, with an allowance of three shillings and fourpence for livery, and one shilling and eightpence per week for commons—higher remuneration than that of any member of the College except the Dean and Sub-Dean.

He was only at Oxford three and a half years; his religious views changed drastically, he repudiated all the old forms for which he had composed so much fine music, and forsook his musical career.

---

[1] By 'Friswides' is meant St. Fridiswide's Abbey, the building of which was incorporated in part by Cardinal Wolsey in his new foundation.

Most of his remaining years were apparently spent at Boston, the chief town of his native district, and in these after years he was evidently one of Thomas Cromwell's chief agents in the suppression of monastic establishments and the martyrdom of religious opponents. He was buried at Boston.

Taverner comes at the end of the highly developed and flourishing school which was definitely broken off by the Reformation, 1547–1560. Whereas, what foreign influence was accepted by the new school was Italian, Taverner's period has more affinity with the Flemish. 'His command of technical ingenuities and his grim delight in following them out suggest study of Flemish methods.' His work is characterized by extraordinary virility, and an exceptionally outstanding personality, which unceasingly vitalizes everything —even in his duller moments.

His music survived into the post-Reformation period, and 'Long after the names of his contemporaries had vanished from the part-books of the late 16th century, his name remained.'

THOMAS WEELKES

Born *c.* 1575; died 1623. Organist of Winchester College, and then of Chichester Cathedral. Hence he did not, like most of the English Choral and Keyboard composers of the period, live the London life. But he died whilst on a visit to London, and left his friend with whom he was staying fifty shillings 'for meat, drinke and boardinge and such like necessaryes', asking him to 'see me buried like a man of my profession'. The place of burial was discovered by Dr. Fellowes—St. Bride's, Fleet Street. Weelkes wrote a large number of Madrigals, a good deal of Church Music which is at present unprinted and unsung, and String Music, also still in manuscript.

He is one of the very greatest of the Madrigalists.

JOHN WILBYE

Born 1574; died 1638. Wilbye was born at Diss, Norfolk, the son of a well-to-do tanner, who was evidently himself something of a musician, since he bequeathed his lute to his son. When about twenty years of age Wilbye became household musician to the Kytson family of Hengrave Hall, Suffolk, and he continued in the service of this family for thirty years. The Hall still exists and its records give particulars of the musical instruments and music books in use during Wilbye's control. Sir Thomas Kytson had a town house, and in this way some of Wilbye's Madrigals came to be dated from London. Some time after Sir Thomas's death, Lady Kytson gave Wilbye the best sheep farm in the district as a reward for his faithful service—after which practically no more music appeared ! When Lady Kytson died Wilbye went to live at the house of her daughter, Lady Rivers of Colchester, and there he remained until his death. He died a wealthy man.

All this gives a rather interesting picture of one type of professional life at the period. There were at this time three main opportunities for making a living open to a sound musician in England : (1) Service in the Chapel Royal, (2) Organistship of some Cathedral, (3) Service with a private family. Abroad it was much the same.

Wilbye's output of composition was not great, but he is reckoned the finest English madrigalist, excelling especially in the more serious style (by which he is to-day, as it happens, less known).

NOTE

The leading composers of this period are extremely numerous. I have selected for mention here chiefly those whose music is most accessible. They are thoroughly representative of their period. The major workers are included, and it will be found that the four chief schools of the sixteenth century (Flemish, Italian, English, and Spanish) are all illustrated. Of all those included some compositions can be heard in the larger churches, at the concerts of Madrigal Societies, &c., or on the Gramophone, or broadcast, whilst the Keyboard compositions are within the capabilities of the competent amateur pianist.

PERIOD II

To Bach and Handel

VI

HARMONY *QUA* HARMONY AT LAST, AND THE INTRODUCTION OF OPERA AND ORATORIO

CONTINUING the thought of the last chapter, one may ask—
'Why were the Modes in general, which had had so long and successful a career as the basis of melodic music, found at last to be unsuitable for choral writing?'

The reason is probably this. Choral writing, at first looked at purely as Counterpoint (as a *weaving of melodies*), was gradually tending more and more to be looked at as Harmony (as a *building of chords* side by side). And music which is thus felt harmonically seems to call for very definite points of repose interspersed with its passages of activity. Such points of repose we call Cadences. And the growing fashion for dance rhythms in choral music would emphasize the need of such Cadences, for, as already pointed out, a dance piece is necessarily cut up into equal sections ('phrases' and 'sentences'), and, to mark this, Cadences, more definite or less so, are demanded.

The Cadence Feeling

Now the note in any scale which makes the most definite cadence is the Tonic (= key-note, or central note of the piece, or 'Doh'). And the Tonic sounds much more final if approached by a semitone, thus—

than if approached by a tone, thus—

And when harmony is put to it this feeling is strengthened [1]—

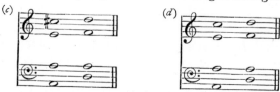

I have earlier in this book made the assertion that all music, even the most complex, has grown out of the simple Folk Song (and Plain Song) and the equally simple Folk Dance. You have gathered that both these influences were active in the sixteenth-century Choral Music, and have now realized that the Dance element, especially, was pushing composers out of their old almost purely Contrapuntal way of looking at things into a more Harmonic way of looking at them. Other factors which tended in the same direction were these:

(*a*) The development of music meant for a keyboard—a medium for evoking tone that inevitably suggests lumps or handfuls, i. e. chords considered as chords and not as by-products of interwoven 'voices' or 'parts'.

(*b*) The popularity of the Lute, a plucked string instrument something like the Mandoline of to-day, and the composition of songs for this, the melody of which was held by the voice of the performer and supported by chords which he played on his instrument. A good deal of simple

---

[1] This remark applies of course to the sixteenth-century harmony almost as much as to that of a later period. Even when the written music did not show a 'leading note', in approaching a cadence the singers inserted a sharp, under certain conditions which we know as the laws of 'Musica Ficta'.—R. R. T.

counterpoint often came into a Lute accompaniment, but the very nature of the instrument suggested the harmonic way of considering music.

The Influence of Drama

About 1600 another and decisive factor entered. The idea of writing upon dramatic themes began strongly to seize composers. Now the old contrapuntal music could express long-drawn moods, such as joy or sorrow, but was necessarily too formal in its construction to express very rapid and dramatic changes of thought, to give point to particular words, and so on. And it was obviously unsuitable as a musical setting for dialogue.

The Renascence takes Effect in Music

This rather sudden plunge into definite Music Drama had an historical cause behind it. The Renascence, which for a century and a half had urged men to the study of Greek thought and the expression of it in painting and sculpture, and which had for some time also influenced architecture, now began to exert its power upon music. Up to this time it had done little more than supply composers with some new literary subjects for their composition, and they had written many Madrigals and Lute Songs the words of which were treatments of classical subjects (Venus and Cupid, and Phoebus and Philomel, are common enough names in their verses), and had also set to music spectacular Masques and Pastorals upon classical subjects. But they had never seriously tackled Greek Drama, and now they began to want to do so.

A little group at Florence, that was in the habit of meeting regularly in a palace there, especially set the fashion. They studied the ancient Greek Drama, and came to the conclusion that it was chanted by solo voices with some simple instrumental support, such as that of the lyre, and they saw that it

made provision for occasional chorus passages. So they devised
an entertainment on these lines, setting such stories as that of
Orpheus and Eurydice.   Similarly they applied their ideas to
sacred subjects, and so produced 'Oratorios'.   The examples
that follow (from an Oratorio, Cavalieri's *Soul and Body*)[1] will
give an idea of their methods, and will show how thoroughly
Harmonic (rather than Contrapuntal) they were in their conceptions, the change of view, indeed, being so great as to give
the compositions of the school the name of 'The New Music'.

[1] The extracts are taken from Malipiero's edition, published in the
great *Raccolta Nazionale delle Musiche Italiane* (Istituto Editoriale
Italiano, Milan).

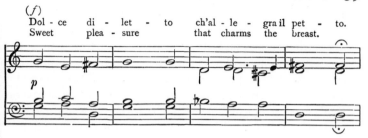

(f)

Dol - ce di - let - to ch'al - le - gra il pet - to.
Sweet plea - sure that charms the breast.

p

An Intermediate Type

I do not propose to dwell upon the music of this period, because it is music which can practically never be heard to-day and the avowed purpose of this book is to explain and place in proper relation such types of music as the ordinary listener can find opportunities of hearing, merely touching upon previous and intermediate types sufficiently to draw from them the necessary explanations of the genesis of the music that *can* be heard. The 'New Music' is an intermediate type. To-day you can hear Palestrina and the English Elizabethan composers, and you can hear Purcell, Bach, and Handel. These 'New Music' people, Peri, Caccini, Cavalieri, Monteverde and Company, you cannot hear. So they are in this book quickly passed over. But note the following:

i. There is a curious analogy between the change from Gothic Architecture to Renascence Architecture, on the one hand, and from the Contrapuntal Madrigal-and-Mass style to the new *Dramma per Musica* style on the other. The first in each case was a weaving of lines, the second a placing in juxtaposition of masses. Both came about from the same dual cause, (a) the exhaustion of the resources of the previous type, and (b) the introduction of Greek models.

ii. An overlapping, of course, occurred. In architecture the quadrangle of St. John's College, Oxford, in a Renascence style, dates from 1630; and Inigo Jones's purely classical gateway to the Botanic Gardens at Oxford from

1633. Yet the chapel of Brasenose College, with mixed Gothic and Renascence features, dates from 1656. There are such overlappings in the history of every art. They are bound to occur, for as long as Providence continues to ordain that 'every little girl or boy that's born into this world alive is either a little Liberal or else a little Conservative', some people will dearly cherish the old and some wish violently to break with it—sometimes with an intention of reverting to a still further past, as here in the case of both architecture and music.

The point to remember, then, is that the break between the contrapuntal and the harmonic was not so clear cut as is sometimes supposed by those who read concise histories and records of dates and facts. Madrigals in the old style were still written up to at least 1620, and the contrapuntal never died out of church music, although the harmonic came in.

iii. The declamatory style for solo voices was called 'Recitative'. The aim was to imitate more or less closely the natural inflexions of the speaking voice, supporting it with mere chords. In Oratorio and Opera, both of them forms which grew up out of the *Dramma per Musica*, Recitative has always continued to form a very important ingredient. Purcell, Handel, and Bach made good use of this means of securing dramatic expression in solo song ; so did Gluck, Mozart, and the Opera writers who followed them ; so did Wagner, who, however, modified it, making it more continuous and giving it a very elaborate (and sometimes contrapuntal) accompaniment. And Debussy's opera *Pelléas et Mélisande* is entirely written in a type of Recitative. With those examples in mind, the innovations of the early seventeenth-century Opera and Oratorio composers cannot be thought of lightly. We do not hear their work nowadays, but we profit by it.

iv. The Orchestra, which had been in a chaotic condition through the previous century, remained in such a condition. But the desire of the Opera writers for direct expression and varied ' colour' caused experiments from which good was later to come.

v. An important social change in relation to music came about through the invention of Opera. There were as yet no public concerts anywhere, but in 1637 an Opera House was opened at Venice, and others followed elsewhere (London, 1656; Paris, 1669; Rome, 1671; Hamburg, 1678). For good and ill the initiation and continuous multiplication of opportunities for the aristocrat, the merchant, and the tradesman and his wife to hear a musical dramatic entertainment, ' at prices to suit all pockets', has been a great influence in musical development. And the wide popularity of Oratorio from the end of the sixteenth century downwards has been another great influence.

(A comment upon this chapter, and a reply to it, will be found in Appendix III, page 169.)

VII

THE CENTURY OF PERFECTION, 1650–1750.

(a) FUGUE

IN travelling quickly along the course of the development of music, what have we so far seen ?—

i. Unison song (church song and folk song) developing into choral song on contrapuntal lines.

ii. Contrapuntal choral song reaching its highest point of development about the turn of the sixteenth–seventeenth centuries.

iii. Then, as the harmonic principle came more and more into light, a partial and temporary decay of the contrapuntal principle and the invention of a form of solo song modelled on speech (Recitative) with a simple chordal accompaniment and the addition of choruses similarly conceived and of rough-and-ready orchestral passages, all with a dramatic intention behind them—a turn over from the more or less impersonal style of the Mass and the Madrigal to the direct dramatic utterance of the early Opera and Oratorio.

iv. Keyboard music brought to its first early stage of coherence, but orchestral music still left incoherent.

Nothing New but nearly Everything Better

The period we are now to enter is a period which offers us, in a sense, nothing new, but instead a gradual perfecting[1] of every style (dramatic, devotional, solo vocal, choral, instrumental) developed previously. The greatest works of the end

---

[1] One of my kind critics raises an objection to the title of this chapter. Simply to call this period ' The Century of Perfection ', without explanation, might, indeed, lead to misconception. I think, however, that the present paragraph, if carefully read, will be found to guard the point sufficiently. See also page 72, 'What Perfection means', and Appendix V.—P. A. S.

of this period (say, 1700–50) are immeasurably beyond the
greatest works of the previous period (the operas, oratorios, &c.
of, say, 1600–50). Instrumental music takes a leap forward
far in advance of anything it has previously attained. Solo
vocal music does the same. The Choral Music alone cannot be
said to be greater than the greatest previously written; it is
not finer than that written just before and after the year 1600,
but only different—in its more direct mode of expression and
its bigger scale. In Choral Music we have climbed the second
great peak on the journey; in Instrumental Music the first
great peak has been reached.

And not only is this the period of a gathering up and
perfecting of all that has gone before: it is the period of their
final gathering up. After this period (or rather overlapping it,
as everything does overlap in the history of art) there comes
into musical composition a new outlook. In Bach and Handel
we see the culmination of centuries of musical development;
in Haydn and Mozart, who are immediately to follow them,
we see the foundations laid of the musical development of
the century that is to follow.[1]

The Period of Fugue

Typically, this is the period of the Fugue. You have seen
a good deal of both the spirit of the Fugue and the body of
the Fugue in such pieces as that Mass of Palestrina, some
of the Madrigals, and the keyboard piece of Gibbons (p. 26),
which, as was pointed out earlier, was nothing but an instrumental adaptation of the mass-madrigal style.

In all these things we had—

   i. A strict adherence to a fixed number of 'voices' or
      'parts', all of equal importance;

  ii. A tendency (particularly noticeable in the Palestrina Mass)
      to 'grow' a long piece out of a short melodic subject;

[1] For another way of looking at the musical development of this period
see Appendix V.

iii. An incipient tendency to obtain variety by moving from the main key to some nearly related key or keys, returning, at intervals or at any rate finally, to the main key.

An Understanding of Keys

The close study and consequent greater understanding of Harmony *qua* Harmony that came about as a result of the Florentine experiments of 16co, had an enormous influence upon the 'incipient tendency' mentioned under (iii). Effective ways of relating chord to chord and key to key came to light. Harmony and key relationship began to codify and, it may be said, to conventionalize. It became realized that keys had natural relationships, in a sort of family system, each key having closely connected with it in aural effect five other keys, as for instance—

Key C

Key G		Key F
(i. e. one sharp added)		(i. e. one flat added)

and the 'relative minors' of these (i. e. those with the same 'key signatures')—

Key A minor

Key E minor		Key D minor

Bach and Palestrina Compared

Now, roughly speaking, a Bach fugue is, in form and style, much the same as a Palestrina movement, such as one of those we have been examining, but with more definite 'point' about every detail of its construction.

It has one main 'Subject' (a snatch of melody like that which we found to be the chief 'Subject' of the Palestrina Mass).

This subject appears successively at the opening in all the 'Voices' (which may be real voices, but which even in an instrumental Fugue still retain this name).

Look back at the Kyrie of the Mass and you will see that the Subject there enters at different pitches, beginning on F in the Tenor, then five notes higher on C in the Alto, then on F in the Soprano, and on F in the Bass. Were this a Bach fugue it would open in much the same way, but instead of the second (Alto) entry opening on the note C, it would most probably start later and be actually and definitely in the *Key* of C, the Soprano entry then bringing the composition back to the Key of F, and the Bass taking it again to the Key of C.

Keys of five notes apart, like these, are in the closest possible relationship, and alternation between them at the opening of the Fugue gives us the sense of variety without disturbing us by taking us far afield.[1]

A Typical Bach 'Exposition'

Here is an example of the opening (or 'Exposition') of a Bach keyboard fugue (from the '48'), chosen because it is similar in style and Subject to the Palestrina piece—

---

[1] In not quite every case, however, even in Bach, do we find actual modulation (i.e. change of *key*) when the 'Answer' (= second entry of 'Subject') comes in. There are cases where the 'Answer' is rather a pitch-transposition of the subject, than an actual key-transposition.

The device of alternation of pitches was, as we have seen (pp. 10 and 15), originally dictated by convenience.   A piece of melody that lay just right for Tenor would be too low for Alto if untransposed, and if transposed an octave up would be too high.   An obvious way out of the difficulty was to transpose it up, not an octave, but a fifth.   This alternation of entries a fifth apart in pitch then became a convention to be frequently followed, though not invariably adopted (Palestrina, in that very passage, as you have noticed, has not transposed his bass entry).   Then the use of the key-changes, as a means of lending variety, became understood, and the convention was carried over into the new period ; thus what had originated out of vocal convenience was now continued, with improvements, from motives of artistic advantage.

How Bach Continues his Fugue

And so with later entries of the Subject.   In some of the Palestrina movements a *number of different Subjects* entered, as the movement proceeded, in similar ' imitative ' fashion (that is, one voice imitating, or copying, as it entered, the theme of the preceding voice): in other movements the *first main subject* of the piece was given greater importance, and ' entered ' frequently throughout the piece. By the time we get to the Bach period composers have learnt how to arrange the various sets of entries each in a different key from the others, passing more or less round the little circle of related keys. The variety which formerly they had often been able to gain only by the use of a *different Subject* for each set of entries is now supplied by the use of a *different Key* for each set of entries. This enables them to use the same main ' Subject ' throughout, and so to give the piece greater coherence. A typical scheme of entries in a shortish Fugue might be something like this—

        Entries in C–G
          „   „ A minor
          „   „ F
          „   „ C

Bach's ' Episodes '

All this, as will have been realized, is simply a closer organization of the old sixteenth-century contrapuntal choral piece. The closer organization is carried out, too, in another important detail. In the old type of contrapuntal piece there were brief passages between the entries, connecting one with another, and architecturally serving no other very definite purpose. In the Bach fugue these intermediate passages are organized into definite ' Episodes '. And no longer do they consist of indeterminate material ; they are now closely and cleverly constructed out of some *motif* or *motifs* of the previous material. For instance, Bach's 7th Fugue of the ' 48 ' has this Subject—

And the first Episode, when it comes, is found to grow from
out of that little figure at the end of bar 2—

The last example shows how the episode serves as a link
between two sets of entries. Yet observe that it fits so neatly,

at its opening, to the close of the last entry, and so neatly, at its closing, to the opening of the next entry that no break is felt. Except for some special and, as we may call it, oratorical reason, a good Fugue goes right through without break. It is a seamless piece of fabric, with the same figure woven into it at intervals and in different colours—not a number of separate pieces sewn together. To use another metaphor, it is organic. It grows out of a seed planted in the first bars. It extends into roots and branches, but it is all one tree.

Stages in the Fugue's Evolution

The Fugue, as we find it in Bach, represents the climax of a process of development, stretching over the period of about eight hundred years that had elapsed since some churchman was struck with the idea that Providence had not given all monks tenor voices or all of them bass voices (page 10). The stages in the development are represented by—

i. The Churchmen of the ninth and tenth centuries, who devised the plan of singing their Plainsong in parallel 5ths and 8ves instead of in merely unison or octaves. (Older Organum.)

ii. The Churchmen of the eleventh and twelfth centuries, who varied from parallelism in the voice parts that accompanied their Plainsong. (Newer Organum.)

iii. The Churchmen of the twelfth century, who wove quite florid choral accompaniments in quicker notes around their Plainsong, strongly held in slower notes. (Descant.)

iv. The Churchmen of the fourteenth century, who sang their Plainsong accompaniment at the gentler intervals of parallel 3rds and 6ths. (Early Faburden.)

v. The Churchmen of a little later, who reverted to an unparallel accompaniment, now (in the light of all the experiments previously made) of a fairly free character.

vi. The Englishman, John of Dunstable (fifteenth century), who revolutionized musical composition by devising more artistic methods for the movement of the voice parts, often departing from the practice of using Plainsong continuously throughout the composition.[1]

vii. The sixteenth and early seventeenth-century Church Music and Madrigal writers, who carried this style of pure Contrapuntal art to perfection, and some of whom developed it in Instrumental as well as in Choral compositions—Palestrina in Italy, Byrd and Gibbons in England, Victoria in Spain, &c.

viii. The early seventeenth-century writers in many countries (Monteverde and others), who emphasized the Harmonic idea.

ix. The later seventeenth-century writers (e.g. Purcell in England), who combined the Harmonic and Contrapuntal aspects.

x. Bach and Handel, who, in their great choruses and their instrumental works, brought to perfection this combined Harmonic-Contrapuntal art (with the emphasis again on the Contrapuntal).

---

[1] Another point, often overlooked, is that Dunstable when he did use the Plainsong *Canto fermo* (placed by him in any voice) often used it in a floriated manner instead of as the usual mere succession of breves.—R. R. T.

VIII

THE CENTURY OF PERFECTION (1650–1750)

(b) THE ARIA, THE SUITE, THE OPERA, AND THE ORATORIO; THE ORCHESTRA.

THE Fugue then, choral or instrumental, is a development from early Church Song. Another development from early song, but this time from the Folk Song, not the Church Song, was the extended Vocal Solo, as introduced into Opera and Oratorio. The determination to write for the singing voice in a manner imitating the inflexion of the speaking voice had by now weakened. The object of that kind of song was *dramatic expression*, and quickly it had been realized that the other object of *melodic beauty* was not, after all, to be despised. So songs that were dramatically expressive and songs that were melodiously beautiful came to exist side by side, and the convention grew up (a rather sensible one, on the whole, and one that had enough touch with the vital requirements of art to give it a life of at least two-hundred-and-fifty years) of joining the two kinds of song. In this way we got the Recitative and Aria—the half-spoken dramatic song, conveying to the audience a clear idea of the situation of the moment, and the melodic song, immediately following, supplying a lyrical reflection upon it.

Take a well-known example of this, a 'Recitative and Air' from Handel's *Judas Maccabaeus*—

RECITATIVE—*Israelitish Woman.*

To Heav'n's Almighty King we kneel,
For blessings on this exemplary zeal.

Bless him, Jehovah, bless him, and once more
To Thy own Israel liberty restore.

(All this is sung tersely, without elaboration or repetition.)

AIR—(*the same Israelitish Woman*).
O Liberty, thou choicest treasure,
Seat of virtue, source of pleasure ;
Life without thee knows no blessing,
No endearment worth caressing.

(This is expanded, by repetition of the words, into a longish Aria.)

Aria Form

Gradually the Aria took on a general (but not quite invariable) form. It became usual to cast it into three sections ; the first and last of these were identical, and to them the middle one gave musical relief. This is a very stereotyped and formal procedure, in strong contrast with the free utterance of the Recitative. When we speak of ' Aria Form ', or Ternary Form, that simple three-part plan is what we mean.

I have called this period ' The Century of Perfection '. Fugue, as has been seen, had been brought to a stage which we may call perfect, and the Aria, too, reached such a stage. Dull Fugues and Arias were, at this period, written by the thousand, but the *forms* had been perfected (which, of course, was just the circumstance that made it easy for inferior composers to turn out such music wholesale).

What ' Perfection ' means

Thus by ' The Century of Perfection ' I do not mean a period when ' everything in the garden was lovely ', but a period when, the rough digging and manuring having been done and well done by others, the horticultural genius had everything prepared for the production of perfect plants and flowers.

The work of three outstanding composers is especially in mind. Purcell (born 1658) arrived in the garden before it was *quite* ready, but grew some fine blooms notwithstanding.

Handel and Bach, arriving a little later (both born 1685) and both being skilful gardeners, soon produced a wonderful show of blooms. A good deal depends on a wise choice of birth date. Bach, if born in 1658, would probably have done much what Purcell did. Purcell born in 1685 would probably have done much what Bach did: Purcell, Handel, and Bach, born in 1585, would have been Peris and Caccinis and Monteverdes, turning over the soil and making the hitherto almost virgin harmonic wilderness fruitful for the harmonic-contrapuntal gardeners who were to follow a century later.

Keyboard Music

Now for the Instrumental Music, and especially the Keyboard Music. The keyboard instruments of Purcell, Bach, and Handel were the same as those of their sixteenth-century predecessors, but improved. Purcell and Handel wrote for the Harpsichord. Bach wrote both for the Harpsichord and the Clavichord, the latter a gentler keyboard instrument with its sound-production apparatus devised according to a rather different principle. (See Appendix IV for a brief description of these instruments.)

Dance Influence again

So far this chapter has been concerned with what grew out of Song. We now turn to what grew out of Dance. Glance back at Chapter IV, and recall the early influence of the Dance on Instrumental Music. Once a form had become stereotyped as a Dance Form it was natural that it should aspire to rank as a pure instrumental form.

If you were a wandering fiddler, playing dances on village greens, some of your tunes being traditional and some made by yourself upon the traditional forms, you would not be likely to confine your playing of them to occasions when the company was prepared to dance. Those tunes would constitute a great part of your professional repertory, and when called on for a little music you would dip into the repertory and perhaps bring up as an instrumental piece something originally designed as a dancing measure. And so, too, with the Harpsichordist. From that it is a small step to providing pieces in these dance forms *meant for performance as pieces of music*, rather than for performance as dance accompaniments. And freed from the restrictions of the dance, the music would tend to develop into complications a little beyond what would be suitable for the purposes of dancing.

Thus, by Queen Elizabeth's day composers were producing pairs of contrasted pieces in dance form but already departing from full dance style, such as a (slower) Pavane, followed by a (quicker) Galliard, and were sometimes preceding this pair by a Prelude, i.e. a short piece not in any dance style at all, but serving as a suitable introduction.

An Example from Byrd

Thus in *Parthenia* (1611), the first music ever printed in England for the Virginals, we find Byrd providing a short three-section piece as follows:

PRAELUDIUM.

PAVANE.

GALIARDO.

The Variety of Dance

Other dance forms used at this period in England were Allemandes, Courantes, Espagnolettes (or Spagnolettas), Jigs, Toyes, Voltes, Rounds, Marches, and Morrises. The varying national origin of these various dances is plainly indicated by their names: the Allemande was of German origin, the Espa-

gnolette of Spanish and the Morris of Moorish, the Courante of
French, the Toye of English.   These things spread from their
country of birth all over Europe, in the same way as Tangos
and Fox Trots have spread in our days from the American
continent.   And having become accepted as dance forms they
passed into the resources of the purely instrumental composer,
who used most of them for separate and independent little
pieces but connected others in the way we have just seen Byrd
doing.

Purcell's ' Lessons '

By the time of Purcell we find the idea of connecting into
sets extended, and so we see him writing Suites of pieces
(which he calls Lessons) such as this :

SUITE I

Prelude

Almand

Corant

Minuet

SUITE II

Prelude

Almand

Corant

Saraband

Purcell's Modern Feeling for ' Key '

All Purcell's pieces are comparatively short, and are simple
both to play and to listen to.   And they are in modern
tonality.   Those short extracts of Byrd's strike one to-day as
a little confused in tonality.   Byrd at the time he wrote these
was between two periods.   The old Modes were going out and
the new Major and Minor Scales had not fully come in.   But
a piece of Purcell's is quite clearly and definitely in some
particular major or minor key, with its definite modulations

into related keys, as for instance this little Minuet, from Suite I, which begins in Key G, modulates at the half-way cadence to Key D, then passes momentarily into Key B minor, and ends in the key in which it began—

(*The marks of expression in this and some other pieces quoted do not appear in the original, but are the additions of a modern editor. They are, however, allowed to stand, as useful suggestions to the reader in his playing of the piece.*)

How Bach did it

With Bach, too, and with the other composers of Bach's period, we find this modern system of keys and key relationships fully established.   But Bach, being a little later, and being gifted with a supreme musical instinct, was able to arrange his musical material with much more skill, and consequently to write much longer pieces, and to put more of them into a Suite, without losing the listener's attention.

For instance, the first of what he calls his *English Suites* consists of the following pieces :

> Prelude.
> Allemande.
> Courante I.
> Courante II.
>   (with two ' Doubles' or Variations).
> Sarabande.
> Bourrée I.
> Bourrée II.
> Gigue.

Altogether this makes ten pieces (counting the ' Doubles'), and some of the pieces are in themselves of considerable length.

An Agreeable Long-windedness

And here occurs an interesting thought—looked at in one way all the efforts of composers through the centuries have been directed to learning how to write longer and longer pieces without losing the attention of the audience.   In Queen Elizabeth's day the longest keyboard piece lasted perhaps five minutes, in Charles the Second's the longest piece lasted perhaps ten minutes.   By the time of Bach there were pieces lasting, say, twenty to twenty-five minutes.   Or, reckoning by single pieces (or ' movements '), the Elizabethan wrote pieces that lasted, at the most, perhaps, three minutes, and Purcell wrote pieces that lasted a still shorter time, because he was restricted by the determination to get the newly understood key relationships perfectly clear and to secure a perfect balance of parts. Bach, however, stepped into the inheritance left by the men of Purcell's period (we will not say of Purcell, for Bach probably knew nothing of Purcell's music, but of Purcell's contemporaries, the Italian violin composers and the French harpsichordists), and so he was able to write single movements that lasted as long as five or six minutes, and yet flagged nowhere, e. g. the Preludes of some of the 'English Suites', which are the longest of his keyboard Suite movements.

Bach's 'Binary' Form

The form of almost all Bach's Suite movements was that which has been exemplified in the Purcell Minuet (page 77). Setting out from a main key he moved at his half-way point to a nearly related key (almost always the key of the Dominant, i. e. the fifth above—e. g. beginning in C he would modulate to G ; but if the main and opening key of the piece were a minor key, the half-way modulation would often be to the relative major, e. g. A minor to C major).

Generally he would there draw a double bar and mark the whole section to be repeated, as Purcell does in the little Minuet just quoted. Then, in the second half of the piece, he would modulate back to his first key (or 'Tonic'). And usually he would mark this second half to be repeated also. This we call Binary Form, and it should be clearly grasped, for it had been growing up and settling itself for a long while and was to be the basis of the next great development in the forms of instrumental music.

The Economies of a Composer

Now if interest is to be maintained in any piece of music the composer must use a comparatively small amount of material. The reason for this is the very human one that the brain cannot be always taking in something new without getting tired.

Look at the Purcell Minuet again, and you will see that the tune of the thing is almost all grown out of this little seed—

Sometimes this figure occurs as just given and sometimes it is so changed as to descend instead of to ascend.   And when the figure itself is not going on, whatever *is* going on will generally be seen, on a little examination, to have been evolved from either the first half or the second half of it. Then if the bass be examined it will be found to be largely made out of the three-note descending scale figure first heard in the second bar.   So there is extreme economy here and this little piece is made out of a quite tiny amount of material.

The Thrifty Bach

Compare now a Minuet of Bach (that from the second French Suite)—

G

I choose this one for quotation because it is one of the shortest movements in all Bach's Suites, and can be given here in full, but short as it is you will find that Bach's idea of a Minuet is a considerable extension of the idea of Purcell. You will, for instance, notice that Bach has lengthened out the second section very greatly, and if you play, or hear, the piece thoughtfully two or three times I think you will find that he has done it by 'developing' his initial 'germ theme' after the double bar. Bear this in mind, in view of a further extension of this sort which you will find carried into effect in the next period.

Bach's Harmonic Foundation

Note, too, that the little piece is laid out, looked at in one aspect, as a series of chords on this basis—

I do not mean that no other chords than these are to be found in the passage represented, but such others as do occur may be called incidental, and considered as having been neatly brought into existence as intermediate chords by the motion of the parts. This harmonic basis is what Bach was consciously or instinctively working to, and the fact that there is a so clear harmonic basis is typical of this Harmonic-Contrapuntal period.

Counterpoint *ex* Harmony

Having investigated the harmony of the passage, now look into the counterpoint. The Purcell Minuet was in three parts (or voices) : this Bach Minuet is in but two. Yet you do not feel it to be thin, because there is something going on all the time in one or other of the parts.

Generally the parts stand out well from one another (which is the essence of good counterpoint), and this is achieved by giving walking notes to the bottom part when the top part has running notes, and *vice versa*.

Note, too, a certain amount of imitation ; e. g. at the outset, at the second bar, the left hand imitates the right hand of the preceding bar, and the right hand imitates the left hand (walking *down*, however, instead of up).

Many of the Bach Suite movements are even more contrapuntal than this, and the Gigues which end these Suites are especially so.

An Example of 'Imitation'

For instance, the very next movement to the Minuet just quoted is a Gigue opening as follows :

Here, as you notice, the left hand imitates the right pretty exactly for a stretch of four bars, and the whole piece is constructed upon the same principle. Many of the Gigues in this way almost step over the line into the domain of Fugue ; they probably come as near to actual Fugue as any piece in dance rhythm and dance style could do.

Opera

A few words must now be said about some other forms of music popular at the period. Opera has been alluded to. After but a century's development it had almost left behind its original aim of being very dramatic and free, and was tending rather to musical beauty and to formality. Consequently practically no opera of the period is to be heard to-day, out of the hundreds that were written (Handel alone wrote fifty) ; Purcell's *Dido and Æneas* may still be heard performed from time to time, and there has been some attempt to revive one or two of Handel's operas in Germany (see page 90), but that is all. (The whole big subject of the growth of Opera will receive a brief generalized treatment in the succeeding volume of this work.)

Oratorio

Oratorio had reached its first great development, and was very popular. The Oratorios of Handel retained popularity for over a century and a half, but are at present (except *Messiah*) under a cloud. Bach's settings of the Passion were enveloped in such a cloud immediately after his death, but are now revived, and enormously valued by all music-lovers. They employ an 'Evangelist', who carries on the narrative in Recitative, and the various characters of the story step into the dialogue whenever their actual words are given in the sacred text. There are reflective Arias, somewhat like that of Handel described on page 72, and both reflective and dramatic choruses. The traditional Lutheran Hymn-Tunes, or Chorales, appear at intervals, set to verses of reflective comment, generally in the way of applying the lessons of the story to the individual, or of expressing collective feelings of prayer or praise.

The Mass

The Mass was now often developed into a form of Oratorio, especially in the hands of the German (Lutheran) composers. The Palestrina Mass we examined was entirely for unaccompanied Choir, and its various sections were short and involved little repetitions of the words. Bach's famous B minor Mass includes not only Choruses, but solo Arias and Duets, and not only has it orchestral accompaniment, but there are in it short passages for orchestra alone. It rises to great heights of almost dramatic expression in some places, and to heights of musical splendour in others, whereas Palestrina's was throughout somewhat quietly devotional.

The Orchestra

The orchestra had emerged out of its early chaotic condition, as a collection of chance instruments, and was on its way to standardization.   The Strings were becoming the basis, as they remain to-day, but behind their tone was that of the Harpsichord.   (This is fully explained in Chapter X.)

The various instruments were now being written for pretty intelligently, more or less on the lines dictated by their several individual characters and powers, but no composer had yet a clear idea of his forces as four distinct bodies—Strings, Wood, Brass, and Percussion, to be combined or heard separately, as fancy might suggest.   Nor was it yet realized what a chance lay in passing appearances and disappearances of particular instruments, and the tossing from one to another of some little phrase so as to show it in varied tone colours.   (This also is made clearer in Chapter X.)

The Violin family had now been brought to perfection, and the efforts of composers (particularly Italian composers) to provide its members with suitable music had great effect in the development of suitable styles and forms.   This was soon to react upon instrumental composition in general, as will shortly be seen.

LEADING COMPOSERS OF THE PERIOD

HENRY PURCELL

Born 1658 or 1659; died 1695. Purcell was a London boy. He came of a musical family. His father may have been that Henry Purcell, 'Master of Musique' mentioned in Pepys's Diary as one of a party of friends who, with music, celebrated at a tavern the decision of the Long Parliament to recall Charles II, but was more likely his brother, Thomas.

Purcell.

Both father and uncle became 'Gentlemen of the Chapel Royal', and Henry senior was also appointed Master of the Choristers at Westminster Abbey. The boy, Henry, at six or seven years old, was admitted as a chorister of the Chapel Royal. Here he received the best kind of musical training, a practical one, learning not merely to sing but to play the Organ and Harpsichord and to compose. The equipment of the Chapel included a band of twenty-four Fiddlers, a band set up by Charles in imitation of the Vingt-quatre Violons du Roi of Louis XIV which he had heard whilst in exile. Charles was musical and encouraged performers and composers.

On Purcell's voice breaking, he remained for a time upon the roll of the Chapel, as it was not the custom to turn a promising boy adrift. There are records of his doing occasional work as music-copyist at Westminster Abbey.

At eighteen or nineteen Purcell was appointed composer to the Chapel Royal and a little later he became, in addition, organist of Westminster Abbey. His genius was thus recognized by appointment to two of the most considerable musical positions in the country.   At this time he composed a great deal of Church Music, some of it serious and devotional and other of it rather lighter in style—the latter possibly written to meet the tastes of the King.

On the death of Charles II, Purcell was retained in the service of James II, and on his exile in that of William and Mary.   He died young—at the age of thirty-seven.

Purcell had a very considerable connexion amongst theatre managers and wrote a large amount of incidental music to the plays of the Restoration dramatists.   Many of the songs he thus wrote are still popular, being very tuneful in a straightforward and thoroughly English way.   He also wrote a number of Odes—many of them of a complimentary nature to royalty on occasions when it went for its holidays or returned from them.   (The opening of one of these Odes, 'Welcome, dread Sir, to Town', indicates roughly the level of their verse.)   His Church Music has been alluded to ; some of it provides abundant opportunity for orchestral activity, in interludes and accompaniments.   His Choral writing in the bigger scale pieces is imposing. The Harpsichord Music is all fresh and delightful, but primitive ; in it Purcell appears as a sort of boy-Bach (note that he was born a quarter of a century before Bach and Handel).   There are a number of 'Sonatas' for two Violins, 'Cello, and Harpsichord that show the greatest ingenuity and musicianship, yet are to-day little played.   And there is one admirable Violin Sonata, re-discovered at the end of the nineteenth century.

Recitative comes a good deal into Purcell's Church and Theatre Music.   It had been introduced into English Church Music by Purcell's master at the Chapel Royal, Pelham Humphrey.   This was Pepys's '*little Pelham Humphrey, lately returned from France, and is an absolute Monsieur as full of form and confidence and vanity, and disparages everything and everybody's musick but his own*'.   Humphrey had been sent to France by the King, and had there studied under the Italian Lully ; this is one of the direct connexions between the Italian musical renascence, the French developments from it, and England, but, in addition, Purcell was all his life a close student of Italian models, and profited by their study.   Nevertheless, though in some senses cosmopolitan, his music has the English directness, and his somewhat plain but massive choral style influenced Handel, who came to England but fifteen years after Purcell's death and found his music in full fashion.

GEORGE FREDERICK HANDEL

Born 1685; died 1759. Handel was born at Halle, in Saxony. His father was a surgeon, who took practical means to stifle his son's musical aspirations, but finding himself unsuccessful, gave way gracefully, and allowed him the best teaching available.

At eighteen the youth went to Hamburg, and became a Violinist in the Opera Orchestra, getting also incidental experience in conducting (at that time carried on at a Harpsichord, by the playing of which the control of the band was effected); he also wrote some Operas, and had them performed.

Handel.

At twenty-one Handel went to Italy, and absorbed operatic traditions nearer their source. On his return the Elector of Hanover made him Kapellmeister, or chief musician.

Shortly afterwards, obtaining leave of absence, Handel came twice to England, where he performed the opera *Rinaldo* and became too popular and prosperous to wish to return to his Kapellmeister duties. Then, his Elector becoming George I of England, Handel found himself in disfavour with the reigning sovereign. He regained favour, and the new approval took the acceptable form of a life pension of £200, as an addition to a pension already bestowed by Queen Anne.

London operatic enterprises carried Handel to a great pitch of popularity and wealth—and then to difficulties. Opera became a party matter, the King supporting Handel's house and the Prince of Wales a rival establishment. Competition led to excessive expenditure upon high-priced vocalists, and at fifty-two Handel was financially ruined. He re-established himself by writing Oratorios, and the best few of these had a clear run of 150 years' popularity before, at the nineteenth-twentieth turn of the century, their vogue fell almost completely away. The Operas had been dropped long before this.[1]

At sixty Handel began to suffer ill-health, and a little later his eyesight failed. He died blind at seventy-four.

This is the merest summary of a life that was full of incident, and that deserves study, especially since its details throw much light upon musical-social conditions in England in the first half of the eighteenth century.

JOHN SEBASTIAN BACH

Born 1685 ; died 1750. The first musical Bach of whom we have knowledge was Veit Bach, born during the fifteen-fifties. He was a

Bach.

miller in Thuringia, and used to play the Zither as the wheel went round. The last was Wilhelm Friedrich Ernst Bach, who was a London piano-teacher for some years, and died, a very old man, in 1845.

That gives Bach musicianship a very satisfactory run of seven generations, covering nearly three centuries. Johann Sebastian belongs to the fifth generation ; the musical miller was his great-great-grandfather, and the London piano-teacher was his grandson. Until Johann Sebastian's sons set the fashion of travel, the family had never stirred far from its native Thuringia.

These Bachs supplied the churches with organists and the town bands with fiddlers ; indeed, in those parts to say ' a Bach ' was to say ' a musician ', and to say ' a musician ' was almost to say ' a Bach '. There were frequent gatherings of the Bach clan to make music. The members of it taught one another. Perhaps they partly ' lived by

[1] *Ottone* and *Rodelinda* were revived at Göttingen in 1921, *Cesare* in 1922, and *Orlando Furioso* at Halle in 1922. Other performances have followed.

taking in' one another's children as music pupils, for they were a fecund as well as a musical race, and any older Bach could always find a swarm of young ones who needed teaching and any younger one a swarm of older ones to give him lessons. Refer to the sketches of Purcell and Couperin for contemporary instances of music as the family trade, and note antithetically that Handel, Bach's exact contemporary, and (in early life) near neighbour, had, so far as we know, no musical ancestry and left no descendants.

John Sebastian became a double orphan at the age of ten, and was then adopted by an elder brother—a professional musician, of course. He made a hobby of holiday pedestrianism, tramping off to hear the organists of greatest fame (see reference to this in sketch of John Bull, p. 46). When he was eighteen he became a fiddler in the private Orchestra of a prince.

Then he obtained a post as Organist, and got into trouble because one of his absences (to hear the great Danish organist, Buxtehude, at Lübeck) lasted three months. All his life through Bach was learning from others—hearing them or studying their works; North German and Dutch and Danish Organ composers, Italian Violin composers, French Harpsichord composers—all were put under contribution, and exercised their influence upon him.

Another grumble of the church authorities was that his juvenile exuberance found expression in too elaborate accompaniments to the hymn-tunes, or Chorales, and the Lutheran Chorale is another great influence in Bach's music. He was constantly 'arranging' Chorales; he put them into his Choral works, either in comparatively simple form or much adorned with flowing 'parts'; he wrote dozens of Organ pieces developed out of Chorales in various ways. The Chorale is a distinctively German thing; Handel became very much Italianized, but Bach, though he picked up composing technique wherever he found it at its best, remained intensely German and even North German in his general outlook.

Other Organ posts succeeded, and then a Kapellmeister post (i. e. a general musical directorship) to a prince whose religious exercises were of a sort that did not call for musical adornment, but who, like many of the English Puritans of sixty or seventy years earlier, revelled in music out of church. This counts as the second artistic period in

Bach's life: in the first his efforts were concentrated on Organ composition; in the second on Chamber Music of all sorts, and on Orchestral Music.

When Bach approached forty he moved to Leipzig. Here he had the music of three churches under his control, played the Organ, composed sacred Cantatas galore, trained Choirs, taught Latin to the small boys in the Choir School, and conducted the University Musical Society. Also he no doubt gave a little occasional attention to his numerous family. Bach has been described by some English schoolboy under examination as (the happy phrase is becoming classic) 'an habitual parent'. He had, in fact, twenty children. The new science of Eugenics has, in this case, surely, no fault to find. Could they have chosen a better father?

This Leipzig period is the third and last. As the others had been devoted largely to the production of, firstly, Organ music and then instrumental music of other kinds, this one was devoted to the production of larger-scale or smaller-scale church compositions—the Cantatas that have been mentioned (300 of them!), and settings of the 'Passion'. Like the productive Handel, he probably used his eyes too much, for he too died blind.

After Bach's death his works were neglected, music having, with his sons, with Haydn, with Mozart, and with their contemporaries, definitely left the distinctively contrapuntal style for another which will be described in the following chapter. Nobody henceforward thought much of Bach until, in the early eighteen hundreds, interest began to revive in Germany and a group of organists in London (Kollmann, C. F. Horn, Jacob, Samuel Wesley—may their names never be forgotten!) became enthusiastic about him and began to pester others to share their enthusiasm. Samuel Wesley, in particular, was indefatigable in his propaganda in favour of 'our matchless Man (if Man he may be called)', and circulated writings intended as 'a thorough defiance of all the Snarlers and would-be Criticks, howsoever dispersed throughout the British Empire'. Then the twenty-year-old Mendelssohn performed the *St. Matthew Passion*, and musicians in Germany became fired with zeal which led in another twenty years or so to the formation of the great Bach Society for complete publication of the works, and, in time, to the present-day Bach worship, the only complaint against which is that in setting up the altar to Bach it has thrown down that of Handel.

A NOTE ON BACH AND HANDEL, AND ANOTHER ON BACH AND PALESTRINA

A brief comparison between Handel and Bach may here fittingly be made.

Handel was more of the practical man, and Bach more of the idealist.

Handel's was the polished, travelled, cosmopolitan mind, Bach's the more rugged mind of the deep student who has spent solitary days and nights in intensive work in his own study.

Handel always had some (quite legitimate) money-making scheme in view when composing; he was thus directing his activities to the winning of the suffrages of a large public, whereas Bach, very frequently, composed merely to satisfy his own need for self-expression or to solve to his own satisfaction some problem of musical form or style.

Bach's choral-writing is more genuinely contrapuntal than Handel's; the one is to the other as the Northern Gothic (organic—'growth' of lines into structure) to Southern Gothic (the Gothic shapes but cut out of the flat): in other words, Handel's harmonic basis is simpler and is more clearly before his mind.

Bach's keyboard writing is much more thorough than Handel's, which, though effective, is often 'sketchy'; Bach was obviously prepared to spend time on the writing of a fugue, whilst Handel wished to 'throw it off' and have done with it.

Handel's Solo vocal music is usually much more graceful than Bach's, but Bach's often attains the deeper expression; here again Handel was fluent, Bach 'thorough'.

A good deal of the difference between Bach and Handel might be expressed in this way—Bach was an organist widened out, and Handel an opera-manager deepened.

Essentially Handel is more modern than Bach.

Both Handel and Bach have religious feeling and great dignity, but Bach's is that of some fine old 'Friend', rising in his Quaker Meeting House, because the spirit moves him, and Handel's that of an Anglican dean, decorously, sincerely, and perhaps just a little pompously officiating in his vestments.

It is also interesting to compare the religious music of Palestrina and Bach. Both were mystics, but Bach's was the more 'human' expression and in places it became even naïve. Palestrina's mysticism lifted the soul of man to heaven and set it before the throne of God, whereas the mysticism of Bach brought heaven to earth, and showed God as 'The Son of Man' in the surroundings of everyday life. In Bach's treatment of sacred subjects there is an intense personal element, and he brings sacred things into touch with himself as the Dutch painters did; Bach is, in religious spirit, a Peter Breughel; Palestrina, a Fra Angelico. As for Handel, it would not occur to one to set up any comparison between him and Palestrina, and in seeking one between him and the painters one thinks of the vigour of Michelangelo and the grandiose suavity of Raphael.

All these are rough generalizations, but they may be suggestive.

FRANÇOIS COUPERIN

Couperin.

Born 1668; died 1733. Born and died in Paris. The Couperins were a family of musicians (five generations) like their contemporaries, the English Purcells (four generations), the Italian Scarlattis (three generations), and the North German Bachs (seven generations).

At twenty-five François became organist of Louis XIV's private chapel at Versailles, and at twenty-eight, as an additional post, of the Paris church of St. Gervais. The St. Gervais organistship had been held by his father and two of his uncles, and was afterwards held by his nephew, grand-nephew, and great-grand-nephew. The Versailles organistship was held by his daughter after him. (Another daughter was organist of Montbuisson Abbey.) To distinguish François from his crowd of organist relations he has been nicknamed, like his monarch, 'Le Grand'.

Couperin le Grand's special reputation as a composer rests upon a large quantity of fine Harpsichord Music, and a 'Method' which he wrote for the Harpsichord, *L'Art de toucher le Clavecin* (1717). The works of Couperin are concise, neat, picturesque in their titles, and *spirituel*. They are typically French. So far as the notes go, many are not difficult, and they deserve a more frequent place on the piano of the amateur and the programme of the public pianist. Bach studied Couperin's work diligently, and was a good deal influenced by it.

JEAN-PHILIPPE RAMEAU

Born 1683; died 1764. His father was organist of Dijon Cathedral. At seven the boy could read any piece of Harpsichord music put before him, but this was about all he would read, which did not please his head master, who asked his father to remove him. He never learnt to spell until the time came for him to write love-letters, when shame drove him to self-improvement. In order to give the love-letters a longer journey and allow them to cool a little on the way, his father sent him to Italy when he was seventeen or eighteen, but he took up with a theatrical

Rameau.

party, and accompanied them, as first violin, to various towns in southern France.

Then he became organist of various churches in Paris, but being disappointed in obtaining a certain post (for which Daquin was preferred) he went to Lille and afterwards to Clermont, in the mountains of Auvergne, where his brother held the post of cathedral organist but was willing to give it up in his favour. Here he had leisure and began to study Acoustics and Musical Theory, accomplishing the first real systematization of Harmony and putting this into a book, which he went to Paris to publish (1722); in this book first appeared the suggestion of 'inversions' of chords, i. e. that E G C and G C E are the same chord as C E G, and so on. Later he published other scientific-musical treatises, and his work in this branch is the foundation of musical theory to-day. In Paris Rameau held an Organ post, and a position of influence as a fashionable Harpsichord teacher.

At the age of about forty Rameau began composing theatre music, but by the age of fifty he had attained no real celebrity in this line. Soon after that age, however, he gained full recognition, became conductor of the Opéra Comique, and wrote Operas and Ballets for the Court of Louis XV. He met with opposition from the supporters of the older operas of Lully (who, as an opera composer, will receive some mention in the second volume of this work). He published a book of pieces of Harpsichord Music, which is worth the attention of pianists.

DOMENICO SCARLATTI

Born 1685 (the same year as both Handel and Bach); died 1757. He was a son of the great Neapolitan Opera composer, Alessandro

Scarlatti.

Scarlatti, who wrote to Ferdinand de' Medici of his son, in 1705, that at Naples—

'His talent found scope indeed, but it was not the sort of talent for that place. I send him away from Rome also, since Rome has no roof to shelter music, that lives here in beggary. This son of mine is an eagle whose wings are grown; he ought not to stay idle in the nest, and I ought not to hinder his flight. Since the *virtuoso*, Nicolino, of Naples, is passing through Rome on his way to Venice, I have thought fit to send Domenico with

him; and under the sole escort of his own artistic ability (which has made great progress since he was able to be with me and enjoy the honour of obeying your Royal Highness's commands in person, three years ago), he sets forth to meet whatever opportunities may present themselves for making himself known—opportunities for which it is hopeless to wait in Rome nowadays.'

At Venice he met Handel, became his close friend and travelled with him back to Rome, where a Cardinal held a sort of competition between the two, in which it was agreed that as Harpsichordists they ranked equally, but that as Organist Handel was the greater (the organ was much more cultivated in Germany than in Italy).

Scarlatti then entered the service of the Queen of Poland and wrote for her theatre at Rome a great many operas. At thirty he became choirmaster of St. Peter's, Rome ; at thirty-four he travelled to London and then to Lisbon, where he became a great favourite at the court. After further years in Rome he went to the Spanish court. He returned to his native place when about seventy, and died there in poverty, having gambled away his large earnings.

Scarlatti wrote a large number of very delightfully bright and vigorous short harpsichord pieces. There is in some of these pieces a good deal of crossing of the hands, and as their composer was very stout one wonders how he played them ; probably they belong to the earlier years.

PERIOD III

To Beethoven

Evolution of Music up to the Mid-Eighteenth Century

(A.) CHORAL MUSIC.

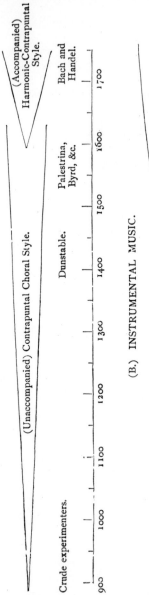

Crude experimenters.

Dunstable.

Palestrina, Byrd, &c.

(Accompanied) Harmonic-Contrapuntal Style.

Bach and Handel.

(Unaccompanied) Contrapuntal Choral Style.

900 — 1000 — 1100 — 1200 — 1300 — 1400 — 1500 — 1600 — 1700

(B.) INSTRUMENTAL MUSIC.

Crude experimenters (English, French, Flemish, Italian, Spanish, &c.).

Gradual improvements in { instruments, performance, methods of composition.

English Virginalists (Byrd, Lull, &c.).

Italian Violinists (Corelli, &c.).

German School (Bach, &c.).

900 — 1000 — 1100 — 1200 — 1300 — 1400 — 1500 — 1600 — 1700

(C.) NOTATION, &c.

Crude Notation (Retarding Progress).

gradually improving to something like our present notation.

Music Printing (Speeding Progress).

IX

THE NEW STYLE IN INSTRUMENTAL MUSIC— SONATA AND SYMPHONY

BEFORE entering the next period let us rapidly survey progress to the present point. The diagram opposite will help us to recapitulate.

The Diagram Considered

i. Note the long, slow development of the unaccompanied, contrapuntal choral style.

ii. Observe one cause of this slow evolution—the lack of recognized and flexible Notation. Obviously, so long as composers had to teach their music by ear, and to hand it down by tradition, accuracy was impossible, and a high degree of elaboration of detail extremely unlikely to come about. Moreover, skill in weaving parts was unlikely to be developed until the composer could note down exactly what he wished to be sung, and could *see* his composition grow before his eyes.

iii. Then, when notation was developed into something very like the present complex (imperfect yet fairly definite) system, music still circulated with some difficulty, because in manuscript. Thus, composers had not the full opportunity of learning from one another, of profiting from their predecessors' and contemporaries' faults and happy inventions.

iv. The development of instruments was going on all the time, but Vocal Music had a great start over Keyboard or String or Wind Music since the *instrument* of Vocal Music had been invented and perfected so long ago as 4004 B.C. according to Archbishop Ussher's chronology, and a very great deal earlier, according to the evolutionists. Naturally, then, when Instrumental Music did rise into artistic importance it is found to have been modelled a great deal on choral music, and it has never entirely discarded its model to this day.

v. Note the greatly increased speed of progress in the development of Instrumental Music at the period when (*a*) the early Keyboard Instruments had been brought to a state of perfection, (*b*) Choral models of high value were now available.

vi. Remember that the date 1600 marks a turning-point. As you observe, the old Contrapuntal Style did not at once die. Rather the new Harmonic Style grew up inside it and then developed into a full Harmonic-Contrapuntal Style.

vii. Remark that when one style comes to its point of perfection, another always grows up inside it. So, a style that was to culminate in Bach grew up inside the style which had culminated in Palestrina. Similarly we shall now find that a style which is to culminate in Beethoven is to grow up inside the style which had culminated in Bach. And, necessarily, the new style has always crude, narrow beginnings, that to some contemporary observers may appear to offer a very unfavourable contrast with the splendour of the existing style then at its apogee. There are two mistakes made by two different classes of people at such a period—In considering the new productions (*a*) the 'Liberals' over-exalt *relative* value, and (*b*) the 'Conservatives' over-exalt *absolute* value. If these people were really intellectually balanced in respect of the musical movements of to-day, they would form a Coalition that would agree to support the older works for their absolute value and the newer ones for their relative value, and disputes would cease.

Why the New Developments were Instrumental

By the year 1750 Choral Music had passed its grand climacteric. Youth and middle age had brought it great riumphs; henceforth it was to have a quieter existence. We cannot say that an art was exhausted that was yet to produce Beethoven's great Mass in D, the choral passages of Wagner, Elgar's *Gerontius*, and Holst's *Hymn of Jesus*.[1] But its period of independent exploration was ended and henceforth the striking developments in music are instrumental in character.

Instruments and Voices Compared

There is an obvious reason for this. The point of perfection is at once starting-point and winning-post. The human voice was waiting from the beginning, and composers only needed to learn how to write for it passages such as it could effectively sing and audiences could enjoy. Meantime instruments had an unlimited course of improvement lying before them.

Another point—Instruments are more reliable interpreters than voices. Pay the piano shop about two guineas a year and your piano will play in perfect tune. If you are a composer writing a Piano Sonata you do not suddenly stop and say, 'Now can I rely on the player to carry out these difficult modulations without flattening? No, on reflection, I can't, therefore I must simplify the passage, or in a percentage of its performances it will lead to the ruin of the effect of the whole composition.'

And a still further point—there is only one kind of human voice (in its four pitches, with their slightly varying *timbres*), but there are innumerable kinds of instruments, with an

---

[1] 'By the year 1750 Choral Music had passed its grand climacteric.' E. W. comments on this, 'Strictly speaking, until the seventeenth century, I suppose, Choral Music in the Beethoven-Holst sense had never existed. All sixteenth century "Choruses" were pretty well solo voice concerns, were they not?' This point is worth making. It is generally agreed that the Madrigals were intended to be sung with one voice to a part, and though the Church Music was probably generally sung with more than one voice to a part (certainly more than one treble boy!) yet the idea of actual chorus singing appears to come in with the Purcell-Handel-Bach period.

enormous range of *timbres*, and the possibilities of combination
of their *timbres* are unlimited.   Moreover, instruments have a
wider range of pitch than voices (i. e. from the lowest note of
the double-bass to the highest of the piccolo).   Here are the
two ranges compared :

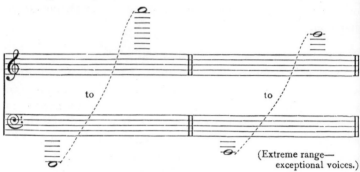

(Extreme range—
exceptional voices.)

Then many instruments can perform rapid passages that
would be quite beyond voices (see some of the Virginals music
quoted in chapter iv, for instance).

And so we could go on.   There are plenty of reasons why
(*a*) Choral style should make an earlier start, and why (*b*) Instrumental style should have a longer run of development.

Of course, the manner of writing for voices is still changing
and, for all we know, may go on changing.   But it can never,
in the nature of things, change as much as Instrumental Style ;
and moreover, whereas Instrumental Style was at the outset
founded on the accepted Choral Style of the period, modifications that occur in the Choral Style of to-day are a good deal
suggested by the changes that have previously occurred in
Instrumental Style.

At any rate, whether or not you agree with all I have just
written, it must be admitted that the middle of the eighteenth
century saw the *perfection* of the second, and perhaps last,
great stage in Choral Style, and merely the *beginning* of the
second stage in Instrumental Style.   And this second stage

in Instrumental Style is a stage of independence, of shaking off more than ever had been dared before of the clinging relics of the choral models.

The Influence of Social Demands

The period is that of the Sonata and Symphony (a Symphony = a Sonata for Orchestra), the greatest attempt as yet made to provide instruments with large-scale pieces, entirely adapted to their resources.

To some extent (more, perhaps, than can be explained here) the Sonata and Symphony grew up in response to a demand arising out of social conditions connected with music. In the early eighteenth century Central Europe was full of petty kingdoms, princedoms, prince-bishoprics, and electorates. And nearly every king, prince, prince-bishop, and elector kept, as a part of his royal state, a Royal Chapel Choir, a Royal Orchestra, and a Royal Opera Company.

Eighteenth-Century Composers as Royal Servants

The Central European composers of that period were nearly all attached to courts as members of the staff maintained to minister to the luxury and display of the rulers. Bach at one time held such a position, Handel in early life held one, Haydn held one, so did Mozart. Beethoven's grandfather and father were musicians in a royal 'Kapelle' (= a body of musicians associated under such auspices as those above mentioned). Beethoven, except in boyhood, was not; he marks the beginning of the break-up of the system, for though such combinations continued to exist (Mendelssohn and Brahms both held positions which were the more modern equivalent of that of a 'Kapellmeister') music from Beethoven's time onwards became more and more democratized, so that to-day music is composed for public concert audiences and not for private and princely court parties.

What kind of Music was wanted?

Naturally there was a great demand for music of a fairly graceful, not too heavy kind, with pith and point, enough 'science' to please cultured people, and Melody, Rhythm and (if Orchestral) effective Orchestration.   So came into existence—

    (*a*) The Harpsichord Sonata,

    (*b*) The Duet Sonata for Harpsichord and Violin, and similar combinations,

    (*c*) The String Quartet and Trio,

    (*d*) The Orchestral Symphony,

    (*e*) The Concerto, for solo instrument and orchestra.

The form of all these things was much the same.   It grew out of what had been going on before, but took on a more definite shape of its own, and, above all, a definite style.

Earlier Sonatas

The word 'Sonata' (literally, a *Sounded Piece* as distinct from a *Sung Piece* = 'Cantata') was already in use. Purcell had written a 'Sonata' for Violin and Harpsichord, and Sonatas for Two Violins, 'Cello and Harpsichord.   Corelli and other Italians had written Chamber Sonatas (Sonate da Camera) and Church Sonatas (Sonate da Chiesa), both of them but modifications of the Suite, the Church Sonatas being (naturally) modified in the direction of a somewhat greater seriousness, and the Chamber Sonatas much less modified, if modified at all.   There, then, is the Dance-Suite influence persisting, though of course in the Church Sonatas it was somewhat disguised.

The Influence of the Overture

Another influence was that of the Opera or Oratorio Overture.   It had become the fashion to write such an Overture in several movements, contrasted in speed and character and hence approximating to a Suite. Take down from your shelf Handel's *Messiah* or *Judas Maccabaeus* and play the overture, and you will get a pretty good idea of how such pieces were written in those days. These two Overtures have but a couple of movements apiece, and neither movement very 'dancy'; but *Jephtha*, you will find, has three, and one of them a Minuet.

C. P. E. Bach

One of Bach's sons, Carl Philipp Emanuel Bach, was the pioneer in this Sonata-Symphony style. On his works were founded those of Haydn, on Haydn's were founded those of Mozart; Mozart's, in their turn, influenced Haydn again, and on Haydn's and Mozart's were founded Beethoven's. On Beethoven's were founded those of Brahms and Elgar, and eventually (though with increasing deviations in smaller matters of form) those of Scriabin and even those of the young men of to-day.

Peasant Ancestry

In general a Symphony composed at the present day is not so very different in essentials from a Beethoven Symphony. People may at first or second hearing call such a piece over-sophisticated, and so it may be (who can yet decide?). But it can be traced back by any reader who has grasped the preceding chapters, stage by stage, to the village green, whence it has reached us by something like the following stages—

1. Folk Dances.

2. Court Dances.

3. Suites (from the Elizabethans to old Bach).

4. Opera Overtures, Sonatas and Symphonies (from young Bach to the present-day writers).

Everything in the way of formal arrangement that you find in the most modern of Symphonies or Sonatas can be seen in embryo in the Folk dance, and everything that you see in the Folk dance can be seen in a higher development in the modern Symphony and Sonata.

The Principles of Instrumental Form

What are the principles of Form in any composition, little or big?

(*a*) You must have Variety.

(*b*) You must have Repetition (= Unity).

In a Sonata or Symphony movement of Haydn or Mozart you find both Variety and Repetition exemplified in two matters—

(*a*) KEY (the movement begins and ends in the same key, but in between wanders into other keys).

(*b*) MATERIAL (the movement, roughly speaking, opens and closes with the same material, but in between gives us something different).

The New Plan of Construction

Out of the Simple Binary Form explained on p. 79 grew something more elaborate, and capable of sustaining interest through a longer piece of work. Here is the scheme—

A. i. A definite FIRST TUNE or SUBJECT.

ii. A passage (often called a ' BRIDGE PASSAGE ') leading to some related key, in which key appeared—

iii. A SECOND TUNE or SUBJECT.

iv. Some little closing passage, or CODETTA, to round off this section.

(As this portion of the piece introduced the chief Tunes, it was often repeated in order that they might be thoroughly grasped.)

B. A DEVELOPMENT, i. e. a shorter or longer passage in which portions or the whole of one or both of the Subjects already given out were 'developed', the music meanwhile passing through various keys, and often in tonality getting quite far afield.

(Thus there is here introduced into the piece the element of Variety in both (*a*) treatment of Tunes, (*b*) Keys.)

C. i. A repetition of the FIRST SUBJECT.

   ii. The 'BRIDGE', but altered so as *not* this time to lead to a different key.

   iii. The SECOND SUBJECT, but this time (as we are nearing the end of the movement) in the 'home-key', like the First Subject.

   iv. Another closing passage (or CODA) probably more extended and final than the first one.

Names for this Form

A little comparison with pages 76 to 82 will show how all this has developed out of Simple Binary Form.   From this origin it is called 'Compound Binary Form', yet in effect it is surely a Ternary Form.   After all, the ear and not history ought to decide musical terminology, and to the ear the feature of this form is its division into *three* clear parts.

Another name for the form is 'First Movement Form', because the first movement of a Sonata or Symphony or String Quartet is so often in this form.   For a similar reason (but not so reasonably) it is often called 'Sonata Form', because it generally (not always) appears in at least that one movement of a Sonata.

How 'Simple Binary' became 'Compound Binary'

If this developed out of the Simple Binary Form used by Bach and others for so many of the movements of their Suites, &c., how did it do so?

Well, the general key system is much the same. The first section, for instance, begins in the main key and ends in a related key. But in the Compound Binary Form this first section has definitely organized itself into two 'Subjects' in the two keys, with a connecting passage and a closing passage.

Then in Simple Binary Form the place where any extensive modulation was likely to occur was just after the half-way-home of the double bar that closed the first section. In Compound Binary Form this has grown into a definite section of 'Development' or 'Free Fantasia', or, as it has been called, a 'Modulatory Section'.

Then in Simple Binary Form the movement, of course, ended in the first and main key of the piece, often with some repetition of the chief material. In the Compound Binary Form this is organized with a more or less exact repetition of the whole of the first section, with a change of key for the Second Subject, in order that the movement shall end in the key in which it began.

What is the advantage of the New Form?

Why is the Compound Binary Form a better form than the Simple Binary Form for a long movement? Because it is much more definitely organized in all points, and, moreover, gives far more opportunity for variety and for striking contrast. Now that the composer has two distinct subjects he naturally gives them different characters. Look at any Sonata-form movements and see how frequently one of the subjects might be described as masculine and the other as feminine.

Consider, for instance, an example from Mozart. Here is the First Subject, rapid and bold—

(Piano arrangement
from Litolff edition.)

And here is the opening of the Second Subject—

Those examples are from Mozart's Overture to *Figaro*, which is in 'Sonata Form'. Get it as a Gramophone Record, if you like, and realize more vividly how the composer has contrasted the melodic and general character of his two subjects.

Variety of Mood now Possible

Note, too, how much more variety of mood could be expressed in this new Compound Binary Form, as compared with the old 'Simple Binary'. The older form, roughly speaking, ran right through with only one break. It had only one piece of main subject - matter, and if, occasionally, it reached the verge of a division of this into two, the parts into which the subject-matter fell were little contrasted. *The whole principle of the thing was homogeneity.* The main variety introduced was that of Key, and in so far as the material was varied, this came about rather as variety of treatment of the details than as variety of actual 'Subject'.

But the more elaborate Binary Form, as it grew out of the earlier Binary, quickly changed character. Sometimes in the hands of Bach's son and even in those of Haydn, you could hardly put your finger on a definite tune to be called by the name 'Second Subject'. But this phase did not last long, and we soon find the Second Subject quite clearly defined and even, on occasion, find it splitting up into several well defined tunes, as also the First Subject does occasionally.

Take one of Beethoven's early Sonatas as an example of this—one which almost everybody knows (the one in E flat, Op. 7).

Here are the openings of Beethoven's various pieces of subject-matter for the First Movement—

FIRST SUBJECT.

A name, however trivial it may be, is a useful thing in discussing subject-matter, and if this piece is being played, fix that subject in your mind as the 'Drum-tap' Tune.

SECOND SUBJECT (*a*).

Call that (from the left-hand part, again) the 'Leap-up-and-run-down' Tune.

SECOND SUBJECT (*b*).

Call that the 'Happy-hymn' Tune.

SECOND SUBJECT (*c*).

Name that the 'Trumpet-call' Tune.

SECOND SUBJECT (*d*).

Name that the 'Harp' Tune.

Even the reader who is lazily disinclined to get down the
Sonata in question, and look it through or play it, will see
at once from the mere openings of these five subjects (for that
is what they really in a sense amount to) what variety of
mood, and style, and treatment the new 'Compound Binary'
form allowed.

And as Beethoven connected many of these Subjects by
the use of 'Bridge' matter, then 'developed' some of them,
and repeated them (with their 'Bridges'), and last added an
extensive Coda, made out of *motifs* from some of them, you
will see after a moment's calculation that his scheme provided
for twenty or more changes of mood (greater or smaller), and
will realize what a step towards *freer* expression was made
by the bringing into existence of this new form.   I would not
like to say that Beethoven could express any *deeper emotion*

than Bach, but he could, in one movement, express a *greater range of emotions*, and express them pretty definitely. As a matter of fact, in this particular movement you may perhaps feel that Beethoven, who was only a young man when he wrote it, and still comparatively inexperienced, has overdone the variety and overlengthened his movement.

Other Forms used in the Sonata

So far we have only been examining one of the several Forms which might come into a Sonata, or String Quartet, or Symphony. As has been said, the First Movement was usually in this form. The last movement, too, was sometimes in the same form; if not, it was generally in the form of a RONDO, a form in which the main subject, or subjects, come round again, time after time, with intermediate matter.

The middle movements would generally be two—a slow expressive movement (possibly in a shortened 'Compound Binary Form', or possibly in some simpler form), and a Minuet and Trio, like that of Bach, but now in a (slightly or considerably) different style—to be shortly discussed.

Sonata compared with Suite

So was made up a string of three or four pieces, a series very like one of the older Suites, in that there was a good contrast between the various movements, but unlike it in that only one of the movements was definitely based on a dance.

Another little point of freedom introduced into the Sonata and Symphony was this. Whereas in the old Suites all the movements were in the same key (or very occasionally in keys that were relative or tonic majors and minors of one another), in the new Sonatas and Symphonies the movements might be in any related keys, and latterly even in unrelated keys.

The New and Improved Minuet

Now about that Minuet. The Bach (Suite) Minuet given on p. 80, being in the old Simple Binary Form, could not

offer much variety. With the new (Sonata) Minuet we find
Ternary Form usual, and the consequent opportunity for far
greater variety.

We have already had Minuets from a Purcell Suite and from
a Bach Suite; let us now look at one from a Mozart Sonata—

It is easy to see how that has grown out of the Purcell and Bach-period Minuet. But where does it differ? Chiefly after the double bar. Where Purcell and Bach, at this point, resumed their first main Subject, Mozart gives us a distinct change of subject-matter. Then, after six bars of new Subject, he returns to the old one. For variety, in this particular Minuet, he reverses the hands, you will notice, and you will also see that whereas the First Subject, on its first appearance, modulated to another (the Dominant) key, on its second appearance it is changed at the end so as to remain and close in the original (or Tonic) key.

Mozart follows this with another and contrasting Minuet and then returns to the first Minuet. Thus the whole Minuet and Trio, as it is called (Trio is the foolish name for the second Minuet), falls into Ternary Form.

Minuet I : Minuet II (= Trio) : Minuet I.

And each Minuet falls into three :

Subject I : Subject II : Subject I.

But the portions bracketed are followed by repeat marks, as you see in the case of the Minuet here given. These repeat marks are, by custom, understood in the case of Minuet I to apply only to the first performance of the Minuet, not to its repetition after the Second Minuet.

The Whole Thing laid out

So putting all together we get :

Minuet I.   1st subject.

1st   „
2nd   „
1st   „
2nd   „
1st   „

Minuet II.   1st subject.

1st   „

2nd   „

1st   „

2nd   „

1st   „

Minuet I.   1st subject.

2nd   „

1st   „

Altogether fifteen changes !

But now look at one of those Subjects and you will see that in itself it contains variety, falling into two or three distinct *motifs*. In all then we get from thirty to forty-five changes of material in one little Minuet and Trio, and this happy restlessness is one of the striking new season novelties introduced by the Sonata-Symphony firm, Messrs. C. P. E. Bach, Haydn, Mozart and Co.

The Beginnings of Modernity

A change of Form had brought with it a change of spirit, or a change of spirit had brought with it a change of Form (have it as you will), and the result (just characterized as 'restlessness') is a much greater feeling of modernity. Bach represents the days when a man usually stuck at the same job, in the same place, all his life. Haydn, Mozart, and Beethoven prefigure our own later period when a man is usually born in a different place from his father, spends his working life a year or two in one place and a year or two in another, and goes for abundant holiday journeys, now to Blackpool or Atlantic City, now to Biarritz or Florida or California, to Florence, to the Fjords, to Montreux and Madrid.

Note that with all this comes a simplification—of Harmony and Counterpoint. In Bach we saw cleverly and effectively moving parts laid out on a basis of a few main chords to each phrase but producing by their movements other, subsidiary, and, as we may call them, by-product chords. In Haydn and Mozart and even Beethoven we see far less of this. The pendulum has again swung over to the Harmonic side, and what Counterpoint we see is evolved out of the succession of chords the composer felt was needed in that particular place. Moreover, the harmonies are now (in Haydn and Mozart especially) clarified and simplified, and follow one another a good deal according to a definitely established and elaborate convention, and yet, though a convention, one that we feel to have a logical basis in the natural relationship of diatonic chords.

In a similar way Orchestration was systematized and clarified. But that calls for another chapter.

X

THE ORCHESTRA FROM THE BEGINNING OF THE WORLD TO THE BIRTH OF BEETHOVEN

MAN had probably not been man more than a few years before he made some sort of a musical instrument. Soon he was making many and they fell into three great classes— Percussion (I put them in probable order of early importance), Wind, and String. Almost every country in the world, even those least in contact with European civilization, has instruments of the three classes.

Slow Progress in Combination

The idea of combining instruments of various classes must have come into man's head early in his existence, but for a long time he bungled the business. Some reasons for this have already been suggested (pages 23 and 86). Two most potent reasons are: for any real progress in combination you must (a) have standardization of instruments, and you must (b) have an intelligible and reliable notation.

As regards (a): there was for long no settled standard as to the size, the number of strings, and so forth, on a Stringed Instrument, and Wind Instruments varied quite as much. Some instruments were so near to one another in their tone qualities and their capabilities that a capable musical Martian looking down on our world would have remarked at once that until process of time had brought about a survival of the fittest no coherent orchestral combination would be likely to arise.

Then Wind Instruments were excessively difficult to bring to perfection, and, indeed, never reached it until the end of the nineteenth century—if they reached it then. For long it was almost impossible to play some of them in tune, and, in addition, for centuries the Brass Instruments were restricted entirely to the production of the wide-spreading 'harmonic series' such as to-day may be heard from a military bugle.

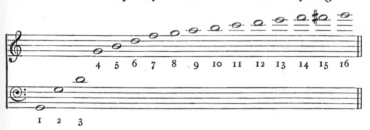

Examples of Early Orchestras

In the sixteenth and early seventeenth centuries all was still in a muddle.

The first real Oratorio (Cavaliere's *Soul and Body*, 1600) was scored for—

> Harpsichord.
> 1 Double Lira (a bowed instrument).
> 2 Flutes.
> 1 Violin.

Monteverde's opera, *Orfeo* (1607), was scored for a much larger Orchestra—

Plucked Strings
- 2 Harpsichords.
- 1 Double Harp.
- 2 Large Lutes.

Bowed Strings
- 2 Violins.
- 10 Tenor Violins (= Violas).
- 2 Viole da Gamba (= roughly speaking, our 'Cello).
- 2 Bass Viols (= our Double-Bass).

Wind
{
1 Clarion (small high Trumpet).
3 Trumpets.
2 Cornets (wooden instruments, not our modern Cornets).
1 Small Flute.
3 Portable Organs.
}

Glaring Anomalies

A glance at that list reveals what are to us curious anomalies, as, for instance :

(*a*) The importance of Plucked Strings and Organs.

(*b*) The lack of balance amongst the Bowed Strings, showing that they can hardly have been used *as a family*, as we to-day use our strings.

(*c*) The absence of Bass Wind Instruments.

Some of the anomalies partly disappear when it is realized that this force was hardly intended to be used as a whole. Various groups were used at one time or another during the Opera, to give one tinge of colour or another to the music.

But the parts for the Keyboard Instruments were not fully written out, a ' Figured Bass', or musical shorthand, indicating the harmonies of any passage, and the player being often left to elaborate his part out of this.

And whilst we know pretty well what we mean by ' Orchestra ', Monteverde could hardly use the word as a sufficient business description of his forces, but would, on any particular occasion, have to define exactly what he meant, since on some other occasion he would use some other very different combination.   To us all this is chaos.

Purcell's Orchestra

By the time of Purcell things were a good bit more settled, but these peculiarities remained ·

(*a*) The constant use of a Keyboard Instrument to supply a background of tone and to 'lead' the other instruments.

(*b*) A lack of differentiation, i. e. Purcell often showed little sense of the fact that different instruments have different capabilities, and, for instance, often gave Trumpets the same passages as Violins (this by using almost exclusively the upper range of the instruments, where the notes of the harmonic series come close together; see diagram on page 123).

(*c*) The combination to be called Orchestra was still not standardized, so that in one work it would mean one set of instruments and in another another set. Moreover, one solo or chorus in a work would be scored for one combination and the next for another, and some instrument included in the orchestral body engaged might be called for only once or twice in the whole performance. Yet there is this beginning of modernity —that the Strings are tending to assume first importance, and to be treated as a family instead of as unrelated individuals.

When we come to Bach and Handel we find a little progress beyond Purcell, but the same general conception in methods of Orchestration.

The best plan for the rest of this chapter will be to take actual specimens of Orchestration of (*a*) Bach, (*b*) Mozart, and (*c*) Beethoven, which will show us in a graphic way some of the changes that took place over the period of about a century which saw the gradual establishment of the modern Orchestra.

Bach's Orchestration

Example I. Opening of *St. Matthew Passion*.

The Figured Bass indicates the chords out of which the Organist is to evolve his part, which is to serve as a tonal background. This Figured Bass goes on (with one or two trifling exceptions) throughout the whole work (hence one of the names given to Figured Bass—*Continuo*). In this particular extract the chords are, as it happens, all to be erected upon one note, which lasts throughout the first five bars of the piece.

The **String Basses** play the same notes as the **Pedals of the Organ,** and this latter instrument, too, persists throughout the work. Even when all the other Strings are silent the Basses (backed by the Organ) stick grimly at their job.

Obviously this ever-enduring, tonally unvaried (or little varied) background and this obstinate, steadily plodding String Bass part are musical weaknesses. They show Bach as willing to take over, almost unthinkingly, relics of an earlier period, a century or a century and a half earlier, when ideas about instrumental tone and tone combination were very crude.

Upon this background Bach has drawn a contrapuntal pattern in five lines. Three of these are taken by the **Upper Strings,** and two by **Flutes** and **Oboes** doubling one another.

The modern plan in such a passage would be to give all the six lines to divided Strings, or all to Wind (choosing such wind instruments as would balance one another in tone quality and quantity), or to Strings doubled in each part by Wind, i.e. in some way to secure homogeneity in a passage where all the moving parts are evidently, as parts, on equal terms. Bach, you see, treats unequal forces as equals.

Example II. Introduction to Alto Aria, *Buss und Reu* (in English version, *Grief for Sin*) in the *Matthew Passion*.

Flute I.

Flute II.

Organ, 'Cellos, and D. Basses.

Here upon the background of **Organ** and **String Bass** tone Bach draws two lines, for two **Flutes** (generally running parallel). He has chosen these instruments to give their particular colour to this particular piece, and he continues

them in exactly the same way throughout the whole long
piece.

In other solo movements in this and other works he uses
two Oboes, or two Horns, or Violins in unison, or Viola da
Gamba (a sort of 'Cello), in each case against the same Organ
and String Bass background.   All this is very pleasant when
heard occasionally by us to-day, as a change from modern
more varied colourings.   But it is, undoubtedly, very 'primitive'.   Note, however, that in one respect Bach's method of
orchestration was in keeping with his method of part-weaving.
Up to his time a movement was more or less seamless from
beginning to end, and it was therefore natural to treat the
orchestration as a continuous whole.   The Symphony period
brought a much more broken style in both structure and
orchestration.

Example III.   Recitative ('*But on the first day of un-
leavened bread*'), in the *Matthew Passion*.

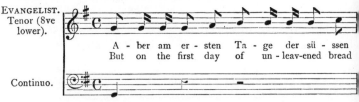

Here the whole accompaniment is left to the **Organ** and
String Basses, supporting the voice by occasional chords.

Haydn's and Mozart's Orchestration

Let us take as our illustration of the next period a passage
near the opening of Mozart's *Figaro* Overture.   I have, without
changing a note of the music, rearranged the orchestral score

of the passage, so as to make it easier to read. Note the
following points :

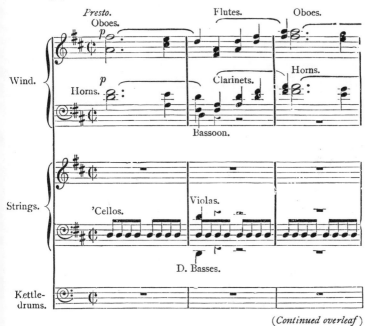

(*Continued overleaf*)

The Keyboard Instrument has now disappeared from the
Orchestra.

Whilst a mere throbbing 'Pedal' note goes on in the
Lower Strings, a play of Wind Instrument colour goes on
above, **Oboes** and **Horns,** on the one hand, alternating with
Flutes and **Clarinets,** on the other. Consider how kaleidoscopic an effect these changes produce, and compare with the
Bach method of choosing certain instruments at the beginning
of a piece, discarding the rest, and continuing the same tonal
colours from beginning to end.

Observe at the fifth bar a 'Tutti' or Full Passage. The
throbbing continues in the **Lower Strings.** The **Violins,**
partially doubled in two octaves by the **Wood Wind,** carry

K

* Horns doubled by Trumpets playing same notes an octave higher.

(*Continued on opposite page*)

the tune in two-part harmony. The **Trumpets** and **Horns** sustain a note (the 'Pedal' just spoken of) in three octaves. The **Kettledrums** come in for the purpose of accent.

Note in this 'Tutti' the differentiation that is taking place. Florid passages are here given to **Violins**; Wood Wind play rather simpler melodic passages; Horns and Trumpets are recognized as excellent instruments for holding long notes. In this Tutti, Mozart intends the Strings to be most heard, and the Wood and Brass count as reinforcements to them.

The **Brass** parts are very simple. The Brass Instruments of the day are limited and can play conveniently only the notes of the harmonic series. The composer has, in each case, dictated the use of a 'crook' in the key of the piece.

This gives him notes which will come in handy in any full passage in the main key and made out of the chief chords of that key, but in other places these instruments are almost useless. Indeed, we may say that they are hardly used except in these 'noise passages'.

The Kettledrums are tuned to Tonic and Dominant, and can therefore only be used when these notes form part of the harmony; thus they are available in much the same way as the Brass, and generally serve as companions to this.

Many Steps Forward and one Backward

Only fifty-seven years separate the composition of Bach's *St. Matthew Passion* (1729) and Mozart's *Figaro* (1786), but Orchestration has been revolutionized. In one respect, and one only, has there been retrogression. Trumpets and Horns in Haydn, Mozart, and earlier Beethoven are very much limited in usefulness by the constructional limitations mentioned. In the days of Bach and Handel trumpet players had developed the technique of playing freely in the highest register of the instrument, where the harmonic series includes the full scale. In the later part of the eighteenth century, however, composers took to using the instrument more for filling in the harmony with sustained notes: high florid passages, such as that well-known solo in *Messiah* ('The Trumpet shall sound'), were no longer written, and so the special skill needed for playing them was no longer cultivated. With Bach and Handel the trumpet had been a melodic instrument; with Haydn and Mozart it was, as a rule, no longer such.

When the keen revival of interest in the earlier music came, in the latter part of the nineteenth century, there were no players capable of performing the music of the period, and the myth grew up of a legendary 'Bach Trumpet' upon which alone such music could be played.

Beethoven's orchestration, though it is only a logical development from that of Haydn and Mozart, demands many examples to illustrate it, and calls for a chapter to itself.

XI

BEETHOVEN'S ORCHESTRA

THE marks of Beethoven's orchestration are:

(1) A bigger and more varied Orchestra ;

(2) Greater freedom for all the instruments—every one being treated as a responsible party capable, on occasion, of acting ' on its own ' ;

(3) Rapid kaleidoscopic changes of orchestral colour, largely due to much freer use of the orchestra as a dramatic agent, i. e. as an instrument for the direct, forceful expression of emotion.

Let us look now, and look carefully, at a series of examples. They are not comprehensive, but they illustrate pretty well in a general manner the characteristics of Beethoven's Orchestration and show in what ways it differs from or advances upon that of Mozart and Haydn. All the illustrations are chosen from one work, the **Fifth Symphony**—a characteristic work of Beethoven's mature period. Study these examples here given, and then, if you are inclined to carry the matter further, buy the cheap miniature score of the work and go through it repeatedly with the Gramophone.

Example 1.

Here is a running passage covering, in short space, a range of about three and a half octaves. Note the contrast introduced (1) between the clear notes of the **Flute** and the richer notes of the **Clarinet**, (2) between **Wood** and **Strings**, (3) between **High Strings** and **Low Strings**.

Example 2.

¹ Actual Notes.

The **Bassoon** treated seriously. (The flowing melody in the rather cadaverous Bassoon tone stands out clearly from a detached-chord String accompaniment.)

Example 3.

Violoncellos and **Double-Basses** taken seriously. Quite unaccompanied they run about the stave rapidly and humorously. This strikingly effective bare treatment of the Lower‑Strings is one of the outstanding features of the Scherzo of the Symphony.

Example 4.

and so on for many bars.

The **Kettledrum** taken seriously. A passage is wanted between the Scherzo and the Finale, so that the one may merge effectively into the other. Beethoven makes what would, with many composers, have been a mere link, into one of the most poetic moments of the whole work. Whilst the Strings play *pianissimo* the Kettledrum's tap is heard, first in broken rhythms and then continuously. Above it, soon, there creeps a soft Violin melody; there works up very gradually a

crescendo in all the instruments and we dash into the opening
of the Finale (see next example).

Example 5.

Here three **Trombones** and **Piccolo** are added. These were old instruments in Beethoven's time. Bach and Handel sometimes used Trombones: Mozart used them, but generally for some special dramatic effect (e. g. the Statue Scene in *Don Giovanni*, the famous three chords in *The Magic Flute*, and the last trump in the *Requiem*). Beethoven accepts them (in his later works) as a pretty normal constituent of the Orchestra. He uses them not only (as here) to give power and body to a forceful passage, but also (as in the 'Benedictus' of his great *Mass in D*) as a *pianissimo* effect of beauty and solemnity. The Piccolo, though the smallest wind instrument, can make its voice heard above the wildest orchestral storm, as it does here.

Note the disposition of the parts. The **Brass** supply the over-riding factor. The **Kettledrums** double the Brass bass, and point the rhythm. **Wind** and **Strings** add their quotas.

Example 6.

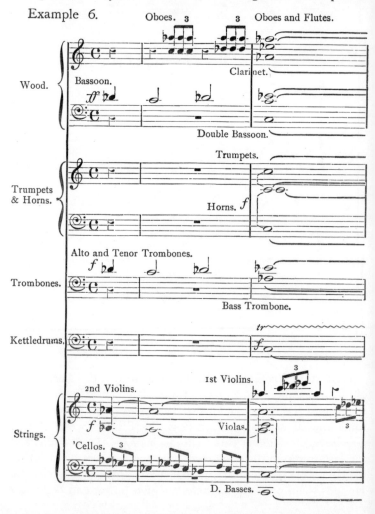

Oboe.

Trombones used melodically. They have here a long melodic passage, of which the example gives but the opening.

Trumpets and **Horns** come in to emphasize a point of high force. In bar 4, **Horns** also strengthen the melody. **Bassoons** also double the melody throughout, but do not really count: they are given something to do to keep them happy, but nobody hears them. The rest of the **Wind** and the **Strings** accompany.

Example 7.

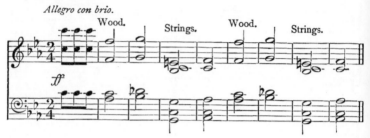

This is an instance of Beethoven's surprising contrasts. Here are **High Wood** chords suddenly alternated with **Low String** chords. The passage continues for over thirty bars, latterly lapsing into alternations of single chords, in Wood and Strings respectively.

Example 8.

Here, in a quiet passage, are seen the **Middle Strings** (Violas and 'Cellos) entrusted with a melody. The **Double-Basses** (note another emancipation) are detached from the 'Cellos, and supply the sole accompaniment (a *pizzicato*[1] bass).

Example 9.

This example gives the melody to the **Flutes, Clarinets,** and **Bassoons** (in three octaves), and the accompaniment to *pizzicato* chords on the **Lower Strings**, with a broken-chord passage in the **First Violins**.

---

[1] *Pizzicato* = plucked ; *arco* (see next page) is used to contradict this, meaning *bow*.

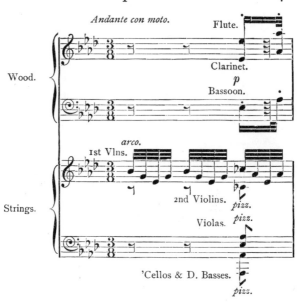

Example 10.

In the first two bars of the example we see the dying of a previous passage. A new passage is about to enter, a running melody by **Violas** and **'Cellos,** accompanied by *pizzicato* chords (Double-Bass again on its own) and a held E flat in three octaves in **Wood.** *But note the intervening little octave leap given in three octaves and three colours in the space of one bar.*

The above examples are but dips into a lucky bag. With score and Gramophone record the reader may go on dipping for himself. He will find that it takes some time to exhaust the bag's contents.

LEADING COMPOSERS OF THE PERIOD

FRANZ JOSEPH HAYDN

Born 1732 ; died 1809. It is hard for a rich man to enter heaven,
so most of the great musicians have come either out of poverty or

Haydn.

out of the merely relative ease of lower-
middle-class-dom. Haydn's father was a
wheelwright, and his mother a cook, and he
was born in a small village in Lower Austria.
The population was largely Slav, his ancestry
also, and for some years now it has been
recognized that the Croatian folk-tunes he
heard around him as a child constantly
entered into his composition, either in body
or in spirit.

The father and mother were unlettered
musicians, and the boy soon showed musical
leanings. A relative from the neighbouring
town of Hainburg, noting this, took him

there at the age of six, and entered him in his choir school. ('Almighty
God, to whom I render thanks for all his unnumbered mercies, gave
me such facility in music that by the time I was six I stood up like
a man and sang masses in the church choir, and could play a little
on the Harpsichord and Violin.')

A further move occurred two years later, when the choirmaster of
St. Stephen's Cathedral, Vienna, being on holiday in Hainburg, heard
him and claimed him. At Vienna he had good teaching for Singing,
Harpsichord, and Violin, but had to make shift as well as he could
in the early attempts at Composition to which he felt impelled.

When his voice broke he was cast out. He took an attic, secured
a few pupils, and spent hours in composition, basing his efforts on the
Sonatas of J. S. Bach's son, C. P. E. Bach, which embodied the new
style, and were at considerable variance with that of the older Bach.
Invited to a nobleman's country house, he found there a small

orchestra and for it wrote his first Symphony, on the model laid down by C. P. E. Bach. Whilst he was about it he wrote, in the lavish wholesale manner of the time, eighteen such Symphonies, mostly, however, for Strings alone.

On returning to Vienna, he gradually became popular as a teacher, and at last, elevated to the lofty position of 'Herr Musikdirektor and Kammerkompositor' to a Count in the neighbourhood, became passing rich on twenty pounds a year, and rashly married the daughter of his wig-maker—a step he ever afterwards regretted, since the lady proved to have as great a gift of fluent self-expression in words as he himself had in tones.

Later he took a similar position under Prince Esterházy, with the duty of controlling Orchestra, Choir, and Solo Singers, and directing the music in the private chapel and the private concert-room and opera-house. The opportunity of putting into performance his works as fast as they appeared was a stimulus both to production and to improvement. By the time he was forty his works were known to connoisseurs in most of the capitals of Europe.

On the death of his Prince, in 1790, Haydn was induced to come to London, where his reception by society, the larger public, and the press was most flattering. He fell in love with an English widow, and but for that unfortunate wig-maker's daughter (who showed no disposition towards decay, but, on the contrary, wrote to him asking for money to buy a nice little house she had seen, which would be just the thing for her when she became a widow) there would have been an English Mrs. Haydn.

Another visit to England took place a little later. He got on splendidly with nearly every one he met in England except the Italian violinist, Giardini (Giardini said, in his hearing, 'I don't want to see the German dog'; Haydn wrote in his diary, 'Giardini played like a pig'. Such are the amenities of musical life!). Haydn used to go to Carlton House to perform at the Prince of Wales's parties, but he could not get his fee, and on his return to Vienna sent a bill for a hundred guineas, which was at once paid by Parliament. Haydn's finest Symphonies were written for London performance.

In his old age Haydn twice saw Vienna occupied by the enemy. The last song he heard was from a French officer, attached to the army of occupation, who came to sing him his own 'In Native Worth', from *The Creation*, and the last music he performed was his own 'Emperor's Hymn' (the 'Austria' of our hymn-tune books), to play which, a few days before he died, he had himself carried to the piano.

Haydn's works are generally light and tuneful. Rarely does he attempt the expression of deep emotion. His Harpsichord and Piano works are of less account than his String Quartets and other Chamber works and his Symphonies. His oratorio *The Creation* has had a great popularity.

WOLFGANG AMADEUS MOZART

Born 1756; died 1791. Leopold Mozart, of Salzburg, Violinist, composer of Operas, Oratorios, and Instrumental Music, and author

Mozart.

of the then standard 'Violin School', out of seven children had but two who survived their first year—Anna Maria, born 1751, and Wolfgang Amadeus, four and a half years younger. We know not what we have lost through the terrible mortality, and especially infantile mortality, of the centuries before ours. Of Purcell's six children, but three survived him, and of Bach's twenty, but nine.

Both of Leopold's surviving children inherited his musical talent, with something added, and when Wolfgang was eight, father and children set off on a tour of Europe, which, with occasional intervening periods of rest and study at home, lasted several years. They were received with applause at the courts and at concerts at Munich, Vienna, Paris, London, and many other centres of musical culture. Their performances on the Harpsichord were famous ; Wolfgang also played the Violin and the Organ, extemporized and composed, and Anna Maria sang. The advertisement of the first London appearance stated of Wolfgang that 'his father had brought him to England not doubting but that he will meet with success in a kingdom where his countryman, Handel, the late famous virtuoso, received during his lifetime such particular protection '. The father falling ill, and no Harpsichord practice being therefore possible in their Chelsea lodging, the nine-year-old Wolfgang put in the time usefully by knocking off a few Symphonies : on the father's recovery more concerts were given, at the last two of which 'all the Overtures were of the boy's own composition '.

The brilliant childhood was not without its severer side. The father, as a sensible and instructed man, gave both children a very careful training. Later tours, in Italy and elsewhere, were made by father and son, or by the son alone, or by the son and his mother. When Mozart was twenty-two his mother died whilst with him at Paris.

So far Mozart's life had been nearly all glory ; after this it had much vexation and sorrow. He settled at Salzburg, as a member of the Archbishop's household, and he who had in childhood played with Marie Antoinette and received gifts from Emperors now dined at the servants' table, and, as 'the villain, the low fellow', received hard words from the patron at whose private concerts he was expected to shine. In the end this ' vile wretch ' was discharged by the Archbishop, and kicked out of the room by the steward. He was, however, morally supported by many members of the nobility and by the Emperor, and by the composition of several Operas he had achieved a wide public reputation.

The point to observe here is that practically no composer yet mentioned in this book lived upon public support ; in almost every case it will be found that aristocratic patronage or some ecclesiastical position was a necessity. Public concerts were still a comparatively new thing, and the sale of printed compositions was still insufficient to provide a livelihood. Handel had achieved a high degree of independence not by ignoring the aristocracy but by using them, and, as will shortly be found, Beethoven did the same thing. But there was as yet nothing equivalent to a Queen's Hall or Carnegie Hall public, and the musician was, thus, socially and financially in fetters.

Mozart's acquaintance with Haydn dates from about this time. The musical results of the connexion are unusual in their way— Mozart's compositions (especially instrumental) were necessarily based upon those of Haydn, who had had nearly a quarter of a century ' start ' of him, and had had a great influence in popularizing the principles and improving upon the style of C. P. E. Bach, in the Symphony, the String Quartet, and the Sonata. Coming fresh to the task, aided by a very delicate musical sense, and profiting by the study of Haydn's work, Mozart was able to introduce refinements in harmony, structure, and orchestration from which Haydn himself, in turn, profited. This is, then, a game of leap-frog—a lending of one another's back in turn for a jump in advance. There is a sense in which such games are always going on amongst composers everywhere, but this instance is a little more definite than most. Haydn said to Mozart's father, ' I declare to you before God as a man of honour, that your son is the greatest composer that I know, either personally or by reputation ; he has taste, and beyond that the most consummate knowledge of the art of composition ' ; and Mozart dedicated six quartets to Haydn, 'for from Haydn I first learnt how to compose a quartet '.

Opera composition brought Mozart much applause and has contributed to his lasting fame His works in this form are referred to in the next volume. Symphonies, Concertos, Chamber Works, Harpsichord and Piano Music (not, on the whole, so great) have also contributed to an undying reputation. There is a simplicity, a clarity, a grace, and a melodic charm about Mozart's writing that makes a very strong and wide appeal.

Mozart had celebrated his dismissal by the Archbishop by marriage to an affectionate and musical but undomesticated wife, whom he had great difficulty in supporting.

To the end pecuniary straitness embittered Mozart's life. To some extent, perhaps, he was himself to blame for this. He was ever too unworldly. From the Emperor he received about £80 per annum as Court Composer ; then the King of Prussia offered him a position as Musical Director at a salary of about £600, and Mozart replied ' How could I desert my kind Emperor ? '

When but thirty-five years of age Mozart died of typhus fever. The severest economy marked his funeral ; the friends who accompanied the coffin turned back before a storm which arose ; the burial took place in the common grave allotted to paupers and nobody marked the position. Mozart's last work was his *Requiem*.

LUDWIG VAN BEETHOVEN

Born 1770; died 1827. Beethoven was born at Bonn, where his father was a musician in the service of the Elector of Cologne.

The father was weak, harsh, and a drinker, and on the child's musical gifts becoming evident compelled him with severity to practise hard. At the age of seven years and three months (modestly understated on the announcement as 'six years') the child appeared at a concert. At nine he had learnt all the father could teach and was transferred to another teacher. The British *Chargé d'Affaires* at Bonn assisted the family, which lived in something approaching poverty.

A good musician, named Neefe, being appointed Court Organist, Beethoven came into his charge, to his great advantage. When the Elector left Bonn on a visit, Neefe accompanied him, leaving Beethoven, now in his twelfth year, as his official deputy at the organ. Neefe's own opinion is thus stated: 'This young genius deserves some assistance that he may travel. If he goes on as he has begun he will certainly become a second Mozart.' Shortly after this Beethoven received the post of Harpsichordist (which implied a degree of conductorship) in the orchestra of the Court Opera House; this gave him operatic experience. He became active also in composition.

When Beethoven was seventeen he travelled to Vienna and there met Mozart, from whom he had a few lessons in composition. On Mozart setting the boy to extemporize on a given theme he was much astonished at the result, and, stepping into the next room, said to some friends there: 'Pay attention to him; he will make a noise in the world.'

Whilst absent in Vienna Beethoven lost his mother. He quickly returned, and was fortunate in securing the friendship of a cultured family, the Breunings, who helped him greatly by making him free of their house, and awoke in him some interest in literature. He also became acquainted with the young Count Waldstein (to whom he afterwards dedicated the well-known Sonata). Henceforward the boy, born in poverty, was never to lack highly placed admirers and friends, but it became his habit to treat them with great (and sometimes exaggerated) independence. Haydn, when passing through

Bonn on his journey to and from London, fraternized with the Elector's musicians and encouraged Beethoven with approval of a Cantata he had written.

When Beethoven was twenty-two or twenty-three he went to Vienna again, this time at the Elector's expense. He at once bought a wig, silk stockings, boots, shoes, overcoat and seal, hired a piano and started taking lessons from Haydn at about $9\frac{1}{2}d.$ per hour. He grumbled, however, feeling that, as Haydn left some of his exercises uncorrected, he was not getting his full money's worth. In the end he sought another teacher. Many of his exercises are extant, and they prove great diligence and a complete willingness to 'go through the mill'. Yet his new teacher, Albrechtsberger, thought little of him. ('He has learnt nothing and will never do anything decently.' Probably the young man was too 'modern'.)

Vienna became Beethoven's permanent place of residence—the Vienna of Haydn and Mozart, and (shortly after this period) of Schubert. Gradually his abilities were recognized and he made influential friends. For some years he lived in the house of the Prince and Princess Lichnowsky, and received from them a stipend. At this time he was famous rather as an executant than as a composer. He was developing into a 'character', and was becoming independent, irritable, self-willed, fond of joking but unready to see a joke when he was the victim. The independence and jocularity often come out in his later music. One who knew him described him as giving the impression in society of a very able man, reared on a desert island, and suddenly introduced to the civilized world. There is much recorded which justifies this. Yet his is nevertheless a life that inspires respect and admiration, for it was filled with high purpose and achievement.

From about his thirtieth year Beethoven began to become deaf. Finally the deafness became total. He had other troubles—particularly with a scapegrace nephew whom he adopted and upon whom he lavished all the affection denied outlet elsewhere. And he manufactured some trouble by his intense suspicion and his unreasonable animosities. When he died, his liver was found to be shrunk to half its size. A good deal must be pardoned in life on half a liver !

His method of composition was 'painful' in its effort. Musical ideas came to him in a very simple and even crude form: sometimes they germinated for years and only grew to perfection after infinite tending and watering. Yet, in his best works, the effect of spontaneity is as fully achieved as in the work of any composer who ever lived.

The instrumental works are the greatest—the 17 String Quartets, the 32 Piano Sonatas, the 9 Symphonies, &c. One Opera, *Fidelio*, exists, and it continues to be performed. And there is the great *Mass in D*, one of the noblest of all choral-orchestral works.

FRANZ SCHUBERT

Born 1797 ; died 1828. Schubert, as will be noted, was a younger contemporary of Beethoven ; he was born twenty-seven years later than Beethoven and died one year later than he. He was born, lived, and died in Vienna, which, as has now surely been noticed by every reader, was Europe's greatest centre of musical culture in the period of the development of the Sonata-Symphony style. (Note that Haydn, Mozart, Beethoven, and Schubert all lived in and about that city. And note the personal connexions—Mozart and Haydn in more or less close touch with one another; Beethoven in touch with Mozart and actually taking

Schubert.

lessons from Haydn ; Schubert living in the same city as Beethoven ; for years reverencing him at a distance, and at last visiting him, upon his death-bed, to be greeted by him as his successor—'*Franz has my soul*'. Haydn, Mozart, Beethoven, and Schubert constitute the 'big four' of the Viennese School.)

Schubert's father was a schoolmaster and a keen amateur musician, the family String Quartet parties being famous in the neighbourhood ; later the Quartet was enlarged into an Orchestra by the addition of musical neighbours, and Franz played the Viola in it. At the age of eleven he underwent in brilliant style the tests for admission into the Royal Chapel Choir School, and here took a very full part in the very varied and abundant musical activities of the boys. Underfed and underwarmed, he had a hard time of it, and one may guess that his resistance to disease in after-life was weakened by the almost Dotheboys Hall conditions, but those were days when almost all schools 'did the boys'.

Composition began early ; Church Music, String Quartets, Songs, Piano Pieces poured out, and were rehearsed and performed as soon as finished by Franz and his schoolfellows.

The word 'finished', however, is, in one sense, out of place. It suggests labour and careful thought, such as Beethoven found necessary, whereas Schubert 'lisped in numbers, for the numbers came'. He achieved 'finish', when he did achieve it, by the perfection of his inspiration and the reliability of his constructive instinct, not by the sweat of his brow or the burning of midnight oil. Much of what he wrote, all through his life, never was 'finished', since it lacked the close logic and coherence of thoughtfully designed and thoroughly considered work. Smaller things were often perfect ; larger ones sometimes suffered by undue length and disproportion. Schubert is, indeed, the very type of the spontaneous musician. He sang as the lark sings, with the same abandon and exuberance. It is even on record that a week or two after composing a song he could fail to recognize it as his own when it was put before him.

On leaving the Choir School, Schubert, for a time, helped in his father's school. Then he made friends who helped him, and was able to give up the school tasks, never, however, obtaining a position of financial independence.

He wrote Songs, Songs, Songs—poured them out by 'mass production'. During his whole life he wrote more than 600, to good words, indifferent words, and poor ones. His special gifts were melody and 'characterization'. At first these Songs were unacceptable to the publishers. They offered him absurd prices of a few shillings when they offered anything at all. A group of his intimates and admirers therefore formed a sort of Schubert Song Society ; they would print a song, hold a concert, have the song sung, sell copies of it to the audience, and so raise money to print another.

Schubert's Piano Music was much of it lyrical in form, and all of it (indeed all his music) was lyrical in impulse. He wrote a good deal of Chamber Music, nine Symphonies (of which but two can to-day usually be heard), a number of unsuccessful Operas, some Masses, a good many Part Songs for Male Voices, and a quantity of Piano Duets. Of course he over-produced, but the best of his work will always charm by its melody, its refined harmony, and its easy, happy spirit, or, if more serious, by its not too deep yet sincere expression of more sober feeling.[1]

Schubert carried a torch at Beethoven's funeral, and a few months later the friends who had accompanied him carried torches at his. On his death-bed he read all the novels of Fenimore Cooper that he could borrow, and studied Handel's scores, which determined him to work hard at counterpoint and make up for lost time! His last thoughts were of Beethoven, and he was buried near him, as he desired. The property he left (including his clothes and hundreds of unpublished compositions) was valued at sixty-three florins, or about £2 10s. But he had been rich in friendships and in the affection of an elder brother who throughout life was his warmest admirer and strongest supporter.

---

[1] E. W. comments as follows on the words 'not too deep': 'Personally I know nothing deeper than some of the really great songs (too often quite unsung).' It is fair to quote this, though it does not destroy the force of the generalization.

XII

BEETHOVEN AND THE EXPRESSION OF EMOTION IN MUSIC

IT is commonly, and quite fairly, said that Beethoven's great contribution to music was to show how it could be made more vividly to express emotion.

His immediate predecessors, Haydn and Mozart, had perfected the Sonata-Symphony form, and within this form had expressed their sense of beauty and often also a good deal of sentiment and of humour.

But Beethoven expressed within the form deeper emotion than they had ever felt called upon to express, and perhaps than they had ever felt. Where Mozart would have been plaintive or, at most, pathetic, Beethoven was able to be tragic. Where Haydn might have been quaintly humorous, Beethoven would be boisterously uncontrolled.

Now, of course, this deeper expression would have been impossible to Beethoven if C. P. E. Bach, Haydn, and Mozart had not prepared the way for him. They had solved for him the main problems of the effective arrangement of material, so that it might contrast well, and yet 'hang together'. In Orchestral music they had, further, found out the sound general method of combining or contrasting the various tone colours. Beethoven born earlier could not have been Beethoven. The expert who designs liners, if born in A.D. 1, would have been content with making a coracle a foot longer than any Briton before him, and making it a little less circular and a trifle better balanced. Bach in 1400 would have been a Dunstable (see page 70), showing the way to a somewhat better counterpoint. Beethoven in 1600 would have been a Monteverde (see page 70), showing the way out of pure Counterpoint to a more direct expression through chords struck as chords, and vivid declamation. All these men were dependent for their opportunity to do what they did upon the chance of being born when they were. We do not know how many Beethovens have been lost to us through their unlucky coming to birth at a wrong time or in a wrong place.

Beethoven, then, wrote music outwardly much like that of Haydn and Mozart, but longer, broader, and deeper (by length here I mean actual length, by breadth I refer to style, and by depth to emotional significance). To some people, necessarily, his music was, by its all-round bigger calibre, incomprehensible ; they could follow the sonata road as far as Haydn and Mozart had taken it, but when they reached the Beethoven section, they became alarmed at leaving trim hedges and well-kept gardens and finding themselves in the open country.

Moreover, Beethoven's music was necessarily more difficult to perform. In keyboard music he was the first to introduce a true Pianoforte style, since Haydn and Mozart had both been brought up on the Harpsichord. As one example of this, consider say a Mozart sonata and a later Beethoven one and see the greater use of, and even dependence on the sustaining pedal, which is, of course, a distinct Pianoforte contrivance, corresponding to nothing at all in the Harpsichord. Big spread harmonic arpeggios, bass notes struck by the left hand and then given to the pedal to sustain whilst the left hand occupies itself otherwise—this sort of thing is constantly seen in Beethoven but hardly to any extent in Mozart, and, of course, it is a great addition to the opportunities of forceful expression. Similarly Beethoven's use of the Orchestra, as has already been explained, was an intelligent modification of that of Haydn and Mozart, largely directed by the wish to express more. The two older men sought to express themselves with crystal clearness; Beethoven often sacrificed their sort of clarity for the purpose of gaining force.   All these three composers had a strong sense of

Beauty; but with Haydn and Mozart beauty came first and expression second, and with Beethoven, perhaps, expression first and beauty second.

All that has just been said about Beethoven naturally applies more strongly to the later than the earlier compositions.

The Minuet has, on account of its compactness, been chosen throughout this book as a convenient illustration of style in various periods. We have examined together a Purcell Minuet, a Bach Minuet, and a Mozart Minuet. Beethoven retained the Minuet as a movement of his early Sonatas, &c. But the Minuet can hardly express much beyond a very formal beauty, and Beethoven longed for a deeper manifestation of emotion. Soon he had so changed the Minuet that he abandoned the name, and the movement that appeared in the Minuet-place in a Sonata or Symphony was now called a 'Scherzo'. This word is the Italian for joke. Many of Beethoven's Scherzo movements were actually jocular; others whilst retaining the feeling of unexpectedness which is the chief element in a successful joke, verbal, practical, or musical, passed out of jocularity into something more tremendous. The Scherzo of the Fifth Symphony (see its opening on the previous page) is a good example of this. It is wildly extravagant in its modulations and bold in its harmonies and orchestration. Humour does come into it (see the example on page 135, where the clumsy double-basses are made to scamper like elephants, and are then abruptly pulled up and started again), but the predominant feeling is something beyond humour, and at the end, where a link is needed to carry us from the Scherzo to the Finale, the composer has soared right away into the mystical (see page 135).

Hear this movement and recognize the coming of the element of the Romantic into music. Such a passage as that which ends this Scherzo and leads into the Finale is the equivalent in music of such lines as those of Keats—

'magic casements opening on the foam
Of perilous seas in faery lands forlorn.'

Romance can be found in Bach ; much more rarely in Handel.
It can be found in Mozart, and, more rarely, in Haydn.   But
with Beethoven Romance begins to become a common and
vital element in the stuff of music.   He was, if you like, the
last great Classic, but he was, at the same time, the first great
Romantic.   You will find it quite interesting to compare
chance pages of Mozart and Beethoven, and in this way to
test the change in the matter of *feeling* which Beethoven
brought about.   For example, here is the opening of a Mozart
Piano Sonata Slow Movement (Sonata V) contrasted with
a very similar movement from Beethoven (Sonata XI)—

Adagio con molt' espressione.

And that Sonata of Beethoven is but a rather early one. If you will test the later ones you will find much deeper feeling than that.[1]

[1] E. W. questions whether the quotation from Mozart is a quite fair one. He suggests that the quotation of the slow movement from (say) the E flat Quartet or the G minor Quintet would be more favourable to Mozart. Nevertheless, I allow the quotation to stand, since there is point in the comparison of two passages from the two composers, technically so similar in appearance (in each case a turn-adorned melody in the right hand accompanied by chords in the left). E. W. adds that to him, speaking generally, late Mozart, and late Haydn too, are deeper than early Beethoven. He is not, however, in these remarks contesting the general sense of my passage, but only trying to prevent false inferences from it, and I am glad that he should do so.

Compare now the sort of air Mozart takes for the purpose of making a set of Variations (Sonata XII)—

That is plaintive and charming.

Now look at one of Beethoven's airs (again a rather early work—Sonata XII)—

These are but one or two, almost chance, examples, but they are sufficient to indicate what is meant by the statement that with Beethoven we see the coming of 'Romance' and deeper feeling into music.

Schubert must be classed with Beethoven as partaking of both Classic and Romantic characters.

A period of but sixty-three years separates the composition of the first symphony of Haydn and the last of Beethoven. What a change of spirit and a growth of mastery in so short a time !

The composers who immediately followed Beethoven and Schubert were those who are now classed as the definite 'Romantic School' in music, and with them, i. e. Weber, Schumann, Chopin, and their contemporaries, will open the next volume of this 'Listener's History.'

APPENDICES

APPENDIX I

GRAMOPHONE RECORDS

The present author's *Columbia History of Music through Ear and Eye* gives a survey of the development of music by means of selected examples, specially recorded for Gramophone by eminent performers, and with the original instruments (viols, lutes, virginals, &c., down to the instruments of to-day and the full modern orchestra). There are five Albums of Records. Accompanying booklets, with explanations of the music, pictures, &c., are included in the Albums. Any Gramophone dealer can supply particulars of this History. A booklet *Practical Lesson Plans* (Oxford University Press) gives hints on the class use of the History.

The monthly journal, *The Gramophone*, reviews Records as they appear: the most important records are also reviewed in the various musical journals.

APPENDIX II

HINTS ON THE CLASS AND LECTURE USE OF THIS BOOK

The main thing is to base all the teaching upon the actual hearing of music of the various periods, and Gramophone Records should help greatly towards this. Encourage keen listening and active questioning and discussion.

A suggested Twelve-lesson, or Twelve-lecture, Course is the following:

1. The Basis of the Art. The Beginnings of Music in Song and Dance. Chapters I and II. (Illustrated by one or two Folk Songs and Folk Dances, and by one of the Bird Song Gramophone Records mentioned on p. 4.)
2. The Climax of Pure Choral Music. Chapter III.
3. The Beginnings of Keyboard Music, Chapter IV, with, as an addendum, About Modes and Scales. Chapter V.
4. Harmony *qua* Harmony at Last, and the Introduction of Opera

and Oratorio. Chapter VI. Also, in order to make up enough material for a lesson, and to introduce some music, give a very general sketch of Fugue, and so anticipate the next lesson.

5. The Century of Perfection, (A) Fugue.   Chapter VII.
6. The Century of Perfection, (B) the Aria, the Suite, the Opera, and the Oratorio.   Chapter VIII.
7 and 8. The New Style in Instrumental Music—Sonata and Symphony.   Chapter IX.
9. The Orchestra—from the Beginning of the World to the Birth of Beethoven.   Chapter X.
10. Beethoven's Orchestra.   Chapter XI.
11. Beethoven and the Expression of Emotion in Music. Chapter XII.
12. A Recapitulation, illustrated by typical examples re-performed.

' Leading Composers of the Period' will be drawn upon as the teacher or lecturer finds advisable—chiefly in introducing any musical example.

The author cannot too strongly urge that, in the class or lecture use of the book, a copy should be actually in the hands of each student : (*a*) Because the teacher or lecturer cannot possibly personally convey in a short course all the book contains ; (*b*) because the lavish music type illustrations are intended to come before the eye of the student himself, and to be closely analysed by him.   In cases where the lesson or lecture lasts but one hour the time should be spent largely in further explanation, discussion, and musical illustration of the prescribed passage of the text-book *previously read and thought over by the student.*   In cases where the lesson or lecture time is longer the teacher or lecturer may perhaps introduce and musically illustrate each subject, and then insist upon the students' re-studying it from the text-book at home.

APPENDIX III

A NOTE ON 'THE INTRODUCTION OF OPERA'

Sir Henry Hadow very kindly made the following comment upon this chapter :

' You repeat the old story of the " Florentine Revolution "—i.e. the beginning of Opera as a deliberate imitation of Greek Tragedy by a party of scholars about 1600. Has not this story (which appears in all the histories of music) now been discredited by Romain Rolland? See his paper "L'opéra avant l'opéra" in *Musiciens d'autrefois*, in which he develops the idea that there was no initiative movement in 1600, and that the thing began earlier and developed gradually.'

Readers who wish to get to the bottom of this very interesting subject might well see the book to which reference is made above (Hachette, Paris), of which an English translation is available (*Some Musicians of Former Days*, translation by Mary Blaiklock ; Curwen, also Kegan Paul). The question is decidedly one of those about which individuals must make up their own minds. My own argument in favour of the traditional view would be somewhat as follows :

The Florentines considered themselves initiators, as Rolland admits at the opening of his paper. And they were, as cultured men, assuredly not ignorant of the three forms preceding Opera, to which Rolland calls attention :

(*a*) The Sacra Rappresentazione (I take it our Miracle Play, pretty nearly).

(*b*) The Latin Comedy (merging into Masque).

(*c*) The Dramma Pastorale (perhaps nearly approaching Opera).

The whole subject is more fully discussed by Henderson in his *Some Forerunners of Italian Opera*. Much of Henderson's matter is a more detailed setting forth of the facts given by Rolland. On page 91 he puts Rolland right on a point connected with Poliziano's *Orfeo* ; yet in the main his facts and Rolland's tally. But Henderson, by his very title, and by his treatment of Caccini in the last chapter, supports the traditional view that Caccini and his colleagues were 'innovators'.

Of course, all innovators have what Henderson calls 'Forerunners', and hence, in *The Second Book of the Great Musicians*, I have preceded the chapters on 'Oratorio' and 'The Earliest Operas' by one 'About the Old Miracle Plays and what sprang from them', showing that I am not unmindful of the existence of the operatic instinct before the days of actual opera. But the operatic instinct and actual opera are two different things, and though I recognize that the Rolland view is a corrective to some of the perhaps too clear-cut statements of the historians, I feel that it is also itself too clear-cut I am very grateful to my critic for raising this point, because the subject is not one upon which I would wish to be thought dogmatic, and because his objection has led to my referring the reader to two very interesting discussions of the subject.

APPENDIX IV

A NOTE ON CLAVICHORD, HARPSICHORD, AND PIANOFORTE

Some confusion exists in the public mind concerning the differing principles of these instruments.   A full description, with many illustrations, has been given in *The Third Book of the Great Musicians.* Briefly it may be summarized as follows :

The three instruments are alike in all having wires and all having keys, and are unlike in the manner in which the keys set the wires in vibration.

The **Harpsichord** is really a kind of Keyboard Zither.   Each key of the keyboard has at its farther end a small piece of wood called a ' Jack ' (B).   Each Jack has in it a Quill.   When the key is depressed the Jack rises and the Quill plucks the string.

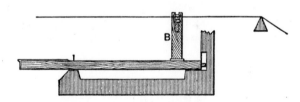

The plucking action is the essential feature, but late Harpsichords had many complications and elaborations, such as two keyboards, stops controlling the use of more than one string to a note, &c.   The **Virginal** or **Virginals** is a primitive Harpsichord.

The **Pianoforte** is a kind of Keyboard-Dulcimer.   It has an action which is merely a mechanical development from that of the Harpsichord, but *the strings are hammered instead of plucked.*

The **Clavichord** action is a little more difficult to describe, though it is in itself quite simple.   *Instead of a Quill or a Hammer we have a ' Tangent '*—a piece of metal (A) at the farther end of the key, *which strikes the string and then remains stretching it so long as the key continues to be depressed.*

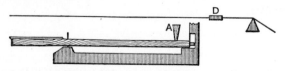

The string would, of course, thus acted upon, normally vibrate in two portions, producing two notes; but a piece of felt (D) prevents the vibration of the hinder portion.

It will be noted that the Clavichord differs from the Harpsichord and Pianoforte in that the vibration-causing agent itself defines the length of string to vibrate and, hence, dictates the pitch of the note. Further, this agent remaining in contact with the string (instead of passing beyond it, as in the Harpsichord, or recoiling from it, as in the Pianoforte), it is possible for the player to influence the tone even after the blow has been made, sustaining the sound by a slight movement of the tip of the finger without leaving the key. This explains the long-held notes which sometimes occur in Bach's '48', which were written for the Clavichord—notes which on the Harpsichord ceased to sound almost at once, which on the modern Pianoforte begin to die as soon as they begin to live, but which on the instrument of Bach's preference could have their life indefinitely prolonged at the will of the player.

APPENDIX V

OTHER VIEWS ON 'THE CENTURY OF PERFECTION'

Sir Henry Hadow writes: 'I do not quite like the title of Chapters VII and VIII, "The Century of Perfection." I feel that you make rather too free with that dangerous word "perfection". And the sixteenth century was as near perfection in its way as the seventeenth–eighteenth (1650–1750). And there will probably be more to come. So why be exclusive?'

And Dr. Ernest Walker writes: 'On page 62 you speak of your "century of perfection" as lasting from 1650–1750. Of course, these things strike different people in different ways; but (purely personally) I should have been inclined to take the whole seventeenth century (at any rate its latter four-fifths) as something of an interlude. Anyhow, 1650–1700 is a very different kind of thing from 1700–1750; and you say later, on pages 72-3, something about Purcell not finding things quite ready for him. And was the *dramatic* side "perfected" in any sense? All that I mean is that I don't think I would myself have put the thing quite in this way: that's all!

'Similarly on page 63 you say, "In Bach and Handel we see the culmination of centuries of musical development; in Haydn and Mozart, who are to follow them, we see the foundations of the musical development of the centuries that are to follow." I wouldn't myself quite have made this sharp demarcation at 1750 or thereabouts, or, indeed, anywhere. The break at this time is, of course, in a way palpable: the New Instrumentalism leaps to the eye, especially in its structural aspects. But is it very much more than this, and was the break anyhow more than temporary? The pre-1750 folk have got a good deal of their own back by now. And as to "the final gathering up and perfecting of all that has gone before", is anything final, and *are* Bach and Handel the culmination of the sixteenth century? But it is only, after all, a question of emphasis.'

I have carefully considered these views, and it is right that I should reproduce them—especially as one object of this book is to provoke readers to think for themselves, and nothing is more likely to do this than the giving of a choice of view. On close inspection it will be seen, however, that little more is involved than a matter of terminology, and it seems to me that the way in which I am using my terms is pretty clearly defined on page 62 in the paragraph headed 'Nothing new but nearly everything better'. There I have made it clear that I am speaking of a 'perfecting of style', and have made it clear that, even so, I except Choral Music, which in its different manner was clearly as perfect in the sixteenth century as in the seventeenth–eighteenth.

Until I came to work out the plan of this book I felt, as Dr. Walker still does, that the sixteenth century was one thing, the first half of the eighteenth another, and the seventeenth an intermediate, or interlude. This, I imagine, is the way most of us have been accustomed to look at the matter. But when I began to think about it I saw clearly that Purcell, Handel, and Bach, differing from one another not in style (in the broad sense) but only in degree of perfection of this style, must be classed together as composers whose works, with those of their contemporaries, make up one definite period.

I find to my surprise that a good many people (though not my two critics here discussed) loosely connect Purcell with the sixteenth and early seventeenth-century composers ; e. g. Goossens' pamphlet, *Modern Tendencies in Music* (page 5), speaks of 'the short period of musical ascendancy during the Elizabethan era which gave to the world the music of Purcell and his splendid contemporaries'. Of course, this writer knows that Purcell was not a (literal) Elizabethan, but the general classification his mind has adopted is significant of his feeling on the matter. Now Purcell has very little in common with the Elizabethans. Apart from questions of date, his art looks forward to that of Handel and Bach, not backward to that of Byrd and Palestrina. He is an example of early flowering in the harmonic-contrapuntal school, and any broadly generalized classification must, I think, recognize this.

Dr. Walker's question, ' And was the dramatic side "perfected" in any sense ?' is pertinent. Personally I think it was. Lully's Operas, Purcell's dramatic music, Scarlatti's Operas, Handel's Operas and dramatic Oratorios, and Bach's Passions show a ' perfecting ' of the somewhat crudely experimental methods of the early seventeenth-century dramatic experimenters—Peri, Caccini, &c. Looked at in one way they close a period in dramatic music, and Mozart and Gluck open another. (I will say more on this point in the second volume, when considering the evolution of the opera.)

Again, however, it is all very much a question of terminology, and whilst I admit that my way of stating the facts concerning the dramatic work of the period is debatable, I think that it cannot mislead any student, but will indeed help him. One must, in a student book, adopt some clear classification of period, such as this, although one may be aware that in history no lines of demarcation are absolutely clear.

To Dr. Walker's question ' and *are* Bach and Handel the culmination of the sixteenth century?' I would reply by quoting a passage from Parry (*Evolution of the Art of Music*, page 159), which will show what I mean, leaving it simply a question for readers to settle as to whether the word I have used ('culmination') is the best one:

'The old methods were resumed under the influence of the new feeling for tonality. Composers began anew to write free and characteristic parts of the several voices in choral combinations, but they made the harmonies, which were the sum of the combined counterpoints, move so as to illustrate the principles of harmonic form, and thus gave to the hearer the sense of orderliness and design, as well as the sense of contrapuntal complexity. And it is not too much to say that their attitude soon changed the principle of their work. Where formerly they had simply adapted melody to melody they now often thought first of the progression of the harmony, and made separate voice-parts run so as to gain points of vantage in the successive chords.'

The word 'culmination' is justifiable, I think, in the sense that the period marks the farthest development of the diatonic contrapuntal style which had been slowly growing up for centuries; no further real contrapuntal development took place until Wagner, a century later, initiated a great chromatic-contrapuntal movement.

I feel that all these questions of classification and description are very fascinating, that several differing yet quite rational classifications and descriptions are generally possible, and that (here I know my critics will agree with me) the important thing is that the student should get the facts into his mind and, having done this, re-classify for himself in the way that to him seems most convenient and most true.

INDEX

The Listener's History of Music

A BOOK FOR ANY CONCERT-GOER
GRAMOPHONIST OR RADIO LISTENER
PROVIDING ALSO A COURSE OF STUDY FOR
ADULT CLASSES IN
THE APPRECIATION OF MUSIC

by

PERCY A. SCHOLES

With incidental comments by

SIR W. HENRY HADOW · SIR RICHARD R. TERRY
DR. ERNEST WALKER · EDWIN EVANS

IN THREE VOLUMES

*Volume II. The Romantic and Nationalist Schools
of the Nineteenth Century*

FOURTH EDITION

LONDON
OXFORD UNIVERSITY PRESS
NEW YORK   TORONTO

Oxford University Press, Ely House, London W. 1

GLASGOW NEW YORK TORONTO MELBOURNE WELLINGTON
CAPE TOWN IBADAN NAIROBI DAR ES SALAAM LUSAKA ADDIS ABABA
DELHI BOMBAY CALCUTTA MADRAS KARACHI LAHORE DACCA
KUALA LUMPUR SINGAPORE HONG KONG TOKYO

First Edition 1929
Second Edition 1936
Third Edition 1943
Fourth Edition 1954
Reprinted 1956, 1960, 1967
and 1974

Printed in Great Britain
at the University Press, Oxford
by Vivian Ridler
Printer to the University

THE AUTHOR'S INTRODUCTION

THE present volume of *The Listener's History of Music* sketches the rise of the Romantic and Nationalist Schools in music. Without claiming that it advances any new views one may at least claim that it places the emphasis rather differently from most existing treatments of the subject.

As I have worked at the preparation of the volume I have been more and more impressed with the fact that the Romantic Movement in Music has usually been discussed rather superficially and in a somewhat detached spirit. It seems to be a pretty common practice with authors of histories to pass over it hurriedly, and partially or entirely to neglect the vital connexion between the growth of the romantic temper in literature and painting with the growth of that temper in music. To take the most glaring example: Parry's epoch-making *The Evolution of the Art of Music*, a very valuable book to which many of us are indebted for our first intelligent conception of the development of the art, entirely ignores the connexion between the Romantic movement in music and that in the other arts—never even mentions it. Indeed, I think I may say that nowhere in the book does there occur even the word 'Romantic'.

To take another example. The third and fourth editions of our admired and indispensable *Grove's Dictionary*, under the heading 'Romantic' give a mere forty lines or so, in which no reference whatever is made to the early nineteenth-century romantic schools in literature and painting [1]

An outstanding element in the development of the arts at the opening of the nineteenth century, as it seems to me, is the new interaction between them. We do not know much about

[1] The second edition was better. It gave nine columns, and gave a number of literary references, though not enough

what Mozart read or what pictures he looked at (if any), and if we did it would probably not affect our view of his music. But we do know that Berlioz read and associated with Dumas and Hugo and Vigny, and looked at the pictures of, and associated with, Delacroix and Géricault, and if we did not know this we could not thoroughly understand his music. And similarly with Schumann's reading of Jean Paul and Hoffmann, and Weber's friendship with Hoffmann and his early connexion with the romantic stage at what we may call its 'Wilhelm Meister' period, and Mendelssohn's family relationship with the Schlegels, pillars of the German Romantic School in literature and protagonists of Shakespeare in Germany. The student's acquirement of this kind of knowledge is not a mere satisfaction of intelligent curiosity; it is vital to his understanding of the music of the period.

And, similarly, when one comes to consider the growth of the Nationalist spirit in music and to look for the incentives behind the work of Smetana and Dvořák, Grieg, Mussorgsky and Rimsky-Korsakof, and Albéniz and Granados, one is driven to a preliminary study of the growth of the national spirit in European literature and political life.

That, then, as I understand my second volume, is its leading motive—the fresh fertilization of the art of music by a closer contact with the sister arts, and, moreover, a contact with them in a phase when they represented the expression of a changed and changing view of life. And that explains in large measure, what some readers of the first volume may at once observe—the larger space given to the biographical matter, which takes on a new significance at a period when life and art have come so very near together.[1]

One close relationship between music and the other arts has

[1] E.E. writes : ' You might have remarked that "advanced" opinion of to-day regards the extra-musical elements here referred to as having temporarily diverted music from its true destiny. This is a truer explanation of the present linking up of the twentieth to the eighteenth century

always existed—the stage relationship. It will be recalled that in the first volume Opera received only passing treatment. The present volume has offered the opportunity of gathering up the threads of that subject and weaving them into a connected fabric.

The previous volume in its earlier editions bore the words, 'In two Volumes ; Volume I, to Beethoven'. I found myself unable to fulfil that promise of a reasonable brevity, largely from the very fact, just mentioned, that a proper study of nineteenth-century music involves frequent and lengthy reference to nineteenth-century life and literature. A third volume proved to be necessary. It brings the subject down to our own day—the day of 'Polytonality' and 'Atonality', of 'Impressionism' and 'Expressionism', an attempted Anti-romanticism and 'Futurism'. An unusual feature of this third volume is the reproduction of a number of paintings of the Romantic, Impressionist, Cubist, and Expressionist schools, with a brief discussion of the parallels between the trends of the musical arts during the past century. Some of these illustrations properly concern the present volume, but it has been thought better to mass them together.

Where I expect criticism (and where any author of a book of this kind *must* expect it) is in the division of the subject into 'Periods'. Some such division is inevitable and necessary if the student is to retain any clear idea of what he has read, yet any method of division is debatable. I may say frankly that my divisions are not perfect, that no division could be perfect, and that I look to the reader to turn backwards and

than the common vague remark that the preceding century is always out of favour. The 'out of favour' in the present case does not of course imply any disparagement of the great men of the intervening period in question. It is a mere question of aesthetic. In this observation seems to me to lie the key to the present-day situation which you discuss in Vol. III.'

forwards, to compare the statements and the dates in one division of my volume with those in another, and to realize that the word 'Period', though the best I could find, is not to be understood too literally as a space of time.

Any attempt to state historical truth is open to debate. Perhaps there *is* no such absolute as 'historical truth', but a syndicate may approach nearer to its discovery than an individual, and so, as in the first volume, I submitted my work to the criticism of certain authorities in whose knowledge and competence we all have confidence, asking them freely to dissent where dissent seems to them to be necessary, and suggesting that their views should be publicly brought forward, as in the first volume, in footnote or appendix. I must gratefully acknowledge the kindness and care of these gentlemen, who will be found to be identified with their remarks throughout by the use of their names or initials. Further, I have to thank Mr. C. M. Crabtree, B.A., B.Mus., for much help in the choice of music examples, in the reading of proofs, in the reduction of extracts from full scores to a piano version, and in other time-exhausting tasks that go to the making of a book of this type.

CONTENTS

Contents

PERIOD V—ROMANTICS AS NATIONALISTS

LIST OF ILLUSTRATIONS

List of Illustrations

PERIOD IV

The Romantic Movement

XIII

THE ROMANTIC ATTITUDE

'MUSIC', says De Quincey, relating his London Saturday night visits to the Opera House, 'is an intellectual or a sensual pleasure, according to the temperament of him who hears it.'[1]

And he goes on equally intelligently (for he was a Lancashire music-lover, and hence not merely an enthusiastic, but also an arguing one), to assert:

> The mistake of most people is, to suppose that it is by the ear they communicate with music, and therefore that they are purely passive as to its effects. But this is not so; it is by the reaction of the mind upon the notices of the ear (the *matter* coming by the senses, the *form* from the mind) that the pleasure is constructed; and therefore it is that people of equally good ear differ so much in this point from one another.

The precise meanings of De Quincey's individual terms need to be apprehended if the meaning of his argument is to be clearly grasped.

By 'sensual pleasure' he seems to refer to the mere beauty of sounds—single, or combined in chords, or linked in melodies. (We may, perhaps, elucidate this thought by putting this pleasure upon the same plane as that of eating or drinking.)

By 'intellectual pleasure' he seems to refer to that further stage in enjoyment, where the sounds have come to *mean* something; not to 'mean' *ideas* ('Ideas! my dear friend! there is no occasion for them '), but to mean something in that more 'sublimated' way which gives the best kind of music-listening the character of a combination of conscious and sub-conscious, of wide-awakeness and dream.

---

[1] *Confessions of an English Opium Eater*, Part II.

It is sufficient to say that a chorus, etc., of elaborate harmony displayed before me, as in a piece of arras-work, the whole of my past life—not as if recalled by an act of memory, but as if present and incarnated in the music; no longer painful to dwell upon, but the detail of its incidents removed, or blended in some hazy abstraction, and its passions exalted, spiritualized and sublimed. All this was to be had for five shillings.

In other words, De Quincey as music-listener was a romanticist. When, hearing 'elaborate harmony' displayed before him 'as in a piece of arras-work', he felt the passion of his life 'exalted, spiritualized and sublimed', he was in much the same mental state as his friend Wordsworth, looking at a stretch of Wye Valley scenery and experiencing

> A sense sublime
> Of something far more deeply interfused,
> Whose dwelling is the light of setting suns,
> And the round ocean and the living air,
> And the blue sky, and in the mind of man :
> A motion and a spirit that impels
> All thinking things, all objects of all thought,
> And rolls through all things.[1]

The Range of Romance

That is the very spirit of Romance—an emotion which all in some measure feel, and which ranges the whole distance from the happy excitement of the little servant girl, reading for the first time of the doings of duchesses in Mayfair, or the schoolboy imagining the tropical dangers and delights of desert islands, to the sympathetic emotion of Burns contemplating a mouse, or of Wordsworth observing a daisy, or, rising higher, the hopes and fears of a young mother watching a cradle, or, carried right away from earth, the rapt vision of ' I, John . . . in the isle that is called Patmos . . . in the Spirit on the Lord's Day.'

[1] *Lines Composed a Few Miles above Tintern Abbey.*

For Romance does range all that distance, and when the one end of its range is compared with the other it almost seems as though the word 'Romantic' has two pretty distinct meanings.

The Romance of the Distant

It was of the first kind of Romance that Byron was thinking when he spoke of Horace Walpole's *Castle of Otranto* as the first Romance in our language, a description of it which has been repeated in other words by a later critic:

> Frowning castles and gloomy monasteries, knights in armour and ladies in distress, and monks and nuns and hermits, all the scenery and the characters that have peopled the imagination of the romantic school, may be said to have had their origin on the night when Walpole lay down to sleep, his head crammed full of Wardour Street curiosities, and dreamt that he saw a gigantic hand in armour resting on the banister of his staircase.[1]

The distant (in point of time or of space) can generally be conceived romantically, and whether or not Walpole was our first literary romanticist, he was perhaps our first literary medievalist. He was almost the first modern Englishman to discover that a Gothic cathedral was beautiful. He actually realized it in an age when 'the very word "gothic" was synonymous with barbaric, and the admiration of an ancient abbey as ridiculous as admiration of Dante'. So to dwell in he built on the banks of the Thames his Strawberry Hill, 'with its gimcracks, its pasteboard battlements and stained paper carvings'.

'Vathek' Beckford did the same thing. He pulled down the Georgian mansion he inherited and instructed his architect to design for him 'an ornamental building that should have the appearance of a convent, be partly in ruins and yet contain

[1] Leslie Stephen on Horace Walpole, in *Hours in a Library*.

some weatherproof apartments'. Five hundred workmen, by the light of the sun by day and that of torches by night, toiled to give Beckford the domestic romance his imagination craved. Twice a great tower was reared and twice it fell, so that this Romantic author soon had around him all the Romantic ruins for which his heart could yearn.

It was a similar Romantic instinct that sent the Bristol musician, R. L. Pearsall, to live in a Swiss monastery, and to compose madrigals in the sixteenth-century style, and, again, that inspired the Bristol boy-poet Chatterton to write his poems in fifteenth-century idiom, to 'find' them in an old chest in a church, and to give them forth as 'written by the good priest, Thomas Rowley, 1464'—much as Walpole had first published his *Castle of Otranto* as a reprint of a black-letter publication of 1529. On a lower plane, it is the knowledge of this existence of a craving for Romance that impels certain second-hand booksellers to adopt the title 'Ye Olde Booke Shoppe', furniture dealers in Tottenham Court Road to make 'gate-legged' tables, and screen impresarios to film scenarios of the Far West.[1]

We may call this kind of Romantic, 'Operatic Romantic'. It is, indeed, welcomed on the Opera stages of all nations, but Germany has been particularly successful in the genre, as is exemplified by, for instance, the libretto of Weber's *Der Freischütz*, or of Wagner's *Tannhäuser* or *Lohengrin*.

The Romance of the 'Sublime'

This Walpole type of Romance, or Operatic Romance, is by no means to be despised. Yet in aesthetic value it is surely far below another type. Compare the Walpole-Beckford 'reaction' to the Gothic with Wordsworth's. He sees an old castle—

---

[1] E. W. is anxious that the allusion to Pearsall shall not be read to accuse him of trading in mere 'sham antiques'; 'his madrigals seem to me the expression of a very genuine and fine musicianship.'

this huge Castle, standing here sublime,
I love to see the look with which it braves,
Cased in the unfeeling armour of old time,
The lightning, the fierce wind, and trampling waves.[1]

or he meditates in a great College Chapel—

> These lofty pillars . . . that branching roof
> Self poised, and scooped into ten thousand cells,
> Where light and shade repose, where music dwells
> Lingering—and wandering on as loth to die;
> Like thoughts whose very sweetness yieldeth proof
> That they were born for immortality.[2]

The two kinds of Romance, though, of course, they often merge, can, for purposes of classification, be clearly differentiated. One of them, we may say, is more ' external ' than the other or, to use other words that mean the same thing, one is more *objective* and the other more *subjective*. Taken together they represent a phase in literature that came about at the end of the eighteenth century and the beginning of the nineteenth—a phase of revolt against the severer, colder style then in vogue.

The Growth of the Romantic Spirit

Our English poet Thomson (1700–48) is an early instance of the coming of the Romantic spirit into poetry. The Romantic tinge in his work seems to us to-day, who know the Lake Poets and all that they brought in their train, to be rather faint and faded; let the comparison, however, be not with them, but with his contemporary, Pope, and we realize that his claim to the title of a romantic pioneer is secure. From classical to romantic has in no art been a sudden revolution, and in literature its stages may be displayed in a simple way by some such juxtaposition as that which follows, of three or four poets' treatment of the same subject.

[1] *Elegiac Stanzas suggested by a picture of Peele Castle in a storm, painted by Sir George Beaumont.*

[2] *Inside of King's College Chapel, Cambridge.*

For me kind nature wakes her genial pow'r,
Suckles each herb, and spreads out every flow'r:
Annual for me the grape, the rose renew
The juice nectareous, and the balmy dew.

That is Pope (*Essay on Man*), and he wrote it in 1732.

And in yon mingled wilderness of flowers,
Fair-handed Spring unbosoms every grace;
Throws out the snowdrop and the crocus first;
The daisy, primrose, violet darkly blue,
And polyanthus of unnumber'd dyes;
The yellow wall-flower, stain'd with iron brown;
The lavish stock, that scents the garden round:
From the soft wing of vernal breezes shed,
Anemones, auriculas, enrich'd
With shining meal o'er all their velvet leaves;
And full ranunculus, of glowing red.

That is Thomson (*The Seasons*). It was written at about the
same date as the previous extract. It certainly possesses
a greater warmth, and might have been written by a romantically-minded seedsman, inspired by an imaginative
reading of his own catalogue.

There scattered oft, the earliest of the year,
By hands unseen, are showers of violets found;
The redbreast loves to build and warble there,
And little footsteps lightly print the ground.

That is Gray; it was written in 1750. It offers us our one
genuinely romantic thrill in our favourite *Elegy in a Country
Churchyard*. 'And having written this beautiful stanza, full
of the true romantic temper, having printed it in two editions,
Gray cancelled it, and no doubt the age of acceptance and
gentility approved the omission. For what are . . . . . .
violets and robins warbling round a grave compared with "the
muse's flame" and "the ecstasy" of the "living lyre", and such
elegant things?'[1]

[1] Theodore Watts-Dunton.

And now listen to the true romantic note—Wordsworth in 1807, singing of daffodils by a lake—

> Continuous as the stars that shine
> And twinkle on the milky way,
> They stretched in never-ending line
> Along the margin of a bay:
> Ten thousand saw I at a glance,
> Tossing their heads in sprightly dance.
>
> The waves beside them danced, but they
> Outdid the sparkling waves in glee:—
> A poet could not but be gay
> In such a jocund company;
> I gazed—and gazed—but little thought
> What wealth to me the show had brought:
>
> For oft when on my couch I lie
> In vacant or in pensive mood,
> They flash upon that inward eye
> Which is the bliss of solitude,
> And then my heart with pleasure fills,
> And dances with the daffodils.[1]

The treatment of any aspect of nature by various poets offers an easy means of tracing the growth of the romantic spirit. We might take rainbows: Thomson's scientifically conceived description, his 'grand ethereal bow', his 'show'ry prism', and his appeal to 'awful Newton' giving way to Wordsworth's impulsive—

> My heart leaps up when I behold
>   A rainbow in the sky:
> So was it when my life began;
> So is it now I am a Man;
> So be it when I shall grow old,
>   Or let me die!
> The Child is Father of the Man;
> And I could wish my days to be
> Bound each to each by natural piety.

Or we might take mountains; the aesthetic appreciation of

---

[1] Wordsworth's *I wandered lonely as a cloud.*

mountains belongs almost distinctively to the romantic period,
Thomson's ' horrid mountains '—

> all the tract
> Of horrid mountains which the shining Alps,
> And wavy Apennines, and Pyrenees,
> Branch out stupendous into distant lands—

giving place to Wordsworth's—

> Farewell thou little nook of mountain-ground,
> Thou rocky corner in the lowest stair
> Of that magnificent temple which doth bound
> One side of our whole vale with grandeur rare.

' The Renascence of Wonder '

To Theodore Watts-Dunton, who has left us the standard
treatment of the subject, the coming of the romantic spirit
into poetry (or shall we say the return of the romantic spirit,
for Shakespeare and the Elizabethans were full of it) was
' The Renascence of Wonder':

> The phrase ' Renascence of Wonder' merely indicates
> that there are two great impulses governing man, and
> probably not man only but the entire world of conscious
> life: the impulse of acceptance—the impulse to take un-
> challenged and for granted all the phenomena of the outer
> world as they are—and the impulse to confront these
> phenomena with eyes of inquiry and wonder. . . . It would
> seem that something works as inevitably and as logically as
> a physical law in the yearning which societies in a certain
> stage of development show to get away—as far away
> as possible—from the condition of the natural man ; to get
> away from that despised condition not only in material
> affairs, such as dress, domestic arrangements and economies,
> but also in the fine arts and in intellectual methods, till,
> having passed that inevitable stage, each society is liable to
> suffer (even if it does not in some cases actually suffer) a
> reaction, when nature and art are likely again to take the
> place of convention and artifice.[1]

[1] Essay on *The Renascence of Wonder in Poetry*, by Theodore Watts-
Dunton, in Chambers' *Cyclopædia of English Literature*, vol. iii.

In Painting, in Sculpture, in Architecture, and in Music, too, this Antithesis of Classic and Romantic is to be found—and this gradual (or occasionally almost sudden) growth of the one into the other, only to be succeeded in time by the decline of the other into the one.

Formal Beauty and Imaginative Beauty

There are two elements in all art, the element of formal beauty and the element of imagination. Reynolds and Romney were Classics, Constable a Classic-Romantic, Turner a Romantic. The Greek and Roman architects were Classic, the Gothic architects Romantic, the Renascence architects would-be Classic, and the Gothic-revival architects would-be Romantic. Shakespeare was a Romantic, Milton a Romantic-Classic, Pope a Classic, Thomson a Classic-Romantic, Wordsworth a Romantic. Mozart and Haydn were Classics, Beethoven and Schubert Classic-Romantics (or Romantic-Classics), Schumann and Chopin Romantics, and so forth.

The divisions vary in character in the different arts, and I am not at all sure that every reader will agree with my effort to apply them above, but the general fact will not be disputed that in all the arts (and by no means least in that of Music) the tendency of the artist leans in one direction or the other, partly according to his natural temperament, and partly (perhaps more) according to the period in which he happens to live.

Art and Nature

Essentially, as the above poetical quotations will have suggested, the Classic leans more towards ‘art’ and the Romantic towards ‘nature’. Listen to a Frenchman on gardens:

Kensington Gardens . . . has something of the solemn grandeur of a wood about it—something uncultivated that delights the eye. It is like a good mile of the Forest of

St. Germain in the heart of town.   In France, our public gardens are placed under the care of some ex-sergeant, whose ideas never soar beyond obeying the orders of his superior, and keeping everything in line. If a refractory leaf does but attract his attention, *une, deusse*, it disappears! Our trees in the Tuileries look like little green imitations that are put into children's toy farmyards.   Good old Abbé Gaultier, from whom we have all learnt a little geography, speaks of the famous park of Versailles, 'where Art has forced Nature'. Over here, Art leaves Nature alone, because the English respect and appreciate her much more than we. Nothing is more imposing than the exuberant beauty of the English parks.   Take a walk across them in the early morning, when there is no one stirring, and the nightingale is singing high up in some gigantic tree; it is one of the rare pleasures that you will find within your reach in London. If the morning be fine, you will not fail to be struck with a lovely pearl-grey haze, soft and subdued, that I never saw in such perfection as in the London parks.[1]

We must all go to Kensington Gardens to hear the nightingale ! . . . And such, in effect, at the opening of the nineteenth century, was the impulse of the school of Composers now to be discussed.   Only sometimes, as they approached, they stopped too long to gaze at the Albert Hall and the Albert Memorial. That, at least, was what Mendelssohn occasionally did.   But Chopin and Schumann, arm in arm, passed within the gates —the one of them to stand under the tree and listen to the song, and the other often to be drawn away into sympathetic contemplation of the moods and humours of the holiday-crowd.

[1] *John Bull and his Island*, by Max O'Rell.

ROMANCE IN MUSIC

To define ' Romance' in poetry is difficult. To define it in music is impossible. Words will not explain what can only be grasped by the feelings ; examples only will serve. And so in this Chapter are given a series of passages from the Romantic composers, passages chosen almost at random, and, when that is realized, marking all the better the swift transition that took place in musical expression during a period of forty years or so at the opening of the nineteenth century.

In the year before Beethoven died was written Weber's Opera *Oberon*. This is how the Overture opens :—

What could be more romantic? From the first note of the
horn we are transported into a magic realm. Our minds are
at once prepared for the later rising of the curtain upon the
'Fairy garden in Oberon's kingdom; luxuriant blossoms;
butterflies; birds; Oberon on a bed of flowers, watched by
spirits and fairies'. And unless the stage manager has done
his work exceptionally well we shall find that the first bar of
the Overture, with its fairy horn call, and the sixth bar, with
its Flute and Clarinet fairy footsteps, have done more to evoke
the desired atmosphere than all the stage decoration, and,
indeed, may feel a sense of disappointment when Fairyland, at
first audible, becomes at last also visible.

Beethoven and his Juniors

Beethoven, it is sometimes said, was the first romantic composer. He was in reality both a great classic and a great romantic. Just where the line is to be drawn between the classic school and the romantic school can be decided only arbitrarily, and Beethoven, Janus-like, gazes in two directions. Beethoven's romance is undeniable; a thousand favourite passages come to mind—the bold opening theme of the early ' Heroic' Symphony, the eerie passage between the Scherzo and Finale of the Fifth Symphony, the opening themes of the so-called 'Pastoral' Sonata and the so-called 'Moonlight' Sonata, and so forth. Yet in Weber we get a certain quality of Romance that is lacking in Beethoven. What is it? Is it romance free from its moral implications? Beethoven is in places sublime and in places pathetic and in places very humorous, but there is always a rather formidable 'bigness' about him. Perhaps it is a suppressed didacticism that we feel. Perhaps there are lingering relics of the classic restraint. Perhaps this composer, usually regarded as the creature of impulse, never quite surrenders himself.

Mendelssohn and the Romance of Fairyland

Adequate explanation eludes us, but explanation there must be of this subtle difference between the most romantic passages of Beethoven and the romance of his younger contemporary, Weber. With Beethoven music was (as Carlyle put it, in his attempt to describe music in general) ' a kind of inarticulate, unfathomable speech, which leads us to the edge of the infinite'. With Weber and Mendelssohn comes an airier type of romance, for with the Overture to *Oberon*, and the Overture to *A Midsummer Night's Dream* (both written in 1826) 'the fairies entered the orchestra'. Could Beethoven have given us in music Oberon or Puck?

Those four opening chords, said Sir George Grove, 'represent moonlight as well as sound can represent an object of sight'. We are apt to fall in with the suggestion of Beethoven's romantically-minded contemporary, and agree that the opening movement of Op. 27, No. 2 entitles that work to be spoken of as the 'Moonlight Sonata'. But if this be night it is the night of cloud as well as moon, of velvety half-darkness, whereas Mendelssohn's night shines full, clear, and silvery.

The moonlight established by the four chords, there enter Mendelssohn's fairies, tripping lightly, much as do those of Weber. Here again, in the one composer as in the other, is an illustration of the new type of feeling which was coming into music at the opening of the nineteenth century. Bach (particularly), Mozart, and Haydn (e.g. the F minor Piano Variations) had shown some romantic susceptibility. Romance has indeed never been absent from music. But with the group, Weber, Mendelssohn, Schumann, Chopin, Berlioz, and others, Romance instead of remaining an occasional commodity became the very staple of music, existing freely in its own right and not as a mere attribute of sublimity.

Of the romance of fairyland Mendelssohn has been quite
the best exponent the world has seen.   In many a *Presto* of
his do we get the fairy feeling.   Here, in the Scherzo in E
minor for Piano Solo (suggested to him by a creeping plant
with blossoms that seemed to him like trumpets for fairies to
blow) is surely again heard (as in Weber) Oberon's fairy-call
followed by the trip of his subjects as, in response to the call,
they crowd upon the scene.

Presto (Very fast).

And in another Piano Solo, the popular *Andante and Rondo
Capriccioso* (written, it is thought, in the same year as the
Midsummer Night's Dream Overture) we surely get the fairies
again.   The Andante Introduction ends with slow arpeggios
and long-held single notes, and then there bursts upon us
the fairy troop :

The Reflective Romance of Schumann

And what of Schumann? Again there is a Romantic quality different in essence from the Romance of Beethoven, though Schumann's frequent reflectiveness and 'moral' tinge bring him nearer to Beethoven than Mendelssohn or Chopin ever came. The three Piano Solos (Op. 28) which bear the actual titles, *Romances*, may be taken as the very epitome of Schumann romance, above all the second:

There is the magician's secret word that in a twinkling carries us from the concert room to some distant shore. But it is not the same fairy shore as that to which Weber and Mendelssohn so often carry us. There is more of the *brooding* quality in Schumann. His touch is not so light as theirs. Schumann has drawn his inspiration less from nature and more from books—the fantastic novels of E. T. A. Hoffmann (himself a minor composer), and the satires and idylls of Jean Paul Richter.

Often Schumann achieves gaiety and light-heartedness, but it is the gaiety and light-heartedness of the fancy-dress ball rather than of fairyland, as in *Reconnaissance* from the *Carnival* set of pianoforte pieces:

sempre stacc.

etc.

Ped.　　＊　　Ped.　　＊

A sort of romantic boldness, particularly at the opening of a piece, is a common thing in Schumann. He steps out courageously, the world before him where to choose his place of rest, and he with a staff in his hand and eager curiosity in his heart. Take for example the opening of *Carnival*:

Quasi maestoso (Majestic).

or, better still, the opening of the great Quintet for Pianoforte and Strings:

Allegro brillante (Quick, brilliant).

etc.

The Tenderness, Gaiety, and Boldness of Chopin

And what of Chopin? The strange thing is that it seems to be natural to us to class together composers so diverse as Mendelssohn, Schumann, and Chopin, and even to associate with them Weber. These composers differ markedly in their idioms, and, in some subtle way, in the quality of the emotion expressed; somewhat exaggerating, perhaps, we almost say that no piece of any one of them could possibly be mistaken for a piece by another. Individually they stand apart from one another, and, grouped, they stand apart from Beethoven who was at work before them, and from the French, Scandinavian, and other romanticists who were at work after they themselves had lived out their too brief lives.

To take two of the group; is there a piece of Schumann that any one has ever thought for a passing moment to be one of Chopin (unless, just possibly, it be the page of deliberately intended imitation in *Carnival* that he himself called 'Chopin')? Is there a page of Chopin that one has ever thought for a moment to be a page of Schumann? And yet when, in 1831, Schumann offered Chopin the first journalistic recognition he had ever received, with the never-forgotten words, 'Hats off, gentlemen, a genius!' he did so because he undoubtedly saw in him another manifestation of the very romantic spirit that was moving himself. The Yorkshireman and the man of Kent seem to have little in common, but let them meet abroad, surrounded by alien minds, and they foregather as Englishmen. The Englishman and the Frenchman seem to have little in common, but send them to Central China and they associate as Europeans.

The romance of Chopin is very varied. Like Schumann he has seized and expressed the romance of the ball-room, with not only its decorations and shining candelabras and gay costumes, but also its tender whisperings and its sitting-out on the balcony (Valse in C sharp minor, Op. 64, No. 2):

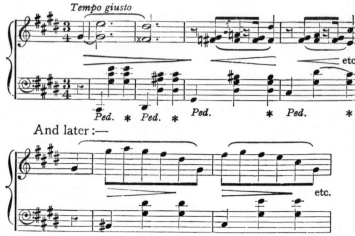

And later:—

The Valse was then in the heyday of its youth, and by comparing the Valses of Weber, Schubert, or Chopin, or the actual dancing valses of Strauss and Lanner, with the Minuets of Haydn and Mozart, we get the measure of the new romantic influences in art and social life. Like Schumann, Chopin has expressed the romance of the bold break-away (Scherzo, Op. 31, generally described as in B flat minor):

Like Mendelssohn, Chopin has been affected by the romance
of the moonlight night (Nocturne in D flat, Op. 27, No. 2):

And he has expressed the romantic aspirations of patriotism
(Polonaise in A, Op. 40):

He has beautifully expressed, too, the romance of watching, brooding motherhood (*Berceuse*):

What, after all, *is* romance in music? How *is* it achieved? Why *should* this strangely simple piece of Chopin, with its underlying oft-repeated left-hand figures and its plain-sailing right-hand melody (which in repetition develops more and more elaborately into broken-chord passages and chromatic scales), why should it at once lull and fascinate us? Can any one say? Perhaps if they could there would be no romance. Is romance the employment of a sixth sense? Is it the perception of the unknown?

XV

THE MUSICIAN AS LITERARY MAN AND PAINTER

'PROGRAMME MUSIC'

THE change of feeling which came over music during the first third of the nineteenth century is now clear to us. Yet the usual and handy way of defining the change as one from the Classical to the Romantic implies perhaps a change of balance rather than a change of character. By the Classical in any art we chiefly mean that manifestation of the art which places the bigger stress on beauty of form and style; by the Romantic we chiefly mean that manifestation of it which places the bigger stress on expression of emotion. The change, as has already been hinted, came at the same period over all the arts, perhaps not quite simultaneously, but rather in this order—Literature, Painting and Sculpture, Music. In each of them it had a dual character; there was a change both in the ideas expressed and in the manner of expression.

The Expression of ' Ideas ' in the Arts

Now, as concerns music, what do we mean by the expression of ' ideas '? Strictly, ideas are the stock-in-trade of the literary man. His very starting point is the 'idea'. Let him lay hold of an original and valuable idea and express it clearly and beautifully and he is completely fulfilling his function.

With the painter or sculptor the 'idea' is less important. The writer discusses, the painter describes. That at least is the primary function of each, for in such literary passages as attempt mere description the writer, however successful in his aim, is engaged in something which the painter can do better, and in such pictures as attempt to tell a story or ' discuss ' a principle of life the painter, however successful, is engaged in something in which he must fall somewhat below the writer.[1] Of course the practice of any art must necessarily be carried out on varying levels; the higher level of literature is, then, discussion (in the widest sense), whilst the higher level of painting is representation (also in the widest sense—not necessarily photographic, of course). When Meredith describes in words the outward charm of his heroine he is, whether he knows it or not, compelled to work upon his lower level, where a painter engaged in the attempt to make us realize those same charms would be working on his higher level.[2] And when Watts pictures 'Hope' he is, though he does not realize it, working upon his lower level, where a poet or prose writer would be working upon his higher level.

Strangely, this sensible theory of the limitations of the various arts, though apparently subconsciously more or less recognized by the greatest artists of all ages, was never clearly

[1] Instead of quoting here from any formal treatise on Aesthetics, let me quote (with a use of italics to make clear the purpose of the quotation) from the personal experience of a philosopher who, at a period of mental suffering, has turned to poetry for relief. John Stuart Mill, in his Autobiography, speaks thus of his study of Wordsworth:

'In the first place these poems addressed themselves powerfully to one of the strongest of my pleasurable susceptibilities, the love of rural objects and natural scenery; to which I had been indebted not only for much of the pleasure of my life, but quite recently for relief from one of my longest lapses into depression. In this power of rural beauty over me there was a foundation laid for taking pleasure in Wordsworth's poetry; the more so, as his scenery lies mostly among mountains, which, owing to my early Pyrenean excursion, were my ideal of natural beauty. *But Wordsworth would never have had any great effect on me, if he had merely placed before me beautiful pictures of natural scenery.* Scott does this still better than Wordsworth, and *a very second-rate landscape does it more effectually than any poet. What made Wordsworth's poems a medicine for my state of mind, was that they expressed, not mere outward beauty, but states of feeling, and of thought coloured by feeling, under the excitement of beauty.*'

[2] How many male readers, even those most susceptible to female charm, can recall being strongly moved by a writer's description of his heroine—even Homer's of Helen?

formulated until comparatively modern times.   Simonides, the
great arbiter of ancient thought upon art, is alleged to have
said ' poetry is a speaking picture and painting a dumb poem '.
If he ever did say it (as Plutarch reports), and meant it to be
considered a practical statement, then either he must have
qualified it greatly by adding explanation to epigram, or else
he was talking with so little consideration of the media and
methods of the two arts he mentioned that one would have
supposed his fallacy would have at once been exposed by any
intelligent chance bystander.

Unfortunately the epigram, in all its crudeness, was accepted,
and its misleading analogy seems to have been unquestioned
until, in 1766, Lessing published his famous *Laokoon, or the
Boundaries of Painting and Poetry*, an unshakable monument
to the value of ordinary commonsense and close reasoning even
in the study of aesthetics.   It is, perhaps, a pity that the
composers of the Romantic Period seem to have paid little
attention to a philosophical work that was already in their
time a classic. They set out upon a journey which had an end
worth attaining, but for want of the guidance of reason they
often strayed from the direct path.

The Expression of Emotion

If Literature's trump card is discussion (including narrative
and drama), if the Pictorial Art's trump card is delineation,
what is Music's ? . . . Surely the direct expression of emotion.
Beauty and Truth are aims of all the arts.   They are liberated
by Literature chiefly by means of discussion and the dramatic.
The Plastic Arts liberate them chiefly by delineation.   And
the Musical Art liberates them in immediate emotional expression.

Literature or Painting without emotion would be dead, but
these two arts express their emotion respectively through the
media of ideas and of pictorial reproduction.   With them
there is the interposition of the concrete, whereas with Music

there is no such interposition. Shakespeare conveys emotion to us by (it may be) the dramatic reproduction of a moment in history ; Turner conveys it by (it may be) the pictorial representation of a sunset ; Beethoven conveys it direct.

It may happen that some deeply moving incident in Beethoven's own life has aroused an emotion of passion : he can transfer the emotion to us without first informing us of the occurrence which aroused it—therein, in a sense, excelling the dramatist. It may be that some natural scene of placid beauty has aroused in him an emotion of peace; he can transfer the emotion to us without first painting the picture—therein excelling the pictorial artist.

That is precisely where music stands supreme, and as it is the duty of each of us to do most what we can do best, Music's main duty is the evocation of our sense of the beautiful through the expression of emotion.[1]

Music as Illustration

To that ideal composers had generally remained faithful. Bach's and Handel's achievement, or Haydn's and Mozart's, might be very adequately described in those very words—the evocation of our sense of the beautiful through the expression of emotion, or, changing the figure a little without much changing its sense, the expression of emotion by means of tonal beauty.

But in an Opera or an Oratorio these composers had a series of literary or pictorial ideas to work upon, and to some extent they made their music an illustration. In his

---

[1] 'You can attach any ideas you please to music, but music, if you will forgive me saying so, rejects them all equally. Art has to do with emotions, not with ideas, and the great defect of literature is that it can only express emotions by means of ideas. What makes music the greatest of all the arts is that it can express emotions without ideas. Literature can appeal to the soul only through the mind. Music goes direct. Its language is a language which the soul alone understands, but which the soul can never translate.'—ARNOLD BENNETT.

Matthew Passion Bach, accompanying the Recitative that tells how the veil of the Temple was rent in twain gives the organist or harpsichordist very rapid left-hand scales to accentuate the thought of tearing. Haydn in *Creation* is very pictorial or literary. He vividly suggests the creation of light, he offers musical hints of thunder, wind, the river, the sea, the tiger, the horse, the dove, the lark, fish, and insects—naïvely yet by no means altogether unsuccessfully. Mozart is less fond of the pictorial and the literary, but in his operas his orchestra often vividly underlines the sense of the words.

Composers in all ages have done this sort of thing and have then, on occasion, gone a step farther in attempting pictorial or literary suggestion in purely instrumental music. Thus Bach has a *Capriccio on the Departure of a Beloved Brother*, with (*Adagio*) 'A coaxing by his friends, to persuade him to give up his journey'; (*Andante*) 'A Representation of the various occurrences that might happen to him in a strange country'; (*Adagissimo*) 'The general lamentation of his friends'; (*Alla Marcia*) 'The friends gather to take leave of him, since they see it cannot be otherwise, and bid him farewell'; (*Adagio poco*) 'The Postillion', and lastly a 'Fugue in Imitation of the Postillion's Horn'.

Bach's contemporary, Kuhnau, published in 1700 a *Musical Representation of some Biblical Stories in Six Sonatas*. Before each Sonata he tells the story in letterpress and then in the Sonata repeats it in music, with some further literary indications added as he goes along. Thus the First Sonata is *The Fight between David and Goliath*, and the various movements are headed 'The Boasts of Goliath'; 'The Trembling of the Israelites before the Giant, and their prayer to God'; 'The Courage of David and his longing to lower the pride of the terrible enemy, with his confidence in the help of God'; 'The Fight between the Two—the pebble is slung from the sling into the giant's forehead—Goliath falls—flight of the Philistines, who are pursued and annihilated by the Israelites';

'The joy of the Israelites over their victory'; 'The Musical Performance of the women in honour of David'; 'The general rejoicings and the happy dances of the populace'.

Similarly, but with less dependence upon detailed representation, Haydn wrote for Good Friday use in the Cathedral of Cadiz a series of seven slow orchestral pieces on the Seven Words from the Cross, followed by a quick one entitled 'The Earthquake'.

Then came Beethoven with his Pianoforte Sonata (Op. 81 a, in E flat) of which the three Movements are entitled, 'The Farewell', 'Absence', and 'The Return'; his '*Rondo a capriccio—Rage over a Lost Penny*;[1] and his *Pastoral Symphony, or Recollections of Country Life*, which he described as ' more expression of feeling than painting', but which yet included a placidly flowing 'Scene at the Brook' Movement, the imitation of bird songs, a 'Happy Gathering of the Peasants' (with a hint of a village orchestra), a 'Thunderstorm' and a 'Shepherd's Song—Gratitude and Thanksgiving after the Storm'.

Beethoven's description, 'More expression of feeling than painting' would apply to large stretches of all such pieces before and during the period, except perhaps some cheap battle-pieces and other feeble efforts, and so it would apply, too, to large stretches of most of the 'Programme Music' (for so we call music of this class) of the Romantic Period, now to be discussed.

The Growing Literary Interests of Composers

The Romantic Period brought with it an immense increase of composition of this kind, and one reason is obvious. Composers were becoming less narrowly composers; they

---

[1] E. W. remarks—'The Op. 129 Rondo is posthumous, and I can't myself believe that Beethoven would have retained in print the queer joke he scrawled on his MS. When it came to publication he discarded such ebullitions, as in the case of the Adagio of the first Rasoumovsky.'

were becoming active readers and writers; their interest was increasingly shared between music and literature. Bach, Handel, Haydn, Mozart, and even Beethoven had not been 'bookish' men; Weber, Berlioz, Schumann, Liszt, and Wagner decidedly were such. Weber and Schumann (the latter the son of a book publisher) dipped deeply into the writings of the German romantic novelists, poets, and philosophers, and both of them themselves wrote a good deal, so that they ranked not merely as composers and performers, but also as active music critics. Amongst the French composers Berlioz, for one, read largely; he revelled in Shakespeare, Byron, and Scott, he was for years the official music critic of an important Paris newspaper, and he left a number of volumes on musical subjects. Liszt associated much with literary men and women in Paris, steeped himself at different times in the works of Hugo, Lamartine, George Sand, and others, and left a large body of literary work. Wagner made a deep study of national legend, read extensively on all manner of subjects, and fancied himself a philosopher; his literary works fill as many volumes as those of some men whose whole lives have been given to literary composition.

It was a new type of musical mind that had arisen, a mind teeming with literary images, and the result was seen in the music of the period.

Weber and Schumann

Weber's instrumental works are not his most important, but are not to be neglected. Such pieces as the *Invitation to the Dance*, with its 'Approach of the dancers' (bars 1 to 5), 'The lady's evasive reply' (5 to 9), 'Her consent' (13 to 16), and so forth (he himself supplied these indications in a spoken commentary when playing the piece to his wife), and his *Concert Piece* (Op. 79), with its story of a crusading knight and his lady, show plainly this literary tendency.

Such a tendency is, however, much more marked in

Schumann, the titles of whose pieces make up a very different looking list from that of any predecessor. We have *Butterflies* ('Papillons'), a set of twelve pieces suggested by a description of a masked ball in Jean Paul Richter; *Carnival*, a similar set with such titles for the separate movements as 'Pierrot' and 'Harlequin', some movements named after living persons, and some others named after imaginary characters; *Novelettes, Pictures from the East, Woodland Scenes, Fairy-tale Pictures* ('Märchenbilder'), *Kreisleriana* (suggested by E. T. A. Hoffmann's fantastic musical novel of the same name)—and so on. Some of Schumann's romantic titles came to his mind after he had finished his compositions, but the definite way in which his musical imagination was sometimes stimulated by his reading may be seen in his account, in a letter, of the composition of the last number of *Butterflies*.

> You remember the last scene of *Flegeljahre* [1]—masked dance—Walt—Vult—masks—Wina—Vult's dancing—the exchange of masks—confessions—indignation—revelation —hurried departure—final scene and then the departing brother. I kept turning over the last page, since the end seemed to me to be merely a new opening, and almost without realizing it I found myself sitting at the piano, and then one *Papillon* after another came to life.

Mendelssohn and Chopin

Mendelssohn was less directly influenced by his reading, though we do see its influence in his *Midsummer Night's Dream* Overture, his *Calm Sea and Prosperous Voyage* Overture (based on Goethe), his *Melusina* Concert Overture (based on

[1] Jean Paul Richter's romantic novel, much in the style of Goethe's *Wilhelm Meister*, which had been published eight or nine years earlier. It expresses ideals idyllically. The characters Walt and Vult are representative of two sides of the author's personality just as are Schumann's Eusebius and Florestan in the *Carnival* already alluded to. Indeed Eusebius and Florestan were evolved by Schumann out of Walt and Vult. ('Flegel', literally 'flail' = a rough, unmannerly person; 'Flegeljahre' = youthful years.)

legend) and elsewhere. He was very responsive to natural scenery, and the recollections of his travels inspired such works as the *Italian* and *Scottish* Symphonies and the *Hebrides* (or *Fingal's Cave*) Concert Overture.

Chopin, though associating much with writers and painters, was less literary and more purely musical than either Schumann or Mendelssohn. Like these two contemporaries he wrote a great number of short characteristic pieces, but where these were not based on dance forms, such as the Waltz, the Mazurka or the Polonaise, they bore vague titles such as 'Prelude', 'Study', or 'Nocturne'.

Berlioz

In Berlioz we find a very distinct example of literary influence. He based works on Shakespeare (Overture to *King Lear*, Dramatic Symphony—*Romeo and Juliet*) ; Scott (Overtures to *Waverley* and *Rob Roy*) ; Byron (Overture to *The Corsair*, and *Harold in Italy*, the latter a symphony with viola obbligato).

With Berlioz we see a more definite application of literary ideas than with (say) Schumann. He often sticks pretty closely to a story. How is such a thing to be done—in a piece of serious music ? The instrumental music discussed in the First Volume of this History consisted chiefly of Fugues, Suites, and Sonatas : all forms which have come into existence as a response to a psychological need for variety combined with unity (see Vol. I, p. 108), and also for a sort of symmetry. that we may call an architecture in time as cathedral building is an architecture in space. Can such a demand be met whilst at the same time a 'programme' of incidents or thoughts (and here we see the meaning of the technical term 'Programme Music') is also followed ?

How is the old form of symphonic 'First Movement', with its contrasted 'subjects', its 'development' of them and its 'recapitulation', to be superposed on a dramatic and emotional scheme the sections of which may happen to fall quite differently? Roughly speaking a 'First Movement' or 'Sonata Form' piece ends as it began (with the same two tunes in the same order in relation to one another), whilst a drama or story moves ever forward towards a conclusion which may differ widely from the opening. A simple 'Concert Overture', such as those of Mendelssohn or some of those of Berlioz, may aim at nothing beyond a representation of the general emotional tinge of the literary work upon which it is based *plus* a suggestion of some main characters or incidents in the 'themes', 'tunes', or 'subjects' and in one or two passages in which this subject matter is treated by processes of 'development'. But such music as this, though we may call it 'Programme Music', is not such in the severest application of the term, since it is not fitted in detail to a previously existent 'programme' of events or of literary ideas.

Obviously for the fullest programmatic' treatment of music some more flexible method is required, and Berlioz invented one. He introduced what he called the 'fixed idea' (*idée fixe*). Let us examine cursorily his 'Fantastic' Symphony.

Here (translated into English) is the 'Introduction' which Berlioz himself supplied for this work.

EPISODE IN THE LIFE OF AN ARTIST
FANTASTIC SYMPHONY IN FIVE SECTIONS

The Composer's aim has been to develop, *in such a way as they may be musical*, different situations[1] in the life of an artist.

The plan of the instrumental drama, deprived of the help of words, needs to be set out in advance. The following programme must then be considered like the spoken [*sic*], text of an opera, serving to pave the way for pieces of music, and providing the motives for their character and determining the expression.

---

[1] M. Adolphe Boschot, in *La Jeunesse d'un Romantique*, remarks that Berlioz has already contradicted his title in explaining that we have here not one episode, but several episodes.

It would be beyond the scope of this book to discuss all that is or is not implied by Berlioz' various procedures ; but it is easy to realize that the full Programme would have very great value to those who first heard this novel work ; and there can be no harm, and nothing but interest for us, in taking in the full Programme, if we remember that Berlioz subsequently eliminated all but the titles of the movements.   At any rate, here is the whole thing.

I.—*Reveries.   Passions.*

A young musician possessed of a weakly sensibility and an ardent imagination finds himself in that state of soul which Chateaubriand has so admirably depicted in *René.*   Vague reveries ; turns of melancholy and joy without precise cause ; delicious troublings of a sentimental adolescent.—Suddenly he sees a woman : the ideal woman, such as he had dreamed of, ' Ideal of beauty and charms for which his heart had long cried out '.—Straightway, volcanic love, delirious anguish, fury, jealousy ; then returns of tenderness, tears, and, at last, religious consolations.

II.—*A Ball.*

The Artist is placed in utterly different circumstances of life, in the midst of *the tumult of a Fête* . . . The cherished image appears before him and casts trouble into his soul.

III.—*Scene in the Country (Adagio).*

It is evening.   In the distance two herdsmen answer one another, in dialogue, with a *ranz des vaches.*[1]   All things join to give back to his heart a long-lost serenity. Then *She* appears.   His soul is filled with painful forebodings.   Will she prove false to him ?   One of the herdsmen takes up his tune again, but the other does not reply . . . Sunset . . . distant thunder . . . solitude . . . silence.

IV.—*March to the Scaffold.*

He dreams he has murdered the woman he loves, that he

---

[1] ' Calling the Cows.'   Melody played by Swiss herdsmen on the Alpine horn.   Cf. the famous *Ranz des vaches* in Rossini's Overture to *William Tell.*

is under sentence of death, and is being led to execution. The procession moves on, to a March that is now sombre and savage, now brilliant and solemn.

V.—*Dream of a Witches' Sabbath.*

He sees himself at the Witches' Revels, surrounded by fearful ghosts, sorcerers, and monsters of all sorts who have come to attend his funeral. Weird noises, groans, shrieks of laughter, and distant cries answered by other cries. The Tune of the Beloved recurs, but it has no longer its noble and timid character; now it is no more than a trivial, grotesque dance-tune, a low cabaret tune; it is *She* who joins the Witches' Sabbath. Howls of joy welcome her. She joins in the hellish orgy. Funeral bells and a mocking parody of the *Dies Irae*.

Such is Berlioz' Programme for his 'Fantastic' Symphony. Now he manages, in the First Movement, to express very powerfully and vividly the emotions which he has indicated, while yet keeping very close to the usual form—of Exposition of subject-matter, Development, and final Recapitulation (see Vol. I, pp. 108–9). Here is his musical expression of the *Fixed Idea* of the beloved one who inspires the whole work:

Allegro agitato e appassionato assai (Quick, agitated and very passionate).
1st Violins & Flute.

In this form, with some extension, but with practically no accompaniment, it constitutes the First Subject of the First Movement. How truly this is the 'fixed idea' of the First Movement may be imagined when one finds that it is also used

for his Second Subject, and sees how the Development Section
begins.   Thus :

It is remarkable that in such a piece as this Berlioz is able to make the usual formal repetition of the Exposition, though this repetition (from the double-bar) cannot well be shown here.

This *Fixed Idea*, this theme of the Beloved, is indeed made, in this Movement, to express the violent and conflicting emotions which the Artist's soul undergoes. The final 'religious consolations' (a succession of very soft, slow, solemn chords) are thus prepared :

The Beloved haunts the gay Ball of the Second Movement:

The role of the *Fixed Idea* in the next two Movements must now be passed over. But its hideous travesty in the Witches' Sabbath (see the Programme above) must be quoted. It is given to the shrill E flat Clarinet.

Liszt.

Liszt was quite as much affected by literary and pictorial influences as Berlioz, and more ready to disregard existing forms. He was inspired by Dante, writing a *Dante* Symphony, with movements 'Inferno', 'Purgatorio' and 'Magnificat', and by Goethe, writing a *Faust* Symphony (dedicated to Berlioz, himself, by the way, the composer of a notable choral-orchestral treatment of the same subject), with movements 'Faust', 'Gretchen', and 'Mephistopheles'. He also wrote a number of what he called 'Symphonic Poems' (the first use of a term which has since become very common). The titles of a few of these will show the detailed literary bent of their Composer's mind—*Tasso* (after Byron and Goethe), *The Preludes* (after Lamartine's 'Poetic Meditations'), *Mazeppa* (after Hugo, after Byron), *Slaughter of the Huns* (after a fresco by Kaulbach, in Berlin), *The Ideals* (after a poem by Schiller), *Hamlet*. There is also a *Dance of Death* (with piano) after Orcagna's fresco at Pisa.

In his pianoforte music Liszt was almost as literary and pictorial—*Benediction of God in Solitude* (after Lamartine), *Years of Pilgrimage* ('William Tell's Chapel', 'On the Lake of Wallenstadt', 'The Valley of Obermann', 'Sposalizio'—

'The Betrothal'—on Raphael's picture, 'Three Sonnets of Petrarch', 'After a Reading of Dante', &c.), *Legends* ('St. Francis of Assisi' and 'St. Francis of Paola') *Consolations* (after Sainte-Beuve), and so on . . . and so on!

Quite evidently with Liszt we have entered fully into the domain of literary and pictorial music, and are hundreds of miles from the Fugues of Bach and the Symphonies of Mozart.

Liszt sometimes gives us an actual 'programme', which he carefully defines as 'any preface, in intelligible language, added to a piece of instrumental music, by means of which the composer intends to guard the listener against a wrong poetical interpretation, and to direct his attention to the poetical idea of the whole or to a particular point in it'.

The Liszt Symphonic Poem, whilst it may embody all the variety of the several Movements of a Symphony, is one piece from beginning to end. A device much akin to that of the 'fixed idea' of Berlioz enables the composer to express all his ideas on the different aspects of a literary subject and yet to bind the piece into unity. It is the device of the 'metamorphosis of themes'—the same tune or subject appearing over and over again, varied melodically, harmonically, and rhythmically, yet not sufficiently so as to preclude the listener's recognition of it. He may, on occasion, relate his themes to persons and then vary them as different aspects of personality or different emotional states are to be represented. And he has other devices. An actual Liszt 'Programme' as printed on the score of one of his compositions may be given. That which is prefaced to the score of *Tasso* may be thus rendered into English :

TASSO

LAMENT AND TRIUMPH

In 1849 all Germany celebrated with splendour the hundredth anniversary of the birth of Goethe. We [1] were

[1] Liszt uses the First Person Plural—authorial or royal ?

then at Weimar, where, among the commemorations, was planned, for the evening of 28th August, a performance of his Drama *Tasso*.

The misfortunes of fate of the most unfortunate of poets had fired the imaginations of the most powerful poetic geniuses of our time, Goethe and Byron ; Goethe, whose lot fell among the most brilliant successes : Byron, whose advantages of birth and fortune were counterbalanced by such lively sufferings. We cannot deny that when we were commissioned, in 1849, to write an overture for Goethe's Drama, we were more directly inspired by the reverent compassion [*respectueuse compatissance*] of Byron for the spirit of the great man that he was evoking, than by the work of the German poet. All the same, Byron, while transmitting to us in some sort the groanings of Tasso in his prison, was unable to unite with the memory of his poignant sorrows, so nobly and eloquently expressed in his *Lamentation*, that of the Triumph which awaited, by a tardy but shining justice, the chivalric author of *Jerusalem Delivered*. We have wished to indicate this contrast in the very title of our work, and would have liked successfully to give form to this great antithesis, of the genius who, ill-treated during his life, shines forth after his death with such power as would crush his persecutors.

Tasso loved and suffered at Ferrara ; he was avenged at Rome ; his glory is yet living in the popular songs of Venice. These three stages are inseparable from his immortal memory. To render them in music we have first conjured up the great shade of the hero, even as it appears to us to-day haunting the lagoons of Venice ; we have then caught sight of his haughty, saddened countenance as he glides through the fêtes of Ferrara, where his masterpieces first saw the light of day ; finally we have followed him to Rome, the Eternal City, which in crowning him glorified in him the martyr and the poet.   F. LISZT.

Liszt tells us that Tasso's 'glory is yet living in the popular songs of Venice'. As a matter of fact, the very theme out of which he makes the whole Symphonic Poem is a tune which he heard the Venetian gondoliers singing on the lagoons to verses of Tasso.

Here is the first and most important part of the song:

Here are the opening bars of the work, using the characteristic close of each 'sentence' of (a):

Before we leave this work, three of the most significant 'metamorphoses' of the theme may be quoted.

(c) is the beginning of the Second Section of the work—Ferrara (see Liszt's programme).

(d) is the beginning of the final triumph at Rome. This form of the Tune is worked up until it is loudly declaimed by the whole Orchestra.

(e) is the complete climax. At the top is (a), broadened out and put into major, below the bass accompanies with the triplet figure shown in (b), itself taken from (a). (There are also several Percussion effects, and surging Upper Strings arpeggios, not shown here.)

(c)

Allegretto mosso con grazia (quasi Menuetto) (*Fairly quick, with grace—like a Minuet*).

2 Solo 'Cellos.

Other 'Cellos, Violas & D. Basses, all *pizz.* *mf espress.* *p*

Bassoons & 2nd Vlns. added. etc.

(d)

Allegro con molto brio (*Quick, with much vigour*).

p

All Strings.

(e)

Moderato pomposo (At a moderate pace, pompous).

The Romantic Forms

The Romantic Movement in music may be said to have brought into existence three new forms, (1) the Concert Overture of Mendelssohn, (2) the Set of Characteristic Piano Pieces, such as Schumann's *Papillons* and *Carnival*, and (3) the Symphonic Poem of Liszt. All these are, in their varying degrees, forms of ' Programme Music '. And in addition there was (4) a great increase of activity in the writing of independent short piano pieces such as the ' Songs Without Words ' of Mendelssohn and the Nocturnes and Studies and Preludes of Chopin.

Improvements in the piano and in orchestral instruments,

giving the composer greater scope for free poetical expression, were a great factor in the increased romanticization of music, but of course a far greater one was the coming together of literary men, painters, and musicians, so that their minds reacted on one another ; and the greatest of all was the influence of the Romantic School in literature—the two Schlegels, Tieck, Novalis, Uhland, Jean Paul Richter, E. T. A. Hoffmann (himself a composer) and others in Germany, Chateaubriand, Lamartine, Hugo and others in France, Scott and Byron in Britain.

The Romantic Temper

Hugo said that Romanticism was 'simply liberalism in literature'. The Lake School in English Poetry, Blake, the Oxford Movement, Christian Socialism in religion, both Turner and Pre-Raphaelitism in painting, the Gothic revival in architecture—all sorts of manifestations of the romantic temper are bound up together in the history of the first half of the nineteenth century, which, curiously, was also the period of railway development and of the growth of a huge crop of tall chimneys. That the age of Shakespearean romance should have been an age of exploration and conquest is not surprising ; that the age of the revival of the romantic should have been the age of steam power seems at first sight not quite so natural. Perhaps it is owing to the chance that at the moment when the romantic temper of the Shakespearean period became due for a re-birth the movement for scientific investigation initiated by Shakespeare's contemporary, Bacon, had attained a development which enabled it to emerge fully into the field of practical affairs. Besides, there is a romance of science and a romance of commerce, and perhaps we are too apt to forget the workings of romantic impulse in realms other than those of Art.

In closing this chapter a few words may be added as to the principles upon the observance of which success depends in the composition of Programme Music.

Success and Failure in ' Programme Music '

Earlier in the chapter was made the passing suggestion that in some measure the Romantic Composers went astray in their application of the Programme Music conception. The places where they went astray were the places where they put too much weight on the ' programme ', making enjoyment of the music too entirely dependent upon a following of the series of incidents or ideas bound up with it.

When Chekov told a brother novelist to ' cut out all those pages about the moonlight, and give us what you really feel about it ' he gave good counsel, and counsel which becomes still better when offered to the musician. As Prior put it, more than two centuries ago,

> Your musick's power your musick must disclose
> For what light is 'tis only light that shows.[1]

Unless the music *quâ* music is intelligible and strong and beautiful no ' programme ' will avail to save it—at any rate to save it for more than the period of a generation that is carried away by its novelty. Very much of the enormous mass of Programme Music of the nineteenth century is already dying or dead because its composers did not realize the difference between illustrator and artist. And some of that of the twentieth century is bound to follow it.

---

[1] *To the Countess of Exeter playing upon the Lute.* Strictly, Prior intended this as a reflection upon the impossibility of describing musical performances in words, but it seems fair to widen the application a little. ' Music must speak for itself ', and no critic, nor even the composer himself in the most carefully drafted ' programme ', can speak for it.

Wagner, with all his admiration for his father-in-law, Liszt (Programme Music's very prophet), said (1877), ' In instrumental music I am a reactionary. I do not like music that requires explanation beyond the actual sounds.' But then Wagner found his outlet for music and explanation elsewhere than in instrumental music. If he had not been the greatest music-dramatist the world has known he would certainly have been its greatest Programme Music composer.

XVI

ROMANTIC SONG

SOMETHING must now be said about the German 'Lied'.[1] It is a product of Romanticism, being due to the rise of the Romantic School in German poetry and the development of Romantic feeling in music, and especially of Romantic harmony through the work of Beethoven and Schubert.

Beethoven himself was hardly a song-writer; the few songs he wrote bulk as nothing against his instrumental music, and in quality are far surpassed by it. Schubert, however, was a born song-writer, and must be regarded as the founder of the German *Lieder* school. As already related in the previous volume, he wrote over 600 songs, and with him began the wholesale song production of the German composers; e.g. Schumann over 200, Franz over 300, Brahms about 200, Wolf over 500. Frequently the songs were composed as series, being settings of either a definite cycle or at least an ordered collection of poems, e.g. Schubert's *Miller Songs* ('Müllerlieder'), settings of twenty poems from *The Lovely Maid of the Mill* ('Die Schöne Müllerin') by William Müller; Schubert's *Winter Journey* ('Winterreise'), settings of twenty-four poems by the same poet; Schumann's *Poet's Love* ('Dichterliebe'), sixteen settings of Heine; Schumann's *Woman's Love and Life* ('Frauenliebe und Leben'), settings of poems by Chamisso; Brahms's *Fifteen Romances from Tieck's 'Magelone'*; Wolf's *Songs of Mörike*, forty-four settings; *Songs of Eichendorff*, twenty settings; *Songs of Goethe*, thirty-seven settings; *Spanish Song Book*, forty-four settings—and so forth.

[1] Properly 'Lied' means simply 'song'; 'Volkslied' means 'Folk Song', 'Volkstümliches Lied' means 'Folk-like Song', 'Kunstlied' means 'Art Song', &c. The word 'Lied' has come, however, to possess a somewhat specialized meaning, the character of which will be gathered from the present discussion of the subject.

Songs had been composed since music began, but never until now had there been quite such a spate of them. And never had songs possessed the intensely romantic quality of those now composed.

In this last characteristic they merely reflected the spirit of the poetry of the day. Frederick Schlegel, one of the pioneers of German Romanticism, distinguished between the Classical school of poetry, which was then waning, and the Romantic school, that was then waxing, by calling the product of the first 'die schöne Poesie' ('The Poetry of Beauty') and that of the second 'die interessante Poesie' ('The Poetry of Interest').

And so with the music set to the two kinds of poetry : the one aims primarily at beauty of vocal contour and the other at characterization of the spirit of the poem, and often of its minute details—the song music of beauty and the song music of interest.

The German 'Lied' of the early nineteenth century may be of one of two kinds—it may be a Verse Song (the Germans call this 'volksthümlich', i. e. in the folk style, the same setting for each stanza), or it may be 'through-composed' ('durchcomponiert'), the music varying verse by verse and following word by word the mood-pictures of the poem. In either case the chief aim is to express in music the spirit of the poem as a whole, and in the latter case there is an attempt to go beyond this general expression and to treat the poem with a musical-dramatic parallelism.

A powerful means of characterization in either case is the enhanced interest given to the piano part ; song has now become in many cases, not, so to speak, a solo with accompaniment, but a duet between voice and instrument. To quote just one example known to everybody, Schubert's *Erl King* is obviously as much a piano piece as a song.

The subjects treated represent in very fair proportion the subjects popular amongst the poets. There is a great revival of interest in legend, and so we have songs about the Erl King and the Lorelei ; there is a revival of interest in nature, and so we get songs about gloomy forests, and 'Wood Loneliness', and trees in blossom, and birds, and brooks, and moonlight, and meadows, and the wayside spring, and the open road, and the wandering apprentice ; and there is a renewed national feeling (encouraged by the spirit of opposition to Napoleon) and so come songs lauding the sacred Rhine and the German Fatherland.

Of course the thing was overdone. Romain Rolland's hero, John Christopher, when he inherited this huge mass of romantic song, rebelled—

Christopher was passing through that crisis of healthy disgust. His instinct was impelling him to eliminate from his life all the undigested elements which encumbered it.

First of all to go was that sickening sweet tenderness which sucked away the soul of Germany like a damp and mouldy river-bed. Light! Light! A rough, dry wind which should sweep away the miasmas of the swamp, the musty staleness of the *Lieder, Liedchen, Liedlein,* as numerous as drops of rain in which inexhaustibly the Germanic *Gemüt* is poured forth: the countless things like *Sehnsucht* (Desire), *Heimweh* (Home-sickness), *Aufschwung* (Soaring), *Frage* (A question), *Warum?* (Why?), *An den Mond* (To the Moon), *An die Sterne* (To the Stars), *An die Nachtigall* (To the Nightingale), *An den Frühling* (To Spring), *An den Sonnenschein* (To Sunshine); like *Frühlingslied* (Spring Song), *Frühlingslust* (Delight of Spring), *Frühlingsgruss* (Hail to the Spring), *Frühlingsfahrt* (A Spring Journey), *Frühlingsnacht* (A Spring Night), *Frühlingsbotschaft* (The Message of Spring) : like *Stimme der Liebe* (The Voice of Love), *Sprache der Liebe* (The Language of Love), *Trauer der Liebe* (Sorrow of Love), *Geist der Liebe* (The Spirit of Love), *Fülle der Liebe* (The Fullness of Love) : like *Blumenlied* (The Song of the Flowers), *Blumenbrief* (The Letter of the Flowers), *Blumengruss* (Flowers' Greeting) : like *Herzleid* (Heart Pangs), *Mein Herz ist schwer* (My Heart is Heavy), *Mein Herz ist betrübt* (My Heart is troubled), *Mein Aug' ist trüb* (My Eye is Heavy) : like the candid and silly dialogues with the Röslein (the Little Rose), with the brook, with the turtle dove, with the lark : like those idiotic questions : '*If the briar could have no thorns?*'—'*Is an old husband like a lark who has built a nest?*'—'*Is she newly plighted?*': the whole deluge of stale tenderness, stale emotion, stale melancholy, stale poetry. . . . How many lovely things profaned, rare things, used in season or out! For the worst of it was that it was all useless: a habit of undressing their hearts in public, a fond and foolish propensity of the honest people of Germany for plunging loudly into confidences. With nothing to say they were always talking! Would their chatter never cease?—as well bid frogs in a pond be silent. (*John Christopher* by Romain Rolland, Gilbert Cannan's translation).

And yet, when all is said, neither John Christopher nor we would care to be without the many very great things of the nineteenth-century German Lieder school, which constitute one of the most distinctive products of the Romantic period in music.

XVII

OPERA—DOWN TO AND DURING THE ROMANTIC PERIOD

No form of musical art more obviously offers opportunities to the Romantic composer than Opera. Weber took full advantage of these opportunities, and so did Wagner. Curiously, the Romantic Trio, as we may call them, the 1809–10 group, Mendelssohn, Chopin and Schumann, did not profit by the opportunities. Mendelssohn could not find libretti to suit him, Schumann's attempts failed through lack of sense of the stage, Chopin was a piano specialist. The great names of Romantic Opera are those of what we may call the three 'V's', Weber, Wagner, and Verdi. Before we follow their paths it is necessary to take a leap backwards, since in the First Volume of *The Listener's History*, in order to avoid too scattered and piece-meal a treatment of the subject, discussion of all but the early beginnings of Opera was deferred.

In that volume was given (see Chapter VI) a sketch of the first origins of Opera, in the last days of the sixteenth century and the early days of the seventeenth—the days of the Italian dramatic experimenters, Peri, Caccini, Monteverde. Then (in Chapter VIII) occurred a brief allusion to the growth of formalism and artificiality in what had been originally intended to be a very direct and natural means of dramatic expression, Handel's Operas, with their stereotyped Arias, being, for our text-book purposes, accepted as the type of eighteenth-century operatic formality. The passages in question should be, at this point, re-read.

Opera in the time of Handel

It is now necessary to extend somewhat the treatment of opera in Handelian times, and then to move rapidly forward to the time of Weber and that of Wagner.

Opera, which had been born in freedom, had, then, by the beginning of the eighteenth century, been straitly bound by custom and rule. Italy, which had introduced the form, remained its chief purveyor, and the Italian influence was potent outside Italy.

An Opera libretto was supposed to treat some incident or group of incidents from the life of some hero or heroine of antiquity—of ancient history or ancient mythology. That, of course, was a relic of the origin of the form. As will be recalled, the declared intention of the Florentine innovators had been to revive the glories of Greek drama; the invention of opera had, indeed, been a late application to music of the Renascence, or Revival of Humane Letters, which had begun to affect the other arts long before—indeed, to put it no earlier, from the fall of Constantinople and the consequent dispersion of Greek scholars and manuscripts in 1453.[1]

So we find Handel, for one, neglecting all the poetical subjects that lay about him in his three countries, his eighteenth-century Germany, Italy and England, neglecting the legends of his own race, and writing (in Italian—almost always in Italian) *Rodrigo* and *Agrippina* and *Rinaldo* and *Scipione* and *Alcina* and *Serse* and *Deidamia*.

Singers and their Arias

And we find him conforming to a pretty rigidly set scheme, something like this—six solo singers (or occasionally seven),

---

[1] The development of our modern music has been slower than that of any other art. At the time of the Revival of Letters its medieval development was not complete. The contrapuntal style, which has so obvious a similarity of style to medieval architecture, then in decline, needed another century and a half to attain its consummation. We see the effect of the Revival of Learning in the *words* of many of the madrigals, and doubtless music gained by the patronage of the rich and noble families who, inspired by the Revival, cultivated literature and the other arts. But only as the sixteenth century ended did what we may reasonably call the ' Renascence in Music ' begin.

three being women and three being men; three Acts; in each
act an Aria for each of the six characters, but no two Arias
for the same character successively and no two Arias of the
same style successively; few concerted numbers, since the
vanity of the highly-trained and highly-paid singers made
them prefer to shine alone.

In explanation of the above limitation 'no two Arias of the
same style successively' it must be added that Arias were
very scientifically classified as—

1. The *Aria cantabile*, slow and pathetic, with opportunities for the singer to embellish his or her part by the
   addition of decorative passages.
2. The *Aria di portamento*, dignified, with few opportunities
   for embellishment.
3. The *Aria di mezzo carattere*, more passionate, and with
   an orchestral accompaniment which might become
   elaborate.
4. The *Aria parlante*, declamatory, and with orchestral
   accompaniment.
5. The *Aria di bravura*, or *Aria d' agilità*, with showy
   scales, arpeggios, 'divisions', &c.

And there were others! John Brown, a Scottish painter
who wrote on Italian Opera in 1789, gives this partial classification (Rockstro quotes it in his *Life of Handel*). There is no
need for any reader to commit that list to memory; the aim
in setting it forth is merely to make clear in what bonds of
formality and strict limitation dramatic expression was now
fettered.[1]

Add that of the three men's voices two (including that of
the hero of the piece) were always an artificial and unmanly

[1] E. W. thinks I have rather overdone 'the Brown-Rockstro business'
that follows, and would like me to guard myself from too literal an
adherence to its statements by emphasizing my words 'something like
this' above. He suggests a reference to Robinson's *Handel and his
Orbit*, pp. 24-5.

Soprano and Contralto, that the third, when not also artificial, was a Tenor, and that the presence of a Bass was comparatively rare, and it will be realized that the librettist and composer who could contrive an opera that kept the rules and yet possessed dramatic force were very skilful craftsmen. Indeed, for the most part, the original Florentine *dramma per musica* had now degenerated into a sort of vocal costume concert, in which now one performer, now another, took his or her turn at approaching the footlights.   In the boxes of an Italian Opera House people played cards, made love, carried on conversation, ate supper—merely breaking off from time to time as there arrived some musical item that took their fancy, or some singer of special fame.

It is necessary to explain the form of eighteenth-century Opera just a little further.   Its dialogue was carried forward by Recitative, of which there were two kinds, *Recitativo secco* or 'dry recitative', in which the singer pushed on rapidly, merely accompanied (much in the original Florentine fashion) by a few chords on a harpsichord, and *Recitativo stromentato*, or 'instrumented recitative', in which the orchestra was used, often fairly elaborately.   The first kind of Recitative, we may say, was used for rapid 'business', the second for more emotionally eloquent passages.

The *Aria* represented the soliloquy of the characters. As so much soliloquy is rare in real life, and when it occurs on the stage puts every one except the soliloquist himself in the position of having nothing to do for the moment, the extensive use of the Aria was another offence against dramatic truth— especially as the Aria form itself had become stereotyped into a stiff formula of *First Section—Second Section—First Section repeated*.

Convention in Opera

It must not be inferred from anything just said that objection is taken to the fact that Opera was treated as a convention.

As soon as you go upon the stage you are necessarily enmeshed in conventions. The three-sided box in which you act is a convention; to sing, instead of speak, is a convention, and so forth. Every art has its conventions. But conventions can become excessive, and they can become meaningless, and this was the state into which operatic conventions had now fallen.

There were other styles of Opera besides the Italian. There was French Opera, founded by Lully upon the basis of the French mythological Ballet. There was English Opera, founded by Purcell and some contemporaries upon the basis of the English mythological Masque. There was the German *Singspiel* (or musical play). All of these were conventional, but Italian Opera, which was soon dominant throughout Europe, was the most conventional of all.[1] The principal librettist to all Europe was the Italian, Metastasio, whose lifetime took in the first eighty years of the eighteenth century, and was most of it spent in Vienna. His libretti were almost as well known to opera-goers as the words of the Mass to church-goers, some of them being set by as many as thirty or forty different composers. Handel, Gluck, Haydn, Mozart, and, indeed, most or all opera-composers of the eighteenth century were at one time or another customers of the famous Metastasio.

[1] In England, of course, there was the notable revolt against the Italianate operas with which Handel was swaying London. The *Beggar's Opera* (which was followed by countless similar 'Ballad Operas') had an immediate and immense popular success, which lasted a century, and which has been so conspicuously revived to-day. The type is, of course, thoroughly conventional, consisting of spoken plays with set songs interspersed. But this was an unpretentious, spontaneous convention. What a reversion this was to a fundamental naturalness is fully seen in the fact that the popular song replaces the *Aria cantabile* and the like. The English Opera of Purcell and his contemporaries was also carried on by Arne and a few others.

II   E

The Reformer Gluck

The first real attempt at reform in Opera came from Gluck (in round figures we may say that Gluck's lifetime, like Handel's, was one of seventy years, but that it began and ended thirty years later—1714 to 1787, as against 1685 to 1759).

From our modern point of view composers wrote too many Operas in those days, just as a little later they wrote too many Symphonies.   Musical composition was, so to speak, journalism rather than literature.   Audiences wanted something new. Handel wrote about fifty Operas and about twenty Oratorios, Gluck over fifty Operas, Haydn one hundred and twenty-five Symphonies and seventy-seven String Quartets—and so on. Gluck had already produced over thirty of his Operas before there appeared his *Orpheus* (1762), which is not only the earliest written of his Operas that now keeps the stage but also the earliest Opera of any composer whatever that does so.[1]

Then, five years later, came *Alcestis*, in the famous preface to which were laid down the principles of reform, something as follows :

(*a*) The music to be secondary to the poetry and drama, not to weaken them by unnecessary ornaments—to be, in fact, something like the addition of colour to drawing, giving more life to the figures without changing their shapes.

(*b*) Halts in the poetry and action for the sake of any kind of display to be particularly avoided, whether such

[1] Purcell's *Dido and Æneas*, composed at least seventy years earlier, is still sometimes performed.   E. W. calls attention to English revivals of Monteverde and of Purcell's *Fairy Queen* and to German revivals of Handel operas (referred to in Vol. I).

halts be for the sake of vocal display or for that of the added interest of interpolated instrumental passages (' ritornelli ').

(c) The Overture to be of such a character as to prepare the audience for the drama to follow.

(d) The orchestration to vary according to the degree of interest and passion in the words.

(e) Too great a disparity between Recitatives and Arias to be shunned.

In fact, as Gluck himself put it, he had in *Alcestis* tried to show that it was possible to abolish the abuses that good sense had often pointed out and only custom defended, and his general aim he described as ' a noble simplicity '. He had not a perfect command over the technique of composition, and he was often careless about details (so that his scores have frequently been worked over by later composers, such as Berlioz and Wagner, in order to fit them for performance). But he often wrote lovely music—and not at the expense of the drama.

He very much diminished the use of the *da capo* in the Aria (i. e. the repetition of the first part, which repetition has, in most cases, merely the object of musical symmetry and serves no dramatic purpose). He attempted a more natural declamation in the Recitatives. He individualized the *dramatis personae* more than had been common, by giving them music distinctive of their individual characters.

Gluck's orchestration does not sound modern to us, as that of Mozart does, but it was much ahead of that of Handel and his contemporaries ; Gluck abandoned the use of the Harpsichord with its ' figured-bass ' background to the music (see Vol. I, Ch. 6 and Ch. 10), but he relied too much on the Strings. He did not use the Wood Wind in the modern free way, yet he attempted a thoughtful use of ' colour '. He was one of the first to introduce the string mutes pretty freely into the orchestra. He gave more importance to the Trombones than any one had previously done, using a group of three.   He used also the Clarinet and the Harp.

Gluck made use of the chorus, but brought its members right into the midst of the action.   On the whole, as will be seen, the principles dictating Gluck's efforts might have been expressed in the cry, ' Back to 1600 ! ' With the fuller resources of the later eighteenth century he wished to carry out the original aims of the innovators of the early seventeenth.

Mozart as an Opera Composer

Mozart was forty years Gluck's junior.   His whole lifetime covered barely the latter half of Gluck's, and the two died within five years of one another.   Mozart was about six years old at the time of the production of *Orpheus*, and nearly twelve at the time of that of *Alcestis*.   The famous preface to *Alcestis* must have been well discussed in the musical circle of which his father was the centre.

The Operas of Mozart sound to us much more ' modern ' than those of Gluck.   As already hinted, Mozart's superiority of orchestration has something to do with that, but this is only part of an all-round superiority of technique.   And this command over technique enabled the composer to combine musical interest and dramatic truth to a wonderful degree.   The musical characterization of the *dramatis personae* is often masterly, yet the melodic charm is so evident that it appears to be the aim, and the listener is probably only subconsciously aware of the truth of the characterization.   The building up of the finales of the acts goes far beyond anything previously achieved, strings of pieces, solos and concerted items, following one another and piling up to a notable musical climax.

Mozart was no theorist.   He issued no manifestos and followed no one plan.   In *The Marriage of Figaro* only half the items are solo Arias, and the Recitatives are mostly ' Recitativo secco ', i. e. they rapidly carry on the dialogue at the very speed of speech, and with mere chords from the keyboard instrument as their support. In *The Escape from the Seraglio* and *The Magic Flute* there is actual spoken dialogue. Gluck had been willing, when introducing his work in Paris, to abandon Italian on occasion for French, and Mozart was willing to adopt his native German. *Figaro* and *Don Juan* have Italian libretti; *The Seraglio* and *The Magic Flute* have German libretti. (The fact that the latter two works have spoken dialogue has just been mentioned; they may be taken as having nationalist aims, and as constituting a glorification of the German ' Singspiel' or musical play with spoken dialogue.)

The classical nature of the operatic libretti of Handel's time has been alluded to; Gluck continued the tradition. So sometimes did Mozart (*Idomeneus, Ascanius in Alba, The Clemency of Titus*, &c.). But Mozart came nearer to the sentiments of our own day by the acceptance of non-classical subjects, such as the legend of Don Juan, the Figaro story from Beaumarchais, and the fantasy of freemasonry of *The Magic Flute*. Surely humour is one of Mozart's highest powers. *Figaro* is full of it, so is *The Seraglio*; *The Magic Flute* has a good deal of intentional humorous relief to its frequent solemnity, as well as some unconscious humour; *Don Juan* if presented, as it sometimes is, without the intended disinfectant of humour, becomes intolerable to a civilized listener.

Weber and Romantic Opera

We are now in a position to realize what was the task Weber undertook, impelled by the growing Romantic spirit of the literary thought of the opening nineteenth century. ' The germ of Weber's romanticism ', it has been suggested, ' is to be found in Mozart's *Magic Flute*,' and this statement takes on more force if one recalls the magic and fairy element that comes into so many of the libretti Weber loved to set— *Rübezahl*, with its mountain spirit in love with a mortal princess, *Abu Hassan*, an Arabian fairy tale, *The Marksman* (' Der Freischütz '), based on German legend, with its casting of magic bullets in the Wolf's Glen, *Oberon*, with its fairy tale, and others.[1]

It was not merely in the choice of subjects but also in the distinctive *flavour* of the treatment of them that Weber showed himself the first great Romantic. Moreover, the classical implications of a foreign tongue, the Italian that had become conventional for Opera, were entirely forgone. Weber was both the first great Romantic Opera-Composer and the first great Nationalist Opera-Composer. He set to music his native German, set it (with one exception, *Euryanthe*) in the native 'Singspiel' style, and, in one notable case, at any rate, (*The Marksman*) based his whole plot on a native legend.

There is a passage by the late W. S. Rockstro (in his extended article 'Opera' in *Grove's Dictionary*) that may be welcomed here, as defining in some degree the nature of genuine Romanticism in Opera.

> It is by no means indispensable that the libretto of the romantic opera should deal with the supernatural. Though it certainly finds a congenial habitat in the realm of ghosts, demons, fairies, gnomes, witches, mermaids, and sprites of

[1] *Oberon* is a real 'romantic' opera. 'Romance' in its original sense means a literary work in a Romance language. The old 'romans' were full of amour and adventure, and so, at the beginning of the nineteenth century, tales or poems with the same characteristics came to be called 'romantic'.

Now the fairy king, Oberon, first made his appearance in the world in the tenth century in a genuine 'roman', the famous Chanson de Geste, *Huon of Bordeaux*. Shakespeare used hints from the Oberon story in *A Midsummer Night's Dream*, and the German poet-dramatist-philosopher, Wieland, retold the whole tale in 1780. Wieland's treatment was much admired. Goethe said, on its appearance, 'As long as poetry is poetry, gold gold, and crystal crystal, Wieland's *Oberon* will be beloved and admired as a masterpiece of poetic art.'

Weber's opera, written for London, had an English libretto by Planché, which was closely based on Wieland's work, which, in its turn, as already stated, was based upon an actual 'romance' of the original 'romantic' period.

So here is one example, at any rate, of a story from the first 'Romantic Period' being set to music in the second 'Romantic Period'.

all sorts and conditions, it is equally at home among the splendours of chivalric pageantry, in the solitude of the Black Forest, or under the arches of a cloister. Its *dramatis personae* may be queens and princes, a troop of spectres, or a company of peasants with hearts as innocent as their dresses are homely. Only, whoever they are, they must speak in their real character, natural or imaginary. The scene cannot very well be laid in the streets of a modern city, nor must the incidents be such as one would be likely to encounter in ordinary domestic life; but the domestic affections, and all other passions which form the common inheritance of every age and country alike, may, and necessarily must, be represented in their fullest integrity. The only condition laid upon the composer is that when he is called upon to deal with natural things he must be truly and unaffectedly natural. When he soars into the regions of fancy, he must trust entirely to the power of his imagination; and in proportion to the extent of that power will be the measure of his success.

FIVE GREAT OPERA COMPOSERS

(Their lives cover just about two centuries—1685 to 1883.)

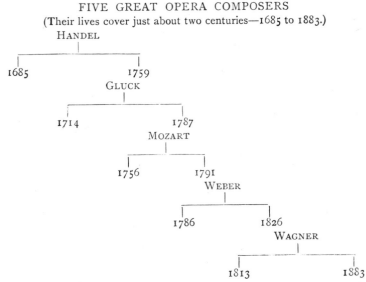

Note that the life of Beethoven (1770–1827) forms a considerable bond. His lifetime overlaps that of Gluck by seventeen years and that of Wagner by fourteen years.

The Work of Wagner

And so, at last, we come to Wagner—the German National Romantic Opera Composer *par excellence*. The language of his libretti is German and his subjects are German legends (or, at any rate, legends of the Northern Peoples). His *Flying Dutchman, Lohengrin, Tannhäuser, The Ring of the Nibelung, Tristan and Isolda* and *Parsifal* are all of this character, and the subject of *The Mastersingers of Nuremberg*, comes, pretty authentically, from German life of the sixteenth century.

In his dramatic aims, Wagner is a nineteenth-century Gluck. He aimed at drama first and music afterwards. He wrote his own libretti, and no longer considered them as mere libretti, i. e. to him the dramatic poems were no longer so much 'composer fodder', but the half or three-quarters of a work of art, which could, as he thought, once he had completed his synthesis of the dramatic and musical elements, hardly be analysed out again. As literature his poems have never won high recognition, yet literary men have welcomed the bringing into Opera of a higher poetical standard.[1]

As the art of Wagner developed it left farther and farther behind it the set divisions into Recitative, Aria, and the like, and made an Act one continuous whole from beginning to end. Where Mozart and Weber had admitted spoken dialogue (in the old German 'Singspiel' fashion) he dropped even formal Recitative, his voice parts being of a character varying with the needs of the moment; if those voice parts somewhat distantly approached the older Recitative style when dialogue was to be carried through, and the older Aria style when

---

[1] See, for instance, Professor Saintsbury, in the *Periods of European Literature*, vol. xii, p. 232, 'The re-knitting of the connection of Apollo's two arts—poetry and music—so long severed from each other by nothing so much as by the frivolity and mindlessness of the older opera itself, is a phenomenon in the history of literature far too important to escape notice here.'

lyrical sentiments were to be expressed, they yet fell completely into neither style.

The Wagnerian 'Leading-Motive'

That Wagner was able to avoid both set divisions and set styles was largely due to his use of the Leading-Motive ('Leitmotiv'), of which, though he cannot be called the inventor, he was certainly the first consistent user.

From the earliest beginnings of instrumental music, by far the most important way of making a long piece has been by the reiteration, with various modifications in melodic, harmonic, and rhythmic treatment, of some tiny germ-theme. Indeed, this was so to a large extent in choral music also, as a glance back at the examples from Palestrina, in Vol. I, Chapter iii, will remind the reader.

With the great Sonata-Symphony-String-quartet composers, Haydn, Mozart, and Beethoven, the device had taken the definite shape which we call 'development'.

Look at an example from Beethoven. Here are the opening bars of his famous Fifth Symphony:

Out of that motive of four notes:

a very large part of the First Movement, indeed a good deal of the whole work is made. Here is the beginning of the Development Section[1] of the First Movement, showing the music's natural, organic growth:

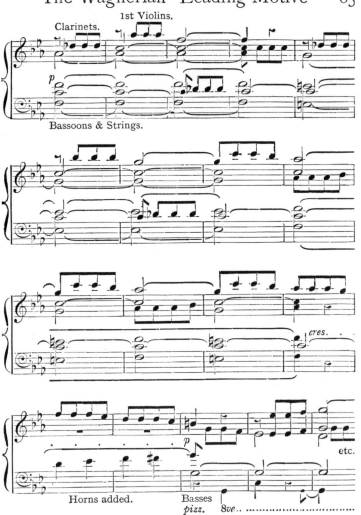

The use of the Leading-Motive is essential to the Wagner scheme. Without so ductile a material he could never have woven his seamless web, nor could he have closely shaped his music to the ever-changing emotional scheme implied by the

words of the drama, nor could he have so definitely characterized in his music the personages of the drama, nor have
brought to the mind of the listener previous happenings,
and so have hinted at their bearing upon the events of the
present moment. But a less skilful craftsman than Wagner
could not have successfully handled the device, and many of
the craftsmen who have since tried to do so have tried only
to fail.

Note that even Wagner could not have done so much with
the device had he lived at a somewhat earlier period, before
the time was ripe for his marvellous development of chromatic
harmony. The Leading-Motive device, under consistently
diatonic extended treatment, would be found stiff and un-
manageable; it is only pliability and variety, the harmonic
facility of a Wagner, that makes so much repetition of tiny
themes possible without boredom. Even this understates the
case; rhythmic and contrapuntal freedom are necessary
also. Indeed, with Wagner as with Bach, counterpoint and
harmony are, we may almost say, merely different aspects of
the same thing,[1] and as Bach was the greatest contrapuntist
since Palestrina and Byrd, so was Wagner the greatest since
Bach.

Let us take a passage illustrative of Wagner's 'Leading-
Motive' method of construction—a passage which, moreover,
compared with the Beethoven passage just quoted, shows
clearly how Wagner's method of development was but the
natural growth of Beethoven's.

In Wagner's Drama of the sixteenth-century Mastersingers,
Walther is a young nobleman who has fallen in love with Eva,
daughter of one of the Masters. To win her, he must be the
victor at a Contest of Song. But as poet-composer he is
more inspired than instructed, and so he has to be befriended

[1] This is still truer of Palestrina and the composers of his time, who
lived before the two aspects had been clearly differentiated in the minds
of either composers or theorists.

and helped by the philosophic cobbler Hans Sachs, himself a Mastersinger.

Now, on the morning of the Contest, Walther comes to Sachs and tells him of a wonderful dream he has had, which Sachs tells him to mould into his Master-Song.

There are three 'Leading-Motives' used in this passage. According to generally accepted labels they are (*x*) the theme of Walther's *Growing Love* for Eva, (*y*) the theme of Walther's *Dream*, and (*z*) that of Sachs's *Friendly Goodwill* for Walther.

Now for the passage itself. First we have (*z*), then (*y*), then (*x*). Notice that (*x*) steals in *before* Walther begins to *tell* his dream, going with his *thoughts*; (*x*) is very briefly developed, then (*y*), but in a changed, *fading* form, with the words, 'For fear the vision fade away', then (*z*) returns as Sachs discourses, and is fully developed—more fully, indeed, than can be shown here. How closely the music is fitted to the thought is shown by the hint of (*y*) again in the very last bars of this extract. This is really brought out by the orchestration, which has been indicated above, as also in the passage itself. The voice parts here are typical—a kind of tuneful recitative, generally coming near to the melody of the moment.

(The words are those of Ernest Newman's Translation, given in Breitkopf and Härtel's Vocal Score.)

The Wagnerian Orchestration

Similarly, Wagner was subtle as a colourist, as, indeed, is fairly shown in the above passage. The sense of orchestral colours was very strong in him, and what he heard in imagination he was determined to realize, though it might imply a great increase upon the normal orchestral resources of the period.

It was customary to employ two of each Wood Wind instrument; he often demanded three (sometimes more), so that he could obtain full harmony in any tone colour. Instead of two Horns he demanded four—when he didn't demand eight. Instead of two Trumpets he demanded three, plus a Bass Trumpet; to the three Trombones he added a Contra-Bass Trombone. The modern use of the Tuba is chiefly due to him; he sometimes used four, plus a Contra-Bass Tuba. The frequent effect of 'fullness' in Wagner's softer orchestration is often largely due to a hardly noticed background of brass chords. For certain special passages he used six Harps. He used percussion freely.

This was all very well, and a world without Wagnerian orchestration is nowadays unimaginable, but—since two wars have so much increased the world's wage bill it has made orchestral concerts almost impossibly costly.

Music and Drama—a Combination of all the Arts

Some incompleteness must be admitted in the definition of Wagner's aim merely as that of a merging of dramatic poetry and music. He intended a merging of *all* the arts—poetry, music, dressing and scenery, and acting. He not only wrote his own dramatic poems and set them to music, but devised his own costumes and scenery and laid down the details of the action.

He attempted too much. His ideas of stagecraft were often childish—rich-childish, that is, not poor-childish, for while the poor child will play with a tin can and in imagination transfigure it into an object of great worth, the rich child must have realistically imitative toys. Wagner did, indeed.

call for stage realism ; he trusted naught to the imagination of the opera-goer. Live horses and sham-live dragons, swans on the river and swans in the air, duels of giants and duels of dwarfs, everything must be shown to the corporeal eye— even to the Holy Spirit descending from Heaven !

Where Wagner's passion for the visual was useful was in pageantry. Of any opportunity such as the gathering of knights for vocal tournament in the Hall of Song, or for spiritual refreshment at the Lovefeast in the Castle of the Grail, he could avail himself with great success. A Dance of Apprentices or a Procession of the Guilds he could carry out splendidly, combining pageant music and a pageant setting in the most effective way, but when it came to Rhine Maidens swimming or Valkyrie Maidens flying he attempted just the same kind of realism, and in the representation of phenomena of this nature even a genius of a stage manager with unlimited funds is bound to fall short of his intentions.

Speed and Length in Wagner

Another fault is long-windedness. He failed to allow for the inevitable slowing-up of drama when set to any kind of music except the old-fashioned *Recitativo secco* that was far below his consideration. One of his Music-Dramas that takes, say, an hour and a half to read aloud (and so, presumably, would take little longer if acted as a spoken play) may take four or five hours when set to music. The wise composer allows for the brake-power of a musical setting and cuts down his libretto accordingly. To illustrate the principle— Shakespeare's *Othello* contains roughly 28,000 words ; Boito's libretto for Verdi's *Othello* contains about 5,700. In other words, Boito has had to discard four-fifths of Shakespeare in order to enable Verdi to get his musical setting into an evening (the four acts of Verdi's *Othello* take about two hours, plus intervals).[1]

---

[1] The late Miss Lilian Baylis told me that Shakespeare's *Othello*, played

Wagner also lengthens his Music-Dramas quite unduly by overlong soliloquies and explanatory speeches. It takes a very pious Wagnerian to listen patiently to Wotan on each occasion of his appearance. Schumann once heard Gluck's *Iphigenia in Aulis* conducted by Wagner. He says, ' I think I heard some of his additions to the music here and there. The close " On to Troy " was also added. This is inadmissible. Gluck would probably make use of a contrary process with Wagner's Operas—he would cut out!' And at that time (1847) Wagner's Wotan was not yet born!

An almost total lack of humour seems to be one of Wagner's faults until, suddenly, when we reach *The Mastersingers* we find him overflowing with it.

Wagner's Success and his Failure

Take him for all in all, Wagner is the greatest man ever born into the Opera world, great in his achievements and great in his failures—and how badly he failed in his main effort is realized when we find that so far from his music and drama merging into one art inseparably, enormous slices of the music are constantly taken for concert pieces and are found to be satisfying as such. Yet nobody ever takes the dramas and performs them without the music, whereby the truth is revealed : Wagner was not, as he thought, a great dramatist. but he was (as he also thought) a very great composer.

Italian and French Opera

A few words must now be said as to earlier nineteenth-century Opera elsewhere than in Germany. We shall expect to find a difference. What the difference is likely to be is hinted at by Weber in his pronouncement *To the Music Lovers of Dresden*, issued on his first taking up his duties as Conductor of the German Opera at the Court of Saxony (see page 82). ' With

at the 'Old Vic' without cuts, took 3 hours 22 mins. net—an hour and twenty minutes longer than Verdi's, which has one-fifth the word-length.

other nations the pleasure of the senses is what is aimed at. Germans, on the other hand, want a complete work of art, perfect in its parts and fashioned into a perfect whole—with them a fine *ensemble* is the first necessity.'

Whilst, then, in Germany the successive efforts of Gluck, Mozart, Weber, and Wagner had tended to bring the Opera on to a level comparable with that of other forms of art, in Italy, 'the pleasure of the senses' had continued to be the aim.

DONIZETTI (1797–1848) wrote nearly seventy operas and operettas, all full of easily-flowing tunes, and of hazardous gymnastics for the singers, vocal display rather than dramatic truth being the aim.

In a brief generalization like the present, BELLINI (1801–35) may be classed with Donizetti. Chopin greatly admired the expressive *cantilena* of Bellini's vocal melody, and his own pianoforte melody was influenced by it.[1]

ROSSINI (1792–1868) also may, for the purpose of so general a classification as the present, be placed almost in the same category, though his sparkling comic-opera masterpiece, *The Barber of Seville* represents a lasting success of a type such as we cannot credit to the other two just mentioned.

All those people, whatever their merits, were essentially musicians first and dramatists a long way after.

MEYERBEER (1791–1864), a personal friend of Weber, had to meet his censure because, in his earlier period, he abandoned the sacred cause of German art and became an imitator of the Italians. Later he made Paris and Berlin his centres of activity, and brought out the series of heavily spectacular and musically glittering works that we to-day associate with his name : (*Robert the Devil, The Huguenots, The Star of the North*, &c.). Auber and Hérold also catered for the Paris public.

---

[1] It must be obvious to everybody that the elaborate arabesques with which Chopin decorated his melodies had their origin in Italian vocalism, whether the style came to him direct or through John Field, the Irishman (1782–1837), the 'inventor' of the Nocturne.

BERLIOZ (1803–69) was a composer of very different aims. He genuinely represents the French romantic movement, just as much so, in fact, as Victor Hugo or Delacroix (see page 115). He was as self-sufficient and as genuinely original as Wagner. His chiefest gifts were the histrionic and the orchestral, and he had a great love of size, often in his works calling for a huge force.   His countrymen thought him mad, as perhaps he was. So was Beethoven—his great hero and Wagner's.   (It is a very interesting thing to see the Beethoven boldness and the Beethoven love of 'big' ideas in music influencing these two composers, who, French and German as they respectively were, showed the effect of the influence in totally different styles and idioms.)

One very important composer of this period remains to be named.   VERDI (1813–1901) had he not been so long-lived would not have so imperatively demanded treatment in this book.   Of his twenty-odd operas, all were in the conventional Italian style until, in 1871, he produced the gorgeously dressed and vividly orchestrated Egyptian Opera, *Aïda*, a piece of equal spectacular and emotional appeal, written for per-formance at Cairo.   *Othello* followed, showing, miraculously, the power of a seventy-four year old Composer to adopt a new style—for *Othello*, though it has all the Italian melodramatic force, is greatly influenced by Wagner in the attempt to put drama first, in some use of the Leading-Motive system, in a greater general continuity, and in a very much more subtle orchestration.   Finally, when the composer was eighty, there appeared that incredibly adroit piece of musical humour, *Falstaff*, in which the use of the Wagnerian system is carried still farther.

Perhaps it will be well to include in this chapter the French-man GOUNOD, whose *Faust* (1859), though it does not satisfy the lovers of Goethe, has become one of the greatest favourites of the sentimental, tune-loving big public (it is decidedly 'dramatic' but rather, perhaps in the way of dramatic effectiveness than of dramatic truth). And there must be a word, too, about another Frenchman, BIZET, whose Spanish Opera, *Carmen* (1875), is not loved by Spaniards, but, by its expressive tunefulness, charms everybody else.

PUCCINI (1858–1924) brings the tale down near our own day. He had a great flair for the popular appeal; he could achieve a style which, essentially, was the traditional Italian style, whilst twisting it just out of the tradition by a touch everywhere of the pseudo-original and 'modern'.

As for the Massenets and Charpentiers, the Leoncavallos and Mascagnis and other second and third-raters, however respectable their achievements, there is not room in a small book like this to do much more than register their existence. (A short biographical sketch of Massenet, with some opinions of Debussy upon his work, will be found on a later page.)

Already in fact this Chapter has departed somewhat from the general plan of the book, which is to sketch the development of the art only in broad outline. So far as Opera is concerned, the enumeration of the Florentine group, of Gluck, of Weber, of Wagner and of Verdi are almost sufficient to do that, but it is well to remember that Wagnerism proved to be, in a sense, the end of the road, and that the composers mentioned on the last pages, and some others to be mentioned later, have found it necessary to some extent to retrace the lines of march, in the attempt (often vain) to find main roads branching off in other directions. The reaction against Wagnerism is best represented by the recantation of Wagner's close friend, Nietzsche, who, after years of enthusiasm for everything that Wagner wrote, turned and proclaimed that he had suffered a change of heart and had found salvation in the simple gospel of Bizet's *Carmen*.[1]

---

[1] E.E. feels that my book gives insufficient attention to the Latin composers as compared with the German. See his note inserted later, after the biographical notice of Verdi.

LEADING ROMANTIC COMPOSERS
WEBER

WEBER's life lasted less than forty years, but as it was one of intense activity it saw a great deal accomplished. He was born in 1786, and died in 1826. He was born near Lübeck, and died whilst on a visit to London.

Weber.

The Weber family, in its extended devotion to music, closely resembles certain families discussed in Volume I of this book. We can trace musicianship in seven generations of Bachs, five of Couperins, four of Purcells, three of Scarlattis, three of Beethovens, two of Mozarts, and four of Webers. The sisters Josepha Weber (for whom Mozart wrote the high-lying, florid Queen of the Night music in *The Magic Flute*), Aloysia Weber (his first love, for whom he wrote the part of Constanza in *The Escape from the Seraglio*), Constanza Weber (whom he married), and Sophie Weber (also a good singer) were cousins of the Weber now under consideration. It is to be noted that the passion for music was in the Weber family accompanied by an equal passion for drama, and the course of this passion can be traced back as far as the sixteenth century.

Weber's father, noble by descent, as the family 'von' indicates, was a handsome, jovial, reckless fellow, at one time a successful soldier, at another a business man (but a pretty poor one) in the employ of an Elector-Bishop, then the exploiter of the new process of lithography (the composer himself, as a boy, was expert at the process, introduced technical improvements, and later almost lost his life by the accident of drinking some of the acid used in the work). For long years this Jack-of-all-Trades was a wandering actor-musician—of the Crummles type, with a strong strain of the Micawber merged. His troupe ('Weber's Company of Comedians') was more or less favourably known over a large part of Germany.

He was an energetic seeker after popular artistic glory, and had an overmastering desire to place before the world a musical child-genius of the type of his nephew by marriage Mozart. Two of his sons were placed under the instruction of Haydn, and another, the subject of this sketch, first under Haydn's brother Michael (Cathedral Organist at Salzburg), and later under the Abbé Vogler at Vienna (the much-travelled organist-composer-theorist, half genius and half charlatan, whom Browning has idealized in his *Abt Vogler*).

As Weber's life was destined to be so brief it is fortunate that productivity began early. At the age of eleven he published a Set of Six Fugues, and henceforward he was constantly publishing—unfortunately, by the business customs of the day, compelled to sell outright, and sometimes, from lack of any copyright law, seeing his compositions pirated and occasionally even grossly rearranged. No impresario could be found for his first Opera (imagine a boy of about twelve engaged upon *The Power of Love and Wine* !) but the second (composed at thirteen), 'A Grand Romantic Comic Opera, *The Dumb Girl of the Forest*', was duly mounted at Chemnitz, Freiburg, Vienna, Prague, and St. Petersburg, and the third, *Peter Schmoll and his Neighbours* (composed at fourteen or fifteen) really attracted considerable attention ; the Overture of this last is still occasionally heard and is, perhaps, the earliest work of its Composer now known to audiences.

The study under Vogler involved residence in gay Vienna, and if the youth, now seventeen, did not busy himself upon a second edition of *The Power of Love and Wine*, he at least acquired the most intimate knowledge of everything the representation of which would have been necessary to a realistic treatment of that subject. He was always of a convivial bent, and had, like his Irish contemporary Thomas Moore, a social gift for the composition of light, pleasant songs and the performance of them, to his own accompaniment (in Weber's case on the guitar, an instrument to which he was long devoted). This in youth was probably a snare. It gave him too much social popularity.

A separation from Vienna companionships soon came, however, through Vogler's recommendation of him for the conductorship of the Opera House at Breslau. Here his boyish impetuosity led him towards undesired improvements. For instance, the existing arrangement of the Orchestra was Wind in front and Strings behind, and he arranged it, apparently in something like the way now universally accepted, to right and left of his conductor's desk. This caused him trouble, and so, too, did the gambling and love-making with which he beguiled his leisure hours.

Another Opera was composed, *Rübezahl* ('Turnip Counting', —a fantastic fairy-tale subject), now long forgotten, though its Overture, remodelled, was long popular in this and other countries, and is still occasionally heard, as *The Ruler of the Spirits*.

There followed a short period at Carlsruhe, at the court of the Duke of Würtemberg, 'a brilliant little court, where powdered and pigtailed courtiers, with cocked hat and sword, wandered hand in hand with high-wigged and high-heeled beauties through the wondering green forests' (to quote from the biography of the composer by his son). Weber's musical talents were appreciated here, and he was encouraged to compose a great deal of music for princely consumption. A title of Ducal Intendant was given him, as a kindly effort towards providing him an official footing for a further leap forward.

The Napoleonic Wars recalled the Duke to army duties, but he recommended his 'Musik-Intendant' to his brothers at Stuttgart, the King of Würtemberg and Duke Ludwig, the latter of whom appointed the young man as his private secretary, with the difficult duty of soothing existing creditors and effecting further loans. Here was a kingdom where the common people languished in misery and the court wallowed in luxury, and when we hear of 'the warming of whole lakes in winter for the ducal duck-shooting' (why, by the way, cannot historians be more detailed—one would like to ask 'How?') we can imagine that money in that court became scarce.

Weber's frequent secretarial intercessions with the King on behalf of the spendthrift Duke brought him no favour, and when, irritated and reckless, he directed an old woman who was seeking the Royal Washerwoman to the room of Royalty Itself, he promptly found himself in prison, where, with the greatest appropriateness, he beguiled himself by the composition of his song *Life is Strife* ('Ein steter Kampf ist unser Leben'). Later he was charged (it is believed quite unjustly) with taking bribes to excuse men from military service, again arrested, and finally thrust into a carriage and deposited on the farther side of the frontier, with the warning that he was banished for life. It was time! The court life was of the most corrupt and he not the man, as yet, to defy demoralizing influences.

But he had done some work at Stuttgart. Guided by the Court Librarian he had read Kant and Schelling; he had also composed another Opera, *Sylvana*, and a sort of Recitation-Cantata, *The First Tone*, which for a few years remained one of his chief means of introducing himself to the musical public of any new locality.

Mannheim was the next place of residence. It was a place of great musical reputation, and there and in the neighbouring Heidelberg he made many friends and had much artistic success, specializing somewhat, as an essentially dramatically minded musician, in the composition of a more elaborate form of 'Lied', or Song— one in which the music, instead of being repeated verse by verse, should adapt itself continually to the thought and feeling of the poem. In this musical form Weber may be said to be one of the pioneers.

At Darmstadt, shortly after, he made many friends, particularly one Jakob Liebmann Beer, son of a rich banker, later known to fame as Meyerbeer, and long an intimate friend of Weber, who, however, in later years felt it necessary to protest against the Italianizing influence of his colleague's operas. (Weber was, before everything, a patriotic German musician). At Darmstadt Weber completed his one-act comic Operetta, *Abu Hassan.*

About this part of Germany Weber continued to wander, active in concert-giving, composition, and literary work. For many years he occupied himself very energetically in musical criticism, almost as Schumann did a little later. The growth of the literary faculty amongst musicians at this period is significant. They both read and wrote, and a connexion between the arts of literature and music was established which strongly influenced the course of the latter. For years Weber intermittently worked upon an autobiographical novel, *The Wanderings of a Musical Artist*, but it was never completed. At various times, too, he planned a musical dictionary, a musical review, a history of music in Vienna, and a life of his old teacher Vogler.

At Munich, a friendship sprang up between Weber and the celebrated clarinettist, Bärmann, whence many joint concerts and the presence of much well-written clarinet music in the list of the composer's works. Adventurous ups and downs marked this period of Weber's life. Is it not on record that during one of the 'downs' he pawned his best trousers?

And so youth wore on. In the years before Waterloo our hero reaped much fame by the composition of patriotic songs for men's voices, under the title of *Lyre and Sword*,[1] which gave a great impetus to male choral society activities. His other compositions began to attract more and more attention. He became a 'coming man'. Royalty gave him frequent passing recognition—and in those days courts were very numerous in Central Europe. 'Weber will soon arrive', wrote Prince Frederick to his officials at Gotha. 'Let the blue chamber be prepared for him; hire a piano and put pens, ink, paper, and candles in his room. Provide his meals until my return, when he shall daily have a place at my table.' Music had not yet emerged from the period of patronage; Beethoven, at Vienna, had nominally achieved independence, but in this he was merely a half-successful pioneer.

At last came Prague. At the age of twenty-six, Weber settled there as Opera Director. Bohemia was musical, and Weber worked hard to provide it with the Catel, Méhul, Spontini and Cherubini performances that it liked. Amongst the singers engaged was a fine soprano, Caroline Brandt, who some time later became Weber's wife. She was an admirer of Napoleon, and *Lyre and Sword* was at first a barrier. But love conquered.

Sometimes Weber met Hoffmann, the musician-novelist whose strange, romantic fancies were to have so much influence upon music (chiefly, however, through Schumann). Said Weber, in a letter to his fiancée, 'There is a look of a little demon gleaming in his face . . . Have you read the *Phantasiestücke*? . . . it shows an exuberant fancy, but (if I dare say so) a want of all settled purpose in the carrying out of the whole.'

On Christmas morning, 1816 (Weber was then thirty) came what the elated composer described as 'A joyful Christmas-box'—the appointment as Court Capellmeister at Dresden. And at the same

[1] Settings of Körner, the patriot poet who was killed in action in 1813, and whose death made a great stir.

time as this communication arrived from the King of Saxony, there arrived also a costly ring from the King of Hanover, and a snuff-box from the King of Bavaria. Weber was getting on!

So to Dresden Weber went. He married his Caroline and settled down, still gay-hearted but now a respectable citizen and—a Court Capellmeister.

There is, however, no silver lining without a cloud, and over this Dresden life hung several clouds. Weber's duties were connected with the new German Opera, but there was also a long-established Italian Opera, in which the Court took a good deal more interest. And it had its own Director, Morlacchi, a schemer and that kind of man who regards a colleague as a competitor. The King was far off; one approached him formally, through ministers, and one never knew whether one's petitions were correctly carried. Innovations were not welcomed. Previous conductors had sat at the piano, Weber determined to use a baton. A 'cellist and a double-bassist sat behind the conductor, read out of his score, and played, the 'cellist into his left ear and the double-bassist into his right, so that he could not hear the rest of the band. But what was wrong with that? Why will young men try to overturn settled customs?

The composition of *Der Freischütz* ('The Marksman') is the outstanding creative activity of Weber's Dresden career. *Der Freischütz* (1820) marks an epoch. It is German and it is romantic. It has tender love-making and magic bullets and a Wolf's Glen. It has spoken dialogue according to the German tradition. Its music and perhaps especially its orchestration were in many ways novel. The first performance took place at Berlin in 1821, and was an enormous success. The performance of the Overture at Dresden in the previous year had been a failure. People could not understand it. It was too 'modern'. The Opera itself did not please every one. Tieck, for instance, great leader in the German Romantic literary movement as he was, could not adapt himself at once to German romance in music, and called *Der Freischütz* 'the most unmusical row that was ever roared upon a stage'. Yet Tieck was a personal friend of Weber, whose relations with most of the foremost men in the German literary world were intimate.

Of *Euryanthe* there is little space to write here. Its production took place in Vienna. The visit there for the purpose of its preparation brought about a meeting with Beethoven—dressed in a shabby, torn dressing-gown, and shouting, as he came to greet the younger composer, 'So there you are, my boy; you are a devil of a fellow! God bless you!' Weber in earlier life had failed to appreciate his senior's work and had sometimes written against it, but that was a passing phase, and later he had won a special reputation as an interpreter of the Piano Sonatas.

Another Viennese composer, Schubert, condemned *Euryanthe* as 'unmusical', deficient in melody, and overpowering in orchestration. The 'book' of *Euryanthe*, by an absurd poetess (one von Chezy)[1] was a drag on the Opera, and the poetess herself, by her imagined slights and frequent financial demands, a constant nuisance to the composer. *Euryanthe* is Weber's one 'grand opera', i. e. everything is set to music, with no spoken dialogue.

An invitation to England now reached Weber—from Kemble, then lessee of Covent Garden theatre. He became busy with efforts to make favourable terms (which he found difficult) and to learn the English language (which he apparently found easy). He had a powerful motive in wishing to make this London visit financially profitable. His wretched wandering childhood, dragged at the heels of his comedian father, his youthful dissipations, and the feverish activities and incessant anxieties of his operatic life had left their mark on a somewhat feeble constitution. Perhaps, too, the accident with the acid had left permanent injury, for his throat was affected. He was not yet forty, yet he felt himself to be already nearing his life's term. The one-time rake had become an affectionate husband and father and longed to provide adequately for his wife and family.

Oberon was the Opera written for this English occasion. The hackneyed phrase 'written with his life's blood' is the most apt available to describe the conditions of composition of this work. Weber gritted his teeth and struggled with the task. To one who asked how he was, he replied, 'How am I? Bless the man, I've got nothing but a galloping consumption.' To another who urged that he was not in a fit state for the journey, he replied, 'Money must be made for my family. I'm going to London to die there.'

[1] The librettist of Schubert's *Rosamunde*.

And so, alas, he did! He was well cared for by his host, Sir George Smart, Organist of the Chapel Royal ('Every possible comfort. . . . Even a bathroom in the house!' he exclaimed in a letter home); he was fêted; crowds cheered him at Covent Garden (for *Der Freischütz* had already made him a popular favourite); *Oberon* was a great success; the audience loved both it and its creator, and jellies, sweets, and lozenges poured into Sir George Smart's house from sympathetic admirers who had noticed the composer-conductor's coughing at the theatre; Weber, indeed, had everything but the health to enjoy what he had. At a party given by a Member of Parliament, Smart and Mori the violinist, had to carry Weber upstairs to the drawing-room, so weak had he become. He longed for home, wife, and children, and insisted that he was well enough to travel. On the evening of 4th June, 1826, Smart, Moscheles, and other friends consulted together as to how they could dissuade him from the journey (then an affair of perhaps three weeks). Their concern was needless, it was not that journey he was to take. They had earlier in the evening helped him to bed, and there he was found in the morning, dead a few hours after they had left him. His last words had been, ' Now let me sleep.'

He was buried in London, but eighteen years later his body was taken back to Dresden, where the young Operatic Composer, Richard Wagner, one of his admirers since boyhood, delivered an address over his second grave, and conducted a Funeral March, on Motives from *Euryanthe*, that he had written specially for the occasion.

As composer, Weber stands, as already suggested, as the definite founder of the German Romantic School; his romantic feeling was expressed not merely in his Operas but in a large amount of instrumental music. As pianist he was brilliant, and his long-drawn, finely graded *crescendo* was a famous characteristic of his performances. As conductor he seems to have been really able. As stage director (born and reared in theatrical circles) he knew his business from A to Z.

Eight years before his death Weber had suggested his own epitaph—' Here lies one who meant honestly towards music and towards men.'

MEYERBEER

Meyerbeer (1791–1864) came of a Jewish family in Berlin, the Beers (he added the 'Meyer' on receiving a legacy from a relative of that name). The father was a rich banker, the mother a highly cultured woman, and the house a resort for thinking and artistic people. One of his brothers became known as an astronomer and another as a poet.

In early years Meyerbeer became locally famous as a pianist. He studied theory under Zelter, the friend of Goethe and the future teacher of Mendelssohn and at that time Director of the Opera in Berlin.

Then he went to Darmstadt to work under the celebrated Abbé Vogler. Weber was there at the time ; he also had been a pupil of Vogler and the two young men, nineteen and twenty-four respectively, became fast friends.

In Vienna Meyerbeer heard Hummel play the piano, and, humiliated by his own inferiority, secluded himself for some months, revising his technique and composing pianoforte music. Then he appeared as a pianist and with great éclat.

At thirty we find Meyerbeer, who has already composed an opera or two, in Italy studying the treatment of the voice by Rossini and other Italian composers. He wrote a number of Italian Operas and had them performed in Italy with a good deal of success. Weber and other old friends in Germany were annoyed by his defection from the cause of German national opera.

Then he settled in Paris, studied French literature and music, took Scribe for his librettist, and wrote French Operas. *Robert the Devil* made a great stir in Paris in 1831, and so did *The Huguenots* in 1836, and *The Prophet* in 1849 (composed, however, six years earlier).

All this time Meyerbeer was dividing his time between the French and German capitals. He was appointed Royal Director of Music at Berlin in 1842. In 1847, he took up Wagner's *Rienzi*, the showy nature of which probably appealed to him, and gave it a Berlin first performance (its first appearance had been in Dresden, five years earlier). Similarly he early performed *The Flying Dutchman*.

He continued to produce showy, glittering, pageant-like operas in Paris, and died there in 1864.

For Wagner's relations with Meyerbeer see page 129. After Wagner had emerged from his first expansive period in opera composition, he found Meyerbeer meretricious. He called him 'a Jew banker who happened to compose music'. As an interesting light on the varying methods of composers, consider, on the one hand, Meyerbeer, who was always fussily making changes in his orchestration and even on occasion supplied the players with alternative readings of various passages in different coloured inks, so that he might try the different effects, and, on the other hand, Wagner, who published the score of *Tristan and Isolda* before he had ever heard a note of it, and never made the slightest change after he did hear it.

The serious Romantics such as Weber, Schumann, and Wagner, came to look on Meyerbeer as a bit of a blackleg. Schumann hated *The Huguenots*. In a famous philippic he said, 'One is often inclined to clutch one's forehead, to feel whether all up there is in sound condition, when one considers Meyerbeer's success in healthy, musical Germany. . . . I place him at once amongst Franconi's circus people'. In his *Operatic Note Book, 1847-50* (see his *Music and Musicians*) he has a number of short critiques such as these:

'OBERON', BY WEBER, MARCH 18TH, 1848.

Too lyrical a subject. The music, too, falls below that of Weber's other operas in freshness. A slap-dash performance.

'FIDELIO', BY BEETHOVEN, AUGUST 11TH, 1848.

Bad performance; inexplicable tempi—under Richard Wagner.

'LE PROPHÈTE', BY GIA. MEYERBEER, FEBRUARY 2ND, 1850.

BERLIOZ

Berlioz (1803–69) was a Southern Frenchman. He was born near Grenoble, in the Dauphiné. But his life was lived in Paris, at the time he entered it the Paris of the waning Classics and the waxing Romantics. And with the Romantics, the Romantics in literature, art, and music, he associated—with Hugo and Dumas and Mérimée and Gautier, Sainte-Beuve, Balzac, Eugène Sue, and Vigny, with Delacroix and the other Romantic painters, with Chopin and Liszt. All these men were his friends, and in their circle he ranked high. Gautier, long after, looking back over the Romantic period through which he had lived, picked out its most notable representatives in three arts and said, 'Hector Berlioz seems to me to form with Hugo and Delacroix the Trinity of Romantic Art.'

Berlioz.

Berlioz was a Romantic from his birth. His father grumbled of him as a small boy, ' He knows every island of the South Sea, yet cannot tell me how many departments there are in France.' At this time a touching phrase in Virgil made him cry.

The bounds of Romance are wide. In English poetry they range from Keats to Byron. In music they range from Chopin to Berlioz. Much of the art of Berlioz marks well-nigh the furthest reach of romance in the direction of horror and the grotesque. This music is drama and often melodrama. Such was the natural bent of his mind. He loved the exotic and the gruesome ; he almost preferred life's mustard to its meat. His whole life was to him a stirring drama played on a stage that often resembled the Musée Wirtz. As a young man in Rome he used a human skull as a drinking-cup and read Byron in a confessional at St. Peter's. At Florence, seeing the body of a dead woman being carried to the mortuary, he bribed the keeper to let him enter, and sat for a long time holding the hand of the corpse.

His love affairs are significant. Leaving out minor adventures, which would take too long to tell and edify nobody, they are as follows :—At fourteen he fell in love with a grown-up young lady with pink shoes. When he saw her he trembled and was tongue-tied. His family, with some amusement, observed his passion, and so did its object, but he never told his love.

At twenty-four, in Paris, his imagination was suddenly gripped by the beauty and dramatic power of the Irish Shakespearean actress, Harriet Smithson. He sent her impassioned letters and moved heaven and earth to get a word with her, but she would have none of him! He nearly went mad. Once, worn out with passion, he slept for five hours on a café table, to the dismay of the waiters.

Then he fell in love with a young pianist of talent (later known to all the world as Madame Pleyel). He became engaged to her, but winning the Prix de Rome had to leave her to take up his residence in the Villa Medici. Then came to him in Rome news that she had married another. Throwing up his scholarship, he hurried off intent on murder and suicide. At Florence he bought woman's clothes and a pistol. They were left behind at one of the stages of the journey, so at Genoa he replaced them. At Nice he suddenly began to cool, changed his purpose, and returned to Rome.

Back in Paris some time afterwards, he found Miss Smithson again. His 'Fantastic' Symphony (see page 34) had been written as an expression of his feelings towards her. He gave a concert, including this composition in its programme, and induced her to attend—allotting her, the heroine of a piece by no means entirely complimentary in its implications, the embarrassing position of a middle front seat of the balcony. At thirty-one, after incredible efforts, he broke down her resistance and married her.

Soon, however, another flame burnt in his heart. A Mademoiselle Recio, a mediocre vocalist, claimed him. He took up residence with her and her mother. With her he toured Europe—ever troubled because, with her poor voice and slender musicianship, she insisted on singing at every one of his concerts, yet unable to break the chains.

At last, when he was over fifty, his legal wife died. Heart-broken he buried the actress and married the singer.

When he was approaching sixty, the singer in turn died. Heart-broken again, he buried her too.

The actress's grave had only been leased for ten years ; at the end of the period the authorities called on him to remove the body. By dead of night, under his supervision, the grave was opened. The coffin broke ; within was but black dust and bones, which with a trowel the grave-digger transferred to another coffin. They carried the actress to the singer's vault, and leaving them side by side, the double widower turned sadly away.

What was there left in life for this poor, feeling, ageing man ? He bethought himself of the pink slippers. He made inquiries. He discovered the lady. She was now a widow, and nearing seventy. He wrote tender letters to her; he paid her visits, travelling from Paris to Geneva where she now lived. He begged her to marry him. She refused. The most she ever accorded him was—to allow him to stand godfather to one of her grandchildren.

And so at the beginning and end of the story we enjoy the romance of the lady with the pink shoes, in the middle of it the romance of the Shakespearean actress, and in the middle of that the romance of the lady pianist. And mixed up with it all there are the romance of the ambitious vocalist and a good many minor romances, too. Berlioz thus carried to near the point of madness the illustration of one principle of the romantic theory—not Rule but direct reaction to Impulse.

Berlioz, who thus, in life, revelled in the romantic, naturally revelled in it also in literature. Look at the list of his works and you see at once the extent to which he depended upon the literary expression of the romantic for his musical inspiration. Shakespeare is there (*Hamlet, King Lear, The Tempest, Romeo and Juliet, Much Ado about Nothing*), Scott is there (*Waverley, Rob Roy*), Thomas Moore is there (settings of some of the *Irish Melodies*); Byron is there (*Childe Harold, The Corsair*), Goethe is there (*Faust*); and so on.

One frequent manifestation of the romantic spirit is the love of the grandiose. Berlioz had this, combined with a Napoleonic craving for 'glory'. He loved to write 'pièces d'occasion' and to produce them in a way that almost entitles him to be called the Barnum of music. His great *Requiem*, performed in the Invalides in memory of the soldiers killed in the Algerian campaign, requires 210 voices, but Berlioz indicates that he advises where possible the use of 700 to 800 ; it also calls for an orchestra of 155 stringed instruments, with wind instruments, sixteen Kettledrums, some other percussion instruments, and four Brass Bands! His *Te Deum*, written for the opening of the Paris Exposition of 1855, is on a similar scale. At the inauguration of the Column of July, on the tenth anniversary of the revolution of 1830, he wrote a Funeral Symphony for a Military Band of 200 players, conducting it with a sword (there was an immense funeral car of fifty coffins, to be placed in the vault under the column—a grandiose idea that must have appealed strongly to the composer-conductor). At the Exposition of 1844, in the Hall of Machinery, Berlioz conducted a force of 1,200 ; for the opening of the Chemin de Fer du Nord he wrote a *Song of the Railway*. He loved to compose music for ceremonies of any kind. He even wrote a piece in readiness for the consecration of a projected Tabernacle in the Champs Elysées for the mulatto quack ' Docteur Noir '—the temple ' predicted by Solomon and described by Ezekiel '. More pleasing is the record of the overwhelming impression made on him by ceremonial music on a large scale in London—the annual singing of the 6,000 Charity Children in St. Paul's (which sixty years earlier had so pleased Haydn). He exclaimed, 'Beyond compare the most imposing, most *Babylonian* ceremony I ever witnessed —a realization of part of my dream, and proof of the still unrealized power of vast masses ! '

Berlioz' ideal orchestra, as sketched in his famous treatise on Instrumentation, would include 242 strings, 30 grand pianos, 30 harps, and wind and percussion to scale. But his romantic tonal ideas were more than a demand for big forces. He studied refinements of orchestral tone as nobody previously had done, and as only his younger contemporary, Wagner, was then doing, and he was the man in all Europe who could best advise whether in a given passage one would (say) best employ a drumstick with a wooden head, one with a felt-covered head, or one with a sponge head. Romantic expression in music is much a matter of colour, harmonic colour and tonal colour ; these things make that direct emotional appeal which is the very essence of romantic art.

And this composer, who studied so minutely the power of every instrument and every combination of instruments, himself played only the flute and the guitar—two of the instruments which, great though their powers may be, least of all impress us by any offer of a large variety of effect.

This brings us to the story of Berlioz' life, which shall be very briefly told.

He was born at Côte St. André, in 1803 (so preceding by six or seven years Chopin, Mendelssohn, and Schumann and by ten Wagner). His father was a doctor. As a child he found amongst the household rubbish a flageolet, and his father taught him how to play it, and later bought him a flute. From a local musician he learnt to play the guitar, and he taught himself harmony from an old elementary textbook.

At eighteen he went to Paris to study medicine, but in opposition to his parents took to the study of music instead (living a cheap vegetarian life in a garret and supporting himself by singing in the chorus at a second-rate theatre). His highest gods were Gluck and (later) Beethoven and Weber. His teacher of composition (first privately and then at the Conservatoire) was Lesueur, who more than thirty years before, had lost the directorship of the music at Notre-Dame by aiming at making sacred music 'dramatic' and 'descriptive' (which was what Berlioz himself decidedly did later), and had enjoyed much success as an opera-composer.

It took Berlioz five attempts to win the Prix de Rome, for his style was too original (and, let us admit, often too lacking in 'finish') to please his judges. In 1826 he failed in the preliminary. In 1827 he passed this but won nothing in the final examination. In 1828 he won a second prize. In 1829 no candidate was adjudged worthy of any award whatever. In 1830 he carried off the First Prize. Here is a characteristic touch : 'As I finished composing my Examination Cantata the Revolution broke out. Grape-shot rattled on the doors and cannon-balls shook the building. Women screamed. I hurried over the last pages of the Cantata and was free to roam the streets, pistol in hand.' The prize, of course, was residence in Rome, and here he remained about a year and a half.

The rest of his life is a story of love affairs, financial losses over concerts to which few came, occasional concert triumphs in Paris, and more often in Germany and Russia, visits to England, where in 1848 Jullien offered him a huge sum as conductor of Drury Lane and then became bankrupt and failed to pay, and where in 1852 and 1855 he was engaged to conduct the New Philharmonic Society (in the latter year in opposition to Wagner, who was conducting the old, original Philharmonic).

His last days were saddened by the loss of his only son and of most of the friends of his youth, and in 1869 he turned his back on the world and gave up the ghost.

The epitaph he had long ago suggested for himself came from his admired Shakespeare :—

> Life's but a walking shadow, a poor player
> That struts and frets his hour upon the stage
> And then is heard no more : it is a tale
> Told by an idiot, full of sound and fury,
> Signifying nothing.

All his life Berlioz had been the stormy petrel of music, or, to use other similes (those of a contemporary Viennese music critic), 'a sort of spiritual yeast that puts everybody's mind in a ferment, or, perhaps, a sort of musical earthquake !'

The fermenting or seismic influence of Berlioz was not only exercised by means of composition but also by means of criticism. For a quarter of a century he served as music critic of the *Journal des Débats*, holding thus a powerful position, of which he made use to the full. He also wrote many books, all of a very personal kind, full of southern romantic exaggerations and of sardonic humour. With all his extravagances there is a vein of solid good sense beneath everything that Berlioz wrote, and this applies also to his music, which, if bold to excess and entirely devoid of reticence, is original to a very rare degree, not always well worked out in its details, not always conformable to the principles of good part-writing, and containing passages very unequal in value, and sometimes commonplace, yet, when sympathetically performed, usually extremely effective, especially perhaps from the skill of the orchestration.

After all, the world of art needs an occasional 'earthquake', and in Berlioz and his friend Wagner it had two at one time.

SCHUMANN

Robert Alexander Schumann was born in 1810, at Zwickau, in Saxony, and died in 1856, near Bonn. He had, so far as we know,

Schumann.

no musical ancestry. One of his grandfathers was a pastor and the other a surgeon, and his father was a bookseller and publisher. What Schumann inherited was, apparently, a tendency towards the intellectual life ; what was individual to him (apparently alone of his family) was the musical gift. This tendency and this gift were intertwined in his being, and he is outstanding as the distinctively literary-minded composer, expressing in much of what he writes as music what he has read as literature, yet (unlike the definitely 'Programme Music' composers) remaining within the natural frontiers of the musical art.

It is worth mentioning that Schumann's mother seems to have been mentally somewhat unbalanced—subject to fits of gloom and silence. A sister, too, became melancholic, and during a paroxysm of an illness drowned herself. As will be seen in a moment, a tendency to melancholia and an indisposition to conversation, which frequently became very puzzling to those who met him, were characteristic of the Composer himself. At the age of forty-four he attempted suicide by drowning and at the age of forty-six he died in a lunatic asylum. There seems to have been a drift to alcoholism during earlier manhood, but that, apparently, was, by an effort of the will, at last overcome. Schumann's temperament was clearly abnormal, and it is surprising that so little trace of this is to be seen in his composition.

Let us return to the father, for much turns upon his character and occupation. Very early he busied himself by writing dramas and learning English. Milton and Young (strange combination as this seems to us to-day) took a hold upon his imagination—the latter so strongly that for a time he believed his intellect to be shaken by his enthusiasm. He wanted to go to the University but could not afford

it, so became a grocer's assistant. But he made a little money by
billiard-playing and by writing a play, and spent it on a short period
of University study. Then he wrote a book, *Scenes of Knighthood and
Tales of Monkish Life*—a title thoroughly typical of the new romantic
tastes of the period, in which he shared. Then he became a grocer
once more. But this grocer wrote novels, seven in eighteen months,
and so gaining capital, set up in business for himself, married,
combined a circulating library with his grocery, turned at last to
publishing, and brought out a series of business manuals, directories,
dictionaries in various languages, a local paper, novels, and translations of those new romantic English writers, Scott and Byron. Whilst
engaged in producing his own translation of *Childe Harold*, in his
early fifties, he died, worn out with the effects of continual overwork
upon a naturally weak constitution.

Zwickau, where Robert was born and spent his first eighteen years,
was during his boyhood a town of only about 4,000 inhabitants. It
had little musical life, but the Town Musicians survived, as, too, the
poor scholars singing in the streets as they used to do in the German
towns in the time of Luther ; there were some rare Oratorio performances (generally of Haydn's *Creation*), and occasional Opera
performances (Mozart, Weber's *Der Freischütz*, Méhul's *Joseph*, light
Viennese Operas, and the old-style 'Singspiel' [1]).

The boy's education was the regulation classical one, and it went
far enough for him to be useful as a proof-reader on a great Latin
dictionary published by the family firm. His early musical instruction he got from small local musicians, his father encouraging him
and buying for him all the music for which he cared to ask—four-
hand 'arrangements' of the Symphonies and Overtures of Haydn,
Mozart and Beethoven, and the like. Some Chamber Music he
heard at the house of a music-loving local manufacturer.

Early literary tastes were very pronounced. He was a leader in
the school literary society, and at sixteen or seventeen became an
enthusiast for the writings of Jean-Paul Richter. There were some
love-silliness, some champagne madness, debts and borrowings and
a general lack of money-sense, with a sentimentality that occasionally
finds amusing expression in correspondence—

[1] See p. 55.

Nature is the great outspread handkerchief of God, embroidered with His Eternal Name, on which man can dry all his tears of sorrow,

and—

Oh friend ! were I a Smile, I would hover round her eyes ; were I Joy, I would skip softly through her pulses ; were I a Tear, I would weep with her ; and if she smiled again, I would die on her eyelash, and gladly, yes gladly, be no more.[1]

(This last series of thoughts, cast into metre and rhyme by some German poet of the time, and set to music by Beethoven, Weber, Schubert, or Schumann himself, would, however, hardly attract our attention as in any way remarkable. It is typically ' Romantic ' ; it definitely represents a part of the spirit of the time.)

Sent to the University of Leipzig, Schumann studied law ('icy-cold and dry ')—or rather he did not study it, preferring the delights of the Gewandhaus Concerts and the company and teaching of the great piano-pedagogue, Wieck. Later, at Heidelberg he was fortunate in finding in the Professor of Jurisprudence, Thibaut, a keen musician who ran a private choral society at his own house and revelled in Palestrina, Handel, and Bach. Schumann as undergraduate still managed his money badly and was once threatened with imprisonment for failing to pay his University dues. And he still drank a good deal.

Soon he returned to Leipzig, determined to be a musician, and settled down to study under Wieck—who once admitted that if Liszt had only had a proper teacher he would have been ' the greatest pianist in the world ', and now promised to put Schumann, if he would only keep his nose to the grindstone for three steady years, into a position of something like the same glory.

Then came an accident. Later, in one of Wieck's books, appeared a guarded reference to ' the finger-tormentor devised by a famous pupil of mine, which he invented contrary to my wish and used behind my back, to the righteous dismay of his third and fourth fingers '. The damage, unfortunately, was permanent, and the virtuoso avenue to fame was thenceforth barred. Composition

---

[1] See Niecks' *Schumann*, from which have been taken the translations of several passages in this sketch.

lessons were, however, pursued under Dorn, Director of the Leipzig Opera House, and another avenue was soon thrown open.

At this time Schumann loved Goethe, Moore, Byron, and above all E. T. A. Hoffmann and Jean-Paul Richter (' When I play Schubert I feel as if I were reading a novel of Jean-Paul set to music '—could there, from a romantically minded musician-littérateur of the eighteen-thirties, be higher praise, for either Schubert or Jean-Paul ?).

Like Weber, thirty years earlier, Schumann itched to express himself in words as well as tones ; he was by nature as much music-critic as practising musician. In 1833, with a band of friends, he started a paper, the *Leipzig New Musical Journal,* or ' Neue Leipziger Zeitschrift für Musik ' ('the tone of the whole to be fresher and more varied than that of the other papers ; in particular we shall block up the old worn-out ways '). Here is Schumann's own after-recollection:

> It cannot be said that musical conditions in Germany at that time were very pleasing. Rossini ruled the stage, Herz and Hünten almost exclusively the pianoforte. Yet only a few years had passed since Beethoven, C. M. von Weber, and Franz Schubert had lived among us. True, Mendelssohn's star was in the ascendant, and wonderful things were being heard of a Pole, one Chopin, but it was not till later that these exercised a more lasting influence. Then one day the thought flashed across the young hotheads : let us not look on idly, let us be up and doing to improve matters, let us set about restoring the poetry of art to its place of honour. So there appeared the first pages of a new musical periodical.

Of this paper Schumann himself soon became Manager and Editor. The 'David's Band' feature of this journal, an ingenious whim of the Editor's imagination, had its counterpart in Schumann's music ; e.g. Eusebius and Florestan, mentioned on p. 32 of the present volume, were two members of this bold company of Philistine-slayers.

As a critic Schumann was one of the first to hail the advent of Chopin (' Hats off, Gentlemen, a genius !')[1] and, more than twenty years later, Brahms (in the famous article *New Paths*—' Neue Bahnen ').[2]

This second stay in Leipzig lasted fourteen years (from 1830 to

---

[1] *Allgemeine Musikalische Zeitung,* 1831.
[2] *Neue Zeitschrift für Musik,* 1853 (see p. 139).

1844, i. e. from the twentieth to the thirty-fourth year of the Composer's age). It saw the composition of many great Piano works (1830–9 especially—in the early part of his career, as will be noted, the Composer tended to concentrate for a time on some one branch of composition), many Songs, Chamber Music pieces (1842), the First Symphony (in B flat), the first Version of what is now called the Fourth Symphony (in D minor),[1] and the First Movement of the great Piano Concerto. It also saw the slow winning of some reputation, one or two abortive love affairs, and—the fight for a wife.

The wife was Wieck's daughter, nine years younger than Schumann himself, her father's show pupil and a really fine pianist who was destined after Schumann's death, by her playing of his compositions, at last to win for them the world's recognition. The engagement was opposed by the father, who, in imagination, after all the years of careful technical and artistic training he had given his daughter, saw a disquieting vision of 'Clara with a perambulator'. He even threatened to shoot Schumann. There was secret correspondence, there was temporary partial estrangement, there were the other concomitants of the 'course-of-true-love-never-did-run-smooth' type of romance. At length legal proceedings were instituted to force the father's consent (or rather to dispense with it), and on the eve of Clara's twenty-first birthday, the musician pair were married. An outburst of song (1840–2) marks the event.

What a wonderful wife to a somewhat wayward genius Clara made, every one knows; what a mother she made has of late years been revealed to us in the memoirs of one of her daughters.[2] 'Clara with a perambulator' was often seen. Seven babies occupied it in turn, but the pianist was never lost in the parent, and domestic and public life ran in a wonderfully fitted double-counterpoint, now one melody and now the other uppermost, but neither neglected.

In 1843 the famous Leipzig Conservatorium came into being. Mendelssohn was its first Director and he at once appointed Schumann to its staff. But Schumann as a teacher was impossible; throughout a lesson he hardly spoke a word.

[1] The second to be written, but later revised and numbered 'Fourth'.
[2] *Erinnerungen von Eugenie Schumann*, 1925 (an English translation is now published).

A visit of Liszt's to Leipzig (1840) is of importance. He fraternized with the active local musical coterie, Mendelssohn, Schumann, and the rest, and he gave some wonderful public performances of pieces of Weber, Mendelssohn, and others, and dazzled people with his 'arrangements' of Schubert's songs, his Fantasia on Meyerbeer's *Huguenots*, etc. 'How extraordinarily he plays', Schumann wrote to his wife, who was away, 'daringly and madly, and again, tenderly and sweetly. But this world is his, not mine. Art as you practise it, and as I often do at the pianoforte when composing, that *expression of an inner mood*,[1] I would not exchange for all his magnificence. There is some tinsel with it, too. You know what I mean.' Schumann said, too, 'Liszt came here much spoilt by the aristocracy, and kept complaining of the want of countesses and princesses and fine *toilettes*, so I became annoyed and told him we had our aristocracy too—a hundred and fifty bookshops, fifty printing houses, and thirty journals.' There spoke the publisher's son and the literary-minded musician.

Concert tours with Clara (one of these through Berlin and on to St. Petersburg and Moscow) broke the routine of Leipzig life. Bad health was frequent, and it was in a state of nervous collapse, suffering from sleeplessness, twitchings, itching, terrors, and delusions, wearied and disheartened, that Schumann left Leipzig, in 1844, to settle in Dresden. It was eighteen years since Weber had led there so troubled an existence as Conductor of the German Opera, and Wagner now occupied this official position. His *Rienzi* had been heard there two years before (1842), his *Flying Dutchman* the previous year (1843), these being the first performances of these works (Weber, it will be remembered, had to go elsewhere for his first performances); *Tannhäuser* was first heard the following year (1845); the libretto of *Lohengrin* Wagner read a little later to a gathering of musicians of whom Schumann was one. A new force in music was becoming powerful, and Schumann only half welcomed it. Of *Tannhäuser*, of which Wagner had given him a copy with a friendly inscription, he wrote to Mendelssohn—

[1] The words here placed in italics represent, in the original, the word 'Gemüthlichkeit'—possibly here translatable 'cheerful intimacy', or something of the sort.

Wagner has another Opera ready. Certainly a clever fellow full of mad ideas and infinitely audacious . . . but he is really incapable of conceiving and writing four beautiful bars (indeed hardly four *good* ones) in succession.

But a few days later he writes again—

I must withdraw much that I wrote to you after reading the score ; on the stage everything works out quite differently. I was greatly affected by much of it.

Some years later Schumann gave what we may look upon as his final opinion of Wagner. This was in 1853, the last year of freedom. *The Ring, Tristan, The Mastersingers,* and *Parsifal* were, of course, still to come, and the judgement must have been founded merely upon *Rienzi, The Flying Dutchman, Tannhäuser,* and *Lohengrin*—

. . . He is, to express myself briefly, not a good musician ; he has no understanding for form and euphony. But you must not judge him from pianoforte scores. If you heard his operas on the stage many parts could not but move you deeply. And if it is not clear sunlight that the genius radiates, it is often, nevertheless, a mysterious magic that overpowers our senses. But, as I said, the music apart from the representation is poor, often quite amateurish, empty and repellent, and it is a proof of the deterioration of taste that these should be put above the many dramatic masterpieces which the Germans possess.

In 1849 came the Dresden Revolution. It saw Wagner hastily slipping out of the town to evade arrest as 'a politically dangerous individual', hurrying furtively first to Liszt at Weimar, then to Paris, and finally to Zurich. Meantime Schumann (no political revolutionary he, though his *Neue Zeitschrift* had always proclaimed him the revolutionary in art), in a village on the outskirts of Dresden was quietly composing. He had, in Bacon's phrase, 'given hostages to fortune'. He had 'five children jumping about and beginning already to listen to Mozart and Beethoven'.

The antipodean difference of temperament of Schumann and Wagner is summed up in their respective reports upon one another. WAGNER ON SCHUMANN—'It is impossible to discuss with a man who will hardly open his mouth' ; SCHUMANN ON WAGNER—'I can't endure a man who talks incessantly.'

Works written at Dresden include the last two Movements of the very romantic Pianoforte Concerto, the 'Second' Symphony (in C), the setting ('a kind of melodrama' as Clara called it) of Byron's *Manfred*, and the *Scenes from Faust*.

At Dresden Schumann had founded and conducted a choral society, which performed Palestrina, Bach, Handel, Mendelssohn, Schumann's own works, etc. Apparently the society was a success, and perhaps, by its success, became the cause of one of the greatest disasters in the Composer's life. He was invited to move to Düsseldorf to conduct its Musical Society. But his health, physical and mental, was steadily declining. Düsseldorf soon found him to be a very poor conductor—no business man, no disciplinarian, and lacking altogether in that readiness of speech which is essential if good and quick work is to be accomplished. The anecdote related by Professor Niecks' father illustrates Schumann's naïve conception of the conductor's art :

> My father told me often how one day at a rehearsal Schumann came up to him as he stood at his desk and showed him a baton with a string attached to it and to his wrist, and said with childlike simplicity and a satisfied and pleased expression on his face and in his voice, ' Look, now it can't fall again ! '

The difficulty of getting rid of an eminent composer whom one has invited to settle in one's town especially to conduct the local choral society may be imagined. There are some situations that are beyond the resources of human tact, and both Robert and his devoted Clara were deeply grieved by the occurrences of this period.

Yet good work was accomplished at Düsseldorf. The Third or ' Rhenish' Symphony (in E flat) was written, the Symphony in D minor (the second to be written) was reorchestrated and became the Fourth. The scattered literary writings were collected and prepared for volume publication. But bad health and the troubles it brought were an oppression. Hallucinations grew more persistent. Before considering the invitation to settle in Düsseldorf Schumann had consulted a guide-book and had found an objection in the town's possession of a lunatic asylum. ' I am obliged to avoid all melancholy impressions,' he said, and explained that in another place his stay had been spoilt by the sight of such a building.

And to such a building he himself came. He begged at last to be taken to it, for he felt the time had come. As · already recorded, a sister had committed suicide by drowning, and he attempted the same end, throwing himself off a bridge into the Rhine, when rescued struggling to cast himself out of the boat, and being brought home by eight men through an excited crowd.

At the asylum he steadily became worse, and after two years there he was one day found dead in bed.

The funeral procession at Bonn was led by two faithful younger friends, both in their early twenties—Joachim and Brahms.

Schumann's was a short life (though longer than Mozart's, Schubert's, Weber's, or Mendelssohn's). But much had been accomplished, and despite the trials inevitable to one who was neither physically nor mentally robust, the daily existence was cheered by much friendship and by unbroken domestic satisfaction.

MENDELSSOHN

Mendelssohn was born and brought up in a circle in which German Romanticism and German love of literature, philosophy and

art in general, were tempered by German-Jewish business solidity and sober middle-class propriety.

His grandfather, Moses Mendelssohn, a poor Jew, born in Breslau in 1729, tramped as a pedlar to Berlin, read and thought and studied incessantly, and won his way to the highest recognition as a philosopher and literary critic. He was the friend of Lessing, and the unconscious hero of his last master-piece, *Nathan the Wise*.

Mendelssohn.

Moses Mendelssohn was one of the early German students of Shakespeare, that great Romantic, just then beginning to receive a long deferred appreciation in continental Europe. His daughter, Dorothea (aunt of the composer) married Friedrich Schlegel, one of the famous Schlegel brothers, the firmest and solidest pillars of the growing German Romantic literary school.

A. W. Schlegel was the great translator of Shakespeare into German; nobody did so much as he and his wife, Caroline, to naturalize the one who was in later days to be claimed as the national German poet. Friedrich Schlegel, the brother whom Dorothea Mendelssohn married, was a brilliant and active writer in the cause of the German Romantic Movement. Like so many of the romanticists he carried his ideas of romantic freedom not only into literature but into life, as is illustrated by the relations of himself and Dorothea Mendelssohn for some years before their legal union. Friedrich wrote a romantic novel *Lucinde*, with his Dorothea as the model of its heroine, in which he defended these principles of freedom in love, and Dorothea's novel, *Florentin*, had the same romantic aim and temper.

Moses Mendelssohn's second son, Abraham (father of the composer) seems to have been less brilliant but more sober than his sister. He entered the solid profession of banking, won a high position in it, married a sensible and charming woman of his own race, and lived a laborious life of strict business principles and keen artistic and literary interests, making his house a centre for gatherings of the highest intellect and artistic ability of the day.

All this suggests, briefly, the background of Felix Mendelssohn's boyhood—an aunt and uncle who were acknowledged leaders in the Romantic literary movement of the time, the proud family memory of a famous literary-philosopher grandfather, dead twenty years before the grandson's birth, friends and relatives who were notable for the positions they had won in literature and the arts, a father who was a model of prudence and a mother who could read many languages, sketch elegantly, entertain gracefully, and teach her children music.

The temperament and character of Mendelssohn reflect those influences of heredity and environment. They show a love of culture in all its forms and a marked romantic tendency sufficiently checked by prudence and common sense.

Mendelssohn was romanticist enough to be able (e. g. in his *Midsummer Night's Dream* Overture) to 'bring the fairies into the orchestra ', but he could never have created a tonal opium-vision like the 'Fantastic' Symphony of his friend Berlioz. Nor was he capable of the love adventures of Berlioz or Liszt. No breath of scandal ever clouded his reputation as a model husband and father, and Queen Victoria and Prince Albert, who would not at one period even go to hear Liszt when he played in London, invited Mendelssohn to Buckingham Palace, where the Prince played his (the Prince's) compositions to him on the organ and the Queen sang, took him to the nursery, and over the cot of the future Edward VII, speaking as one parent to another, discussed mumps and measles.

Mendelssohn was a romanticist but not a headlong romanticist. He was personally acquainted with, and (in varying degrees) in sympathy with Weber, Schumann, Chopin, Berlioz, and Liszt ; as a romantic composer, however, he may be classed with the first three of these but hardly with the last two. And of all six he is, in both life and art, the most discreet.

Jacob Ludwig Felix Mendelssohn was born at Hamburg in 1809.[1] A year or two later, that city being in the occupation of the French, the family escaped in disguise to Berlin, which was their home henceforth. The parents had accepted Christianity and added the name ' Bartholdy ' to their ' Mendelssohn ' (though we never use it now), and Felix was brought up a Lutheran.

His first music lessons were given by the mother, but soon Zelter, the conductor of the historic Berlin Singakademie (or Choral Society) and a noted theorist, was called in to give him lessons in composition, and when the boy was fifteen, Moscheles, then one of the world's most famous pianists, undertook his piano instruction—though, as he admitted, there was by that time little left to teach, the boy's natural aptitude having already pushed him far forward. Another child of the family, Fanny, showed surprising musical talent, and but for the conventional view of the father ('for Felix music may become

[1] By a very curious coincidence the house in which Mendelssohn was born in that year was the scene in the following year of the birth of Ferdinand Hiller, another Jewish musician who played a large part in the Romantic Movement, and the close personal friend of almost all the Romantics—Berlioz, Chopin, Liszt, Meyerbeer, Schumann (whose Piano Concerto is dedicated to him), &c.

a profession, for Fanny it can only be an ornament') might have become better known to the world. In their possession of brother and sister musical prodigies the Mendelssohn and Mozart families resemble one another.

At the age of eleven Felix, as a boy alto, took his place amongst the grown-up members of the Singakademie—'in a tight-fitting jacket, cut very low at the neck, over which the trousers were buttoned, into the slanting pockets of which the little fellow liked to thrust his hands, rocking his curly head from side to side, and shifting restlessly from one foot to another'.

When the boy was twelve years old, his master, Zelter, who was a close friend of Goethe (the Zelter-Goethe correspondence is well known) took him to Weimar to visit that great man. Until Goethe's death, about ten years later, the young musician and the old poet remained intimate. 'I am Saul and you are David; when I am sad come and cheer me with your music', said the King of German Literature to this 'sweet singer of Israel'.

The early compositions of Mendelssohn were prepared for performance at the Sunday gatherings of family and friends. Before Mendelssohn was fifteen he had written thirteen Symphonies for such performances—mostly, however, only for Strings. An Opera, *The Wedding of Camacho*, was publicly performed in Berlin in 1827 (and then never again performed anywhere until 1885, when it was performed in Boston, U.S.A.).

The years from Mendelssohn's twentieth to his twenty-fourth were years of travel. His prudent father wished him before settling down to make acquaintance with the world. He explored Italy and he spent a good deal of time in Paris and in London. His reputation grew rapidly, and in England he became a special favourite. He was a friendly man, and to some extent a 'society man'; wherever he went all houses were open to him.

He conducted his C minor Symphony at the Philharmonic Society in London in 1829 (astonishing the band by using a baton—which he had had made specially for him, no such implement being then on sale in London). His associations with the Philharmonic Society were often renewed, and throughout the remainder of his life London was very dear to him—his 'smoky nest', the 'grandest and most

complex monster in the world'.   He hobnobbed with the organists
(Samuel Wesley, Attwood, and others) and often played the organ
at St. Paul's Cathedral, at Christ Church, Newgate Street, and
elsewhere.

His 'Songs without Words' were published by Novello in London
(simultaneously with their publication in Germany); later they were
to take the name Mendelssohn into every British drawing-room, and
even to annoy their composer by a popularity that overshadowed his
more important works, but at first they had a curiously slow sale. The
leading English critics, Davison (*The Times*) and Chorley (*The
Athenaeum*), always supported Mendelssohn, but for long decried
Schumann and Wagner.

On Zelter's death, in 1832, the Mendelssohn family quite naturally
expected that their young hopeful would be offered the position of
conductor of the Singakademie.   (He had already been offered, but
had refused, the chair of music at the University of Berlin.)   The
wish was not realized and the family, hitherto great supporters of that
institution, seceded.   Compensation came to the young man in the
offer of important work as Festival conductor, especially at Düsseldorf, where success in directing the Festival led in 1833 to the
appointment as permanent director of the town's music—a position
Schumann also, seventeen years later, was to occupy.   The duties
included control of the Opera (soon abandoned in disgust), of the
Choral Society, and of the Church Choirs.   It is rather curious that
two Protestants like Mendelssohn and Schumann should have been
put in charge of the church music of this Roman Catholic city; Mendelssohn roused some opposition by trying to bring into use that
music of which the Roman Catholic Church has most reason to be
proud—the school of Palestrina.

In 1836, at the Düsseldorf Festival, Mendelssohn produced his
Oratorio, *St. Paul*.

About this time occurred the appointment as conductor at Leipzig
which offered Mendelssohn the opportunity of doing what may be
called his life's work, so far as official duties are concerned.   In a
few years he widened his work here by bringing into existence the
quickly-famous Leipzig Conservatorium, of which he assumed the
direction.   Leipzig was the home of Clara Wieck (from 1840 Clara

Schumann); with her and her husband, and with visiting musicians such as Chopin and Berlioz, Mendelssohn was in close touch. (Schumann's passing connexion with the Conservatorium is referred to on page 98.)

The foundation of an Academy of Arts at Berlin, by Frederick William IV, and this monarch's love of music, led to Mendelssohn's oscillation between Leipzig and Berlin; for the latter place he composed the music of several Greek plays.

The marriage and family life of Mendelssohn were of the happiest. There was no financial stress in his life, and the incessant musical activities in which he engaged (and which probably shortened his days) were prompted by love of his art. He was always doing something; if not composing or playing he was dancing or doing gymnastics, or swimming or painting or playing chess or billiards, or writing letters, all of which things he did really well (he was a particularly good letter-writer and the volumes of his published correspondence are important). He exercised to the full the family and racial versatility, and perhaps the flame of his versatility burnt too feverishly to burn long.

In 1847 he conducted the first performance of *Elijah* at the Birmingham Festival, for which it was composed. In the same year, at Leipzig, rather suddenly, he died, apoplexy being the immediate cause. They gave his obsequies all possible municipal honours, and then at night a torch-light procession of a thousand people conducted his body to the station. On the way to his home city of Berlin stops were made at various stations, and local choral societies were in waiting to do musical homage. So popular had Mendelssohn become that (in Germany and Britain at any rate) it seemed at first as though with his death Music had come to an end. There was little in the art of Mendelssohn to rouse opposition. Whilst often finely fashioned it was not too complex to be readily grasped by the hearer. Its orchestration was finished (except in the accompaniments of the choral works, where it was often very perfunctory) but not startling; perhaps the strongest influence in the orchestration is that of Weber. The subjects of the oratorios chimed in with the spirit of the Evangelicalism of the period The composer provided liberally not only for the concert room but for the home, and many of his songs and piano pieces were not too difficult for the amateur.   The orchestral music was 'Romantic', but it rarely ranked as 'Programme Music' in the full sense of the term, and one did not need to be acquainted with a string of literary works before one could understand what the music was 'driving at'; the most frequent 'programme' inspiration, in fact, came not from literature but from landscape (or seascape). The *Hebrides* or *Fingal's Cave* Overture, the *Calm Sea and Prosperous Voyage* Overture, the *Italian* Symphony, the *Scottish* Symphony—in such music as this the emotion is generalized, not particularized in the detailed way that is necessary when a work of fiction provides the basis, and hence intelligent listening is easier.

It may be noted that Mendelssohn was one of the first to write independent 'Concert Overtures'.

A great debt owing to the memory of Mendelssohn is that incurred through his Bach propaganda. Handel was popular in Mendelssohn's day and all his life Mendelssohn was an active conductor of Handel's oratorios. But Bach was then neglected. Mendelssohn, at eighteen, procured from Zelter the manuscript of the *Matthew Passion* (which Zelter had bought at a waste-paper price at the sale of the effects of a cheese merchant deceased), and put it into rehearsal. In the following year he prevailed on Zelter to let his society, the Singakademie, perform it; the youth himself organized and conducted the first two performances, and Zelter the third. As a result of this revival the work was at last published and was gradually taken up all over the civilized world. At Leipzig, the most important scene of Bach's labours, Mendelssohn initiated and carried to success a project for a Bach monument. Berlioz, after a visit to Leipzig, said the creed there was, 'There is one God, Bach, and Mendelssohn is his Prophet.' Everywhere Mendelssohn went he played Bach's organ works—even in England, where at that time very few organs had the now standard compass of pedal board, which is the one required for the proper performance of Bach's pedal parts. Samuel Wesley had for some years been pushing in England the claims of Bach, 'the matchless man' as he called him, and Mendelssohn's propaganda at last brought success to the movement. (Wesley's last performance on the organ was at a London church where Mendelssohn and he played Bach to one another, and then, with a *Nunc Dimittis*, the old man went home and died.)

It is rather curious that it should have been Mendelssohn who accomplished this Bach revival, for although in his writing he adopts Bach devices (the chorales in *St. Paul*, some passages in the Organ works, etc.) yet his own music has rather the 'easy' appeal of that of Handel than the depth and seriousness of much of Bach. Indeed in style and musical mind we may almost say, comparing two composers of the Classical period with two of the Romantic period, as Handel is to Bach, so is Mendelssohn to Schumann.

CHOPIN

By parentage Chopin was half Polish and half French. His lifetime was similarly divided. He spent about half of it in Warsaw and

Chopin.

half in Paris. The combination in his life of Polish and French hereditary influences, Polish and French surroundings, and Polish and French sympathies affected his whole being. We may fairly say that both he and his art were of dual nationality.

For a short period (1738 to 1766) a former King of Poland was Duke of Lorraine ; hence a thread of interest between the two countries, and hence, perhaps, the migration of Chopin's father, Nicholas Chopin of Nancy, to Warsaw in 1787. Here he became book-keeper in a snuff factory. He must have been a cultured and clever man, for he soon drifted into educational positions, some of them of official importance, and as an educationist in Warsaw the rest of his life was passed.

His lifetime and that of his son Frederick saw great changes in Poland. When he entered it, it was an Empire, with a proud record of 800 years' independence. Soon after his arrival, however, began a series of struggles to maintain that independence against the attempts of selfish neighbours. In 1795, seven years after his arrival, and fourteen years before the birth of his son, the patriot Kosciusko was defeated and his country parcelled out amongst Russia, Prussia, and Austria. In 1830, when Frederick Chopin was twenty, Revolution relit the lamp of independence, but within a few months the flame was again snuffed out, and, so long as Frederick Chopin lived (and, indeed, for nearly seventy years afterwards) the word 'Poland' was a geographical rather than a political description.

It was at Zelazowa Wola, about thirty miles from Warsaw, that Chopin was born. The date has been in dispute, but is now settled as 22 February 1810. The other children of the family (five in number) were all girls—a fact which was not without some influence upon the development of the Composer's temperament, which remained ever sensitive and delicate and rather feminine than masculine. All the sisters, by the way, like their father, had intellectual leanings; all (even the youngest, who died at the age of fourteen) occupied themselves in some degree with authorship. The mother was a Pole; little is known of her, except that she was amiable and affectionate.

Within three or four years after Chopin's birth the family moved to Warsaw—the ancient capital with its pomp and dirt, its palaces and huts, its Eastern and its Western habits and tendencies, its proud memories and its unpractical inefficiency. The boy very soon showed unusual musical talent, especially as pianist. At nine he played in public; when he was ten, the great singer, Catalani, heard him, and, amazed and admiring, gave him a watch with an inscription. He became a favourite in aristocratic houses; the Grand Duke himself made much of him.

As teachers he had for piano Zywny, a Bohemian, and for composition Elsner, a Silesian, head of the Warsaw Conservatoire and the principal teacher of composition in the country. To a large extent, however, Chopin was self-taught, since Zywny's lessons ceased when the pupil was twelve and Elsner's method was one designed in the very fullest measure possible to encourage originality ('Leave him in peace; his is an uncommon way because his natural gifts are uncommon'). Chopin always remembered with gratitude and affection his two teachers; when, in early manhood, he was asked in Vienna, the city of Haydn and Mozart, of Beethoven and Schubert, of famous composers and of famous teachers, how he had learnt so much in

Warsaw, remote and near the edge of European civilization, he replied, 'From Zywny and Elsner even the greatest ass must learn something'.

Apart from music the boy's favourite studies (he had the normal high school education of the day) were Polish history and literature. He was a good caricaturist, and a clever actor—all his life popular in social circles as an amusing mimic.

On the whole Chopin's gifts, apart from that of music, seem to have been social rather than intellectual. From his earliest years to his dying day he mingled with people of culture and refinement (and, we may say, with no others), and so he became 'well informed', but he was not the reader that Schumann was, and beyond the inspiration that he undoubtedly got from the history of his native country we can trace no direct connexion (as we decidedly can with Schumann) between what he took in as literature and what he gave out as music. Everything he ever wrote is intensely 'romantic', but the romance is generalized and not, as with his German colleague, particularized by the choice of definitely romantic subjects for musical treatment. Schiller, Goethe, Byron, and Shakespeare were at the moment in ascendancy in Warsaw, as in the other capitals of Europe, but it is difficult to trace the immediate effects of these in Chopin's after-production, and the only poetic stirrings of whose existence in Chopin's mind we may be sure came from the great national writer, eleven or twelve years his senior, Mickiewicz, later exiled for his patriotism, and as an exile to become a member of Chopin's Paris circle, to organize a Polish legion in support of Mazzini in Italy, and to die, a victim of the Crimean War, in Constantinople whither he had gone to oppose the enemies of his country. Not only Mickiewicz's epic writings, but also, doubtless, his adaptations of Polish folk-balladry awakened a response in the youth's ardent mind.

It is worthy of notice that the singing and fiddling and dancing of the peasantry interested Chopin. Other music he doubtless heard in plenty. There was an opera house (of rather second-rate pretensions) in Warsaw, in some of the churches were to be heard the Masses of Haydn and others, and a concert society existed, which gave weekly performances, with a new symphony in every programme —which sounds very enterprising!

At eighteen Chopin visited Berlin. A professor friend was to go there as delegate to a scientific congress, and the youth's parents seized for him the opportunity of travel under escort. He heard Operas better performed than he was accustomed to, and enjoyed Handel's *Ode on St. Cecilia's Day*—which he said represented his ideal of the sublime.

A little later Chopin spent three weeks in Vienna. At Berlin he had modestly kept in the background, neither performing in public nor even seeking introductions to Mendelssohn (who had already won much recognition) and other musicians who were there at the time. At Vienna he gave a concert or two, playing, amongst other things, his Variations on Mozart's *Don Juan* air, *Là ci darem*. He had been delighted, on calling on Haslinger, the publisher, soon after he arrived, to learn that he had already decided to publish this piece, which he had sent him a little time before.

For some time the *Là ci darem* Variations remained Chopin's *cheval de bataille*. He played them at all his concerts, and when they at last appeared in print they inspired Schumann's article, '*An Opus 2*', with its often quoted, 'Hats off, Gentlemen, a genius!'

> It seemed as if eyes, strange to me, were glancing up at me—flower eyes, basilisk eyes, peacock's eyes, maiden's eyes. In many places it looked yet brighter—I thought I saw Mozart's *Là ci darem la mano* wound through a hundred chords, Leporello seemed to wink at me, and Don Juan hurried past in his white mantle.[1]

Something like this warm appreciation was won by the piece at Vienna, and Chopin's reception as pianist was even more hearty than his reception as a composer. One characteristic in his playing was remarked upon here which was often remarked upon afterwards throughout his life—his soft playing. He did not strive for power, but made his effects by delicacy. He was afraid the papers would blame him, 'especially as the daughter of one editor is said to be a great thumper'. For the second concert Count Moritz Lichnowski, apparently thinking that the instrument used at the first one had been at fault, offered his own. This was the younger brother of the generous Prince Carl Lichnowski, the intimate and helpful friend of Mozart and Beethoven. Prince Carl had been dead fifteen years,

[1] From Ritter's translation of Schumann's *Music and Musicians*.

but Beethoven had died only two years before, and Count Moritz had been intimate with him to the last. Vienna had, by the way, lost Schubert only the year before Chopin's visit—but had hardly noticed the loss.

Chopin took his success modestly: 'People are surprised in me, and I'm surprised in them for being surprised in me'. He returned by Prague and Dresden, and at the latter place, Morlacchi, the director of the Italian Opera, who had been such an enemy to Weber, showed himself a friend to Chopin. But then Chopin was in no sense a business rival, as Weber had been.

Although well known in Warsaw as a pianist, Chopin had, strangely, never yet given there a concert of his own. He did so soon after his return from Vienna, playing his Concerto in F minor (also to be a favourite *cheval de bataille*), and playing it on this occasion, as on many others later, divided by the performance of some lighter piece before the second movement. Public taste at that time demanded such a concession. Clara Wieck (later Clara Schumann), when as a girl she played Beethoven's Sonatas in public, was accustomed to ease her audience in this way.

Chopin was now poised for flight. He had resolved to go out into the big world, but hesitated. 'I have a presentiment that once I leave Warsaw, I shall never return.' This presentiment was fulfilled.

His old master, Elsner, with pupils of the Conservatoire, accompanied him out of the town to a village, where they fêted him, sang a cantata Elsner had composed in his honour, and gave him a silver casket filled with Polish earth. It was the only Polish earth with which he was henceforth to have contact. We shall hear of this casket again.

Chopin's most loved friend, Titus Voychihovsky, accompanied him, and their first place of prolonged stay was to be Vienna. A few days after they arrived, there came great news from Warsaw. The 1830 Revolution had broken out. Voychihovsky immediately took flight, to 'do his bit'; Chopin, who, though not at this date an invalid, was of the 'C 3' physical type, sadly remained. The Revolution only gave Poland a momentary independence, and to a land in bondage Chopin never afterwards felt drawn to return.

In Vienna he mingled with musicians of great names—Czerny, in the youth of some of us known by his '101', and then known by bigger things; Thalberg, the giant technician; Hummel, for two years the household apprentice of Mozart, later the successor of Haydn as Capellmeister to his Prince, and the friend of Beethoven, to whom as an extempore player he had been considered a rival; Aloys Schmitt, over whose five-finger exercises some of the older of us have spent many precious hours of our young life ('over forty years old now, and composes eighty-years-old music', said Chopin of him); and Slavik, the wonderful violinist who, as Chopin reported, 'can play ninety-six staccato notes in one bow'.

Of the pianists here mentioned, note that every one of them wrote 'methods' and 'studies' and 'exercises'. Chopin himself in later years laboured intermittently at a 'method', which, however, was never completed.

The old harpsichord was now well in the background and the technique of the newer piano was becoming settled—with as one first result the production not only of these aids to study but of showy pieces of technical exhibition, which many audiences preferred to the more serious compositions, and which at least served as explorations into unknown territory such as could afterwards be occupied by composers of serious intent.

On the whole Chopin was probably a little dissatisfied with Viennese musical taste as he found it. Not only were show pieces popular, but, as he reported in correspondence, so were the Strauss and Lanner waltz productions—which, trivial as they appeared to him, we who have lived to hear a popular dance music so much less worthy would gladly welcome back.

The Concerto in E minor was the great composition of this period; it had been written in Warsaw and now appeared very often in the Composer's programmes. It showed little skill in orchestration, and, indeed, its composer never had much. With him a Piano concerto was a Piano solo with trimmings. His was the aristocratic conception; pianist and orchestra resembled with him a king and his court. Chopin was ever, first and foremost, a Pianist, and his compositions were always a pianist-composer's self-expression.

Other places were visited, and at last (1831) Paris was reached. Louis Philippe had been about a year on the throne. Victor Hugo's famous

Preface to *Cromwell*, that resounding challenge of the Romantic school, was two or three years old; his *Ernani* had led to vigorous fisticuffs at its first performance in the previous year, and he had just written his *Notre Dame*, with its muscular dwarf, its gracious gipsy maiden, its variegated medieval Paris street life and its Gothic architecture. The Romantic school in painting was even more firmly established. Géricault's scene of horror, *The Raft of the Medusa*,[1] was twelve years old. The historical painting of Delacroix, in which every picture tells a story, and tells it very forcibly and sometimes gruesomely, was in full favour. Berlioz had just written his *Fantastic Symphony*. Such manifestations of the Romantic spirit in the various arts find, as already hinted, little or no echo in the compositions of Chopin (the writing of Hugo, he once said, he felt to be coarse and ugly), but he must have agreed with a more sober manifesto of the Romantic attitude, that made some time before by the philosopher-statesman-orator, Cousin, 'The highest aim of any art is to awaken, *in its own way*, the feelings of the infinite.' That statement of the Romantic position, all Chopin's output supported.

In Paris music, the classicist, Cherubini, was still active. The operas of Auber and Rossini were coming in. Meyerbeer was rising well above the horizon. So was Bellini, whose well-shaped Italian melody and whose personal friendship were to give Chopin much pleasure. A host of opera writers now forgotten were then in the full swing of successful careers. Chopin had entered a busy musical hive, and felt his sympathies engaged in certain quarters and repelled in others. Of Cherubini and of Reicha (the famous teachers of counterpoint) he soon disposed. 'These gentlemen are mummies', he said.

The great pianist of the Paris of those days was Kalkbrenner. Chopin played to him and he at once asked if he were a pupil of Field—which, in one sense, he certainly was (see page 75). As a pianist, Chopin, he said, had 'no method' and he proposed to take him as a pupil and put him through a three years' course. Mendelssohn was angry when he heard what had been suggested, Elsner, to whom Chopin wrote for advice, discountenanced it, and Kalkbrenner himself, later, came to see that his proposition had been

[1] Reproduced in Vol. III.

unwise. Chopin's pianistic style followed no rules, but it was his own, and any disturbance of it, at this late stage, would probably have brought disaster.

Chopin's success in Paris was in no way startling. Financially, for a time, he made little headway. Then the tide turned and brought him fashionable pupils. His refinement (of music and of manner) pleased. 'I move', he wrote home, 'in the highest society, among ambassadors, princes and ministers.'

A fashionable piano teacher Chopin, to the end of his days, remained. His career was the antithesis to that of Liszt, whose friendship he at this time made, and who was afterwards to write his life. Chopin shone in the Paris drawing-rooms, in the intimate cultured circle, and was almost a failure in the concert hall ; he travelled hardly at all ; Liszt toured the world, claiming the admiration of crowds.

Gradually Chopin's compositions began to become known, as other pianists than himself began to play them. He paid a very brief visit to London in the year of Queen Victoria's accession, but played only in private.

The intimacy with the woman novelist, 'George Sand', now calls for mention. She had heard some of Chopin's compositions and begged Liszt to introduce him. The friendship that sprang up lasted ten years and then was abruptly broken—to the sorrow of both parties. The nature of the relationship has been much discussed. It seems to have had some resemblance to that earlier friendship between Madame de Warens and Rousseau. George Sand was five years Chopin's senior and had a family of children to care for, and in the main, perhaps, her sentiments were motherly.

In the winter of 1838–9, Chopin accompanied George Sand and her children to Majorca. They fled to escape bad weather—and found worse. The peasantry were antagonistic. Everything was thoroughly uncomfortable. Chopin became really ill, and the medical attention was poor. The food was unattractive. There were many fleas.

At last Chopin, spitting blood copiously, was carried to a boat, whose cargo consisted of squalling and odorous pigs, and in gloom and suffering, reached Marseilles, where his health improved.

Here he played the organ at a funeral service—that of the famous singer, Adolph Nourrit, who at the time of Chopin's first arrival in Paris had been engaged in an effort to win for Schubert's songs the appreciation of the Parisian musical public. The piece Chopin played was Schubert's song *The Stars* ('Die Gestirne'), and, says George Sand, the great body of the congregation was disappointed, for he played it softly and plaintively and like the far-away echo of another world.

The Majorca expedition was in every way disastrous, and unfortunately it left a permanent mark upon Chopin's health.

For many summers Chopin spent three or four months at George Sand's country home at Nohant. On the whole he was happy there, though his hostess declared that he was not very well fitted for a country life, which was probably true enough. There were great gatherings of all that was brightest in Parisian literary and artistic talent, plenty of killing for those to whom a stay in the country meant that particular kind of pleasure (Chopin was not one of these), and, in the evenings, in the private theatre, wordless plays, musically interpreted in turn by Chopin and Liszt, each seated at a piano behind the scenes, one at one side of the stage and one at the other. Those must have been great evenings! In Paris George Sand and Chopin occupied houses almost adjoining, and the social, literary, and artistic gatherings were almost nightly renewed through the winter.

When Chopin was approaching his fortieth year there occurred the events that led to the Second Republic. That was a revolutionary year elsewhere than in France, and Britain was the sanctuary to which refugees of many nations were flying. London was full of distinguished foreign musicians, and Chopin, driven from his Paris circle by the disturbances, joined them. He was now in failing health. When he went to play at some great house, or visited Broadwood's to choose a piano, they had often to carry him upstairs, as they had carried the dying Weber, about twenty years earlier. He played in Manchester, in Glasgow, and in Edinburgh, and spent much time amongst aristocratic friends to whom a Scottish pupil, a Miss Stirling, introduced him. He was much fêted—too much, indeed, for he became very weary. He loved the Scottish scenery but hated the Scottish Sabbath—' The Scots are ugly but good ; their Sunday—no post, no railway, no carriages, no boats, not a dog stirs, all desolate !' Things were now getting very bad with him. He had become physically very weak and mentally very sensitive. He wrote to a friend that he felt worse every day.

At last, almost hysterically, in his boredom and weakness, he fled back to Paris, found himself to be now too much exhausted to compose, play, or teach, and as his providence had been no greater than that of artists in general, lacked means whereon to support himself even during the only too obviously brief remaining period of life. Apprised of this by one of his friends, the admiring and generous Miss Stirling sent him £1,000, of which he consented to retain only a portion. An urgent message to Poland brought one of his sisters to his bedside. George Sand, it is said, strove to see him but was refused admission by those about him, and thus there did not take place the reconciliation which would probably have given both parties comfort.

Two days before Chopin's death (in October 1849) he saw standing at the foot of the bed one of his countrywomen, the Countess Potocka. He begged her to sing, the piano was brought to the door of the room, and she sang pieces by Stradella and Marcello. As she ended it was thought that Chopin was passing away, and all present dropped on their knees. But the dying man lingered two days longer. His favourite pupil, Gutmann, was with him when the end arrived ; Chopin bent to kiss his hand and died in this act of appreciation and gratitude.

There was a great service at the Madeleine, with a congregation of 4,000 and the chorus and orchestra of the Paris Conservatoire, who performed Mozart's Requiem. Chopin's own Funeral March was played as the cortège entered, and two of his Preludes on the organ later. Then they carried him to Père-Lachaise, where, in compliance with his own request, he was to be buried next to his friend, whose music he much loved, the Italian opera composer, Bellini. Meyerbeer, the painter Delacroix, his favourite pupil, Gutmann, and many of his own exiled compatriots made up the funeral procession.

The ' earth to earth ' was Polish—for at last was opened the silver casket given him on that memorable day when, as a young man of twenty, he set out to carve a career for himself, and its contents were scattered over his coffin.

Chopin's heart, however, was not buried in France. It was sent back to Poland, and there it still rests, in a church in Warsaw.

Chopin's was not a life of happiness. We have, perhaps, got a good deal more pleasure out of it than he did.

In Chopin's music French refinement, grace, and elegance tend at the extreme towards effeminacy, and even morbidity. Wonderful as is his genius when the Frenchman is uppermost, it attains, perhaps, even higher flights when the Pole in him bursts forth. Then, indeed, he writes music unsurpassed in its tremendous fire, strength, and even ferocity. Sometimes, too, there are in his music echoes of the tragedies of Poland.

As a composer for the Piano, Chopin stands among the greatest of innovators. Being himself a most accomplished pianist he had a special gift for writing music well moulded to the keyboard and well adapted to the ten fingers—and (very important) to the two feet. The element of crudity which is sometimes exhibited by the pianist-composer was entirely lacking in him; he brought extraordinary subtlety into Piano Music and Piano Playing, and, instead of mere showy brilliance, has given us the most delicate, lace-like elaborations.

Chopin wrote practically nothing of importance apart from Piano Solos.

LISZT

Liszt was a Hungarian—of a sort. As Chopin was a patriotic Pole who left his country in youth and never set foot in it again, so Liszt was a loyal Hungarian who never learnt his country's language. His public career was considered an honour to Hungary, and when he was still under thirty he was presented by the citizens of Budapest with a sword of honour, which henceforward figured in caricatures as did his contemporary Gladstone's collar. He composed Hungarian Rhapsodies based upon national songs, he wrote a big book upon the music of the Hungarian Gipsies, and towards the end of his life he was appointed by the Hungarian Government Director of an Academy of Music, apparently brought into existence so that his presence in the Capital might be claimed for a month or two of every year. Yet despite all these outward signs, Liszt was not a Hungarian but a cosmopolitan—of all composers perhaps the most cosmopolitan who ever lived. He was resident in turn for long periods in France, Germany, and Italy, a great part of his life was spent in a post-chaise hurrying from one capital of Europe to another, and a good portion of his output as a composer was based upon works of French or German literature.

Liszt.

In the account of the life of Haydn in the first volume of this work is a mention of his thirty-years' employer, Prince Nicholas Esterhazy. When Prince Nicholas died, his successor, Prince Anton, disbanded the orchestra and released Haydn on a pension. This Prince Anton had in his service, as a steward, one Adam Liszt, a very keen musical amateur. And in 1811 (two years after the death of Haydn, whom he probably knew) this steward had born to him a son, Franz, who early manifested the most surprising musical talent.

1811 was 'the year of the great comet': all the biographies mention this, sometimes saying that it was Halley's comet, in which they are surely wrong; but at any rate there was that year a big blaze in the heavens, and the poetical suggestion of the biographers is that Franz Liszt was its reflection upon earth. The place of birth was Raiding (or, in the Magyar tongue, Dobr'jan).

The boy's first teacher was his father, but later he had some lessons in Vienna—in piano from Czerny, and in composition from the seventy-year-old Salieri, the friend of Haydn and Beethoven, the teacher of Schubert, and the enemy of Mozart (whom legend for long charged him with having murdered !).

On performing in public, in Vienna, at the age of eleven, Liszt was approached by Beethoven, who greeted him with a kiss (a great compliment, no doubt, but after all Beethoven was now all but stone deaf, so apparently he must have judged the playing with his eyes).

At the same period Liszt made the acquaintance of Schubert. As in later years Liszt was the encouraging friend of many composers of recent times and of a number of pianists whose playing is still remembered, this makes him a notable link between present and past. It is worth mentioning that whilst he was in Vienna, the twelve-year-old boy was a contributor to the Variations Diabelli published.[1]

From Vienna, father and son went to Paris. Here Society, Literature, and Art fêted the boy, ' le petit Litz ', as he was called.

After leaving Czerny, at twelve, he never had another piano lesson in his life, but in Paris he continued the study of composition with the opera-composer, Paër, and the contrapuntist Reicha (see page 115).

He composed an Opera, *Don Sancho*, the only one he ever did compose, and it was duly performed. London and Manchester were then visited, and 'the little Litz' (as we, too, then called him) was fairly launched on the career of virtuoso.

At fifteen he wanted to leave the concert room for the church, but his father dissuaded him. Nearly forty years later, as we shall see, he found a way of keeping one foot in each.

During this early Paris period Liszt was much in touch not only with the literary romanticists (Hugo, Lamartine, Sainte-Beuve, George Sand, and others) and the painter romanticists (Delacroix and others) but also with what we may, without any intended disrespect, call ' the religious romanticists '. Saint-Simon, with his early expression of a form of what was later to be called ' Christian Socialism ', attracted him, and he enjoyed the friendship of Lamennais, the opponent of the doctrine later defined as ' Art for Art's sake ' and the advocate of Art as a means of attaining moral perfection.

---

[1] The idea of this publication was to have fifty composers do one variation apiece on a waltz air by the composer-publisher, Diabelli. If Lenz is correct, Diabelli called on Beethoven with thirty-two of the Variations, whereupon Beethoven wrote thirty-three of his own. These then constituted a set in themselves, and became the First Book, and are what we now hear to-day. Schubert, Czerny, Hummel, Kalkbrenner, and others of the greatest composers of the time appeared in the Second Book, and so did young Liszt.

The death of Liszt's father had now left the youth to develop on his own lines. He brought his mother to Paris, and as a very fashionable piano teacher, and a widely travelling piano virtuoso, easily supported her and himself. Liszt's virtuoso career may be said to have extended to about his thirty-fifth year. It took him everywhere in Europe and brought him perhaps more fame and money than any musician had ever previously earned. The ladies, in particular, flocked to his 'recitals'. He was, by the way, the first musical performer to use this term, and, indeed, probably the first pianist to give 'one man shows', and he was also the first pianist to place himself in full view of the audience, the usual position previously being either with the back to the audience or with the instrument between player and audience. So fervid was feminine admiration that if he dropped his handkerchief it was torn to pieces, as 'souvenirs', and Tolstoi tells somewhere of one lady admirer who removed, framed, and hung on her wall that portion of a chair that had received his sacred pressure.

This brings us to a consideration (as briefly as fair statement will allow) of woman's more direct influences on Liszt's mind and art. Woman figured largely in the Romantic thought of the age, and Liszt had probably as many loves as Byron or Berlioz and nearly as many as Goethe.

Omitting all minor and short-lived amours, there are three that must be mentioned. In early days, teaching music in Paris, the youth fell deeply in love with and was equally beloved by the daughter of a Minister of State, Caroline St. Cricq. The father saw to it that the lovers were parted—yet in heart they never were, for when Liszt was thirty-three they had at last another tender meeting, whilst when he came to make his will, over a quarter of a century later, he left his Caroline a ring. At that youthful parting they had promised to recall each other at the hour of the Angelus, daily for the rest of their lives, and Liszt asserted that he, at least, kept the promise. These little details have more than a mere gossip value ; they are typical of the sentimental expansion of the Romantic period. (Compare, by the way, the return of Berlioz' poor wandering heart to its first love—page 90.)

For about ten years (1834 to 1844, i. e. from about his twenty-third to his thirty-third year) Liszt was in close intimacy with the Countess of Agoult (later, under the name of 'Daniel Stern', to be known as a romantic novelist). They lived together romantically in Switzerland and elsewhere, and of their three children one later married a pupil of Liszt, the great pianist-conductor von Bülow, and then left him for another friend of Liszt, Richard Wagner. Cosima Wagner, the helper and inspirer of Wagner and, until old age overtook her, the 'grande dame' of Bayreuth, was, then, Liszt's daughter.[1]

The friendship with the Princess Sayn-Wittgenstein followed. They settled at Weimar, where Liszt was appointed by the reigning Duke as his musical director. The glories of Weimar's Schiller-Goethe period were revived. On a salary of about £200 a year (but salaries were nothing to him ; he could always make money galore by the clever pot-boiling pianoforte 'transcriptions' that he was now lavishly pouring out), Liszt made Weimar the Mecca of musicians. Wagner's *Lohengrin* had its first performance there (1850). Liszt's orchestra, more than any other orchestra in Europe, gave the compositions of Berlioz their chance of becoming known.

Liszt and the Princess took their love seriously. In its early days he had written to her, 'Without your love I wish for neither earth nor heaven. Let us love one another, my only and glorious well-belovèd in God and in our Lord Jesus Christ, and let men never try to separate those whom God has joined for eternity.' The union had, at any rate, the basis of community of mind. The Princess urged Liszt to creative effort. She wrote for him his books (or great parts of them) ; she pressed him to push forward with his own composition, despite its comparatively languid reception by the public, who to the end insisted, to Liszt's chagrin and hers, that he was a pianist and not a composer (how few men can earn two reputations ?). She took an interest in his friends, and it is said that the term popularly applied to Wagner's music, 'The Music of the Future', was of her coining.[2]

[1] She died in 1930.

[2] Lina Ramann, one of the most important of Liszt's biographers, relates this incident. Brendel (a successor of Schumann as editor of the *Neue Zeitschrift für Musik*) said *Lohengrin* was too advanced for the public of that day. 'Then', cried the Princess, 'let us call it Music of

The Prince of Sayn-Wittgenstein being still alive, the Princess and the Composer could not marry.   In 1861, when the connexion had already lasted about fourteen years, the Princess went to Rome to appeal to the Pope.   There she stayed awaiting her answer, smoking strong cigars and writing religious books by candle light in a shuttered room with fourteen busts of Liszt around her (this was indeed 'the Romantic period'!).   At last annulment of the marriage was definitely promised.   The day was fixed, Liszt hurried to Rome.   On the evening before the expected event the Pope called for the documents and perused them afresh.   The marriage was forbidden !

That happened in 1861.   In 1864 the Prince died and all obstacles were removed.   But the Princess and her long-standing lover, though until death came they took the tenderest interest in one another's affairs, were never joined in matrimony, and in 1865, aged fifty-four, Liszt took the tonsure and minor orders (doorkeeper, reader, exorcist, acolyte ; he could not say mass or hear confession, and he was free to abandon the orders if he wished) and henceforth was known to the world as 'the Abbé Liszt '.[1]

After these events the Princess lived on at Rome, frequently visited by her old friend, who now made a travelling triangle of Rome, Weimar, and Budapest (see reference earlier to the Academy of Music at the last place).   At Rome Liszt was led to expect that the music of St. Peter's would be put under his control, but it never was.   When in 1870 the fight over Infallibility came on, the Princess and Liszt took opposing views, but even this did not bring a complete cleavage.   The Princess was much occupied with a work

the Future '.   Liszt and von Bülow caught up the phrase and it became the catchword title for the compositions of what people then knew as 'the Weimar School', i.e. the compositions of both Wagner and Liszt. In 1851 Wagner gave the term a sort of confirmation by publishing his essay *The Art-Work of the Future* (' Das Kunstwerk der Zukunft ').

[1] 'Liszt, Liszt, O Liszt ', sang Mr. Punch in 1886, when the Composer, after a very long absence, visited London, and to the popular tune of the time, ' Let us be happy together ', welcomed the guest with a stanza ' Let us be Abbé, together '.   It is a ' good forty year ', he added, ' since Liszt was in London, and Erard and Broadwood say it will be a good pianoforte year now he has returned '.

in over twenty volumes on *The Inward Causes of the Outward Weakness of the Church*: it never appeared until 1912, when she had been a quarter of a century dead, and then (O Pathos!) the *magnum opus* of this pious churchwoman was at once entered upon the Index Librorum Prohibitorum!

Liszt's creative powers also were in these later years directed into Christian channels. He threw himself with ardour into religious composition. His two oratorios, *St. Elizabeth* and *Christus*, and such Piano pieces as *St. Francis of Assisi preaching to the Birds* and *St. Francis of Paola walking on the Waves*, represent this phase of his psychological experience.

Liszt's death took place in 1886 at Bayreuth, and there is his last resting-place. The last music he heard was a fine performance of his son-in-law's *Tristan*.

Summarizing Liszt's main activities we have—

To about his thirtieth year—Virtuoso Pianist, and Composer of showy 'Piano Transcriptions'.

Thence to his fiftieth year—At Weimar; Conductor, and Composer of very seriously intended music, some of it very novel in design.

Thence to his death in his seventy-sixth year—Headquarters at Rome, with teaching and other activities at Weimar and Budapest. Composer of religious music.

As a Composer, Liszt has been very variously judged. Some rank him high—necessarily, for this purpose, disregarding a large mass of pieces expressive either of love of technical display or of shallow sentimentality, and dwelling upon the larger and more serious works, and especially the many Symphonic Poems (see page 39). Of the works bearing Liszt's name there are about 1,300, of which about 400 are original and the rest 'arrangements' or 'transcriptions'.

On one point there can be no question—Liszt's abundant influence upon other composers. Traces of the effect of his style and his innovations are easily seen in the works of contemporaries and followers as widely differing as Wagner and Raff, Tchaikovsky, Rimsky-Korsakof, Borodin, Saint-Saëns, Scriabin, and Strauss.

As a Pianist, Liszt was undoubtedly supreme, and this not only in the brilliant style of which he was a recognized exponent.   Wagner, that greatest of all Beethoven enthusiasts, said, ' Whoever hears Liszt play Beethoven's Sonatas must realize that what he is experiencing is not mere reproduction but actual creative effort '.

Incidentally, Liszt as Piano Virtuoso was one of the first resolutely to break down the tradition of the social inferiority of the artist. For a long time he could not return to Russia because of the well-known incident of his rebuke of the Czar.[1]   In passing it may be suggested that the *prima donna* airs of some pianists to-day may be partly due to a perversion of the Lisztian conception of artistic dignity, spread abroad by Liszt's innumerable pupils, and encouraged by their agents.

Liszt's teaching at Weimar was entirely gratuitous.   Every would-be virtuoso of the sixties, seventies, and eighties gravitated there, and if he or she showed capabilities, was accepted as a member of the Liszt pupil-circle, which played for the great master's criticism every week-day afternoon and on Sundays gave a sort of semi-public concert.   Whether either the Liszt teaching centre at Weimar or the later Leschetizky teaching centre at Vienna has made a really valuable contribution to art the present writer (simply from his personal experience of the playing of Liszt and Leschetizky pupils) takes leave to doubt.   If Chopin's pupils had only made their mark (which, curiously, they none of them did), there might have been a leaven of more delicate artistic sensibility and sensitiveness to tone qualities introduced into public pianism.   At the present moment it would be easy to find fifty young players, of no great name, who give more genuinely musical pleasure than did any fifty survivors of the Liszt and Leschetizky régimes.

Liszt's generosity of nature knew no bounds.   He gave recitals for every good cause.   When the public subscription for the Beethoven monument stopped, shockingly, at about 500 marks, Liszt offered to raise, by recitals, the other 50,000 marks required, and did so.   In time of pestilence, flood, or famine, Liszt played

---

[1] The Czar engaging in conversation, Liszt stopped playing, and when the Czar said, ' Pray continue, Mr. Liszt ', or words to that effect, Liszt replied, ' When your Majesty speaks, all others should be silent '. Anecdotes of this sort are numerous.

money out of the pockets of well-to-do Europe into those of suffering Europe. His own pocket was always open. During his lifetime he probably gave away more money than he spent on himself. His was 'a heart of gold' and his fingers were creators of the same commodity.

And in advice and encouragement Liszt was just as generous. His own compositions were relative failures, yet he fought not for these, but for those of Wagner, Berlioz, and others. He helped to make the value of their work known in three distinct ways—by writing about it, by transcribing it for piano, and by performing it at Weimar and at the numerous festivals he was everywhere called upon to conduct. He was the friend and encourager of the rising Russian School, first of Glinka and then of Borodin and others. He applauded the Bohemian, Smetana. The young Brahms found his way to Weimar and so did the young Grieg, and each was enheartened by his reception.

It seems impossible to judge Liszt by any common-sense criterion. He defies classification. *Was he a great composer?* He wrote reams of trumpery stuff and yet his compositions (apart from his personal encouragement) inspired or influenced half the work of the composers of the day, including many whom we must rate much more highly than we do him. *Was he a good Christian?* He accepted Christian ideals, and clothed the naked, fed the hungry, and forgave his enemies ; his sex morality was very questionable, yet all the time he was filled with Christian devotion.

And so on ! The Lisztian mind is a bundle of antinomies. But there was never anything petty about him. He was, for good and for ill, a daring virtuoso both in Art and in Life.

WAGNER

Wagner's father was a minor municipal official at Leipzig. He died in 1813 when the child was a few months old. The mother then married an actor-painter, named Geyer, and the family removed to Dresden, where Geyer had a theatrical position. Geyer died a few years later, and a return to Leipzig was then made.[1]

---

[1] There is a point in dispute as to the paternity of Wagner, which cannot be discussed here.

At Dresden the boy had seen and admired Weber, then in office as conductor of the German Opera.   Beethoven and Weber were to

Wagner.

be the two great musical influences in his life—the composer who had carried instrumental music to a point where, by its vivid presentation of emotion and its strong emotional contrasts, it approached a state of tonal drama, and the first great German Romantic composer for the stage.

The thoughts of Wagner's circle were much engrossed in music and in affairs of the stage.   His father had been, as an amateur, devoted to music and the theatre; his stepfather had, of course, the same interests; his brother Albert, fourteen years his senior, enjoyed a successful career as an actor, singer, and stage manager; his sister Johanna Rosalie, ten years his senior, won distinction as an actress; his sister, Clara Wilhelmine, was a singer; his niece, Johanna, fifteen years his junior, won a very high place as an opera singer and (when her voice left her for a period) as an actress in the spoken drama.   From the first Richard Wagner shared the family leaning, as a child reading Shakespeare (then attaining that popularity in Germany that he has ever since retained—see pages 102–3), and writing plays.   He also revelled in the romantic E. T. A. Hoffmann, the inspirer of his contemporary, Schumann.

Wagner's formal education was a classical one.   Its last stages were carried out at the Thomas School, Leipzig, of which Bach, eighty years before, had been Cantor, and at the University of Leipzig.

The attraction Wagner always felt for Beethoven has already been mentioned.   At the famous Gewandhaus Concerts in Leipzig he heard the Symphonies.   At seventeen he arranged the Ninth Symphony for piano and tried to get a publisher for it.   At this age he also wrote an Overture, which was duly performed—to a derisive audience, for it was, by his own subsequent description, a foolish work.

Up to this point Wagner's musical studies had been desultory and unsystematic.   He now entered a six months' period of study with

Weinlig, the Cantor of the Thomas School, applying himself assiduously and successfully, under the direction of one of whom he ever after spoke gratefully as a very wise master, to the task of acquiring the technique of composition.

At nineteen he wrote a Symphony, which was performed at one of the Gewandhaus concerts.

Soon after this he was appointed chorus master at the opera house at Würzburg, where his eldest brother was then employed as a singer. A series of short-lived opera house engagements followed—at twenty-one Conductor at Magdeburg, at twenty-three Conductor at Königsberg, at twenty-four Conductor at Riga. Thus was gained a varied experience. Two operas were composed and a third begun during this period, of which one was never performed, *The Fairies* (' Die Feen'), the second was performed and quickly dropped, *Forbidden Love* (' Das Liebesverbot '), and the last is still sometimes to be heard in the opera houses of Europe, *Rienzi* (founded on Bulwer Lytton's novel). Meantime Wagner had married one of his opera singers, Minna Planer.

In 1839, aged twenty-six, the conductor-composer resolved to go to Paris, and to try if it was possible to get the Opera on which he was working, his glittering, Meyerbeer-influenced *Rienzi*, staged there. Accumulated debt and the surveillance of the Russian police made departure a problem, but by adventurous means and the exercise of bribery, the pair got at last aboard an English boat and set sail. Storms and legends of the sea supplied inspiration for his next opera, *The Flying Dutchman*.

Eight days were spent in London, and then the crossing was made to Boulogne. Meyerbeer was staying there, and Wagner sought him out and obtained from him introductions which he expected to find useful in Paris.

Paris, however, was a bitter disappointment. Wagner was there two and a half years, and never got his opera performed : sometimes the couple nearly starved. Wagner tried to get a place as chorus singer in a theatre and failed for lack of voice. He corrected proofs and made operatic cornet ' arrangements ' and piano ' arrangements ' for publication, wrote articles on music for the press, heard a lot of Beethoven, whom Habeneck was then popularizing at the Conservatoire concerts, wrote some songs and *The Flying Dutchman*, and had one small work performed, an overture—*Columbus*.

That is the sum of Wagner's Paris experiences at this period, which ended happily with a call to Dresden, where it had been resolved to perform *Rienzi*. It was in 1842 that the performance took place, when Wagner was nearing thirty. It took nearly six hours to get through the piece, and next morning Wagner sat down to contrive 'cuts'. But the 'cuts' he indicated were not used, for the singers said the music was 'too heavenly'. Eventually the opera was tried as a two-evening work. Wagner was always long-winded.

The Composer now began to become known. Articles about him began to appear in the papers. The first big corner was turned.

Next year (1843, aged thirty) Wagner had the triumph of seeing his *Flying Dutchman* on the same Dresden boards. Further (and this was a great step) he received the appointment of Conductor of the Dresden Royal Opera, succeeding Morlacchi, who having plagued his colleague Weber, twenty years before (see page 83), now helped Wagner by an opportune death.[1] It is interesting to recall that Wagner's first official duty was to help Berlioz, then visiting Dresden as a part of a long and triumphal German tour, with rehearsals for his concerts.

For seven years Wagner was busy at Dresden directing performances of all manner of operas, reviving Gluck, giving careful performances to the Beethoven symphonies, trying to improve Church Music by introducing Palestrina (see page 106 for Mendelssohn's similar attempt at Düsseldorf), and cultivating male-voice choral music. He also conducted the music and made an oration on the occasion of the translation of Weber's remains from London to Dresden (see page 85).

In 1844 *Tannhäuser* was completed and in 1845 performed—with

[1] In Weber's day the Italian and German Operas were separate royal establishments; hence the rivalry. Now, apparently, they were merged. Dresden for long had only an Italian opera, being recalcitrant to the growing national influence. It was only in 1815 that the German opera was established there. Later, as we have seen, Dresden struck a shrewd blow for the national operatic movement by giving the greatest of all German opera composers his first real chance.

only fair success, yet it was pretty widely taken up in different parts of Germany. The cloven hoof of modernity was supposed to show itself plainly in this work, and it was much criticized (see Schumann's opinion, pages 99–100).

The Royal Library at Dresden afforded opportunity for the study of the national literature. From *Tannhäuser* onwards all Wagner's work was based on native legend. In particular, at this time Wagner began to work on the Nibelung myth, not to finish his task until twenty-six years later.

In 1848 came political disturbances in many parts of Europe. Everywhere fetters were snapping, and when the Dresden risings began, Wagner's sympathies, royal official though he was, were with the revolutionaries. He took more or less part in the fighting and then had to fly—first to the sympathetic Liszt at Weimar (Liszt, who always helped any worthy musician, and who was at this time engaged in rehearsing *Tannhäuser*), then to Paris, and finally to Zurich.

At Zurich Wagner remained settled for about eight years. Von Bülow was conductor there, and towards the end of this period married Cosima, Liszt's daughter. Wagner was much helped by a wealthy man, Wesendonck, who built him a house on his estate, and in the end the composer had to clear out because he was attempting to tamper with the affections of his patron's wife. He worked hard at the production of much literature (*Opera and Drama*, &c.), he came under the influence of Schopenhauer's philosophy, which left more or less mark henceforth on the text of every one of his works,[1]

---

[1] All that we see about us is merely 'idea'. Only 'will' has actual existence. Suffering is the stimulus of 'will', and only when the 'will to live' is abandoned does 'will' reach its full development.—This central thought of Schopenhauer's system finds its reflection in parts of *The Ring*, *Tristan*, and *Parsifal*. Schopenhauer's *The World as Will and Idea* was published when Wagner was a child of six, but never gained recognition until he was well into the forties. Then it swept through philosophical circles. In 1854 Wagner sent to Schopenhauer a copy of the 'book' of *The Ring* as a token of gratitude and reverence. Many of Wagner's keenest musical admirers must wish that their hero had never become an amateur philosopher. They would in that case have been spared some of Wotan's melancholy long-windedness—to mention only one advantage.

he completed and privately published the immense libretto for his *Nibelungs' Ring* Cycle, and he finished the music for the first and second dramas of the Cycle, *Rhinegold* and *The Valkyrie*, and made great headway with *Tristan*. Wagner's *Lohengrin* was performed by Liszt at Weimar in 1850. He himself could not be present, being under sentence of banishment from Germany. This first performance of *Lohengrin* was really the decisive turning-point in the whole Wagner movement. He visited England (1855) and conducted a season of the Philharmonic Society's Concerts (Berlioz was also there; see page 93).

The summary above of work done at Zurich gives a hint as to the rapid development Wagner's genius was undergoing at this very fruitful period. The tabular statement subjoined will show the order of composition of different works, and, especially, the long period of gestation and of growth of some of them, especially, as stated above, *The Ring*.

In 1859 came an often related scandal—the hostile reception of *Tannhäuser* in Paris. After laborious efforts Wagner had managed to get a royal command for a performance of this work. It was long rehearsed, and great expense was lavished on the production. But the position of the Ballet, early in the work, was an offence to late diners. It was an offence, too, to the *corps de ballet* who wanted to be seen by the same late diners. The ballet girls, then, worked up feeling amongst their gentlemen friends, gilded youth as represented by the Jockey Club was mobilized, and hissing and whistling killed the performance. Wagner, who was, as ever, in need of money, had relied upon having heavy profits from these performances, and instead gained only about £30, which went a very trifling distance towards the liquidation of his ever-accumulating debts, which now stood at a high figure.

In 1861, aged forty-eight, Wagner received notice that his sentence of banishment from Germany was revoked. About this time he separated from his wife, with whom he had, on the whole, lived happily, and took instead von Bülow's wife, Cosima (Liszt's daughter). After his wife's death in 1866, and when at last Bülow divorced Cosima (1870), Wagner was able to contract a legal marriage with Cosima.

A worry of this period of the early sixties was the refusal by every opera house of *Tristan and Isolda*. Vienna gave it seventy-seven rehearsals and then dropped it. It had been completed in 1859 and was first performed in 1865—by von Bülow, at Munich.

This mention of Munich as a centre of Wagner propaganda calls for the brief relation of a romantic episode in Wagner's life, and one of great importance by its influence on his life's work. How did the Munich connexion begin? Head over ears in debt, and dispirited, Wagner found sudden salvation. A high official of the King of Bavaria sought him out when he was travelling and had reached Stuttgart, and summoned him to the King's side, at Munich. The King, a lad of eighteen, a lover of Wagner's idol, Beethoven, and an admirer of Wagner's opera, *Lohengrin*, had read the published libretto of the as yet only half-composed *Ring*, which, as Wagner had come to believe (such were his difficulties), would remain to the end only half-composed. 'Come here and finish your great work', said the King, and offered the Composer a home and a pension.

Wagner's actual stay in Munich was not long (May 1864 to December 1865), for the King's favouritism and the counsel he took with Wagner upon political matters led to the enmity of the men of state, who insisted upon his banishment from the capital. But the connexion between the King and Wagner still continued, more or less openly, and one result is still seen in the existence upon Bavarian soil of the great Festival Theatre—at Bayreuth.

The bringing into existence of this, however, was about seven or eight years ahead, and in the meantime Wagner and his future second wife were living at Lucerne, in the Villa Triebschen. *The Mastersingers of Nuremberg*, first sketched twenty-two years before, was finished at Lucerne in 1867.

The friendship with Nietzsche, then a young Professor of Classical Philology at the University of Basle, began at this period (1868), Nietzsche upon whose loyalty he was to impose many burdens, and who was, by pen and voice, to be for long his greatest non-musician supporter, and at last, disillusioned, to cut adrift from him.[1]

[1] Man, as at present existing, is a bundle of effeminate childishnesses We should strive towards the production of the superman—inflexible will, infinite endurance, determination to enjoy. That is a central thought in

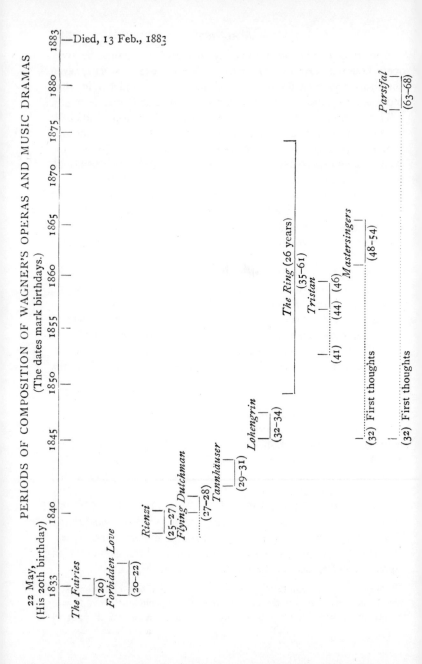

PERIODS OF COMPOSITION OF WAGNER'S OPERAS AND MUSIC DRAMAS

(The dates mark birthdays.)

22 May, (His 20th birthday) 1833

The Fairies (20)

Forbidden Love (20–22)

Rienzi (25–27)

Flying Dutchman (27–28)

Tannhäuser (29–31)

Lohengrin (32–34)

The Ring (26 years) (35–61)

Tristan (41) (44) (46)

Mastersingers (48–54)

(32) First thoughts

(32) First thoughts

Parsifal (63–68)

—Died, 13 Feb., 1883

The foundation stone of the Bayreuth theatre was laid in 1872, when Wagner was in his sixtieth year. The first performance took place there in 1876, when Richter, Wagner's faithful friend and helper, conducted the *Ring*, now, at last, completed. Money was lost, and Wagner and Richter came to England, with the fond idea of regaining it by a series of concerts at the Albert Hall. These, however, brought in only a few hundreds of pounds, a drop in the bucket. British admirers actually began to subscribe towards the liquidation of the Bayreuth deficit, but proceeds from performances at Munich came, and the sums subscribed by the British Wagnerian circle were returned to them with a grateful letter from Wagner.

It was in 1877, when Wagner was sixty-four, that the London expedition took place, and at this period the Composer was engaged on his last work, *Parsifal*. It was to be a 'Sacred Festival Drama', with its performances strictly confined to Bayreuth. It had its first performance in 1882, Levi conducting. Next year, at Venice, Wagner died.

Three years later, Wagner's patron, 'The Mad King of Bavaria', drowned himself, and, also, Wagner's early generous helper, and later father-in-law, Liszt, died. Von Bülow died in 1894, Richter lived until 1916. Then there had passed away all of Wagner's most loyal and effective supporters but one. At the date of the first writing of this book there still lived Cosima Wagner, aged ninety; she had already survived her husband by over forty years, and like that other long-surviving widow of a genius contemporary with Wagner, Clara Schumann, who survived Robert by forty years, had devoted herself to the keeping green of the memory of what her husband accomplished for the world.

Wagner's Music Dramas have already been briefly discussed (pages 62 to 74). He sketched out or actually wrote the libretti of a good many stage works he never set. In his early twenties, he dramatized a novel by König, as *The Exalted Bride* ('Die Höhe Braut'), and sent it, in sketch form, to Scribe, then, and for long after, the most popular playwright in France, hoping that he would com-

the Nietzschean system, and one congenial to Wagner, and (as later events showed) only too congenial to the German nation as it was at that time developing.

plete the work as a finished libretto, and so open to the composer a path to the Paris stage. As Scribe ignored the suggestion, Wagner finished the libretto himself, and a few years after it was set by one Kittl (as *Bianca and Giuseppa*), and, performed in Prague, had a good deal of success.

He wrote the libretto of a Four-Act Comic Opera, on an *Arabian Nights* subject, *The Happy Bear Family, or Man's Cunning greater than Woman's*, but never set it to music. He sketched a Three-Act Opera, *The Mines of Falun*, and completed the libretto of a Five-Act one, *The Saracen Woman*; he sketched a Music Drama *Jesus of Nazareth*, and others, *Frederick Barbarossa* and *The Victors*; he completed in a preliminary prose version *Wieland the Smith*, and offered it to Liszt. The range of subjects in this list (all the way from the *Arabian Nights* to the New Testament) is rather remarkable.

Apart altogether from stage works Wagner's literary activities were very extended. His prose works fill ten considerable volumes. They include fiction (the novelettes *A Pilgrimage to Beethoven*, &c.), critical sketches (on works of Weber, Halévy, Beethoven, Spontini, Gluck, Liszt, Auber, and others), discussion (*The State of Religion, Religion and Art, Judaism and Music, German Art and German Politics*, &c.), technical treatises (*On Conducting*), and, of course, an enormous treatment of his own aims and methods (*The Art Work of the Future, Opera and Drama*, and so forth). Not included in the collected edition is the great Autobiography, *My Life*, begun in his middle fifties (1869), privately printed (very few copies), and only made known to the public when Wagner had been dead nearly thirty years (1911); this work is revealing as to its author's character —not least in the suppressions and distortions which, were no other source of information available, would in many cases convey a very misleading impression. What Wagner here admits without disguise, and what he carefully glosses over, show the possession of a curiously intermittent sense of shame. Wagner was no saint, he was egoistic and egotistic, unself-controlled in matters of sex, wildly reckless in expenditure, shameless in borrowing and careless in repayment. His life stands justified, not as an example to the young (except, decidedly, in the matter of courage and perseverance), but by the musical legacy he left behind him.

BRAHMS

No apology shall be offered for placing the notice of Brahms amongst the notices of the Romantics—no apology, but a word,

Brahms.

perhaps, of explanation. The work of Brahms is sometimes spoken of as a return to the Classics, and its composer as a classical composer born out of due time. Yet open a composition of his anywhere and play a phrase at random and you feel at once that you are in the presence of a most genuine Romantic.

The classical claims of Brahms are indeed based not upon an absence of romantic feeling but upon the presence of a feeling for form and proportion that was very often to seek in the other Romantics.

Brahms showed himself a master of the Sonata and the Symphony. They, too, or some of them, wrote Sonatas and Symphonies, but when they did so paid less attention to the form and proportion of their work than to its romantic contents. They excelled in short romantic piano pieces and in long ' programmatic ' Tone Poems rather than in the Sonata form and style. Brahms also wrote short romantic piano pieces, but he wrote no Tone Poems and no Programme Music, instead of these reverting to the classical Concerto and Symphony and in them attaining the balance and poise we call ' classic ' combined with that type of emotional expression we call ' romantic '.

On the one side Brahms was the continuator of Beethoven, so much so that von Bülow called Brahms' first Symphony Beethoven's Tenth; on the other he was the continuator of Schumann, so much so that Schumann in his last years hailed him as a son or brother, and his widow remained to her death in closest and almost motherly relations with him, as with the musician who of all musicians living best understood her husband's work and best gathered its influences into his own.

The lives of Liszt and Berlioz show the Romantic spirit at its least controlled, that of Brahms, seen in contrast, seems to show an almost Puritan severity.   Look at romance on the side of sex ; consider the long lists of women loved by Liszt, and Berlioz, and Wagner, the quiet yet intense domestic love of Schumann, and the bachelor solitariness of Brahms, who feared to marry and ran away from the only woman we know him to have been in danger of loving, lest with that danger should have been bound up the other one of neglect of his art.   The turbulence and restlessness of Liszt and Berlioz, the brooding spirit of Schumann, the refined drawing-room life of Chopin and the quiet retirement of Brahms are reflected in their music.

Brahms was the son of a poor, plodding double-bass player, who, with effort, had attained a modest footing in theatre orchestras of Hamburg.   There the composer was born in 1833.

Early progress in piano-playing enabled the boy to assist his family by performing in cafés and dancing halls—with a volume of poetry or history propped up before him, for at this time, as through-out his life, he was a great reader, and it is of interest to know that two of his favourite boyhood authors were those who had previously enthralled and inspired also Robert Schumann—Jean Paul Richter, and Hoffmann (see pages 32 and 97).

Some excellent musical training was given him by the then famous theorist and beloved pupil of Schumann, Marxsen of the neighbour-ing town of Altona.   At his hands the boy received a thorough grounding in the classics of music.

At twenty, Brahms set off on a concert tour with the Jew-Hungarian fiddler, Rémenyi.   There were adventures.   At Göttingen the piano was a semitone too low, and Brahms transposed the piano part of Beethoven's Kreutzer Sonata, playing it from memory.   Joachim was in the audience, realized the ability of the youth (who was, he said, the most considerable musician of his age he had ever met), and promised him an introduction to Schumann.[1]

---

[1] E. W. points out that this incident, related as above in Hadow's *Studies in Modern Music* and possibly elsewhere, is differently related by various authorities.   May says Celle, not Göttingen, and the Beethoven Sonata in C minor, not the ' Kreutzer '.   Joachim himself (see May i. 106) speaks of the first meeting as being at Hanover, at his own lodgings, a little while later.

At Hanover a worse trouble than a low-pitch piano presented itself. Rémenyi, a fiddler of the adventurous travelling type, like Paganini and Ole Bull, had been mixed up with politics. Four years before, in that revolutionary period later alluded to (page 165) he had fought for his native country against Austria and had even been adjutant to General Görgei, the successor of Kossuth as Dictator. Görgei was now serving a twenty-years' term of imprisonment, and his former adjutant was not looked upon favourably by the representatives of constitutional authority. Brahms and Rémenyi were expelled from the city and territory.

They went to Weimar, where Liszt reigned. Liszt welcomed them, and such of Brahms' work as he performed there awakened his enthusiasm. Brahms found himself enrolled amongst the young hopefuls of Liszt's 'New German' party, a position from which he definitely seceded a few years later (1860), when with Joachim and two others he signed a bold manifesto against 'the so-called Music of the Future'.

Joachim was now at Göttingen, and Brahms journeyed there to claim the promised letter to Schumann. He got it and then, almost penniless, continued his journey on foot to Düsseldorf, where Schumann was now situated.

Schumann's enthusiasm was immediate. He wrote the now historic article (the counterpart of his earlier article on Chopin ; see page 97), secured Brahms a hearing at Leipzig, and gave him his friendship and loving support. Thenceforward, though the road was an uphill one, it ran straight.

From his twenty-first to his twenty-fifth years Brahms held a congenial post as conductor at the court of Lippe-Detmold. His duties were light and only extended over a short portion of the year. He had leisure to work at composition and opportunity of travel and concert-giving. And he gained experience in conductorship that was to be of great service later. For a period of four years he published nothing, studying incessantly and improving himself in his art with that determination and high idealism that marked his whole life.

Abandoning this post at length, Brahms settled for a couple of years in Switzerland—at Winterthur, where Kirchner, an able

Schumann pupil and a congenial friend, was stationed.   There were
pupils to teach and a publisher for his compositions; life was happy
there.

The performance of the first Piano Concerto, at Leipzig in 1859,
created strong discussion.   There were those who disliked its severity
and lack of solo display.   Some one called it 'not a concerto, but a
Symphony with pianoforte obbligato'.   Many of Brahms' works were
received with hostility, but he went quietly on and gradually made
his way.

In 1862 came the settlement at Vienna which was to last the rest
of the Composer's life.   For a time he held various conductorships
there.   The romantically-conceived and classically-executed Piano
and Chamber Music, the *German Requiem* in 1868, the Four
Symphonies, the Violin Concerto, and other works established his
position.   He came to be looked upon as the main bulwark of the
serious classical school by those who detested the works of Wagner
as new-fangled and outrageous, but he never asked for this position,
and, indeed, was himself a close and admiring student of everything
Wagner wrote.   So far as he personally was concerned, the manifesto just mentioned was directed against Liszt and not Wagner.

The rhythmic complexity,[1] the effective counterpoint, the rich
harmony, the general intellectuality, the warm romanticism, and the
dignity of Brahms' work, the effective combination in him of many
of the characteristics of Bach, Beethoven, and Schumann, gave a
very evident individuality to all he produced, and a Brahms cult
grew up that was practised by his admirers in various countries with
almost excessive fervour.   In England there was a 'highbrow'
Brahms coterie that somewhat resembled the Browning coteries of
about the same period.[2]

---

[1] His music must have seemed rhythmically very complex and varied
when first heard, considering the bondage to musical metre (roughly
speaking, slavery to the bar-line and the accented 'first beat') under
which music had served for about two centuries, and from which it is
not even yet wholly freed.   The rhythmic complexity of Brahms really
amounts to little more than the frequent use of a few set devices.

[2] Perhaps the Brahms cult went on the whole too far.   It 'put people's
backs up'.   George Bernard Shaw, who was a young London music

The picture of Brahms' last public appearance is a touching one. It occurred in Vienna, in 1897. He was dying of cancer of the liver. He knew it and the public knew it, and when, as the Fourth Symphony ended, the Composer was called for, and stood before the audience 'shrunken in form, with lined countenance, white hair hanging lank ', and tears running down his cheeks, there was much sad sympathy. He had had in his time a fight with poverty, and was wont to point to the manuscript of his *German Requiem* in proof of this, for it was made up of pages of various sizes, due to his inability to buy more than a few sheets of manuscript paper at a time. Material comfort had been gained, the public had more and more been won over, critics had ceased to oppose. And now the fight was over, and the end had come, and the parting was near. In a few weeks he was dead.

Brahms was a very human creature. He was often rough and boorish and satirical—partly, no doubt, as a protection against the lion-hunters of whom he went in fear, and partly from an upbringing in working-class poverty. He loved children and peasants, and, like Beethoven, he loved nature, and in it he perpetually sought inspiration. The outstanding characteristic of his life, as one reads it, is the high idealism that permeated it. He sought no publicity and did not defend his work ; he enjoyed many friendships but maintained enough solitude for the growth of his spirit. His art to him was everything, and in the quiet detachment with which he practised it, he reminds one of Bach, or of that César Franck of whom we are later to read.

Brahms' music does not at once carry every one by storm. It is a common experience for men to dislike or disdain the music of Brahms and then, as they grow older, to come to see in it qualities they had never suspected.

critic in those days, never recovered. In 1920 he described Brahms as 'a musical sensualist with intellectual affectation, who succeeded only as an incoherent voluptuary, too fundamentally addle-headed to make anything great out of the delicious musical luxuries he produced' (Article on Elgar in *Music and Letters*).

ROSSINI

Rossini (1792–1868) came of good-humoured parents.   The
father was a musician—or at any rate town-trumpeter of Pesaro on

Rossini.

the Adriatic coast of Italy ; he was also
town inspector of slaughter-houses, and the
head of what was reputed to be a particularly merry home.   The mother, a baker's
daughter, was a woman of resource ; when
in 1796 her husband was clapped into jail
for French and republican sympathies, she
went, with her four-year-old, to Bologna
and came out as a leading lady in comic
opera.   Then the trumpeter was released
and turned himself into a horn player so
that he might be the companion of his wife
in her professional travels, the future composer being left in the
charge of a pork-butcher.

Soon the mother's voice failed, but the horn-playing did not, and
the child, who had had some indifferent musical instruction, travelled
with his father, serving as accompanist in theatres and doing odd
jobs of a musical kind.   He also did a little singing and acting.

By and by he was admitted to the Conservatoire of Bologna, as a
budding composer and violoncellist.   He won a prize for a Cantata,
and had other successes.   Mozart's music had a great appeal for him,
and his companions called him ' the little German '.

Out of his pupilage he quickly made a name as an Opera Composer, his pieces coming out one after another, in various opera
houses of Italy.   His melodic gifts and sense of humour helped him.

In his early twenties he was already director of the great San
Carlo Theatre in Naples, and composer of *The Barber of Seville*, a
witty setting of Beaumarchais' witty play and the most delightful
work of its type since Mozart, which took him thirteen days to complete.   Whilst in the Spanish vein, and full of the inspiration of
Spanish love-making, he married a Spanish *prima donna*, who, by
the way, was also a composer, Isabella Colbran ; she had a bad

reputation for singing out of tune, but probably had domestic qualities that compensated. The two visited London and Paris, and in the latter place Rossini, for a short time, directed the Italian Theatre.

Rossini usually composed an opera every five months or so. In Vienna he had great success. He met Beethoven there and tried to get up a subscription for him.

In 1829, aged thirty-seven, he wrote his famous *William Tell*. Then he stopped. He had made all the money he needed; he had fame and he wanted rest and pleasure. After a time he settled in Paris, and then, after forty years of never putting pen to paper (except for a few trifles, the very Italian-operatic setting of the *Stabat Mater* and some piano music) he died in 1868.

He had a wonderful gift of melody, understood the capabilities of the human voice, and was the best orchestrator Italy had produced up to his time. (Remembering his father, he wrote specially well for the horn.) A certain kind of *crescendo* became a mannerism with Rossini, and it is universally known as 'The Rossinian Crescendo'. Briefly, it consists of the mere mechanical reiteration of a musical phrase or sentence (often more fussy than deeply significant) with an ever-increasing number of instruments, until the whole Orchestra is engaged. Here is a specimen—from the Overture to the otherwise brilliant *Barber of Seville*.

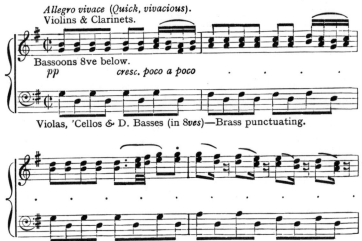

Parry (*Evolution of the Art of Music*) speaks sadly of 'such tricks as the whirling Rossinian *crescendo*, which is like a dance of dervishes, all about nothing', producing 'physical excitement without any simultaneous exaltation of higher faculties'.

DONIZETTI

Donizetti was born in 1797, at Bergamo. There is an absurd story, which appears occasionally in the press, to the effect that he was of Scottish descent (a mythical ancestor Donald or Don Izett has been supplied as the necessary basis of the theory).

He studied at the conservatoires of Bergamo and Bologna. The first opera to bring him real renown was *Ann Boleyn* (1830), *Lucy of Lammermoor* (based on Scott's novel) extended his fame greatly, and *The Daughter of the Regiment, Lucrezia Borgia*, and *La Favorita* carried it still farther. At forty-seven the Composer was struck down by a form of paralysis which developed into mental weakness, and he died at fifty-one (1848)—the composer of sixty operas.

Donizetti made his success by means of a natural gift of facile, taking melody combined with ability to write florid, showy, singable vocal parts, requiring first-rate vocalists to tackle them. He was a poor orchestrator and a poor contrapuntist. Look at a few pages of Donizetti and you will be surprised to learn of his appointment as Professor of Counterpoint at the Naples Conservatoire.

BELLINI

Bellini was a Sicilian. He was born in 1801, the son of an organist. A nobleman sent him to Naples to study at the conservatoire.

At twenty-five he wrote, for the Scala at Milan, an Opera, *The Pirate*, which made him at once famous. He then produced opera after opera in quick succession, *Norma* and *The Puritans* being two that are still particularly remembered.

Rubini, Malibran, Pasta, Tamburini, Lablache, Grisi—all the great names of swell singers, male and female, are associated with the first performances of Bellini's works, which immediately on production became everywhere popular. Their main effect came from their melodies—which Chopin greatly admired, and which (as suggested on page 75) had doubtless some effect upon his melodic style. In Paris Bellini had enjoyed great popularity.

Bellini gravely overworked, and died at thirty-three (1835). He was buried at Père-Lachaise, and fourteen years later his friend, Chopin, was buried beside him.

To some extent Bellini was a follower of Rossini, who supported him with encouragement and advice.

VERDI

Verdi was a North Italian; he was born at Roncole, near Busseto, in the district of Parma, in 1813—the year of the birth of Wagner.

Verdi.

His parents kept a small inn and shop. He must have showed early inclinations towards music, for at about the age of seven his parents provided him with a small spinet (or harpsichord). He tried to pick out chords on it, and failing one day to find again the chord of the previous day flew into a temper and smashed it with a hammer. It was repaired and is still preserved and bears this inscription, hidden within on one of the jacks :—

These jacks were renewed and new-leathered, and the pedals fitted gratis by me, Stefano Cavaletti, in view of the good disposition of the lad Giuseppe Verdi in wishing to learn to play, this being reward enough for me.   Anno 1821.

About the same time Giuseppe was himself the victim of Italian excitability, for the priest of the village church, upon whom he was waiting as an acolyte, seeing him absorbed in listening to the organ instead of attending to his ceremonial duties, kicked him down the altar steps so that he lay at the bottom insensible.

His father allowed him to take lessons from the organist who had so dangerously charmed him, and in a couple of years (aged ten) the boy succeeded his master and began to charm others in his turn. During the week he went to school at Busseto, lodging with a cobbler who boarded him and paid for his schooling for a fee of threepence a day.

Busseto was a very musical town, and its leading musical light was one Barezzi, president of the Philharmonic Society, and, as it happened, the wholesaler from whom Verdi's father bought his supplies of spirits and coffee. Barezzi took Verdi into his employment and encouraged his musical studies. Verdi had lessons from the conductor of the Philharmonic Society and wrote some music for performance by the Society. The local charitable institution promised money for instruction in Milan, so Verdi went there. He tried for a scholarship at the Conservatoire but was refused on the grounds of lack of aptitude for music. He therefore took private lessons—from one Lavigna. In Milan he remained for two years, and then returned to Busseto in the expectation of succeeding the cathedral organist, who had died; another applicant was, however, appointed, whereupon the Philharmonic Society, which, with its orchestra, had been in the habit of taking part in the more important services, removed all its music and opened hostilities which lasted for some years. Although not successful in his claim to the cathedral position, Verdi stayed in Busseto, marrying the daughter of his kind protector, Barezzi.

At twenty-five, with a wife and two children and an opera, Verdi went again to Milan. The opera, now forgotten, was performed at the Scala, and with fair success.

Suddenly, within three months, Verdi lost his wife and both children. A comic opera he had written was a failure and, sad and disheartened, he dropped composition—as he thought, for ever. A clever impresario who had faith in him managed to shake that resolution, and with *Nebuchadnezzar* Verdi made a considerable hit. *The Lombards* followed, and made a still greater one, as it had passages that could be applauded as a demonstration against the Austrian Government that then ruled Northern Italy. Other operas followed quickly, and with three works of the early fifties of the century, *Rigoletto*, *The Troubadour* ('Il Trovatore') and *The Misled* ('La Traviata'), the work of Verdi enters the zone of the still performed.

It would be useless here to detail the whole of the operatic productions of Verdi, or the circumstances in which each appeared, but three outstanding ones must be mentioned.

Aïda, on an Egyptian subject, was composed for the Khedive of Egypt and first performed at Cairo—in 1871 ; it is highly spectacular, very tuneful, and very dramatic.

After *Aïda* it seemed as though Verdi's work was done, since no new opera was produced for sixteen years. Then, in 1887, he astonished the world with *Othello*, a work of a very different kind from any he had previously written. often styled 'Wagnerian', perhaps because it has something of the 'leading motive' element and also frankly aims at a genuinely dramatic presentation of its great story.

At the time of the production of this remarkable work Verdi was seventy-four. Six years later appeared another Shakespearian work, with the same characteristics still further developed—*Falstaff*, the work of an eighty-year-old composer who in it showed both a youthful gaiety and a youthful ability to adapt himself to modern ways that are truly amazing. *Falstaff*, though pretty often performed, is not at present one of Verdi's 'popular' operas. It seems to be 'too good' for the large operatic public, though it sparkles with bright humour, witty counterpoint, and clever orchestration, and has, indeed, been hailed as the greatest modern comic opera. Boito, himself an able composer, was the librettist of *Othello* and *Falstaff*.

Verdi, the Italian melody-maker *par excellence*, had, at eighty years old, learnt from Wagner, both in true, artistic dramatization, and also in actual method (e. g. plastic, continuous, tuneful recitative for the voices, a whole musical fabric of real value, &c.), yet had not dried up his own great melodic genius, and had retained all that is best in Italian Opera (in his case, doubtless, partly inborn, partly acquired).

One major work of Verdi needs to be mentioned—his great Requiem in memory of the romantic novelist Manzoni, the Italian Sir Walter Scott; it is rather theatrical, yet full of real feeling and very effective.

Other well-known works are settings of the Latin hymns, *Stabat Mater* and *Te Deum*, and above all a String Quartet which has much merit and interest, especially considering the wide difference between most of his work and Chamber Music. This Quartet is sometimes performed, and has been recorded for the gramophone.

That Verdi was a good deal influenced by the Romantic movement in literature goes without saying, when one considers the original sources of many of his plots—*Ernani* and *Rigoletto* (Victor Hugo), *La Traviata* (Alexander Dumas fils), *Macbeth*, *Othello*, and *Falstaff* (Shakespeare). He died in 1901.[1]

---

[1] This seems a suitable place to record an objection of E. E. 'I do not think you allot your space quite fairly between the Teutonic and Latin elements in nineteenth-century music. Of course the *greatest* German masters

PUCCINI

Puccini came of a very musical family. There were four generations of musicians behind him. He was born in Lucca in 1858, and trained at the Milan Conservatoire. He reached the honour of performance at the famous Scala theatre in Milan at the age of twenty-six. *La Bohème,* in 1896, based on Murger's well-known novel, was his first outstanding success. Then came *Tosca, Madam Butterfly, The Girl of the Golden West,* and a set of three one-act operas of which a comedy, *Gianni Schicchi,* is the best, and is, perhaps, a little masterpiece. *Turandot* was his last opera, and was unfinished when the composer died in 1924 (it was completed by Alfano). A great melodic facility, of a typical Italian order, effective orchestration, a strong sense of the stage, and a realism sometimes crude are characteristics of Puccini's work. These are all qualities that bring an opera writer a large popular following.

GOUNOD

Gounod's mother was a fine pianist. He was born (in Paris) in 1818 and quickly showed his inherited talent. He studied at the Paris Conservatoire and won the Prix de Rome. At Rome he studied church music with particular interest, especially that of the sixteenth century.

On return to Paris he became an organist, and studied with a view

were by far the more important, and should be treated accordingly, but need the disparity be quite so tremendous as your book makes it? I think, for instance, that you underrate Bellini, your view of whom seems to me quite Teutonic, and Bizet deserves greater prominence, both because he is typical of a definite and valuable element in music, and because his influence has been so great. I also think you omit some very characteristic works. It seems strange to me to mention Donizetti and not his *Don Pasquale.* And the revival of Verdi's *La Forza del Destino* has been hailed as a revelation: he did not suddenly become great with *Aïda* as some people seem to think. What about the Italian *verismo*—not I admit a very high form of art, but still a living force to be reckoned with?'

to the priesthood, which, however, he never entered. His Solemn Mass, which (or part of which) had its first performance in London, in 1851, first brought him the 'publicity' which every composer needs as much as every business man. He was then thirty-four.

Gounod.

A few months later the Opera, *Sappho*, was produced in Paris. The Opera which was to bring him real fame was, of course, *Faust*, which appeared eight years later. It shows much stage-skill and much melody, and these have made it one of the most popular operas ever written, but those who like Goethe do not like Gounod. Other Operas were also written (*Romeo and Juliet* is well known, but those who like Shakespeare do not like Gounod), and a symphony or two had an ephemeral career. There were, further, a number of oratorios, devout ballads, and some popular trifles such as the *Funeral March of a Marionette*, and the *Meditation* on Bach's Prelude in C, which show no signs of dropping out of use.

The oratorios, especially, were popular in England, and here Gounod came at the time of the Franco-Prussian War, staying for five years—till 1875. He was taken up and 'run' by Mrs. Georgina Weldon, the vocalist, a lady so strong-minded and original that in a period of obedient wives she was taken to be insane and only managed to remain outside the asylum in which her husband wished to shut her up by repeated defence in the law courts, which she ably conducted in person. In the end she and Gounod quarrelled, and more fighting resulted. Mrs. Weldon's forty or fifty large cases of legal and other papers (she never destroyed a line of writing) were examined in the 1920's, and they were found to contain a number of smaller works of Gounod, probably never published.

With intervals, Gounod retained his devotion, and a Mass which he wrote for Rheims Cathedral he intended, he said, to write kneeling— on the stone on which Joan of Arc knelt at the Coronation of Charles VII. Gounod, it will be seen, was a true romanticist!

He had a lyric gift and a dramatic gift, and a gift of very pleasant orchestration, in fact he had all the 'popular' qualities, but he veered too much in the direction of the effeminate and sentimental.

Gounod died at seventy-five in 1893.

BIZET

Born at Paris in 1838, he studied at the Conservatoire, won the Prix de Rome, and married the daughter of his composition professor, Halévy.

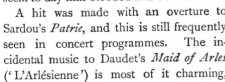

Bizet.

For a long time he toiled in vain to win recognition as an opera composer. Three works still occasionally to be heard are *The Pearl Fishers* (1863), *The Fair Maid of Perth* (1867), and *Djamileh* (1872). They seem to-day thin-blooded and conventional.

A hit was made with an overture to Sardou's *Patrie*, and this is still frequently seen in concert programmes. The incidental music to Daudet's *Maid of Arles* ('L'Arlésienne') is most of it charming, and is known to concert audiences in its form of two Suites for Orchestra. Two other Suites are *Rome* and *Children's Games*.

The now universally popular *Carmen* was a setting of a libretto taken from the story of the same name by Mérimée. It is a Spanish gipsy opera. Its success was not immediate and was never known to the Composer, who died a month or two after its first performance (1875). The tunefulness and delicate, piquant orchestration of Bizet are very attractive, and in *Carmen*, at any rate, he shows dramatic power.

He wrote a good many songs, some of which are occasionally to be heard.

For a further remark on Bizet see the Appendix to Vol. III, *The Two Frances in Music*.

LALO

Lalo was born at Lille in 1823. He studied at the Paris Conservatoire. He first composed drawing-room ballads, then Chamber Music. Then for ten years he composed nothing. At forty-four he brought out an Opera, which had little success, and he then turned to orchestral composition. His *Spanish Symphony* for Violin and Orchestra, and other works, made his name, and his Opera, *The King of Ys*, years after, confirmed it.

His masterpiece is considered to be the ballet-pantomime *Namouna* (also existing in the modified form of an orchestral suite), which awakened the enthusiasm of Debussy, d'Indy, and others, and influenced them a good deal. Dukas, also, owes a good deal to him. Adept orchestration is one of Lalo's strongest points.

He died in 1892.

DELIBES

Delibes was born in 1836, in the Department of Sarthe, and died in 1891. He studied at the Paris Conservatoire and then at once appeared before the public as a composer of successful Operettas, Operas, and Ballets. (Of the Ballets, *Coppélia* and *Sylvia* are favourite specimens. Of the Operas, *Lakmé* has been popular.) In melody, harmony, and orchestration he had that graceful light-handed touch which is always welcomed by musicians and non-musicians alike. He was, as one says, 'typically French'—but in saying it one remembers that France expresses itself in more than one type.

Like Chabrier, but in a lesser degree, Delibes has influenced many composers of very different temperament from himself.

CHABRIER

Chabrier was a Southern Frenchman; he was born in 1841. His mother was fond of music and gaiety, and he inherited her temperament. At fifteen he was brought to Paris. He entered the Civil Service, but all the time enjoyed a high private reputation as an astonishingly brilliant pianist. He also spent many hours in association with the literary men of the Capital, especially the Symbolist Verlaine; he was enthusiastic about the Impressionist School of Painting. He was always friendly with the Franck group of musicians.

At thirty-six he produced a Comic Opera, *The Star*, which had a great success. Other similar work followed. Then he became a Wagnerite. He now resigned his government position and became an assistant to Lamoureux (see Vol. III, under d'Indy) in his early Paris Wagner performances. (At a later date he composed a set of quadrilles on themes from *Tristan!*)

His orchestral Rhapsody *España* greatly enhanced his popular reputation, as did also his Opera *Gwendoline*, which was refused by the Paris Opera as 'Wagnerian' but taken up in Brussels and in Germany. *The King in Spite of Himself* (*Le Roi malgré lui*) had a great success at the Paris Opera.

Then a natural excitability became pathological, and still in his early fifties (1894) Chabrier died paralysed.

MASSENET

Massenet was born in 1842, in the Department of Loire. He studied at the Paris Conservatoire, especially under Ambroise Thomas. He won the Prix de Rome.

He had early Opera successes and was appointed to the staff of the Conservatoire. Amongst his pupils was Debussy, who (it will seem strange, doubtless, to many readers who know something of the music of both men[1]) always acknowledged great indebtedness to him. Debussy, it is true, speaks of Massenet as a composer obsessed by the feminine interest of life, but lauds his conception of the true role of the composer. Says he, ' Music ought humbly to give pleasure ; probably there is great beauty possible within these limits. Extreme complexity is the reverse of art. Beauty ought to be sensitive, to offer us an immediate enjoyment, to impose itself upon, or insinuate itself into us without our making any effort to grasp it. Look at Leonardo da Vinci and Mozart. Those are the great artists !' Surely in this saying, and in others like it, Debussy was humanly influenced by the glamour of old friendship. He put the telescope to his blind eye

[1] E. W. remarks perfectly justly that ' there is a good deal of Massenet in some early Debussy, e. g. *The Prodigal Son*'. But see the biographical sketch of Debussy in Vol. III for a suggestion as to that.

and saw none of the insipidity and facile sentimentality that are mingled with the genuine melodic charm of much of Massenet's work.   Perhaps he did Massenet little service when he mentioned Leonardo and Mozart in the same breath as him ; to read Anatole France's *Thaïs* and then to hear Massenet's operatic treatment of it is to receive a shock.   Amongst other operas of Massenet are *Herodias*, *Manon*, *Sappho*, and *Werther*.   His orchestral Suite, *Picturesque Scenes*, has considerable popularity.

Massenet died in 1912.

MESSAGER

Messager was born in 1853 at Montluçon.   He was a pupil of Saint-Saëns.   His chief fame has come from his very tuneful Light Operas and Ballets, some of which are known everywhere.   He has been director at Covent Garden and also at the Paris Opera. Debussy dedicated to him his *Pelléas and Mélisande*, and he was the first to conduct its performance.   He died in 1929.

SULLIVAN

Arthur Seymour Sullivan was born in London in 1842 ; his father was an army bandsman.   His early musical training was received in

Sullivan.

the Chapel Royal Choir.   He was the first to win the Mendelssohn Scholarship, which enabled him to study at the Royal Academy of Music, and then at the Leipzig Conservatoire (where Grieg was a fellow-student). For a time he was a London organist.

On his return from Leipzig he had brought with him his music to *The Tempest*, which, performed at the Crystal Palace when he was twenty, at once gave him a considerable place in the esteem of musical people.   Various compositions followed, but his real life-work began when, in 1867, aged twenty-five, he produced his setting as a Comic Opera, of

Burnand's play, *Cox and Box*. The great series of Comic Operas to libretti of Gilbert followed, which have never, for pure fun, charming melody, skilfully achieved rhythmic variety, piquant orchestration, and essential Englishness, had their equal.

It is sometimes said that Sullivan was entirely English (see for instance Mr. Edward German's article in the *Dictionary of Contemporary Composers*. 'In everything he wrote he betrayed no foreign influence' —such statements are common). True, the English folk-song style played its part in his development, and so did the Purcell-Arne seventeenth–eighteenth-century straightforward, swinging, simple melodic style ; and in the general form and style of the operas something was doubtless learnt from the English Ballad Operas of the eighteenth century. But he learnt from Mozart, from the French Light Opera, and especially, perhaps, from Offenbach. This cannot be denied—and yet it is ! And listen to the tunes in the *Rosamunde* Overture, and consider whether he did not learn something from Schubert. No harm in that ! As Emerson says, 'The greatest genius is the most indebted man.' What is now wanted is a composer who will learn from Sullivan, and provide some more Light Operas on the same high musical level. But he will need another Gilbert.[1]

Sullivan died in 1900.

GLUCK

(Although not coming properly within the period of this volume, Gluck receives a brief notice here, since his work is considered in the chapter on Opera.)

Gluck was born in 1714 near Neumarkt, in Bavaria. He had some musical education at a Jesuit school and continued it in Prague, where he went when about eighteen, and then, in early manhood, in Milan, under Sammartini. From his twenty-seventh year onwards

---

[1] E. W. comments,' " But he will need another Gilbert." Quite so ! No non-Gilbert opera of Sullivan (so far as I know) now keeps the stage, though I cannot myself see any difference in musical quality. To my mind this seems to involve a reconsideration and lower estimate of Sullivan's own gifts.'

he was composing operas, at first for theatres in Italy.   At the age
of forty-one he came to London where, without much success, and

Gluck.

derided by Handel, then omnipotent there,
he wrote several further operas.[1]   In the
Haymarket Theatre he played a 'concerto
on twenty-six drinking glasses, tuned with
spring water, accompanied by the whole
band, being an instrument of his own invention, upon which he performs whatever
may be done on a violin or harpsichord'.

Passing to Paris, he was much influenced
by Rameau's operas, with their dramatic
recitatives, and this tended towards dissatisfaction with the conventional Italian works
in which he had been brought up.   He
continued his composition actively, bringing out opera after
opera, and was rewarded for one produced in Rome by a Papal
knighthood.   For six or seven years he was settled in Vienna, where
Orpheus and Eurydice appeared in 1762.   At Vienna he taught
Marie Antoinette singing.   His *Alcestis* appeared five years later.
(See page 56).

With the help of Marie Antoinette, now Dauphiness of France, he
settled down to make a Paris career.   *Iphigenia in Aulis* appeared
in 1774, the year his now nineteen-year-old patroness became Queen.
This work had a great success.   *Orpheus and Eurydice* (in French),
a re-casting of the former Opera of the same name (in Italian), also
appeared in 1774.   Gluck was now sixty and at the height of fame.
Alcestis was similarly re-cast and *Armida* and *Iphigenia in Tauris*
followed.

During this period Italian opera began to put up a defensive fight
in Paris ; a young composer of reputation, Piccini, a Neapolitan,
was imported and an Italian attempt at a counter-revolution was

[1] E. W. suggests that the legend of Handel's derision rests upon one
recorded quip, at the expense of Gluck's counterpoint (which was never
his strong card).   He also points out that Handel never knew a note of
Gluck's rememberable things.

begun. He, also, became a favourite with Marie Antoinette, and he, also, became her singing master. He, also, produced a host of operas; he, also, composed an *Iphigenia* (the prima donna who took the name part at the first performance was drunk, and the joke circulated that this was ' Iphigénie en Champagne ').

A war of Gluckists and Piccinists broke out, a pamphlet war which sometimes became a war of fists. Piccini, himself, seems to have admired his rival, and when, rich and famous, and after some years' retirement in Vienna, Gluck died, Piccini wished to institute an annual subscription concert in his memory, for, said he, ' opera is as much indebted to Gluck as the French theatre is to Corneille' (cf. Rossini's attempt to get up a subscription for Beethoven, page 143 ; these unexpected admirations do sometimes occur.)

Gluck died in 1787.

PERIOD V

The Romantics as Nationalists

XVIII

THE ROMANTICS AS NATIONALISTS

IT was bound to come, Schumann saw that. In 1843, welcoming a young Danish composer (Gade), he wrote:

It really begins to look as if the nations bordering on Germany desired to emancipate themselves from the influence of German music; this might annoy a German nativist, but it could only appear natural and cheering to the more profound thinker, if he understood human nature. So we see the French-Pole Chopin, Bennett the Englishman, Verhulst the Dutchman, besides the representatives of Hungarian music, giving promise and performance that must lead them to be regarded as most worthy embodiments of the artistic tendencies of their native lands. And though they all seem to regard Germany as their first and favourite teacher of music, we cannot wonder that they try to speak their own musical language to their own nation, without becoming untrue to their former instructor. For no land can yet boast of masters that equal our greatest ones: who will declare the contrary?

In the further North of Europe we also see national tendencies displaying themselves. Lindblad in Stockholm transcribes old folk-songs for us, and even Ole Bull, though by no means a man of the first rank of talent, has tried to naturalize in our country the tones of his own home. Perhaps the appearance of so many distinguished modern poets in Scandinavia has given a powerful impulse to musical talent there, if the artists of that country have not been sufficiently reminded by their lakes, mountains, aurora borealis, and antique runes, that the North may well dare to speak its own language.

Our young composer has also been nourished by the poetry of his fatherland: he knows and loves its poets; old legends and traditions accompanied him on his boyish wanderings, and Ossian's giant harp resounded from the shores of Britain. A decided Northern musical character makes its appearance for the first time in Gade's music, and especially in his *Ossian* overture; but Gade will be the first to acknowledge all that he owes to German masters. They have rewarded the great industry with which he has devoted himself to the study of their works (he knows nearly all, by all) by the gift they bestow on those who remain true to them—the consecration of mastership.[1]

Before we proceed, a few remarks may be made upon Schumann's statement. Let us first take, one by one, the composers he mentions.

i. 'The French-Pole Chopin' did truly contribute notably to the nationalist movement, in his treatment of Polish national dances, the Mazurka and the Polonaise ; and, as will have been gathered from the brief biography of him already given in this volume, in doing so he was genuinely inspired by patriotic feeling.

ii. 'Bennett, the Englishman' (i. e. William Sterndale Bennett, 1816–1875) never attained the greatness expected of him by Mendelssohn and Schumann, nor did he ever very boldly 'emancipate himself from the influence of German music'. The composer, in fact, was crushed by the piano teacher, Royal Academy Principal and Cambridge Professor, to the gain and loss of British music.

iii. 'Verhulst, the Dutchman', a very intimate personal friend of Schumann, had a most successful German and Dutch career, chiefly as conductor, but attained no great position as a composer, and as such is to-day forgotten. Schumann's expectations as to his contemporaries have often been falsified, but that is no fault of his. He could see promise but could not guarantee temperamental and circumstantial conditions favourable to its fulfilment.

iv. By 'the representatives of Hungarian music' he probably alluded chiefly to Liszt, who had, in 1843, published very little that had any Hungarian flavour, but in some of his meetings with Mendelssohn and Schumann may have revealed, possibly in extemporization, his national interests.

[1] From Ritter's translation of Schumann's *Music and Musicians*.

v. Lindblad (1801–78) was a singing teacher and composer, trained in Germany, as every northern composer then was, and prolific as the author of songs to Swedish words with a Swedish tinge in the melodies.

vi. Of Ole Bull (1810–80) something is said on p. 196. He was certainly a very fervent nationalist, both in politics and art.

vii. 'Our young composer,' Gade, after all this eulogy, never fulfilled his nationalistic promise. His German training, so much extolled by the German who is speaking, was too much for him (see pages 173 and 197).

So much by way of commentary on Schumann's article. It is to his credit that, though somewhat dimly, he perceived a tendency that was only to become strongly pronounced in a later generation—that of Grieg, Dvořák, and Mussorgsky, composers whose works he did not live to know. Observe that in Schumann's 'Rules and Maxims for Young Musicians' he advises, 'Listen attentively to all folk-songs; these are a treasure of lovely melody, and will teach you the characteristics of various nations.' Nothing is truer than that national characteristics are expressed in folk-music, and, as national temperaments are very varied, the movement which was to bring into composition the wider use of folk-song themes (or themes modelled on or influenced by folk-song) necessarily brought also an increased melodic and rhythmic variety of subject-matter, and widened and deepened the scope of music.

The Motives—Patriotism and Primitivism

It may be surmised that there are two motives behind every movement towards nationalism in music, the conscious motive of patriotism, and the perhaps less conscious motive of 'back to the land '.   There is, at once, a revolt against foreign 'domination ' and a revolt against overmuch civilization.

Both these motives are of such a character as to be enormously strengthened by the growth of Romanticism.   For one thing, Romanticism in any art means a general throwing off of bonds, and when bonds begin to be thrown off there are pretty sure to be found amongst them both that of foreign domination and that of highly organized development. And, for another thing, the Romantic temper once aroused finds natural and ready food in the glorious past that every country claims and easily moves on to the idea of a glorious national future, patriotism being, in fact, in itself, like mother-love, one of the romantic emotions.

Returning to the suggested motives of nationalism in music, it may then be said that the chief are a wish to be national and a wish to be natural, though, indeed, the fulfilment of the former wish is probably felt to be dependent upon the fulfilment of the latter, for one cannot build afresh without going down to the foundations.

The two dominations in music during the eighteenth and the early part of the nineteenth centuries were the Italian and the German. Roughly speaking, Italy had for some time dominated the world in Opera and Germany had dominated it in Instrumental Music.

With Weber (and, later, with Wagner) Germany threw off the Italian operatic yoke, and now came the time for other nations to throw off both the Italian Operatic yoke and the German Instrumental yoke.

Who are the ' Nationalists ' ?

It is difficult to fix periods in the development of Art. We found that out in trying to fix the epoch of the Romantic in music; musical styles can easily be divided into the Classic and the Romantic, but in the most Classical period the Romantic temper has never been entirely absent, and in the most Romantic period Classical forms often persisted.

And, similarly, it is difficult to fix the epoch of the Nationalistic. Schumann is decidedly a German nationalist, nurtured upon German literature and German music and expressing

intensely the German spirit.   Are we to call Chopin a definite
Nationalist? Perhaps not, though, as already said, his Mazurkas
and Polonaises, at any rate, are the expression of an ardent
patriotic faith by means of a distinctly national idiom.   If by
Nationalism in music, at this period, we mean, more than anything else, Anti-Germanism, then by such a definition Chopin
was, indeed, the first greatly successful nineteenth-century
Nationalist.

But a group of somewhat later composers of various nations
are as a rule intended when we speak of the Nationalist Movement in music—Smetana and Dvořák in Bohemia ; Grieg in
Norway ; Balakiref, Borodin, Mussorgsky, and Rimsky-Korsakof in Russia ; and Albéniz, Granados, and Falla in
Spain.   These men, more clearly and decidedly and consistently than any predecessors or contemporaries, show us the
national application of the Romantic spirit.

Political Influences

It is impossible to dissect out and separately exhibit all the
closely interwoven nerves and muscles of a complex artistic
organization, and in the study of Nationalism in music we find
the complexity to be extreme.   Literary and political developments have their part.   Amongst the former may be instanced
the growing study of national legend and folk-poetry, amongst
the latter the widespread desire for political freedom that
found expression, as the first half of the century neared its
close, in such risings as those which re-established a republic
in France, drove the Pope out of Rome, massacred the Austrians in the streets of Milan, and snatched Sicily from the
crown of Naples.   In the years 1848–9, not only were these
things happening, but Hungary was rebelling against Austria
and Croatia against Hungary ; there was a revolution in
Saxony in which Wagner was actively concerned ; there was
an insurrection in Posen.   Schleswig-Holstein was rebelling
against Denmark and Smith O'Brien's Army of 'the Irish

Republic' was yielding to a posse of fifty constables in a cabbage garden in Tipperary.

All this constituted the most general outburst of national feeling that the world had ever seen. Everybody seemed to be engaged either in shaking off somebody else's rule or else in opposing the shaking off of one's own. There is no need to try to relate all this very closely to the growth of National feeling and the increased use of National idiom, but there is obviously a connexion—whether one considers that political revolt inspired artistic revolt, or (perhaps on the whole more reasonably) that the two revolts were different expressions of the same surging resolve to attain national freedom.[1]

Literary Influences

As for the growing interest in folk-legend and poetry just mentioned, that in itself is too ample and too complex a movement to be described here in detail. Perhaps British example had a good deal to do with the stimulating of such a movement.

In 1765, Bishop Percy had rescued a manuscript from the hands of the servant who made the fires—a collection, in seventeenth-century handwriting, of national ballads. He published it with other similar material—to the scorn of his friend Dr. Johnson. It soon fell into neglect in Britain, but its contents were translated and imitated in Germany by Bürger, who thus became the very founder of the German Romantic literary movement, and in turn inspired Scott, Coleridge, and others who became the leaders of the Romantic movement in Britain.

[1] It is interesting to note one direct incidental connexion between politics and music. Verdi's name, in 1848-9, became the symbol of Italian patriotism, its letters being perceived to give the initials of the cry, 'Vittoria Emmanuele Rè d'Italia'. One could cry, 'Viva Verdi', with the thought of a cunning *double-entendre*. At the first performance of the composer's opera, *The Battle of Legnano*, at the Argentina Theatre in Rome (January 1849), every piece was welcomed with this cry.

Coleridge's *Ancient Mariner*, Goethe's *Erl King* and *King in Thule*, and Heine's *Lorelei*, and the many other ballad-imitations of the period are the result of Percy's publication, and so are Scott's collection of *The Minstrelsy of the Scottish Border* (1802), and similar collections of actual folk-poetry. We may almost say that whatever has since then been done either in the way of collecting the poetry of the simple people of any country or in that of writing poetry in a simple folk-style is due to Percy. Wordsworth said, ' I have already stated how much Germany is indebted to this Percy's *Reliques*, and, for our own country, its poetry has been absolutely redeemed by it. I do not think there is an able writer of verse at the present moment that would not be proud to acknowledge his obligation to the *Reliques* ; I know that it is so with my friends, and as for myself, I am happy to make a public avowal of my own.'

Roughly speaking, we may say that whatever is natural, uninvolved, and unforced in the poetry of the nineteenth century, as contrasted with the general formality and frequently undue artificiality of that of the eighteenth, is due to the peasant influence which was brought into literature by Percy's re-discovery of the folk-mind.[1]

The Folk-Music Discovery

Naturally with this went a refertilizing of music. Poetry, Music, and Dancing are the three folk-arts,[2] and once the folk were rediscovered as poets it did not take very long to rediscover them as composers of songs and dance tunes. George Thomson of Edinburgh collected the melodies of Scotland,

---

[1] E. W. thinks I here overstate the case.

[2] A folk-drama, once extensive, now lingers weakly in our remote districts in the form of the Easter Play of St. George and such things. Folk painting and sculpture may almost be said never to have existed, unless the church frescoes and statuary of the middle ages be considered as such.

Ireland, and Wales, and engaged Pleyel, Haydn, Beethoven, Bishop and others to write accompaniments for them, and, where necessary, poets like Burns and Scott, Joanna Baillie, and Peter Pindar to prepare the words.   Other nations initiated similar movements.[1]

The folk-musician began to come into his own; there was amongst the composers of many countries the cry, already suggested, of 'Back to the Land!' and not merely that, but 'Back to *our* Land!' The Wordsworthian love of the language of men 'in humble and rustic life' began to have its counterpart in music.   In every country of Europe cultured people began to realize that, after all the court and town life of music during the previous two centuries or so, something was now to be gained by a fresh contact with the soil.

And when one gets in contact with the soil national differences begin to be perceptible.   In the main the manners and diet of the great hotels of the world's capitals are standardized, whilst those of the village ale-houses and cafés are national and local.   Everything we have in literature or music comes originally from the folk, and it is good occasionally to go back to the folk, and regain their simple directness and their local colourings.[2]   If the nations of Europe had grown up in sealed compartments we may imagine that each would have developed its own art music.   But they have not so grown up; at one time the musical style of Flanders had overflowed into the other compartments; at another that of England, at another that of Italy, and at another that of Germany.   And so came into existence a cosmopolitanism, latterly very German-tinged, which needed correction from time to time, if individuals of

[1] The English curiously lagged; it seems to have remained for Lucy Broadwood, Frank Kidson, Baring Gould, Cecil Sharp, Vaughan Williams and other enthusiasts of the late nineteenth and early twentieth centuries to realize that there existed a fine repertory of folk-tune in England.

[2] E. W. protests, 'If "folk" here means "peasantry" then I fear I don't agree.'   (And the worst of it is, it *does*!—P. A. S.)

different nationalities were to be enabled to develop themselves on the lines really congenial to their natures.[1]

The course of the movement in several different countries may now be briefly sketched.

Bohemia

Bohemia lost its independence to the Habsburgs in 1620 and regained it only in 1918, as a part of Czecho-Slovakia. For long the Bohemian language was prohibited ; the growth of Bohemia's literature was stopped and its religion under a ban. In music it had something individual in the folk-song and the Hussite hymns, but conditions were not favourable to any national development in the art, and Bohemian composers had to adopt German and Italian fashions in music. Prague as an operatic centre was the friendly host of Gluck and of Mozart. Its opera-house had, indeed, been established as early as 1725. National aspirations either in political life or in art were, however, discouraged.

In the revolutionary year, 1848, an attempted rising was

---

[1] E. W. (who at this point of his reading of my proofs begins to be a little obstreperous) exclaims, ' Might not somewhere or other a few lines be added, perhaps, on the far from unimportant question of plagiarism ? All composers whose names are known have rights that are respected, but many folk-enthusiasts seem somehow to consider it more morally commendable to get one's thematic material out of a public-house than out of one's own head—and it is so much easier not to have to bother to invent a tune for oneself.'

To this one might reply—The ' rights ' alluded to are *not* always ' respected '; consider, for instance, the many cases (e. g. in Brahms) where a long composition is nothing but a string of ' Variations on a Theme of ——'. Further, the practice of basing compositions on folk (or ' public-house') themes is ancient and reputable. The Elizabethan virginalists did it. Haydn did it in his symphonies, &c. ; so sometimes did Beethoven, as Stanford and others have pointed out.

No doubt E. W. would have some rejoinder to make to this, but the Author being chairman is able to close the debate !

quickly suppressed, but in 1860 a new constitution was won, the Czech language was made compulsory in schools, and, though independence had not yet come, an encouraging measure of national recognition was gained. A musical development took place, including the founding of Singing Societies (still a feature of social life), and of a National Opera-House in Prague.

The Bohemian composer, Smetana (1824–84), then engaged in Sweden, returned. He produced a series of thoroughly Bohemian operas—Bohemian both in literary and in musical subject matter. The one best known outside Bohemia is *The Bartered Bride* (1866), a village farce (for so it may almost be called), with a stirring piece of fresh-air music as an overture that is frequently heard from every concert platform in the world. The most truly characteristic passages in this are in exactly similar style to Dvořák's *Slavonic Dances*, a typical example of which is given on p. 172. His *The Brandenburgers in Bohemia* (1863), and *Dalibor* (1868) treat subjects from Czech history. His *Libuse* (1872) has for heroine the mythical foundress of Prague. His *Two Widows* (1874) is a comedy of Czech country life. His *The Secret* (1878) depicts life in a small Czech town. His other two operas, *The Kiss* (1876) and *The Devil's Wall* (1882), have also nationalistic subjects.

Smetana deliberately abstained from the writing of symphonies and the like, maintaining that a new school must refrain from the adoption of settled academic forms. The new form of the Symphonic Poem, inaugurated by his friend, Liszt, appealed to him, however, and he wrote a series of such Poems, entitled *My Fatherland*—(1) 'Vysehrad' (a mythical castle of Bohemia); (2) 'Vltava' (i.e. the river we know as the Moldau); (3) 'Sarka' (a legendary maiden, commemorated in the name of a valley near Prague); (4) 'From Bohemia's Groves and Meadows'; (5) 'Tabor' (the Taborites are warriors of national legend); (6) 'Blanik' (the Czech mountain in which sleeps an army ready to sally out when the moment comes).

The influence of Czech folk-tune is seen in the themes from which Smetana develops his works, and he made some attempt at the artistic treatment of that popular dance, which arose in Bohemia in the early years of the nineteenth century and then spread all over the world, the Polka. He offers, in all respects, a good example of the Nationalistic branch of the Romantic School.

Smetana's younger colleague, Dvořák (1841–1904), was much influenced by him. He soaked himself in Bohemian folk-music, and then (as a rule) made use not of actual folk-music themes, but of original themes in the folk-music style and spirit. The very titles of a number of Dvořák's works show his nationalistic sympathies, e. g. *Heirs of the White Mountains* (a Cantata) ; *Bohemian Peasants' Hymn* ; Three *Slavonic Rhapsodies*; *Slavonic Dances*; the Overture, *My Home*; piano-duets, *From the Bohemian Forests*.

Dvořák hated the necessity of publishing his works in Germany, with no indication of their Czech origin.[1] He made use in his instrumental works of two distinctively Czech forms, the *Dumka* (a lament, dirge, or elegy) and the *Furiant* (a lively dance). These, he realized, were capable of being used respectively as slow movement and as scherzo of pieces of the sonata type.

Brahms said of Dvořák : ' He 's never at a loss for an idea ', and this is true ; moreover the ideas have freshness, and it is impossible to hear the best works of Dvořák, as it is to hear the best works of Grieg, without being grateful for the nationalistic impulses which sent certain composers to their

[1] When at Cambridge, in 1891, to receive his Hon. Mus. Doc. (and to conduct his Fourth Symphony and his *Stabat Mater*) he indignantly refused a souvenir programme offered him, since in it he appeared not as ' Mr.' but as ' Herr ' Dvořák (C.M.C. gives me this anecdote on the authority of the late Dr. Chas. Wood of Cambridge).

native folk-music for inspiration and so brought into music a welcome novelty and variety.

Novák (born 1870) and Suk (1874–1935), the former Dvořák's successor as Professor of Composition at the Prague Conservatoire and the latter his son-in-law, are amongst the later representatives of the Czech national school.

For music which simply shouts 'Bohemia!' at you, we cannot do better than turn to those immensely popular *Slavonic Dances*, originally written as Piano Duets, by which Dvořák's position was established. Here is the beginning of a typical one (Op. 46, No. 8), one of the most ebullient.

Some of these Slav Dances are extraordinarily lazy and elegant (though without the artificiality which 'elegant' perhaps suggests). But most of them are of this high-spirited type. Note in this one, (1) the great speed; (2) the violent syncopation; (3) the contrast in the hurtling force of the opening and the buoyant flight of what follows—one might perhaps think of the career of an express train and the course of a greyhound; (4) the simplicity, the persistent reiteration, directly taken from primitive dance-music.

Scandinavia

Gade (1817–90), a Dane, was one of several Scandinavian composers with nationalistic aspirations. But in those days the thing was to go to the Leipzig Conservatoire for training, and this meant to return Germanized.

The short-lived Richard Nordraak (1842–66), a Norwegian, was more genuinely national. Edvard Grieg met him in 1864, when they were respectively twenty-one and twenty-two, and said of the meeting, 'The scales fell from my eyes; it was through him that I learnt to know the popular songs of the North and even my own nature. We swore to keep clear of the effeminate Scandinavianism of Gade, mingled as it is with Mendelssohnianism, and we set out enthusiastically on the new road.' Nordraak and Grieg founded in Copenhagen the Euterpe Musical Society for the performance of Scandinavian works.

Gade and Grieg were always closely intimate, and at first Gade approved of Grieg, but when Grieg's second Violin and

Piano Sonata was performed, Gade came round to the artist's
room and said, 'Dear Grieg, the next you must really make
less Norwegian', to which Grieg replied, 'Dear Professor, the
next will be more so'.

The titles of many of Grieg's minor works would be enough
in themselves to show us his thoroughly nationalist aim—his
Norwegian Peasant March, his *Norwegian Bridal Procession*,
his *Wedding Day at Troldhaugen*, his *Norwegian Dances and
Folk-Songs arranged for Piano*, his *Symphonic Dance on Norwegian Airs*, &c. His incidental music for his countryman,
Ibsen's, play *Peer Gynt* is intensely Norwegian.

Grieg insisted that he was a Norwegian, not a Scandinavian,
'I am not an exponent of Scandinavian music, but only of
Norwegian. The national characteristics of the peoples, the
Norwegians, the Swedes, and the Danes are wholly different
and their music differs just as much.' (Letter to *New York
Times*.) When Norway was at length separated from Sweden
in 1905, Grieg wrote, 'What has happened in our country this
year seems like a fairy tale. The hopes and longing of my
youth have been fulfilled. I am deeply grateful that I was
privileged to see this.'

Yet Grieg was the protagonist not merely of Norwegian
nationalism but of nationalism in general. He had soaked
himself in Norwegian folk-tune, not so much to be enabled to
use it as it stood (which he rarely did) as to acquire its spirit
and idiom, and when Percy Grainger, in 1907, showed him his
collection of English folk-tune he immersed himself in that,
too, afterwards expressing the opinion, 'English folk-song is
worthy of the honour of being lifted on to the level of Art,
thus creating an independent English music. The folk-songs
will doubtless be capable of forming the basis of a national
style as they have done in other lands, those of the greatest
musical culture not excepted.' He was deeply impressed
with the earnestness and energy with which the English Folk-
Song Society carried out its objects, and, altogether, showed

himself (as Dvořák did) a convinced believer not merely in the
nationalistic movement but also in what has above several
times been called the 'Back to the Land' movement. He
resented the saying of some German critic, 'Grieg never remembered the ocean, but stuck to the fjord', and well he might,
for if he did 'stick to the fjord', in such a piece as his Piano
Concerto, he drew all the world into the fjord with him.[1]

A few typical turns of Griegian-Norwegian idiom may be
quoted.

It would be hard to find a more characteristic example of
this than the popular *Norwegian Bridal Procession.* In the
very opening section (in which, indeed, the whole piece is
crystalized), hardly one important feature is unrepresented,
excepting Grieg's very personal harmony, and even of that one
simple phase may be considered to be present.

---

[1] A typical anti-nationalist criticism is that of Riemann, 'It is to be
regretted that Grieg has imposed on his art the limits of national
characterization, and that instead of the universal language, he speaks
only a local dialect'. That stick would do to beat Sir Walter Scott or
Dickens ; theirs, too, is a 'local dialect'.

First, there is throughout the well-known Griegian open-fifth in the bass, derived from the playing of the Hardanger fiddle.[1]

Secondly, there is, at the end of each of the two sentences which make up this little paragraph of the tune, the typical little bursting into flower, which takes the form of sometimes a triplet, sometimes a quintuplet, sometimes, as here, a sextuplet. The very work which offended Gade (see page 174) has a notable example of this 'flowering', in the chief tune of the Second Movement. Where but in Grieg would one find such a phrase ending in such a way?

[1] It is an attractive picture, Grieg in a boat with his friend Rontgen and a player of the Hardanger Fiddle, Grieg listening with delight, nodding his head to the rhythm and holding in his hand a cup of wine, which every now and again he offers to the fiddler with a 'Skal'; exclaiming from time to time, ' *This is Norway !* '

Finally, there is the drop from the seventh to the fifth of the scale, as marked at *a*, or from the third to the keynote, as at *b*. These drops often go with the 'flowering', but here is a different, equally characteristic, instance, from the First Subject of the Piano Concerto.

Other Norwegian composers have been Kjerulf (1815–68), Svendsen (1840–1911), and Sinding (1856–1941). (Brief references to the Norwegian violinist, Ole Bull, a great inspirer of the Norwegian school, who founded a National Theatre at Bergen and tried to found a Norse Conservatoire at Christiania, will be found on pages 161 and 196.)

In spite of what Grieg says, the differences between Norwegian, Swedish, and Danish music are not so great as to come within the scope of this book. Finnish music will, however, be found treated separately on pp. 188.

Russia

Russia had always teemed with music—folk-songs and folk-dances, in various styles in the various parts of the vast empire, often with an oriental tinge ; and the music of the Greek

Church was of course prevalent everywhere. Opera and orchestral music were only heard in the larger cities; up to the earlier part of the nineteenth century the opera was usually Italian and the orchestral music German.

The rise of national feeling that followed Napoleon's retreat from Moscow in 1812 had at length an effect upon music, and in 1836 there was issued a nationalist musical manifesto— GLINKA'S opera *A Life for the Czar* was heard at St. Petersburg. It was the deliberate national effort of a composer trained by Italian and German teachers, and thus equipped with the current technique, reverting for his literary and musical subject-matter to the national legends and the folk-music by which in early life in the depths of the Russian countryside he had often been stirred. In its first forty-three years it had 500 performances, and when its fiftieth year came to be celebrated every opera-house in Russia performed it.

Nine years younger than Glinka was DARGOMIJSKY. He stands midway between the founder of Russian nationalism and the later group of downright nationalists of whom we are to hear in a moment as ' The Five '. Glinka directly influenced Dargomijsky, advised him, and helped him in his studies. The early works were not Russian in theme. Then, in *Russalka* appeared an operatic setting of a Russian legend. The poem of this was by the national poet, Pushkin, as was that of *The Stone Guest* which succeeded. Not very strongly Russian perhaps, in some features of his musical style, Dargomijsky yet went to his own national legends and literature for his subjects, and he was at least very anti-Italian in discarding in a great measure set melody, well-turned songs, and the like.

Followed the group of ' THE FIVE ', who, banded together in the interests of musical nationalism, imbibed in varying degrees the notions of Glinka and Dargomijsky. They were:

Balakiref.	Mussorgsky.
Cui.	Rimsky-Korsakof.
Borodin.	

Biographical sketches of all these composers will be found at the end of the present chapter. Their activities may be said to have extended over the period from 1857, when Balakiref wrote his Fantasia on Three Russian Themes, for Piano and Orchestra, to 1918, when Cui, the last survivor of the band, died. We may then put the working life of this school at about sixty years.

Most of these composers were born and reared in the Russian countryside, and in early life soaked their receptive minds in Russian folk-lore and folk-song. Several of them were ardent folk-tune collectors, and published the results of their researches. They were greatly affected by Russian literature (especially by Pushkin) and by Russian legend. They took their opera plots almost entirely from Russian history or Russian fairy-tale, and they wrote orchestral tone-poems on similar themes. Their folk-tune interest was not confined to the products of their own people. Glinka had studied the national music of Spain and based two orchestral pieces upon it (see page 201), Balakiref wrote a Spanish Overture, similarly based, Rimsky-Korsakof wrote an Orchestral Fantasia on Serbian tunes. The oriental strain in Russian life and art is seen in the literary themes and musical style of many works, such as Balakiref's piano fantasia, *Islamey*, and his symphonic poem, *Thamar*, and Rimsky-Korsakof's Symphonic Suite, *Scheherazade*, and his Opera, *The Golden Cockerel*, to mention, almost at random, a few of the works most likely to have been heard by readers of this book.

The crudity and directness, the rapid and violent contrasts of feeling that are characteristic of the Russian temperament are often represented in the works of these composers. They were Russian not merely by intention to be Russian but also by intention to be sincere, which necessarily came to the same thing.

Russian as they were they could not, of course, have done what they did had they not been born into a period when

the Romantic Movement was in full swing. It was the pianistic
genius of Liszt that made it possible for Balakiref to write his
Islamey, and study of the 'programmatic' compositions of
Liszt and Berlioz that made it possible for Borodin to write
his *In the Steppes of Central Asia*, with its strings of approaching horses and camels, its desert immensities, and its army,
whose cries and songs are at last lost in the distance. Romantic
expression in music, 'programmatic' expression and national
expression are all really parts of the one endeavour to attain a
more definite self-revelation.

After the composers just mentioned came TCHAIKOVSKY,
Russian in feeling yet more cosmopolitan in the forms he
adopted, and then, with Glazounof, Liadov, Liapounov,
Rachmaninov, Catoire, Glière, Medtner, and others, the
specifically Russian character, though still often present,
gradually weakened. Younger men, Scriabin and Stravinsky
(to be considered later), were still Russian, the former especially in his open expression of violent emotion, and the latter
especially in barbaric rhythms, use of the folk-element, orientalism and vivid colour. Taking it for all in all the Russian
School has given the world the most definite and the largest-
scale demonstration of the vivifying effect of nationalism that
it has yet seen.

The Russian spirit is well expressed in Mussorgsky's prelude to *Pictures at an Exhibition* (see page 205). This
Movement binds the various Pictures together, recurring
in varied forms. It is called *Promenade*, presumably representing the Composer's passing from one picture to another in
the Exhibition. The character of Russian music is one of the
hardest to analyse. There are in it uncompromising directness, simplicity, solidity, even squareness, though generally
without awkwardness. Such characteristics in the melody of
this example are tellingly emphasized by the accompaniment.
Note also the typical rhythm—plain but unhackneyed.

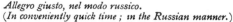

etc.

It would not be right to leave the subject of the birth and growth of a Russian musical art without mention of the business man of the movement, Belaief (see page 207), who, by the foundation of concert enterprises, the offering of prizes for composition, the organization of a publishing firm, and the close personal support of individual composers of promise, enabled his countrymen to achieve more than would otherwise have been within their power.[1]

[1] E. E. makes some general criticisms of my treatment of the Russian composers, in considering which it will be necessary for the reader to consult not only the present chapter but also the biographical notices which follow. He says, 'As for Mussorgsky, I do not think your treatment is at all commensurate with the immense significance which he has acquired as a forerunner of modern music. With regard to other Russian composers you fall into the common error of ascribing their Orientalism to racial heredity. The true explanation is the custom of spending holidays in the Crimea (where there were wandering bands of Tartar musicians) and, still more important, in the Caucasus, where some of them used to get native musicians to play to them. The Orientalism of Balakiref's *Thamar* and Rimsky-Korsakof's *Scheherazade* is entirely Caucasian—not innate but acquired like other folk-music by travelling. So are the " Persian" dances in Mussorgsky's *Khovanshchina*.'

Spain

Spain is one of those countries that possess a very distinctively individual folk-music. Glinka's visit to Spain in 1845-6 (see page 201) had important consequences. He observed that Italian music ruled in cultured circles there as in Russia, yet that the one country, as the other, possessed a marvellously varied and abundant folk-music.[1]

The Spanish musicians' appreciation of their country's own folk-art has come later. In 1850 an association was formed to revive the Zarzuela, the traditional popular form of one-act comic opera. PEDRELL (1841-1922) collected folk-tunes, studied the works of the Spanish composers of the contrapuntal period, and as composer and teacher was active in awakening his countrymen's interest in their musical inheritance. Tenets of his were that every country's art music should be based upon its folk music and that national opera is national song developed on the scale of drama, i.e. is popular song raised to a higher power. ISAAC ALBÉNIZ (1860-1909), a fine pianist, and as such a pupil of Liszt, wrote Zarzuelas, Operas, and, especially, piano pieces, in which he made great play with the characteristic rhythms and melodic turns of various parts of Spain. The national instrument, the Guitar, had its influence upon the rhythms, harmonies, and melodies of composers.

GRANADOS, TURINA, and FALLA followed, and composed music every phrase of which was so distinctly national that heard in isolation it could not be taken as the product of any other country.

The due development of a Spanish musical art has been delayed by a musical inertia amongst the cultured classes, which to a large extent still remains.

The result of this has been twofold—Spain has been rather late in making her contribution to the national movement in

[1] It has been pointed out by Calvocoressi that the oriental element in both Spanish and Russian folk-music is a link probably to some extent accounting for Glinka's ready appreciation of the former.

music, and now that she has begun to do so what she contributes is often somewhat primitive, consisting of an incessant repetition of those highly rhythmic fragments of tune so characteristic of Spanish folk music. After her vivid and eventful history she is so many-sided, and these many sides are so clearly reflected in her music, that musical illustration cannot in this volume go beyond a mere suggestion of characteristics.

We may well pass over certain obvious, though strongly individual, dance-forms, such as the Tango,[1] which have popularly done duty with us as representing Spanish music. True, these *are* representative; but Spanish music has more remarkable, more subtle, more complex features than these. (There are musical distinctions, just as there are racial distinctions, between even the various districts of Spain; but we cannot follow these up in this brief sketch.)

One of the most important facts in Spanish music is that dance and song are almost inseparable—each element is almost always present. This is well seen in the *Seven Spanish Popular Songs* (*Siete Canciones populares Españolas*) which Falla has edited; indeed, in one of these there are a greater number of bars of the dance element than of the actual voice part, and in almost all the two elements are either combined or alternated. In fact, almost all Spanish song is either in recitative-like manner or in strongly marked dance rhythm. At the same time, in our ideas of Spanish music we have taken too much account of the dance element, too little of the song element.

Falla tells us that there are three main, vital influences from outside under which Spanish music has come: they are that of Byzantine church music, that of the Moorish invaders, and that of the gipsy settlers.

The chief results of these influences are (1) the use of many modes and scales which come from the East (and a few of which coincide with some of our Western pre-seventeenth-century modes); (2) the use of finer and more numerous

---

[1] Properly, Argentine.

tonal distinctions than the mere twelve semitones of our
Western octave; and (3) the use of more or less rhapsodical
turns, which, however, are, as Falla says,[1] 'employed only
in determinate moments as outbursts or expansions induced by
the emotional force of the text', and which, therefore, we must
regard 'more as expansive vocal inflexions than as ornamental
flourishes, although they take this last aspect when the music
is reduced to the geometrical intervals of the tempered scale'.

The second of these three points obviously cannot be shown
in our modern Western notation. But of many possible
examples of the influences of the first and third points in
Falla's own music, the *Song of Dolorous Love* (*Canción del
Amor Dolido*) from his Ballet, *Love, the Magician* (*El Amor
Brujo*) seems to illustrate fairly well the first and third points.
(Notice, in view of what has been said above, the presence of
singing in Falla's Ballets.) Throughout, a very characteristic
mode, with the scale of C, D flat, E flat, F, G, A, B flat, is
used consistently (though with some flat A's in the accompaniment and some accidentals in the final bars of this). Here
are the final bars of this Song. (The music of the first two
bars of this extract has already been reiterated three times.)

There remains to be mentioned the most prevalent, most obvious of all features of Spanish music—the influence of the guitar. Every one is familiar with the Spanish guitar-strumming manner; what is less recognized is its important effect on harmony.

A single bar must suffice as an example of Falla's development of this feature. It is from *The Three-Cornered Hat* (*El Sombrero de tres picos*), one of the former Russian Ballet's most popular productions. On this one bar Falla bases a whole passage of a dozen bars or so.

France

The music of France has been only very slightly influenced by the folk element.

French national characteristics have expressed themselves in their varying ways, with the effect of producing a surprising variety of musical feeling, such as the romantic Catholic religious mysticism of FRANCK and D'INDY, the tuneful sentimentalism of MASSENET, the verism of CHARPENTIER, the grace and apt melody of FAURÉ, the delicate impressionism of DEBUSSY, the light, well-turned wit of RAVEL, and so forth. The world's musical publics of to-day, though acquainted with a great deal of French music, have not, however, through it arrived at any clear conception as to the characteristics of French folk-song or folk-dance. Without hearing an actual specimen of folk-tune the concert-goer gets from later nineteenth-century Norwegian, Russian, Bohemian, and Spanish composers a very good idea of its characteristics in the countries of those composers, so that he would easily put into words a few significant facts concerning those characteristics. He could not do this for France.

A national movement dating from about 1870 has been the revolt against German influences and especially against Wagnerism ; but that is negative, and the positive side of French nationalistic musical feeling is less definitely recognizable by the uninstructed because that feeling has never been focussed by any ' back-to-the-land ' attempt, such as that of the countries previously mentioned.

Britain

Britain, though it has at least four very distinctive types of folk-music, the English, Scottish, Irish, and Welsh, has until very lately contributed little to the nationalistic movement in music, except by helping to supply the initial impulse by the production of one of the first great collections of folk-poetry (see page 166). Once the Elizabethan and Stuart periods were over, British composers ceased to show the possession of any strong individuality and consequently of any real nationality. Probably Schumann's allusion to Sterndale Bennett as one of those non-Germans who gave 'promise and performance that must lead them to be regarded as most worthy embodiments of the artistic tendency of their native lands', and as 'trying to speak their own musical language to their own nations', was due partly to his wish to make up a varied list as support of his general thesis and partly to his non-recognition in those early days of what nationalistic expression in music really meant. , Schumann could recognize the difference between the Italian and the German mind in music, he could hear the Pole speaking in a Chopin Polonaise, or the Hungarian Gipsy in a Liszt Rhapsody, and a very little deviation from accepted German idiom in Gade or Bennett would make him, in his inexperience, think that he had got the authentic utterance of the national spirit of the countries from which those composers came.

The real development of British nationalism in music came a good deal later, when PARRY the Englishman (1848–1918), MACKENZIE the Scotsman (1847–1935), and STANFORD the Irishman (1852–1924), in many of their works, made use of the musical folk-idioms of their respective countries and gave national and personal tendencies a freer range. The younger school, VAUGHAN WILLIAMS, HOLST, BAX, and others have gone still farther in the same direction, and there has even, at times, seemed to be a danger that devotion to folk-theme would, by excess, drift into a mere mannerism. The theory attributed to Pedrell (page 182) that every country's art-music should be based upon its folk-music arose independently in Britain and was very strongly maintained there during the first quarter of the present century. ELGAR was a dissentient from this theory, adopting less obvious means of expressing his national feeling.

Finland

Reference has been made (page 165) to the part which political discontents played in the strengthening of national feeling and the bringing of it to a musical expression. Finland, a country of mixed Eastern and Western stock, with a mythology and folk-poetry of its own, conquered by Sweden in the twelfth and thirteenth centuries and ceded to Russia in the early nineteenth century, maintained its desire for political independence and suffered cruelly under foreign rule.

SIBELIUS (born 1865) has in his music strongly expressed the sense of struggle and of gloom, as well as that of bold determination. His music combines the romantic tenderness and the vigour of the North, and without using actual folk themes he has been much influenced by the folk-melody and folk-rhythm of his native land. The literary subjects upon which he has based some of his work have been strongly national. The work of the Finnish poet-scholar, Lönnrot (1802–84), in collecting from the life of the peasantry the scattered lines of the great national epic, the *Kalevala*, was one of the results of the folk-lore movement started by Bishop Percy in the previous century, and it had its part in bringing about a national music for Finland. 'It is hardly too much to say that Sibelius's music seldom gets away from the atmosphere of legend and rune. In idea, rhythm, turn of melody, colour of thought and orchestration, he keeps within touch of the magic halo which surrounds the *Kalevala* . . . the poem which sets forth the mythical history of the Finnish people, just as the *Nibelungenlied* sets forth the mythical history of the Teutonic nations' (D. H., in *Grove's Dictionary*, 2nd edition) .

Italy

Italy has remained very much outside the nationalist musical movement of the later nineteenth and early twentieth centuries. In the sixteenth and seventeenth centuries, Italy made a wonderful contribution to the music of that church which has its headquarters in her capital. At the same period, largely out of her Renaissance poetry grew up the Madrigal. Towards the end of this period, the Opera and the Oratorio were introduced by the Italians—with the new vocal form of the Recitative. Then, as already recounted in Chapter XVII, the Italian love of vocal display and of easily understandable melody triumphed over the attempt to be dramatic, and Italian opera, a very national product, overspread the civilized world. In the opera of the eighteenth and early nineteenth centuries Italy was very plainly expressing some of her national preferences. In a sense, she needed no national musical movement ; it was rather the other nations that needed movements of rebellion against her domination.

A definite national musical movement came about in Italy in the first quarter of the twentieth century, when such men as Pizzetti (born 1880), Casella (1883–1947), and Respighi (1879–1936) initiated a demonstration against the one-sidedness and insularity of Italian musical activities, pleading for a more dramatic opera, a more definitely poetic song-style, and, above all, a cessation of the neglect of instrumental music in a nation that had once boasted a Corelli, a Domenico Scarlatti, a Vivaldi, and, through them and others, had exercised an influence upon Bach and the then rising German School.

Germany

In Germany the conscious nationalist movement was almost confined to a demonstration against Italian Opera (see Chapter XVII and the biographical sketches of Weber and Wagner). In Bach's time German composers had absorbed the influences of the Italian and French instrumental schools of that day, and had developed a national school of instrumental composition that was strong enough for its influence to overspread all other countries that were interested in instrumental music. Except in Opera, then, the Germans were, at the opening of the period with which this volume is concerned, able to cultivate a style in consonance with their national temperament, and to do it without any beating of drums and flourishing of banners. They were nationalists (consider Schumann's very German type of romance), but hardly consciously so. They were in music a governing race and not a rebellious province, and so far from the later nineteenth-century German political nationalist movement (which bound its petty states into one great confederation and worked up feeling towards the 1914 War) stimulating national feeling in music, it rather used music as one of its existing proofs of the virtue of German national Kultur and as one of the justifications of the cry of 'Deutschland über alles'.[1]

There is no sign even now of any German nationalist movement in music, and indeed no such movement has been needed, since, in the main, German music during the twentieth century has continued faithfully to represent the German temperament.

Hungary

The population of Hungary is, of course, very mixed. What we often call Hungarian music is probably a blend of the music of two races, Magyar and Gipsy, the latter being specially responsible for the elaborate melodic embellishments that characterize much of it. Liszt's twelve Hungarian Rhapsodies are based upon Hungarian melodies of various types. There are Hungarian influences in a good many works of non-Hungarians such as Haydn and Schubert. Brahms's Hungarian Dances give a very artistic treatment of Hungarian dance tunes. The Rákóczy March of Berlioz is a treatment of a tune which celebrated a national hero-king. Béla Bartók

---

[1] Properly, 'Deutschland über alles' means 'Germany *beyond* everything', not 'Germany *on top of* the world'. See its original use in von Fallersleben's poem of the eighteen-forties, where it is simply a finely worded aspiration for the unity of the German people, then politically divided. E. W. suggests that I make this clear.

(1881–1945) made a great collection of the folk-tunes of his native country; he published many of them for practical use and based compositions on some of them. At the period with which this chapter is chiefly concerned Hungary was prominently represented in music solely by Liszt.

LEADING NATIONALIST COMPOSERS
SMETANA

The Bohemian national school found its first great protagonist in Frederick Smetana (pronounced *Smet*ana), born in 1824 at Leitomischl, where his father was a brewer. Prague was the centre of his activities. He studied there, under Proksch, an able musician, and established himself there as a fashionable piano teacher. When the National Theatre was founded he became connected with it, at length becoming its principal conductor (1866), and producing there seven Operas of his own of strongly national interest (see page 170 as to their subject-matter). He wrote a series of six Symphonic Poems, with the general title, *My Fatherland*, and other works, and died in an asylum in 1884.

There was an interval of four years during which Smetana was absent in Sweden—as conductor of the Philharmonic Society of Gothenburg.

Smetana belonged to the school of 'The New Music'. He was a follower and friend of Liszt, and adopted wholeheartedly the new Lisztian form, the Symphonic Poem. Wagner to some extent influenced his operatic writing. But he retained his individuality. He himself described his operatic aims as the combination of the simplest melodies with carefully chosen harmonies, the whole work carried out upon a well-considered general scheme, and with a pervading unity throughout, such as would entitle the opera to be looked upon as one great symphony in close relation to a libretto.

Smetana was a good pianist. In addition to the works already mentioned, he wrote a certain amount of Piano Music. He also wrote a good deal of Choral Music. Amongst his Chamber Music is a String Quartet, *From my Life*, which descriptively follows the experience of the composer's career. In the last Movement is a persistent high note which represents the peculiar and very painful form of ear-trouble which overtook him—a symptom of the malady which brought his life to an end.[1] Like Beethoven, Smetana wrote his most mature works with no possibility of ever hearing them.

Smetana's memory is revered amongst the Czechs, and, in 1924, the Centenary of his birth was made the occasion of great national rejoicings.

DVOŘÁK

Dvořák (1841–1904) was born, and in spirit ever remained, a Bohemian peasant. His father was the butcher and publican of

Dvořák.

a village on the Moldau, and he himself began his earning life as a butcher boy.

His interest in music was aroused by his father's zither playing and by what he heard in his village from the travelling bands. He took to singing and to playing the violin, and later got some lessons on piano and organ.

In 1857, when he was sixteen, he went to Prague and became a pupil of the organ school belonging to the Bohemian Church Music Society. To keep himself he played the viola in cafés and the organ in a lunatic

asylum. It was a time of poverty. He lacked money to buy books and music, to hire a piano, to attend concerts. 'As for Mozart and Beethoven, I only just knew that they existed.'

In 1862, when he was twenty-one, a great national event occurred. Smetana returned from his post in Sweden to help to establish the now famous National Theatre of Prague. Dvořák gained admission to the orchestra as a viola player. He spent a good deal of time in composition.

About ten years later he obtained a good position as church organist, gave up orchestral playing, and married. His orchestral

[1] Very similar to a symptom of Schumann's malady.

works began to get a hearing and an opera of his, *King and Collier*, was at last performed at the National Theatre. The Austrian Ministry of Fine Arts now gave him a small pension. Brahms, who was one of the inspectors appointed to examine his compositions, gave him great encouragement and helped him to a publisher. Dvořák now wrote the Slavonic Dances for Pianoforte Duet, the melody and spirit of which caught everybody's attention, so that his name became European.

The *Stabat Mater* made Dvořák known in England, and the various English musical festivals began to give performances of his music under his own conductorship, and sometimes to commission new works.

For three years (1892–5) he was in New York as head of the National Conservatoire. Then he returned to Prague, and a few years later became head of the Conservatoire there.

He died in 1904. An example of his music has been given under 'Bohemia', pages 172–3.

A touch of Negro influence comes into three or four of Dvořák's works as a result of his stay in America. One such work is the popular *New World* Symphony, where, although there are no actual Negro themes, there are a number of themes that suggest the Negro idiom. Dvořák deliberately adopted the view that 'the inspiration for truly national music might be derived from the Negro melodies or Indian chants'. 'What songs belong to the American and appeal more strikingly to him than any others? . . . The most potent as well as the most beautiful amongst them, according to my estimation, are certain of the so-called plantation melodies, and slave songs, all of which are distinguished by unusual and subtle harmonies,[1] the thing which I have found in no other songs but those of Scotland and Ireland.'

This view has been much discussed. If nationalism in music implies the exploitation of the idioms of one's own race, then work by white composers based upon Negro idioms would not be an instance of nationalism. It would, however, offer an escape from accepted conventions as a 'back to the land' movement. It would

[1] This word is probably a mistranslation on the part of somebody who prepared Dvořák's statement for American publication.

be somewhat analogous to the study of Spanish national idiom by certain members of the Russian school, a study which helped to free them from current German influence and so to enable them to 'find themselves'. The nationalistic movement in music, as we have seen, is plainly two things at one time. It is a search for racial expression, and also for primitive inspiration.

After his first Opera, *King and Collier*, mentioned above, Dvořák wrote seven other operas, including *The Water-Nymph* (*Rusalka*). Other important, and sometimes extremely popular, works of his not yet mentioned are the Overtures *Carnival*, *My Home* (*Mein Heim*), *Nature* (*In der Natur*), and *Othello*; a Violin Concerto and a 'Cello Concerto; a String Sextet, a Piano Quintet, eight notable String Quartets (including the popular *Nigger* Quartet, in connexion with which see the foregoing remarks on Negro influence),[1] three Piano Trios, and Dumky (plural of Dumka) for Piano Trio; a Sonata, a Sonatina, a Ballade, &c., for Violin and Piano; quite a number of Piano Solos and Duets, which should be better known than they are; five or six biggish choral works (including the immensely popular though gruesome *Spectre's Bride*); and many good Songs and Part Songs. (The well-known *Songs my Mother taught me* is one of his *Zigeunerlieder*, or *Gipsy Songs*.) Other works include seven Symphonies, of which we sometimes hear the Fourth. The Symphony *From the New World* is the Fifth.[2]

Among Dvořák's gifts, either national or individual, are characteristic harmony, a remarkable, fresh, vital use of the orchestra, and a real genius for chamber music for strings.

SUK

Joseph Suk was born at Cracow in Bohemia in 1874. He became a very fine violinist, and (at seventeen) one of the founders of the soon world-famous Bohemian String Quartet.

He studied composition under Dvořák, whose daughter he married.

---

[1] E. W. points out that the *name* 'Nigger' often given to this quartet was not authorized by either the composer or his publisher.

[2] E. W. pleads for mention of the second in D minor, 'far and away Dvořák's orchestral masterpiece, on lines that he seldom attempted'.

She died early, and his thoughts on his loss of her and of her father inspired a Symphonic Poem, *Azrael* (i. e. the Angel of Death). He also sought consolation in nature, and this also inspired some of his compositions. In the effort to approach nature more nearly he became, in a small way, a farmer.

Suk's earlier compositions are influenced by Dvořák's style; he later escaped from it and became freer both in rhythm and in harmony, sometimes approaching atonality.
He died in 1935.

GRIEG

The chance effects of political events upon art would make too long a list for any one to undertake its compilation. In 1746 the

Grieg.

fate of the Stuarts was finally decided at the Battle of Culloden. That brought into existence an oratorio, wherein the composer, Handel, whilst professedly praising the goodness of God and the patriotism of an ancient Jewish hero-warrior, Judas Macca-baeus, was really celebrating the triumphant butchery of a victorious German-English general, the notorious Duke of Cumberland. The Duke's final defeat of the Young Pre-tender gave a great stimulus to popular musical balladry in which the romantic Highland spirit expressed its loyalty to its traditional ruling house, and it sent to Norway a Fraserburgh mer-chant named Greig, who still kept up his connexion with his native land by an annual visit to take part in the Communion of his Presbyterian fathers, and whose son and grandson maintained the link by serving in succession as British Consuls of Bergen. Edvard Grieg the composer was a son of this grandson of the exiled mer-chant,[1] and thus possessed a one-eighth proportion of Aberdeenshire blood, and also a touch of romance in his ancestry which he valued

[1] The spelling of the name had been changed, so as to secure the correct pronunciation.

and which perhaps had a little influence upon his temperament and hence upon his composition.

Grieg's mother was a Hagerup, a member of a notable Bergen family. The music in his nature came from her. She had studied in Hamburg and London, and, as a semi-professional, played the piano in important Bergen concerts. She began to teach him the same instrument when he was six. She loved Mozart, Weber, Mendelssohn, and Chopin, but whilst she easily awakened his enthusiasm for the music of these and other composers she was not able to overcome a repugnance for steady work that in boyhood seemed a part of Grieg's nature. However, he made some progress as a pianist and experimented in composition. Poetry was a passion with the boy, and he had a childish desire to gild his life with glory by becoming a pastor and shaking the world with pulpit oratory.

The definite turning towards music came with the appearance in his parents' home one day of Ole Bull, the world-famous Norwegian violinist, whose concert triumphs and travelling adventures had made him, in his lifetime, a national legendary figure. Ole Bull looked over some of the attempts at composition and urged the necessity of a cultivation of the native talent he sensed in them.

This was in 1858, when the boy was fifteen. The Leipzig Conservatóire, founded by Mendelssohn in the year of Grieg's birth, fifteen years before, and probably equipped with the best musical educational staff in the world, was pointed at by Bull and by ordinary common sense as the proper institution in which to seek a thorough training, and thither Grieg was now sent.

Not all Grieg's teachers at Leipzig won his equal allegiance. There was the celebrated pianist, Moscheles, appointed by Mendelssohn and admirer of his whilst antagonistic to the music of Mendelssohn's contemporaries, Schumann (a former professor of the Conservatoire, by the way), and Chopin. There was the great E. F. Richter, theorist and writer of text-books, who taught harmony very strictly by rule and struck out of his pupils' exercises whatever did not conform thereto. There were professors who looked upon the rising Wagner even less favourably than Mendelssohn and Schumann had done, thinking him a dangerous revolutionary. But there were other teachers more discerning and, as an incentive to overcome his natural laziness, there was the example (which he after-wards gratefully recalled) of certain hard-working English youths, Franklin Taylor, John Francis Barnett, Walter Bache, and Arthur Sullivan.

The Leipzig training completed, Grieg returned to the North. He settled for a short time in Copenhagen, the birthplace and residence of the Danish composer, Gade, then looked up to as the leader of a Scandinavian School of composition, though now his music sounds to us like that of a somewhat weakened Mendelssohn born in the North and hence with some tendency to the use of northern colour.

Of Gade 'in his best works' Grieg was always an admirer, and he owed to him, in part at any rate, the determination to allow national character to shine through cosmopolitan training.

Soon, leaving Denmark, Grieg returned to Norway, settling in its capital, Christiania. Here he founded a Musical Union, whose con-ductor he remained for thirteen years. He was in frequent touch with Ole Bull, associating much, also, with Richard Nordraak, another very loyal Norwegian musician and cousin of the Norwegian author, Björnson, and with Kjerulf, nearly thirty years Grieg's senior and one of the first genuine Norwegian nationalist composers. Svendsen, violinist, conductor and composer, and also a Norwegian, was another friend.

In 1864 Grieg married a partly Danish bride, his cousin, Nina Hagerup, a good singer and the daughter of a famous Danish actress. (In later years she was to do much for his songs by her sympathetic treatment of them.)

In 1868, when Grieg was twenty-five, came a letter from the ever-generous Liszt. He had by chance seen the First Sonata for Violin and Pianoforte (Op. 8) and spontaneously wrote to congratulate and encourage its composer and to invite him to visit him. The letter was an asset. It turned out to have definite financial value. On the strength of it the Norwegian Government made Grieg a grant, to enable him to visit Rome, where at last he met Liszt in person. Liszt especially approved the national characteristics of the young composer's music; it was passages embodying these that most definitely caught his fancy. The Piano Concerto was now in existence—in manuscript. Liszt took the copy to the piano, played it, combining solo and orchestral parts in masterly fashion, and handed back the manuscript with the words—' Continue in your path ; you have the right stuff in you and—let nobody intimidate you ! ' This encouragement, often recalled, was of permanent effect.

Into Grieg's life henceforth there enters very strongly the influence of some of the nationalist writers of Norway. With Björnson he was in close relations and with Ibsen he was brought into actual collaboration in 1874, when he received a letter from him asking him to write the incidental music to the play *Peer Gynt*. How splendidly the commission was accomplished all the world knows if only from the later recasting of some of the music into the shape of two *Peer Gynt* Suites. Occasional opportunities of hearing the play, with the music, also occur, and offer a perfect proof of the delicate poesy and romance and also of both the genuine national feeling and the high technical equipment of the Composer.

For some years Grieg lived in a country place on the Norwegian coast, working day after day, and summer and winter, in a little wooden hut just big enough to contain a stove, a piano, and a composer. Then he built a villa near his native Bergen, and there, with fairly frequent conducting and performing tours, he steadily worked on. His constitution was frail, and he suffered a good deal of bad health. He got many invitations to visit America, but did not feel himself equal to the strain. His music brought him in a fair income, but, as he once complained, Lehar made as much out of his operetta, ' The Merry Widow ', as he himself made out of a whole lifetime's composition.

A notable incident in Grieg's life was the stand he made on the Dreyfus case. The injustice of the verdict aroused his indignation. In reply to an invitation from Colonne to take part in a Paris concert he wrote that he was at such a time ' unable to enter into relations with the French public '. Colonne sent Grieg a most proper letter in return, to which Grieg replied suitably (with some allusion to the ' abominable letters ' he daily received from the French public). All this was in 1899. Four years later Colonne renewed the invitation and it was accepted. Grieg duly conducted in Paris, before going on the stage taking five drops of opium ' which had a remarkably calming effect!' The audience had not taken opium and was not very calm : there were two parties, of which the friendly one happily turned out to be the stronger. Police protection was provided for Grieg on leaving. The courageous spirit that ruled the frail body was fully revealed both in the 1899 refusal to visit Paris and in the 1903 acceptance of the invitation.

In 1907 Grieg was to pay one of his visits to England to play and conduct at the Leeds Festival. On the eve of setting out he fell ill and was taken to a hospital. 'This, then, is the end', he said as he entered it, and so it turned out. He died a few days later.

Grieg was buried in a grotto, high up a wall of cliff which juts out into the fiord within sight of his home Troldhaugen. The mouth of the grotto was walled up, the words ' Edvard Grieg ' cut upon the stone, and there his ashes were left, in this simplest and most appropriate of all resting places, and one he had himself chosen.

The reception of Grieg's music by the public was usually cordial. From brother musicians and professional music critics it was sometimes less so. Partly no doubt this was because so many of his compositions were slight in length and in scope. He never wrote a Symphony[1] or an Opera. But he wrote one Concerto, one String Quartet[2] and five Sonatas (one for Piano, three for Violin and Piano, and one for 'Cello and Piano). His many songs were such as any one could appreciate and much of his Piano music was such as amateur pianists could play. 'It is surely no fault of mine that my music is heard in third-rate hotels and from schoolgirls', the Composer once wrote. Perhaps the case of Grieg is unique in that he introduced a decidedly new note into music and yet at once won popular approval. His music has been illustrated under 'Scandinavia', pages 175-7.

Although keenly resenting the ill-based criticism to which he was often subjected, to the end he was modest in his claims. In the very year of his death he wrote, 'What I have accomplished, in large works and small, signifies to me personally a continuous develop-

---

[1] Save a juvenile unpublished one, written at Gade's instance, of which two movements exist as the Op. 14—Two Symphonic Pieces for Piano Duet.

[2] And an unfinished second one.

ment, and yet, unfortunately, I am conscious that I have never yet reached what I have been striving after. So to-day I cannot name a single work as decidedly a front-rank composition.' That, however, perhaps only represents a passing mood, and certainly many readers, remembering the Piano Concerto, will dissent.

GLINKA

Glinka was born in 1804, on the country estate of his father. An uncle in the neighbourhood maintained a private orchestra, in whose performances the boy revelled, as he did also in the folk-music he heard in plenty.

Early piano lessons were taken from a governess, later ones, in St. Petersburg, from the Irishman, Field. On return to his country house, the youth made good use of his uncle's orchestra, rehearsing it in some of the orchestral classics, and in this way pushing forward his practical studies.

For a few years Glinka held a civil service position in St. Petersburg; then, at twenty-four, he gave this up and, financially supported by his family, devoted himself entirely to music.

At twenty-six, for reasons of health, he visited Italy. For a year he studied at Milan, making the acquaintance of Bellini and Donizetti and hearing Italian operas under the best conditions.

At twenty-nine he went to Germany, to study, at Berlin, under Dehn, a famous teacher of composition. He had a definite object in view, to acquire the technique to enable him to write a real Russian opera.

Back in Russia, he set to work at his opera. He took a thoroughly national subject—that of the invasion of Russia by the Poles in 1613. At thirty-two he heard his opera performed—*A Life for the Czar*. It has some Italian influences remaining (being lyrical in style) but enough folk-influence to provoke a few of the ultra-respectable to complain of the humble origin of some of the music. Some of the music in the Polish scenes is written in the rhythms of the national Polish dances, the Polonaise and the Mazurka. This work came in time to be accepted as a musical symbol of Russian nationality, and thus to enjoy a huge popularity.

The next opera, *Russlan and Ludmilla*, had a more Oriental tinge. It was based upon a fanciful folk-poem, by the Russian national poet, Pushkin, an older contemporary of Glinka. The work was not a success, and, nettled, the Composer decided on a further sojourn abroad. This had important consequences, since two years of it were spent in Spain, where, besides writing an orchestral work of very Russian character, on a folk theme *Kamarinskaya*, he made a close study of Spanish folk-music, and basing upon it two other orchestral works, *Jota Aragonesa* and *A Summer Night in Madrid*, supplied the inspiration which has led to similar studies and compositions by native Spanish composers.

Glinka's contribution to music was welcomed by the Romantic composers of the day. Berlioz, in his capacity of music critic, praised him, and in return Glinka did something to gain a footing in Russia for Berlioz's music. Meyerbeer, too, admired his work. It was at a concert of Glinka's works in Berlin, arranged by Meyerbeer, that Glinka caught a chill which led to his death in his fifty-third year.

Liszt, too, greatly encouraged Glinka. It will be realized that Glinka's activity was looked upon by some of the leading Romantic composers of the period as that of a sort of Russian branch of the Romantic Movement, and, as has been made evident in the preceding chapter, Nationalism is, in itself, essentially an offshoot of Romanticism.

There is in Glinka's work a new rhythmic freedom. Five or seven beats to a bar are common. For some time this remained a Russian characteristic, though nowadays it is common enough everywhere. Glinka died in 1857.

DARGOMIJSKY

Like Glinka, and only nine years later (1813), Dargomijsky was born on a Russian country estate. He early showed musical talent, and received training in Piano, Violin, and Harmony and Counterpoint.

As an amateur, popular in St. Petersburg drawing-rooms, Dargomijsky composed songs and other music, occupying meantime a position in the civil service.

Then he met Glinka, who inspired him with a desire to shake off the dilettante and put him upon the way towards a mastery of the technique of composition.

The Romantic Movement in French literature was in full swing. Influenced by it Dargomijsky first made an attempt at an opera based on Hugo's *Lucrezia Borgia*, and then, abandoning this, at another on the same author's *Notre Dame de Paris*. The style of this latter work, *Esmeralda*, was French rather than Russian. It had to wait long for a hearing, and then, at length, won success both at St. Petersburg and Moscow.

Russalka which followed, was at least Russian in literary theme, being based upon Pushkin's treatment of a national legend of a water-sprite.

About 1865, Dargomijsky came into touch with a group of younger men. He was then in his fifties; they were only in their varying twenties. They were already his admirers, but they held views which, had Wagner's music and his theories been much known in Russia at the period, would perhaps have been called Wagnerian. They wanted dramatic fitness before musical charm and one might almost say that the only thing Wagner wanted and they did not was a high orchestral development, for they attached more importance to the vocal treatment.[1]

With the definite intention of carrying into effect the principles laid down by this group of bold young thinkers, 'The Five' as they came to be called (see page 178), Dargomijsky began to set as an opera Pushkin's *The Stone Guest*. During its composition he died (1869, aged fifty-six); two members of the group of 'The Five', authorized by him on his death-bed, completed the work. It has never been a great success, lacking sustained melody—'a recitative in three acts' it has been called, and, as such, very different from anything of Glinka's.

In addition to his operatic works, Dargomijsky wrote a large number of songs (he had a thorough understanding of the voice and the problems of musical declamation); and also some orchestral

[1] We might make this sort of a distinction perhaps—Dargomijsky and his friends wanted music-drama; Wagner (whatever his intentions, and the word he coined) wrote, rather, drama-music.

pieces. One of the latter is *Baba Yaga*, a fantasia based on native legend.

BALAKIREF

Glinka and Dargomijsky were men of some means. So was Balakiref. In fact none of the earlier Russian composers were members of the musical profession, in the usual sense of the words, all either enjoying some family income or else earning their living apart from their music. Balakiref was born in 1837. His mother taught him music. Like Glinka he enjoyed the advantages of close acquaintance with peasant music, and again like him the other advantage of experimenting with a private orchestra (that of his friend Oulibichef, a country gentleman who is known to musical history especially as a writer on Mozart). Perhaps partly through Oulibichef's influence he acquired a minute and extensive knowledge of the musical classics.

Then, too, he came in touch with Glinka, the great founder of Russian musical nationalism, who saw him as the Elisha to his own Elijah. Balakiref composed a piece for piano and orchestra on Russian tunes, and a fantasia on a tune from *A Life for the Czar*. Glinka gave him a Spanish tune (see page 201) and he made an Overture out of it. He also wrote a symphonic poem called *Russia*.

He started in St. Petersburg an institution that was to have a great part in the promulgation of nationalistic ideals, the Free School of Music, and, similarly, he started a series of concerts at which might be given more progressive programmes than those usual at the period.

Balakiref may be looked upon as the founder of the group of 'The Five' (*alias* the 'Mighty Little Heap', *alias* 'The Invincible Band'), consisting of himself, Rimsky-Korsakof, Borodin, Mussorgsky, and Cui (see page 178). It is of the nature of a group of this sort to disintegrate, and so it was in the present instance; during the last forty years of his life Balakiref lived, indeed, a very solitary and retired life.

Liszt encouraged Balakiref. Far and wide he played Balakiref's great Russian-oriental virtuoso Piano Fantasia, *Islamey*, and Balakiref dedicated to him his Russian-oriental Symphonic Poem, *Thamar*.

Balakiref never wrote an Opera.   He started one and then abandoned it.

He died in 1910.

BORODIN

Borodin (1833–87) earned his living as a Professor of Chemistry and a medical man, holding many official posts, and, indeed, did more than earn his living at these occupations, since he made several valuable researches in chemistry and helped to found a women's medical school.

At twenty-eight, as a keen but uninstructed musical amateur, he came in touch with Balakiref, and at once became a member of his circle.   He studied and composed with diligence, but complained that, owing to his professional work he could get serious work done only when unwell.   (He tells us somewhere that all his musical works were written when he was suffering the inconveniences and discomforts of a bad cold in the head.)   The complete list of his works runs only to twenty-one.

Liszt appreciated Borodin and encouraged him greatly, and Borodin wrote an account, later published, of his experiences in the Liszt circle at Weimar.   His works include two Symphonies (and part of a third), the Symphonic Sketch *In the Steppes of Central Asia*, two String Quartets, Piano pieces, Songs, and the Opera, *Prince Igor* (left unfinished and completed by Rimsky-Korsakof and Glazounof).

Borodin's death was sudden, unexpected, and deplored.   At a party, dressed in national costume, he fell down dead.   Though in many works strongly national in feeling, Borodin is not, in his forms and the style he adopts, so drastically Russian as some other members of the circle of 'The Five'.   He did not emulate the recitative-like style of Dargomijsky.   He loved melody and preferred bold outlines to details.

MUSSORGSKY

Mussorgsky (1839–81) was first an army officer, then a civil servant. Like some others of the Russian pioneers he got his first inspiration from Russian folk-music heard as a child.   He early came in contact with Dargomijsky, who encouraged and influenced him, and all his life he strove to apply the Dargomijsky principles. He loved not

Mussorgsky.

'art for art's sake', so much as 'art for life's sake'; he was not much of a theorist and believed in intuition rather than training; he sought truth before beauty in musical representation. He was in fact one of the most determined musical 'realists' who ever lived; his country upbringing having given him a strong bias towards folk-lore he was strongly influenced by it in the literary subjects he chose for his compositions. He was almost Tolstoyan in his view that art should appeal to the many, not to the few. In the operas *Boris Godounof* and *Khovanshchina* he took subjects from national history. His songs are strongly characteristic of his mind : they are sardonic, humorous or tender, and always go straight to the mark. Some orchestral pieces exist (the best known being the Symphonic Poem, *Night on the Bare Mountain*), and some piano pieces, *Pictures at an Exhibition* (see page 180), in which he tries to express in tone the emotional content of nine or ten paintings by the Russian, Hartmann.

Mussorgsky was one of 'The Five' and for a time he lived with Rimsky-Korsakof. But he was not a very 'clubbable' man. He was very irritable and excitable, became slovenly and careless, drank and drugged, and died in a hospital on the forty-second anniversary of his birth.

Mussorgsky has been chosen to illustrate 'Russia' in this book (see pages 180–1).

RIMSKY-KORSAKOF

Like Balakiref, Rimsky-Korsakof was born and reared in the country, and like him he enjoyed the double advantage of an early soaking in folk-songs and the enjoyment of a household band of musicians—a small one, in Rimsky-Korsakof's case, merely a group of four Jews living on his father's estate, but enough to set his childish musical imagination at work.

Balakiref was a man of means, Cui a soldier, Mussorgsky first a soldier and then a civil servant, Borodin a scientist, and Rimsky-

Korsakof a sailor, as a young naval officer going on long voyages and studying music between watches. At eighteen (he was born in 1844, so this was in 1862) he was engaged in a three-years' cruise. He had already come into touch with Balakiref, and from port to port he sent to him work he had done, and received from him suggestions as to its improvement. The first symphony Russia ever produced was written under these conditions.

Rimsky-Korsakof.

This Symphony was later (1871) one of the causes of his being offered the post of Professor of Composition at the St. Petersburg Conservatoire, and another was the Symphonic Poem, *Sadko*, an orchestral setting of a legend of the sea. The young sailor felt himself unfitted for the post, since he had never himself undergone any systematic theoretical training, yet he accepted it, and by diligent study equipped himself for the duties. Indeed he made himself the best theorist of 'The Five'.

Rimsky-Korsakof was a prolific composer. He wrote fifteen Operas (including *Ivan the Terrible*,[1] *Sadko*,[2] *The Snow Maiden*, *Kitej*, and *The Golden Cockerel*), three Symphonies, a Symphonic Suite *Scheherazade*, Chamber Music, Piano Music, Choral Music, Songs, &c., and also text-books of Harmony and of Orchestration.

Though a strong nationalist, as the subject of his operas and their musical material equally show, Rimsky-Korsakof was not a revolutionary. He shared a dwelling for some time with Mussorgsky, but did not share his views. He did not fully accept the Dargomijskean principles as to the texture of music ; he willingly wrote an extended tune. He was a great collector of Russian folk-tune, but also a

[1] The Composer's own name for this was *The Maid of Pskof* and so it is called in Russia.

[2] There is a relationship between the two '*Sadkos*', the operatic and the orchestral.

great student of the methods of the classic composers, and a sound and systematic teacher of the young. Much of his work is the expression of a strong dramatic impulse and it both throbs with vital rhythm and glows with vivid orchestration.

When the weakening influence of time broke up the Balakiref circle, 'The Five', Rimsky-Korsakof, who had been one of its most devoted members, became the centre of a new circle with similar aims, Belaief (see page 181) and Glazounof being prominent members.

Rimsky-Korsakof died in 1908.

At least one of Rimsky-Korsakof's greatest claims to a prominent place in the history of music is as an orchestrator. He is the successor of Berlioz, and the founder (if, indeed, Berlioz himself was not) of the instrumentation of Stravinsky and of all moderns except a few who still cling to the now overripe classic-and-romantic German musical outlook (as does, it might quite well be argued, Richard Strauss). From this outlook the orchestra is regarded as a mass, rather than as a collection of individuals to be bound into unity.

Rimsky-Korsakof treats every instrument with the respect due to a soloist—to an individual. In fact, he makes every instrument speak in its own tongue almost as tellingly as does Berlioz. His Treatise on Instrumentation is already almost a classic.

CUI

The long-lived César Cui (born in 1835, died in 1918), was half French, his father having been left, wounded, in Russia at the time of Napoleon's retreat. The son entered the Russian Army, became an authority on fortification, and attained the rank of General. He early joined the group of 'The Five' and was one of its leading members. Born in the same year as Saint-Saëns, he had an almost equally long life, was equally chauvinistic in principle, and equally cosmopolitan in practice. He wrote many Operas (*not* on Russian subjects as a rule), Songs, and Piano Pieces, and also many critical articles. It is his part as one of the leaders of the circle of 'The Five', rather than any strong individuality in his composition, that has given him his place in the history of music.

TCHAIKOVSKY

Tchaikovsky (born 1840) was the son of a civil servant and began his own active life as a civil servant too.   Previously interested in

Tchaikovsky.

music in an amateur way, at twenty-one he began to study it seriously.   At twenty-three he dropped his government work and, in poverty, gave himself up to the art.   His study was carried out chiefly at the St. Petersburg Conservatoire under Anton Rubinstein, and it was at length followed by a period as Professor of Harmony at Moscow Conservatoire under Nicholas Rubinstein, to whose support Tchaikovsky was for long much indebted.

When about twenty-eight, Tchaikovsky came under the influence of Balakiref and Rimsky-Korsakof, but he was never a member of the group of 'The Five', nor was he in full sympathy with the aims of that group.   He is often spoken of as no true Russian composer, yet the romantic attractions and violent antipathies of his life, the gleams of riotous gaiety and clouds of gloom are represented in his art by contrasts just as violent, and are as typically Russian as the temperament of any hero or heroine in the novels or plays of Chekov.   *Au fond* Tchaikovsky is perhaps conventional, but that is a matter of the quality of his music, not of its character.   Very Russian was his marriage, which was followed by a separation after only nine weeks. And very Russian, too, in its apparent eccentricity, was the strange relationship with the music-loving rich widow, Nadejda von Meck, whom he never once met, yet who became and remained for many years his best friend, sustaining him with a yearly allowance sufficient to enable him to give his mind to composition, encouraging him by an incessant correspondence, and giving him hospitality, in her own absence, on her country estate.

Once success had come to Tchaikovsky his time was divided between short concert tours to different parts of Europe and long stays at a small country house he had bought, where he lived the solitary and restful life his nervous temperament found congenial. He paid one visit to the United States.

At fifty-three (1893), Tchaikovsky, to the dismay of friends who were present, imprudently drank unboiled water. Within a week he was dead of cholera.

In Britain and America Russian music first became known to the large public not through the works of the pioneers but through those of Tchaikovsky. His melodic vein, brilliant orchestral colour, and strong emotional expression, quickly captured the ear of concert audiences. Amongst his works are ten Operas, six Symphonies, Symphonic Poems, Suites, three Piano Concertos, a Violin Concerto, Ballets, Chamber Music, and a great many Songs and Piano Pieces.

ALBÉNIZ

Isaac Albéniz was a Catalonian. He was born in 1861, and died in 1909. He made his first public appearance as a pianist at the age of four, and at the age of about seven competed for admission to the Paris Conservatoire, but after successfully passing the tests had the bad luck to be declared too young for admission. At eleven he was touring America as a recitalist. He then studied for a short time at the Conservatoires of Leipzig and Brussels. His whole youth was adventurous and unsettled, but he won great fame as a pianist, obtaining the approval and help of Liszt and Rubinstein. He was notable for his performance of the classics.

After a time he almost abandoned piano-playing for composition, in which he was very prolific. At thirty he began careful study in Paris under d'Indy and Dukas. He composed innumerable Piano pieces (many of them very difficult and some of them needlessly so), four or five Operas and Operettas, and other things. He succeeded both in giving Spanish composers faith in their own national musical style and in leaving the world some music (e. g. his *Iberia* Suite, twelve piano pieces) of that much needed kind which satisfies the connoisseur by its taste and the skilfulness of its construction and the more 'popular' public by its charm of melody and harmony and its rhythmic vivacity.

Albéniz passed some years of his life in London, where he produced several stage works, gave lessons, and published a good deal of effective drawing-room music.

GRANADOS

Like Albéniz, Granados was a Catalonian.   He was born in 1867, and lost his life by the sinking of the *Sussex* by a German submarine when on his way home from America in 1916.

As a composer Granados profited by the teaching of Pedrell (see page 182); as a pianist by that of several Spanish masters and of Charles de Bériot (son of the famous violinist and the teacher of Ravel also) in Paris.   His skill in the latter capacity was very high, and made him well known in France and Spain.   The influence of Albéniz is seen in his compositions, but there is a peculiar simplicity about his work in its comparative lack of both contrapuntal interest and harmonic variety.   It abounds, however, in piquant rhythms and melodic touches, drawn from the folk music of various parts of Spain.   His set of Piano Pieces, *Goyescas*, is based upon pictures of the great Spanish painter Goya (1746–1828); out of these he later fashioned an Opera of the same name—a strange proceeding. It was in returning from New York, where his Opera had had its first performance, that he lost his life as above recounted.

FALLA

Manuel de Falla was born at Cadiz in 1876, and became a pupil in composition of Pedrell (see page 182).   From his thirty-first year to his thirty-eighth he was resident in Paris, where he associated with Debussy and Ravel.   The compositions that have come to very prominent notice have been the Opera *Life is Short* ('La Vida Breve') (written 1905 ; produced 1913), the Ballet performed by Diaghilef's troupe in 1919, *The Three Cornered Hat*, the Ballet *Magician Love* ('El Amor Brujo'), the three pieces for Piano and Orchestra, *Nights in the Gardens of Spain* (composed in 1916) and the Opera *Master Peter's Puppet Show* (a Don Quixote incident), produced in 1923.

Falla was a keen student of his native folk-tunes, i.e. the music of the Southern Spanish peasantry, and his music shows much evidence of this in its rhythms and its melodies.

Amongst his later works is a Concerto for Harpsichord which, like some other works of his, shows strong 'ultra modern' leanings. In fact, though it seems convenient to place the notice of this composer amongst the notices of his fellow-countrymen in this volume, there would be an almost equal propriety in deferring it until the following volume. He died in 1946.

TURINA

Turina was born in Seville in 1882. He studied for many years in Paris with d'Indy. He was also in close touch with Debussy. He has written some works for the theatre, some Chamber Music, Songs, &c. An orchestral piece that has made his name widely known outside his own country is *The Procession from Rocio*. His music is full of the Spanish spirit and idiom.

Turina was a famous teacher of composition (in Madrid) and did much critical writing. He died in 1949.

MACKENZIE

Alexander Mackenzie was born in Edinburgh in 1847. His father, grandfather, and great-grandfather were all musicians. At ten the

Mackenzie.

boy was sent to Germany to study music (especially Violin) at Sondershausen near Weimar. At fourteen he became a member of the Ducal Orchestra, and experienced the manners and the music of a small German Court of the old style. At sixteen he came to London, and re-learned his native language, which he had almost forgotten, and won a scholarship at the Royal Academy of Music. At eighteen he returned to Edinburgh, and supported himself as a professional violinist, composing actively meanwhile. There he remained until his early thirties, when, having begun to make a name as a composer (partly by the support of Manns, the Crystal Palace conductor), he went to Italy, and devoted himself to composition. Many of his works were written for the various English Festivals, and he had a considerable success as an opera composer.

At forty-one Mackenzie was appointed Principal of the Royal Academy of Music, and he retained the position for thirty-six years, retiring in 1924. He was knighted in 1895.

A certain number of Mackenzie's compositions show a desire to use Scottish material, and he has frequently been inspired by Scottish subjects. He died in 1935.

PARRY

Parry was born at Bournemouth in 1848, and died in 1918. His father was the artist, Gambier Parry, a man of high artistic and moral

Parry.

ideals, and a fine type of English country gentleman, as was Parry himself.

The boy began to compose at eight. At Eton he took the lead in musical activities, and he actually took his Oxford Mus.Bac. degree whilst still at school. At Oxford he was equally active in musical doings. He was also prominent in almost every branch of athletics, and throughout his life, as swimmer, yachtsman, motorist, &c., he was by his venturesomeness constantly in danger, and often suffered minor injuries.

Leaving Oxford he entered Lloyd's, but after a few years gave himself to music study under Dannreuther, whose house was a great centre of musical culture in London in those days.

It was with a Festival Cantata that Parry first became known, and to the end he put his best work into compositions of this nature ; often he himself wrote or compiled his own libretti, for he had much literary taste and skill.

At thirty-five Parry was appointed to the staff of the Royal College of Music, and at forty-six he became the head of that institution, to which his genial influence and broad-minded humanity were of the utmost value. At fifty-two he added to his responsibilities that of the Professorship of Music at Oxford. He was knighted at fifty and created a Baronet at fifty-five. He wrote an epoch-making book on the history of music looked at from the evolutionary standpoint (*The Evolution of the Art of Music*), a fine book on Bach, and several other books of importance.

As a composer Parry was very English, not in the sense of making much use of English folk-song, but in the sense that the typical English moral qualities are represented in his work. His music has a Miltonic quality, and it is significant that his magnificent setting for Chorus and Orchestra of Milton's *At a Solemn Musick* ('Blest Pair of Sirens' he calls it, from its opening lines), is usually regarded as his highest achievement. Towards the end he wrote a number of unaccompanied Motets of the greatest beauty. His Solo Songs are by some looked on as classics, and by others little regarded; they are almost all of them settings of English poems. The list of his compositions is enormous; it is in fact far too long; a greater reticence and more revision might have been to the advantage of his work.

STANFORD

Stanford was born in 1852 in Dublin. At eight he began to compose. At eighteen he went to Cambridge, where at twenty-one he

Stanford.

became organist of Trinity College and soon after conductor of the University Musical Society; this under his direction gave the first British performance of many important works of contemporary composers, such as Brahms, of whom Stanford was a great admirer, with whom he was later to be intimate and by whom he was undoubtedly a good deal influenced. For three successive years the College authorities gave their organist leave of absence for a period, in order that he might study in Germany, and he fully profited by his opportunities. Before leaving consideration of these early days it may be well to recall that in 1879, when he was twenty-seven, his Morning, Communion, and Evening Service in B flat marked an epoch in English Church music; its individual style, and its logical form (it introduces a unification of thematic material somewhat akin to the *Leitmotiv* system of Wagner) at once attracted attention, and gave its composer a position in cathedral and church service lists that seems likely to be permanent.

The larger public had heard of Stanford about three years earlier than this, when he composed the music for the Lyceum production of Tennyson's *Queen Mary*. At this time began a friendship with Tennyson that remained very close to the end of the poet's life, and several of the composer's works, such as *The Revenge* and the Wellington Ode remain as testimony to his admiration of the poet.

As an orchestral composer Stanford was very busy, writing eight Symphonies, six Irish Rhapsodies, three Piano Concertos, three Violin Concertos (including one of the Irish Rhapsodies that is in this form), and so forth. As a Chamber Music composer he was almost equally prolific (eight String Quartets, for instance). In addition he wrote much Incidental Music for plays and eight Operas, some of which had successful runs abroad. As a choral writer and a choral conductor Stanford was very active and successful, and as a writer of solo songs almost equally so. As a teacher of composition he could claim that at the Royal College of Music successive generations of young composers had willingly admitted great indebtedness to him. He was for long Professor of Music at Cambridge University.

Stanford wrote a very practical book on *Musical Composition* and published several volumes of collected papers.

In a good deal of Stanford's music he makes use of Irish folk-tune, and he was one of the first to do this.

Stanford died in 1924

APPENDIX

PROGRAMME MUSIC

Here is a classic protest against 'Programme Music' in its cruder and what we may call its more 'material' forms. It comes from the famous treatise, *Of the True, the Beautiful, and the Good*, by Victor Cousin, the French philosopher, statesman, and orator. It says nothing that has not been said before and since, but it says it neatly :

Give the cleverest symphonic writer a storm to reproduce. Nothing could be more simple than to imitate the whistling of winds and the crash of thunder. But by what combination of ordered sounds could he enable us to visualize the flashes of lightning that suddenly tear asunder the veil of darkness, or that most terrifying aspect of storm, the movement of the waves, now rising to mountains, now falling headlong into unfathomable abysses? If the listener has not been previously told the subject of the music he can certainly never guess it, and, indeed, I challenge him to distinguish between a storm and a battle. Despite all the composer's skill or genius he cannot reproduce shapes in sounds. Music, then, wisely directed, will avoid a hopeless competition ; it will refuse the attempt to reproduce the rise and fall of the waves and other natural phenomena, but will awaken in our hearts the emotions that possess us during the different phases of a tempest. Thus Haydn becomes the rival and even the superior of the painter, for it has been permitted to music to move the heart even more powerfully than painting.

This appeared in 1854. Ten years later was born Richard Strauss, who has represented in music the bleating of sheep, the whirring of wind, the clash of battle, the preaching of sermons, the washing of babies, the hanging of criminals, the ticking of clocks, the rising of the sun, the noise of waterfalls, danger on the mountain and the attaining of the peak, and, of course, thunder and storm.

Liszt and 'Programme' Extemporization

'At my last recital [in Milan] a valuable silver cup, of beautiful craftsmanship, said to be by one of Benvenuto Cellini's best pupils, was placed at the door, so that people might put into it their suggestions as to themes. When I began to read the suggestions I found, as I expected, a great number of musical themes from Bellini and Donizetti. Then there came to light an anonymous note from some one who proposed " Milan Cathedral ". " Ah," said I to myself, " here's a man who's learnt something from his reading and remembers what Mme. de Staël wrote, ' Music is an architecture in sound.' ". . . A respectable gentleman gave me the subject "The Railway ". . . . I hurried on to another paper. What did I now find? . . . I read " Is it better to marry or to remain a bachelor? "

INDEX

Aberdeenshire, 195.

Agoult, Comtesse d' (1805–76), 123.

Albéniz (1860–1909), 165, 182, 209–10.

Albert, Prince Consort of England (1819–61), 104.

Albert Hall, London, 12, 135.

Albert Memorial, 12.

Alfano (b. 1876), 149.

Altona, 138.

Amateurism in music, 200–7; see under the various Russian composers.

American music, Dvořák's views on, 193.

Architecture, analogies with music, 45, 52.
  Classic and Romantic, 11.
  Gothic, 5.

Aria, formality of, 54.
  varieties, 53.
  in Wagner, 62.

Arne (1710–78), 55.

Arrangements, 125, 129.

'Art for Art's Sake', 121, 205.

'Art Songs', 47–8.

Auber (1782–1871), 75.

Bach, J. S. (1685–1750):
  Passions, 29, 108; Capriccio, 29; Organ Works, 108.
  Descriptive music, 29.
  Romantic expression, 16.
  French and Italian influences, 189.
  compared with Wagner, 66.
  influence on Brahms, 140.
  efforts of Mendelssohn and Samuel Wesley, 108.
  Gounod's improvements, 150.

Bache, Walter (1842–88), 197.

Bacon (1561–1626), 45.

Baillie, Joanna (1762–1851), 168.

Balakiref (1837–1910):
  LIFE, 203. WORK, 179–81.

as nationalist, 165.
  one of 'the Five', 178, 204.
  influence on Borodin, 204; on Tchaikovsky, 208.

Ballad Opera, 55.

Balzac (1799–1850), 88.

Bärmann, H. J. (1784–1847), 81.

Barnett, J. F. (1837–1916), 197.

Bartók (1881–1945), 190.

Bavaria, King Ludwig II of (r. 1864–86), 133 et seq.
  King Maximilian Joseph of (r. 1799–1825), 83.

Baylis, Lilian, 73.

Bayreuth, 125, 133 et seq.

Bax (1883–1953), 187.

Beckford (1760–1844), 5–6.

Belaief (1836–1904), 181, 207.

Beaumarchais (1732–99), 142.

Beethoven (1770–1827):
  Symphonies, 15, 16, 63; Piano Sonatas, 15, 16, 30, 126; Violin Sonatas, 138; Diabelli Variations, 121; *Fidelio*, 87.
  his emotional expression, 28.
  as Classic-Romantic, 11, 15.
  as song-writer, 47.
  descriptive music, 30.
  as general reader, 31.
  his 'madness', 76.
  monument at Bonn, 126.
  relations with Lichnowski, 112.
  greets Liszt, 120.
  as arranger of British folk-tune, 168.
  decline in German taste after his death, 97.
  popularization in Paris, 129.
  and Salieri, 120.
  Schumann's study of him, 95.
  use of development, 63 et seq.
  influence on Berlioz, 76, 92.
  Wagner's novelette on Beethoven, 136.
  influence on Wagner, 76, 128–9.

Beggar's Opera, 55.

Index

Index

THE LISTENER'S
HISTORY OF MUSIC

Volume III

To the Composers of Today

The Listener's
History of Music

A BOOK FOR ANY CONCERT-GOER, GRAMOPHONIST

OR RADIO LISTENER

· PROVIDING ALSO A COURSE OF STUDY FOR ADULT CLASSES

IN THE APPRECIATION OF MUSIC

by

PERCY A. SCHOLES

With incidental comments by

SIR W. HENRY HADOW · SIR RICHARD R. TERRY

DR. ERNEST WALKER · EDWIN EVANS

———

IN THREE VOLUMES

Volume III. To the Composers of Today

FIFTH EDITION

LONDON
OXFORD UNIVERSITY PRESS
NEW YORK   TORONTO

Oxford University Press, Ely House, London W. 1

GLASGOW   NEW YORK   TORONTO   MELBOURNE   WELLINGTON
CAPE TOWN   IBADAN   NAIROBI   DAR ES SALAAM   LUSAKA   ADDIS ABABA
DELHI   BOMBAY   CALCUTTA   MADRAS   KARACHI   LAHORE   DACCA
KUALA LUMPUR   SINGAPORE   HONG KONG   TOKYO

First Edition 1929
Second Edition 1939
Third Edition 1943
Fourth Edition 1949
Fifth Edition 1954
Reprinted 1957, 1960, 1963
1970, 1971, and 1974

Printed in Great Britain
at the University Press, Oxford
by Vivian Ridler
Printer to the University

THE AUTHOR'S INTRODUCTION
TO THE FIRST EDITION

THE variety of aim of present-day composers has made the writing of this volume a bewildering task. Some clear classification of material had to be found, and as classification is always a very relative process I cannot hope to have satisfied every critic. All I can say is that the effort to classify has done me good, and I hope that the effort to grasp the classification, and if he likes mentally to amend it according to his personal tastes, will also do the reader good.

The warning uttered in the Introduction to the second volume must now be repeated with even greater emphasis. The word 'Period', which was well in place in Volume I, necessarily becomes less and less definite as Volumes II and III proceed. The reader must not take it too literally, and, as I said in the Introduction to Volume II, must 'turn backwards and forwards and compare the statements and dates in one division of my volume with those in another'.

It will be realized that certain composers could be almost equally well treated under one head or under another. Was I to treat Falla (to take but one chance instance) under the 'Nationalist' head in Volume II, or under the 'Neo-Romantic' or even the 'Anti-Romantic' head in Volume III ? So long as composers persist in many-sidedness such problems will face any author who tries to write about them collectively. The reader on any historical subject must be given his material under a classification, for un-ordered facts and judgements are not easily retained by the human mind; but having thus acquired his facts and considered the judgements, it is his business gradually to rearrange them in any way that seems to him to be (for him) more significant and more 'true'.

The choice of composers to be included in the third volume has been extremely perplexing. Apparently almost everybody composes nowadays! And for almost every composer before the intelligent public some claim to consideration in such a book as this can be made. As I wrote the biographical material I soon found that I was getting too far afield, and that a *Listener's History* that had originally been planned as a single volume and had expanded itself first to two and then to three, was in danger of extending its volumes right across the shelf of any book-buyer rich enough to give a wholesale order. Many biographies that I had written I discarded, and I dealt flint-facedly with a conscientious and thoughtful friend who read the book in typescript and presented me with a list of between seventy and eighty living composers worthy of treatment whom I had omitted.

The composers I have included are either typical of some trend in modern music, or are composers of whom 'ordinary' readers in Britain or America are likely to demand information—with a slight preference for the older men whose position in the interests of musical people is of some longer standing and is, perhaps, for the time, less debatable.

I saw no way of drawing a hard and fast line. There are authors upon this subject who announce, 'I have excluded living composers', and others who announce, 'I have excluded composers born since such-and-such a date'. I have adopted neither of these mechanical expedients and, frankly, I stand or fall on my judgement, well aware that the shifting panorama of musical activity will compel me to a good deal of rewriting, addition, and perhaps omission, in any succeeding editions of this third volume of my book.

As some compensation to any reader who is disappointed at not finding here the name of some living or recent composer upon whom he has 'put his money', I would state that it is intended to prepare, as soon as possible, a *Listener's Encyclopaedia of Music*[1]—a handy and comparatively inexpensive

---

[1] Since published as *The Oxford Companion to Music*—nine editions to date.

volume giving, as succinctly as possible, information about all phases of musical work and all composers likely to interest the attendant at concerts, the gramophile, or radio listener—or, for that matter, the intelligent amateur player or music pupil.

As I admitted in the Introduction to the second volume, any attempt to state historical truth is open to debate. Perhaps there *is* no such absolute as 'historical truth', but a syndicate may approach nearer to its discovery than an individual, and so, as in the first and second volumes, I have submitted my work to the criticism of certain authorities in whose knowledge and competence we all have confidence, asking them freely to dissent where dissent seems to them to be necessary, and promising them that their views should be publicly brought forward, as in the first volume, in footnote or appendix.

I must gratefully acknowledge the kindness and care of these gentlemen, who will be found to be identified with their remarks throughout by the use of their names or initials. Further, I have to thank Mr. C. M. Crabtree, B.A., B.Mus., for much help in the choice of music examples, in the reading of proofs, and in the other time-exhausting tasks that go to the making of a book of this type, and Mr. W. McNaught, B.A., and the late Mr. C. Stanley Wise, B.Mus., who read the proofs.

I am also indebted to a number of music publishers for the permission to quote from their copyright publications.

A Bibliography of works in the English language upon the composers discussed in this volume will be found as an Appendix. It does not represent the sources consulted in the preparation of the book, which included the standard works in French, German, and Italian, but it will, it is hoped, be of use to many readers. So far as I know I have everywhere scrupulously acknowledged quotations from brother authors; if I have anywhere erred in this matter I should like to be informed so that I may have the opportunity of repairing the error in any later edition.

What I believe to be a novel feature of this final volume is the provision of reproductions of a number of paintings of various modern schools, inserted in the hope that a little study of their characteristics may suggest illuminating parallels with the contemporary development of schools of composition. For the permissions to use these illustrations I am indebted to the following:

The Trustees of the National Gallery, for Whistler's *Battersea Bridge*.

La Société du Droit d'Auteur and Frank Rutter, for Cézanne's *Landscape in Provence*.

The above Society and Pablo Picasso, for Picasso's *Three Musicians*.

Frank Rutter, for Picasso's *Lady in Mantilla*.

Messrs. Constable & Co., for Kandinsky's *Improvisation*.

Messrs. R. Piper & Co., Munich, for Schönberg's *Visions*.

Messrs. Faber & Gwyer, for *Economy—Dress in 1926 and in 1905*.

In closing this Introduction to the final volume of my *Listener's History* I feel I must say a grateful word about the generous attitude of my publishers, who have allowed me to add very considerably to the expense of production by the inclusion of such a large number of music-type illustrations and portraits—no fewer (in the whole work) than 140 of the former and 65 of the latter.

CONTENTS

Contents

LIST OF ILLUSTRATIONS

xii   List of Illustrations

PERIOD VI
The Impressionist School

XIX

THE IMPRESSIONIST SCHOOL

As Strauss represents a continuation of Wagner, Berlioz, and Liszt, Debussy represents a reaction against them—and a reaction of the most definite and uncompromising character. Never since 1600, when the 'monodic' school sprang into existence as a more or less conscious reaction from the 'polyphonic' school, had there been such a definite secession from the current ideals, methods, and style. It is worth while to recall the essential nature of that earlier secession (fully described in Chapter VI of Volume I), as there are some curious parallels to be noted between these two revolutionary movements, nearly three centuries apart.

Roughly speaking (which is all a book the size of this one can anywhere attempt to do), the chief fundamental technical aim of the 1600 revolutionaries was to present *a truly dramatic vocal utterance*. The primary principle involved in this aim was, they considered, *to make the note express the word*, and the emotional flux of the music thus minutely accompany the emotional flux of the text. The chief process was the casting aside of the old-fashioned contrapuntal art, firstly because it took too long to express itself and hence was unsuited for the quick following of the thought of a text, and secondly because its elaborate interweaving and its throwing from voice to voice and 'development' of musical themes was too elaborate, too purely and *exclusively* musical, holding too much of what we may call *a pattern-interest* to be fitted for close dramatic representation.

The Revolt of Debussy

The revolt of Debussy, and of the few who have to some extent followed him, was not at all unlike that earlier revolt. Debussy, in his Opera *Pelléas and Mélisande*, cast aside all purely melodic considerations, all *specifically musical* expression in the voice parts. He cast aside the contrapuntal and 'symphonic' methods of Beethoven and Wagner, because the process of 'development' by those methods was too slow a process for an always-on-the-spot and up-to-the-minute reproduction of the shifting emotions to be expressed, and also because these methods, again, savoured too much of pattern-making.

Debussy on Bach and Wagner

Debussy received the normal training of a great school of music. He was acquainted with the Classics and the Romantics. He studied counterpoint in the usual way, though without much enthusiasm. He visited Bayreuth and was impressed. Then he turned against the Classics (or at all events against Beethoven) and against the Romantics, and, particularly, against the Master of Bayreuth. With all the fervour of a convert he exclaimed, 'Bach is the Grail and Wagner is the Klingsor, trying to crush the Grail and to take its place'.

This praise of Bach may seem inconsistent with the allusion that has just been made to the essentially uncontrapuntal style of Debussy. And, indeed, to describe without apparent inconsistencies the position of Debussy (or, for that matter, of any composer who theorizes about his art) is difficult. What Debussy liked in Bach may be grasped from the following discussion by him of a Bach Concerto—

Here we find almost intact that style of musical 'arabesque', or rather 'ornamental principle', which is the base of every mode of art. The Primitives, Palestrina, Victoria, Orlando di Lasso, and others, made use of the divine arabesque. They found the principle of it in the Gregorian chant, and supported its frail threads by means of opposing counterpoints. . . . Do not even begin to think there must be something unnatural or artificial in this. On the contrary, it is infinitely more 'true' than the poor little cries that the lyric drama seeks to produce.

Of course you may remark that you never heard anybody whistle Bach. This mouth-glory Wagner has achieved; on the boulevard at that moment of the day when the prisoners-de-luxe of the musical houses of detention are released you may hear gaily whistled the Spring Song of *The Valkyrie*, or the opening phrase of *The Mastersingers*. I know that lots of people think that this is music's promised reward, but may one not claim to hold the contrary opinion without being thought singular?

Apparently, then, it was the decorative quality of the melodic element in Bach (rather than the masterly counterpoint) that appealed to Debussy, and indeed there is, questions of tonality aside, an obvious plainsong or Bach-like arabesque quality about many of Debussy's own themes.

Here is a Flute theme from *The Afternoon of a Faun*.

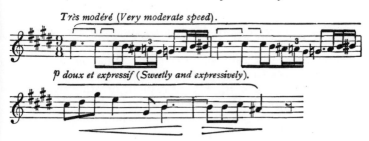

And here is an Oboe theme from the same work.

And doubtless Bach's reticence also appealed to him. Bach could express awe or jollity as well as any one, but he never expressed unrestrained romantic passion. We cannot imagine anything equivalent to the erotic transports of Siegmund and

Sieglinde or Tristan and Isolde as coming from Bach—or, for that matter, Handel or Mozart or any composer of the eighteenth century.[1]

Anti-Romanticism

And Debussy loved the eighteenth century. When a composer or poet takes a dislike to a century (and many do!) it is always to that which immediately precedes his own. The century before that he praises. So Debussy objected to the Romantic Movement in music (including Beethoven, its great herald, but not including Chopin, whose Gallic grace and arabesque-like melodic shapes attracted him) and lauded the 'classical' period, including Mozart and Bach and especially Bach's French contemporaries, Couperin and Rameau, in whom, again, he admired simple 'rightness' and reticence—

> We possess a pure French tradition in the work of Rameau, with its delicate and charming tenderness, its rightly placed accent, its rigorous declamation, its lack of pretence to a German profundity and of a need to emphasize with blows of the fist, to explain breathlessly, which seems as though one were for ever exclaiming 'You are a collection of idiots who understand nothing unless one compels you by force of exaggeration'. It is to be regretted that for so long French music should have taken a road that has led it far from that clarity of expression, that precision and terseness of form that are the particular and significant qualities of the national genius.

In the allusion to 'German profundity' and 'blows of the fist' we see, of course, hints of the distaste for Beethoven and Wagner in particular, and in Debussy's own music we find that in the revulsion from the forcefulness of these composers

[1] W. McN. interjects, 'Why on the side of non-reticence instance only romantic passion and eroticism? The non-reticence extends to all strong feelings: Hate (Alberich), Physical Exaltation (Forging Songs), Loyalty (Kurwenal), Pain (Amfortas), Friendship (Sachs and Walther), &c.'

he has, indeed, often shown himself a master of that most telling forensic art of understatement.

The Influence of Mussorgsky

Debussy's armour against Germany came largely from Russia, his armour against Wagner from Mussorgsky. The un-Wagnerian directness of Mussorgsky appealed to Debussy—

> Nobody has ever spoken of all that is best in us with an accent more tender or more profound; he is unique and will remain so, with his art devoid of system and of dry formulae. Never has so refined a sensibility been translated by means so simple. His music is like that of some enquiring savage discovering music step by step as his emotions develop. There is no question of any particular form, or at any rate what form there is is so many-sided that it cannot be related to the established (or as one might say, administrative) forms; the music is made up of little successive touches, bound together by a mysterious connexion, and by a gift of luminous clairvoyance; sometimes, too, Mussorgsky gives a sensation of trembling and unquiet shadows, which wrap themselves around the heart and press upon it to the point of anguish.

In Debussy's music any kinship with Mussorgsky is, perhaps, not very obvious. It is particularly hard to find in Debussy directness and primitiveness, at any rate of the Russian brands. It is almost impossible to find in him any of Mussorgsky's simple, elemental force. For Russian or Mussorgskyan *feeling* we should, in fact, have to search a long time; but Mussorgsky's influence in *dramatic method*, and above all the parallel of Debussy and the 1600 revolution, are to be seen in the songs, and in the Opera *Pelléas and Mélisande*, the music of which is so glove-like a fit to the words that the work might almost be called one long recitative.

For example, in the first scene Golaud finds Mélisande in

the gloomy forest. Golaud tells Mélisande who he is, she tells him her name, and he persuades her to follow him to the Castle. Yet with none of this are we given so much as the beginning of a set song. (Compare the telling duet of Puccini's Mimi and Rudolf when *they* first meet in Act I of *La Bohème*.) In the whole Scene there is no nearer approach to ordinary 'melody' than this:

Lower Strings, with 8ves below. Bassoons added.

So far we have seen in our study of Debussy three influences, (*a*) a reaction against the fervour and complexity of the whole 'Romantic' school as it then existed, (*b*) a corresponding love of eighteenth-century concision and clarity, and (*c*) an equally corresponding love of dramatic directness, such as that found in Mussorgsky. We now come to some definite influences emanating from sister arts.

The Literary Symbolists

The 'Symbolist' Movement in poetry and the 'Impressionist' Movement in painting were at their height when Debussy, returning in 1887 from study in Rome, settled again in Paris. Baudelaire, the chief precursor of the Symbolist Movement, was dead twenty years before, but Verlaine was alive, as also Mallarmé and a group of younger poets who gathered at Mallarmé's house and looked to him as their leader. Debussy frequented this house and imbibed the ideas there current, so it is of interest to us to get as clear a notion as possible of the nature of those ideas.

To describe in a few words the Symbolist Movement in literature is not easy. On its negative side it was a reaction against the big-bow-wow style of the French Romantic poets, and especially of the latest group of them who were known as the 'Parnasséans'. The Symbolists attempted a product altogether more delicate. To an English reader the change of feeling and method from Byron to Rossetti may convey a rough-and-ready idea of the change of feeling from (say) Hugo to Verlaine. And, too, as to 'content' the comparison between Ruskin and Pater may help. Ruskin was the apostle of what has been called 'moralized beauty'—a sort of Christian-statesman-critic. Pater was aesthetic and a frank hedonist—not the fruit of experience but experience itself is the end. 'A counted number of pulses only is given to us of a variegated and dramatic life. How may we see in them all that is to be seen in them by the finest senses?'[1]

There was, then, a good deal of the sensuous and the voluptuous about the Symbolist group, but they were a delicate sensuousness and a refined voluptuousness, expressing themselves with an aristocratic grace.

Nothing was coarsely or bluntly expressed. Indeed, what a poem said was almost less important than what the reader was led to think between the lines. There was a constant stimulus to the imagination, and herein lies the force of the title the Movement adopted. Words were used as symbols. They suggested rather than expressed. This often led to obscurity, and in some cases obscurity actually seemed to be the object.

Poetry like this approaches the quality of music. More than any other art, music (at its best) is the art of the subconscious. Try to find words with which to express the changing emotional shades of a Chopin nocturne, phrase by phrase of the music, and you will soon realize that in 'appreciating' that nocturne, as you have done, perhaps hundreds of times, you have been subconsciously following a play of emotional expression that you cannot with any completeness or exactitude consciously re-express.

This musical attribute was deliberately sought by the Symbolists in their poetry. Baudelaire had, in his time, counselled that poets should 'take possession again of their lost estate in the realm of music' ('reprendre à la musique leur bien'). Paul Valéry, writing about the Mallarmé group, said 'Music had been our very food, and our literary minds dreamt of nothing but to draw from language almost the same effects that sonorities produced on our nervous system'.

---

[1] From the conclusion of Pater's *Renaissance*. He omitted it from the second and third editions, as he 'conceived that it might possibly corrupt some young men into whose hands it might fall'. In the fourth edition, somehow reassured (or grown reckless), he restored it.

This, then, may be looked upon as a movement in literature the very opposite of the programme-music movement in music. As in programme-music the composer borrows and tries to re-express more or less definite literary ideas, so in Symbolist poetry the poet tries to achieve expression of emotion denuded, to the limits of possibility, of definite literary ideas. Mallarmé said, 'To *name* an object is to sacrifice three-quarters of that enjoyment of the poem which comes from the pleasure of guessing bit by bit. To *suggest* it—that is our dream.'[1]

The reader who is pretty well acquainted with even three or four of Debussy's compositions but has not previously grasped the connexion between his style and the aims of the Symbolist poets must surely now see a little light. The Symbolists were attempting a poetry like music, and Debussy, inspired by them, attempted a music more musical than had previously (or, at any rate, recently) been written, in that it eschewed, as far as possible, those Beethoven-like or Wagner-like complexities of development of theme which resemble argument or rhetoric, those Lisztian emotional passages that can easily be re-expressed in words, and those detailed 'programmatic' attempts which belong most properly to the short story or novel.[2]

The Painter-Impressionists

So much for the Poet-Symbolists; now as to the Painter-Impressionists, a closely allied group. Their aims differed

---

[1] It seems to us to-day rather strange that Mallarmé and his colleagues were at one period enthusiasts for the romantic Wagner. Presumably the mythology, with its suggestions of mysterious forces of nature behind the happenings of life, was what attracted them.

[2] Debussy certainly wrote a good deal of music that can be called 'Programme Music' (*The Cathedral under the Sea, Minstrels, Evening in Granada, The Wind across the Plain,* &c.). But, in it all, the musical condition is paramount, and though stories can legitimately be read into some of the pieces it is easy enough to see that their passages were not modelled upon any definite scheme of 'events'. It is, then, only 'Programme Music' in the more general sense of the term.

from those of the Symbolists, one may say, merely as the art of painting differs from the art of poetry. Sir Edmund Gosse has said of the Symbolist poets that their verse was 'a murmur of waters flowing under a veil of rushes', and we may say of the Impressionist artists that their painting was a play of light. They shunned drama ('Light is the chief personage in a picture' was one of Manet's maxims), 'literary' subjects, classical formality, and all established conventions, and sought to make out of the representation of effects of luminosity a kind of beautifully painted music. A technical procedure which is of interest, because in a moment we shall find a slight musical analogy to it, is the process of painting in pure, unmixed colours in such a close juxtaposition that at the proper distance the eye sees them merged into their intended composite. Like the poets they tried to achieve delicacy of nuance; as an example, they discovered that shadows are not necessarily black, but have their varying colours.

Manet may be considered the founder of the School, other members being Monet, Degas, Renoir, Pissarro, Sisley, and Cézanne.

At first the Impressionist painters had no popular success. They got their name as a nickname, from a painting of Monet's, *Sunrise, an Impression*, at the historic 'Salon des Refusés' of 1863; the idea of the term is that the painter records what a quick glance can see, i.e. he does not unnaturally assemble in one picture a mass of details each of which could have been observed only by its own particular glance. The pictures of this exhibition were sold by auction at the end and fetched an average of four pounds apiece. Later, to help Monet, who was in poverty, Manet, who was well-to-do, with a friend of his, anonymously bought ten of his pictures for forty pounds.[1]

[1] In 1923, Monet, aged 83, visited Paris to see, with his old friend Clemenceau, the building at the Tuileries that had been prepared to house nineteen of his paintings which a grateful nation had accepted as a gift from him. So does time bring its triumphs!

'Impressionism' in Tone

The comparison between the Impressionist painting and Debussy's music is quickly made. Debussy, too, as has already been said, avoided the dramatic, the narrative, the formal, the conventional, the involved. The preoccupation of the Impressionist painters with light *quâ* light had its parallel with this Impressionist musician in a preoccupation with tone *quâ* tone.

To take an example: frequently his chords are separate entities, their notes chosen and spaced on the piano (or distributed in the orchestra) in such a way as to produce the desired momentary tonal effect, and with little or no regard to their neighbours in such matters as the 'preparation' or 'resolution' of discords.

For the most part the harmony of Strauss is an extension of that of Wagner, whose harmony is an extension of that of Beethoven, whose harmony is an extension of that of Haydn. But Debussy's harmonies very frequently indeed can be derived from nothing heard from previous composers. Gifted with a very keen ear, he had listened to bugles and particularly bells, and had studied the 'overtones', the components of what we wrongly term a single note—those overtones the particular character and relative strengths of which, in any particular performance of a note, give that note its 'timbre'. And often he reinforced some of those overtones by the addition of notes, and so arrived at tonal effects by a synthetic process somewhat similar to the technical process of the Impressionist painters above referred to.

An influence in encouraging Debussy's freer conception of harmony was the music of his contemporary, Erik Satie, to be briefly discussed later in this volume.

Like the Poet-Symbolists and the Painter-Impressionists, Debussy is generally very 'atmospheric', and so, like them, he has been charged with vagueness. There is abundant design in a picture of Monet or a composition of Debussy, but (to quote *The Times* obituary of Monet in 1926, for the sake of its interesting allusion to Debussy)—

> It stands to reason that if an artist is designing in atmospheric values, in veils of light, the design will not be so emphatic, so easily grasped as if he were designing in solid forms, but nobody can look with attention at a picture by Monet and regard it as a mere representation of the facts and conditions. In this respect his work might well be compared to the music of his countryman, Claude Debussy, in which, under an atmospheric shimmer, the melodies are not so immediately recognisable as they are in the works of Bach and Beethoven, but are nevertheless present to an attentive ear.

The Whole-Tone Scale

A special technical device of Debussy to which allusion is often made is his use of the whole-tone scale.

There are two pitches at which this scale is available. It will be seen that, with enharmonic changes (reading F sharp = G flat in (*a*), C flat = B in (*b*), and so on), there is no note in our musical system which cannot be found in one of these two pitches of the scale.

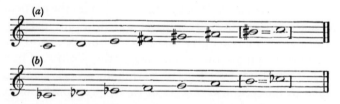

This scale is necessarily the most fluid possible. As all the intervals are the same, it may be said to have no features. Its effect, then, is vague, and so it contributes to the 'atmospheric' or 'remote' effect that is characteristic of Debussy.[1]

[1] E. W. recalls his foot-note to vol. i, p. 35, and says, 'I myself always seem to feel this whole-tone business not as a scale but as a chord (in arpeggio or in harmonic blocks).'

Debussy was not the inventor of this scale, but he made more systematic use of it than had any one before him. Here are two typical examples of his use of it. The first is from *Bells sounding through the leaves (Cloches à travers les feuilles)* from the Second Book of *Images* for Piano Solo. We have a whole-tone-scale melody at the top, supported by harmony which is merely made to fit the melody. (Notice the complete descending whole-tone scale at the outset; there appears to the eye to be a gap between the first two notes—such notation will generally be found necessary in practice.)

Two other points are illustrated in this example; firstly, Debussy's interest in bells, which we have just noted, secondly, his use of chords simply as blocks of sound, as shown in the lower part in the first bar. Debussy was really the inventor of this typical modern practice.

In our second illustration, we have a few bars, from *The Afternoon of a Faun* (*L'après-midi d'un faune*), of purely diatonic melody, with whole-tone chords arbitrarily introduced into the accompaniment at the second and fourth bars.

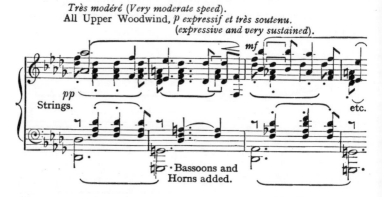

Très modéré (*Very moderate speed*).
All Upper Woodwind, *p expressif et très soutenu*.
(*expressive and very sustained*).

pp
Strings.
etc.

Bassoons and Horns added.

Debussy's Subjects

The subjects Debussy has chosen for his composition are, in the main, just what one would expect, given his style. It is a style with limitations. No 'Fate knocking at the door' symphony, no 'Hero's Life' tone-poem, could be achieved by Debussyan methods, even if such subjects were in consonance with the composer's general trend of mind.[1] The mystical

---

[1] E. W. protests, 'Beethoven is no doubt reported to have said that the first four notes of the C minor Symphony represented Fate knocking at the door; he is on equal authority reported to have said that they represented the note of some bird or other—but the latter interpretation is usually forgotten! I imagine that more pseudo-emotional nonsense has been written about the "fate-meaning" of this Symphony than about any other imaginary "meaning"—which is saying a good deal. The *Hero's Life* interpretation being definitely, even anxiously, authenticated in all its details isn't *pari passu*, is it?'

Maeterlinck symbolist play, *Pelléas and Mélisande*, is a natural choice as the subject of an opera; his style suits it perfectly. The opera is a masterpiece that can never be repeated, for the combination of librettist and composer will assuredly never occur again. Mallarmé's *Afternoon of a Faun* is another obvious choice as the subject for an orchestral piece, and its summer haze and heat are wonderfully suggested. It is very interesting to recall that Manet illustrated the first edition of this poem, so that we have here a concentration upon one and the same subject of the efforts of a leading Symbolist poet, a leading Impressionist painter, and the leading Symbolist-Impressionist composer.[1]

Clouds and *The Sea* are other orchestral examples of nature 'impressions', and amongst the piano pieces are *Gardens in the Rain, Reflections in the Water, Goldfish, Mists, Dead Leaves*, and many others.

There is in everything Debussy has written a suggestion of aristocratic refinement. The Symbolists and Impressionists were a sort of aristocracy. Mallarmé scorned the crowd and administered the duties of a sort of esoteric priesthood. There was a certain superiority about all these subtle practitioners of the three arts and perhaps they loved art rather than humanity. This apt remark has been made about Debussy's music—'It is lonely music; there are no *people* in it.'

Properly considered Impressionism is a Phase of Romanticism, but it is Romanticism become reticent, or at least more impersonal. The heart is there, but it is no longer worn on the sleeve.

NOTE

At one time, particularly in France, protests were made against the labelling of Debussy as an Impressionist Composer.

Such protests seemed to be based mainly upon the idea that by the

---

[1] It is terrible to imagine what things the realist Strauss would have done had he attempted a tone-poem on that subject. What an afternoon that Faun would have had!

application of the word 'Impressionist' there is implied something dero-gatory to Debussy as a master of musical form. Those who made the objection appeared to believe that Impressionist painting is formless; this matter is put upon the right footing in the quotation from *The Times* above given, and nothing need be added to that.

Another idea seems to be that the word 'Impressionist' as applied to Debussy suggests that he was a painter of musical landscapes, whereas it is rather the *emotional suggestions* of a landscape that he conveys. This second objection seems to be really stupid, since apart from the fact that to paint a landscape in sounds is an impossibility, it is Debussy's very skill in conveying the emotional suggestion of a scene of nature that is so marked, and that most entitles him to the description 'Impressionist'.

In any case, the critic Debussy, introducing his mythical character of Mr. Quaver (Monsieur Croche), into whose mouth he was accustomed to put his own opinions, was able to say of him, 'that he spoke of a score as if he were speaking of a picture, hardly ever using technical terms', so that the parallel between Debussy's art and that of a certain school of painters would not be entirely repudiated by the composer himself.

It is amazing that any one should cavil at one of the aptest labels ever yet attached to the baggage of any composer as it started its travels down the ages, and the objections are alluded to here only so that it may not be thought that this chapter has been written in ignorance of them. As has been shown in this chapter, an approach to parallelism between Debussy's music and the poetry of the Symbolists and the painting of the Impres-sionists is clearly defined, and the personal relations between Debussy and the Symbolist poets and Impressionist painters were close.

The Art of Ravel

Having discussed at some length the nature of Debussy's contribution to the art of music, it is comparatively easy, by defining differences, to discuss that of Ravel. Yet if this handy method be adopted, with it must go the warning that Ravel is no mere secondary Debussy and no mere disciple. Ravel is discussed second on purely chronological grounds, and described relatively on grounds of convenience.

Debussy and Ravel are both 'Impressionists', but Ravel is less truly so than Debussy, inasmuch as his music is less 'misty' or 'atmospheric'. Put Franck and d'Indy on one side and Debussy and Ravel on the other and you seem to have two distinct styles; then take Franck and d'Indy out of the discussion altogether and look only at Debussy and Ravel, and their distinction of style becomes clear enough. (Put red on one side and various blues on the other and you have an evident contrast; put red out of sight and your various shades of blue begin to sort themselves into classifications of their own.)

Debussy and Ravel—a Comparison

Comparing any sufficiently large body of mature work of the two composers, it will be realized that Debussy's is more 'fluid' and Ravel's somewhat more 'solid', i.e. more firm and clear in its outlines. Or Debussy's work is rather more 'subjective' and Ravel's more 'objective'. Partly this shows itself in differences of harmonic idiom. A good way of realizing the differences would be to hear, on consecutive evenings, Debussy's Opera, *Pelléas and Mélisande*, and Ravel's Opera, *L'Heure Espagnole*. It would then be found that Debussy was much more occupied in evoking emotional 'atmosphere', and Ravel in musically characterizing the sense of words which expressed clear thoughts or described dramatic 'events'. To this the rejoinder may be made that the literary subjects are very different and call for widely differing treatment, but to that may be re-rejoined that nobody imposed these subjects upon the respective composers, and that their very choice of them emphasizes the psychological difference between the two men.

The Italian composer, Casella, has drawn a fairly apt parallel by suggesting that as Schumann stands to Mendelssohn in German Romanticism, so does Debussy stand to Ravel in French Impressionism.

One great distinction between Franck on the one hand and Debussy-Ravel on the other is that the Franck music is charged with Christian feeling (mystical Christian feeling, that is), whereas the Debussy-Ravel music is an expression of

Paganism. Analysing further, Debussy represents the more shadowy side of Paganism (take *The Afternoon of a Faun* as an example) and Ravel the more clean-cut type of Pagan mythology (take *Daphnis and Chloe* as an example).

Both composers were opposed to the 'big' ideas of the Beethoven-Brahms school, both were careful manipulators of scraps of detail, but Ravel is a little more concerned with the planning and arrangement of his detail. To use the cant phrase, he is a trifle more 'cerebral'; he keeps command over himself and plans very exactly, and he tends to observe rather more closely than Debussy the principles of classical musical form.

Somebody has compared Ravel as a composer with Poe as a poet—Poe who maintained that there was no 'chance' in art any more than in mechanics, and that a poet's 'happy find' is as much the consequence of a train of reasoning as an engineer's 'invention'. When Poe wrote his famous essay on *The Philosophy of Composition* he was ignorant of what a more modern psychology has revealed to us of the workings and relations of the conscious and subconscious mind. It is now clear to us that one poet may depend much more than another on (conscious) reasoning and less on (subconscious) 'intuition', which is, after all, probably only a concealed reasoning; and so, in musical composition, Ravel seems to depend more upon the conscious than Debussy, and as a consequence the workings of his mind are seen by us in a whiter light. Debussy's music seems to 'grow' like an organism where Ravel's is more worked out to a scheme. Another Italian composer-critic, Pizzetti, has said that Ravel interests the listener's intelligence rather more than he interests his heart, and that is, perhaps, the same thought expressed in another way.

It seems strange to any one who knows the 'indolent voluptuous Massenet' to be told that he influenced Debussy, yet we have Debussy's word for this, and going back to his earlier works can find confirmation. Ravel, on the other hand, was more influenced by the colder, less sensuous style of the classically-minded Saint-Saëns.

Debussy's frequent use of the essentially vague 'whole-tone' scale has been mentioned; Ravel uses it practically not at all. This is typical.

Both Debussy and Ravel are ironists—especially Ravel. They both look on at life rather than throw themselves into it, and somewhat lack the large sense of humanity, of fraternity.

Like Debussy, Ravel is a great inventor of novel 'effects'. From *Fountains* (*Jeux d'eau*) onwards his additions to the stock-in-trade of the piano composer have been frequent and valuable. In orchestration he is equally original. Roland-Manuel has said that of all beings Ravel and Stravinsky best know the weight of a soft trombone chord, a 'cello harmonic, a *pianissimo* touch of the Tam-tam in relation with such-and-such an orchestral grouping. He makes a distinction between Debussy and Ravel as to orchestration which confirms from another side all that has just been said as to the difference between temperaments and methods—Ravel's music is fairly easy to conduct; follow the composer's direction and his effects are produced: Debussy's music is very difficult to conduct; the securing of the effects is a matter of extremest delicacy and requires enormous ability, and even the possessor of such ability seems to be somewhat in the hands of 'luck', succeeding on one occasion and, with the same orchestra in the same room, failing on another.

Like Debussy, Ravel is a harmonic innovator. Both men use parallel thirds, fourths, fifths, &c., very freely, but Debussy inclines more to the use of parallel ninths than Ravel, who favours parallel sevenths.

No composer has gone further than Ravel in the suggestion of economy—in giving the impression that every note of his music is essential.

As to literary influences, Ravel (despite what has just been said about his Opera) has accepted much the same as Debussy, with a slightly greater appreciation of some less definitely 'impressionistic' and 'symbolist' poets. He has compositions based upon Mallarmé, Verlaine, Verhaeren, Henri de Régnier, Jules Renard, 'Tristan Klingsor', Franc Nohain, and others, but he has also felt the value of some poetic inspiration of the past—Marot, Perrault, Mme d'Aulnoy, and the Princesse de Beaumont.

OTHER IMPRESSIONISTS (OR PARTIAL IMPRESSIONISTS)

Amongst French composers, Dukas, Florent Schmitt, Roussel, Séverac, and others, are more or less closely allied with the Impressionist party.[1]

Amongst British composers, Delius reflects Impressionist influence. (The late Philip Heseltine's remark in the *Dictionary of Modern Musicians* that Delius' art is 'the reverse of impressionistic' because with Delius 'Nature is interpreted not as a series of external phenomena, but rather as an integral part of the soul itself', and so forth, is not overlooked when this statement is made, but it is made nevertheless—on the view that the writer referred to has implied so narrow a definition of Impressionism (confusing it with the cruder forms of Realism) that it would actually exclude Debussy himself.)

Charles Marriott remarked in his *Modern Movements in Painting*—'Whatever Impressionism is, or is not, it is a form of Realism; but if we describe Impressionism in painting as a refinement of Realism with particular reference to conditions of light and atmosphere, we shall be near enough the truth for practical purposes.' Yet by 'Realism' and 'Impressionism' we commonly mean two very different things; it would sur-

---

[1] E. W. thinks Séverac deserves a little more notice here, 'if only in virtue of that very great little piece, *A Corner of a Cemetery in Springtime*'.

prise most listeners to hear Delius described as a 'Realist' composer, and satisfy most listeners to hear him described as at least an Impressionist-influenced one.[1]

As a side-light it may be remembered that Ravel and Florent Schmitt, themselves composers of the Impressionist School, were admirers and helpers of Delius before the world knew much of him.

There are strong traces of Impressionist influences in Vaughan Williams also, and it may be recalled that amongst the many teachers whose advice he sought, as a young man, was Ravel.

Perhaps, too, Bax had something of the Impressionist in him, and certainly there is an analogy to be traced between the Celtic literary influence in his work and the Mallarmé-Maeterlinck mistiness that appealed to Debussy.

It is impossible to hear John Ireland's (Orchestral) *Forgotten Rite* or his (Pianoforte) *Island Spell* without thinking that the work of the French Impressionists has counted for something in his development.

Cyril Scott has, in some of his compositions, shown very strong Impressionistic influences, so that he has occasionally received the decided compliment of being called 'The English Debussy'.

The Alsatian composer, Loeffler (American by adoption), showed very distinct Impressionist leanings in many of his works.

And so one might go on! Pure musical Impressionism is now a waning force, but it is a force nevertheless.

The German composers have been little influenced by the French Impressionists, the Italians and Spaniards more so.

---

[1] Definitions of Impressionism are sometimes blurred by the interaction of the influences on its literary, pictorial, and musical exponents. In this connexion it may surprise some readers to recollect that the literary 'Realist', Zola, was the great inspirer of Impressionism as a creed for painters.

Respighi and Falla are examples of the modern partial application of Impressionist methods. Respighi some years since alluded to Debussy as follows—'The spirit, the aesthetics and technique of modern music were not established in a precise, lasting, and definite manner until the appearance of the *Nocturnes*, the G minor Quartet, *The Afternoon of a Faun*, and *Pelléas and Mélisande*. . . . Debussy's work represents the greatest revolution in modern musical art.'

LEADING IMPRESSIONIST COMPOSERS
DEBUSSY

Debussy was almost a Parisian by birth, as he was decidedly one by spirit. He was born in 1862 at Saint-Germain-en-Laye.

Debussy.

At twelve he was sent to the Paris Conservatoire, and here he did well, winning honours in pianoforte and other subjects. His harmony professor was Guiraud, the then popular opera-composer, whose favourite pupil he became.

In 1884, aged twenty-two, Debussy won the Prix de Rome, which entitled him to a period of three years of quiet work at the Villa Medici. The work which brought him the distinction was the biblical Cantata *The Prodigal Son*, which has occasionally been staged as an opera. It offers little suggestion of the 'impressionistic' style which we now consider to be characteristic of the composer.

One of the conditions attached to the award is that the recipient shall send home each year a composition of some serious value. The first work so sent by Debussy was the Symphonic Suite, *Spring*, the second the delicate setting for orchestra and female voices of a translation of Rossetti's *Blessed Damozel*. Neither of these works was well received by the tribunal appointed to report upon it, and neither was allowed the usual public performance. From a comparison of these works with the one which won him the prize it would appear as though the prize work, however able, had been deliberately 'written down' to a style thought to be acceptable to the examiners.

Two strong influences on Debussy's development were that of Wagner, afterwards pretty completely cast off, and that of the Russian national school, especially Mussorgsky. There was even a short stay in Russia (at seventeen, as private pianist to the wife of a railway contractor), and the Russian influence was a vital factor in the composer's development. Debussy had met Balakiref, Borodin, and Rimsky-Korsakof in Russia, but not Mussorgsky, whose works, however, he closely studied. He made some little study of the Russian gipsy music.

At the period when Debussy left Rome for Paris, the Mallarme coterie was in full strength there. Debussy, as already related, became an habitué of the Mallarmé salon, associating with the poets, painters, and sculptors whose innovations were, as they intended, to prise the world of literature and art out of the groove of routine in which it was heavily rolling, and give it a freer course. The world of literature and art is rarely without some little band of workers of this type, but the trouble seems to be that when prised out of one groove, instead of running free it simply falls into another and runs in that until the next group of indignant enthusiasts takes it in hand. All this Providence has apparently ordained! It is a process of nature that on the whole works for the enrichment of the art.

Gradually Debussy made his way. A music-loving music publisher, Hartmann, encouraged him with needed money help (to save the composer's pride the publisher took IOUs, and when he died, his executor, more 'hart Mann' than Hartmann, insisted on their being redeemed).

In 1894, when Debussy was thirty-two, his *Afternoon of a Faun* was performed and created much discussion by its freedom of harmony and of form, and the novelty of its general style. So did a String Quartet (the only one he ever wrote), some Piano Pieces and Songs, and also some further orchestral works.

When in 1902 (aged forty) Debussy produced his Opera, *Pelléas and Mélisande*, the stir aroused by the *Afternoon of a Faun* broke out anew. To begin with, Maeterlinck, whose Drama Debussy had thus set to music, although he had given permission, now objected because Debussy had omitted certain scenes. Then the style of the vocal solo work was very new; it was like one long recitative, and that of what seemed to many people a very unvaried sing-song or plain-chant character. Further, the frequent absence of the customary 'tonality' (or adherence to a key) made the harmony sound very vague. Moreover, the orchestration was 'economical'; there were no rousing outbursts of tone, the work seemed to be tinted rather than coloured, and the tints seemed to be all greys. The fact is, *Pelléas* is a triumph of understatement, and understatement, though an effective method in argument with an intelligent individual, will not do with, say, the crowd at an election meeting. *Pelléas* is a masterpiece, but it will assuredly never be the work for the society dame or the 'tired business man'.

The piano compositions of Debussy are of very great importance. He really understands the instrument—as Chopin had understood it. He writes piano music, not orchestral music for piano, yet he obtains effects of sonority and colour that approach the orchestral; important use of effects of the pedal (or rather of both pedals) is a characteristic, so that the feet become almost as important as the fingers.

The many songs of Debussy are delicate and 'impressionistic' rather than 'tuneful'.

Amongst the most important of the orchestral pieces not already mentioned in this biographical sketch is *The Sea*.

There is some Chamber Music in addition to the Quartet just referred to—a Sonata for Violin and Piano, another for 'Cello and Piano, &c. And there are other things.

Debussy died in 1918 after a long and painful illness during which he continued bravely at work.

RAVEL

Ravel was of Basque descent, and was born in 1875 at Ciboure, near St. Jean de Luz, among the foothills of the Pyrenees. From childhood, however, he lived in or near Paris. He entered the Conservatoire and studied the piano with Charles de Bériot, counterpoint with Gédalge, and composition with Fauré.

As a boy he had become an enthusiastic admirer of the vivacious melody, bright rhythms, and clear orchestration of Chabrier, whom he met and whose influence on him was great, as was that of his master Fauré, with his respect for classic forms. Erik Satie (1866–1925), nine years his senior, the most daring harmonic innovator of the time, a composer who feared neither God nor man but did what seemed good in his own eyes, also exercised influence on him, both personally and through his compositions. Ravel tried later to help Satie, who was always miserably poor and never knew how to win public recognition, but, like other wayward geniuses, Satie was unhelpable. As already mentioned Satie's influence on Debussy was considerable.

Ravel.

Satie was a born iconoclast. He was one of those who are always 'agin the government', and the government of those days, as it happened, was largely Wagnerian, that is, it approved 'big' ideas, highly developed on the 'Leitmotif' system, with heavy orchestration, whereas Satie and his disciples (of whom Debussy and Ravel are only two of a large number) looked upon those things as opposed to the Latin temperament, and desired a greater directness. The mad whimsicality of Satie was one thing that stood in the way of his own recognition—writing his scores in red ink, often without bar lines, giving them incomprehensible titles, &c. Ravel also had a whimsical strain—but he had also common sense and balance.

As a competitor for the Prix de Rome, Ravel was unlucky. At twenty-six he won only the second prize, which did not entitle him to take up residence in Rome. At twenty-eight his failure aroused strong protests, in which his teacher, Fauré, joined. At thirty, still persevering, he was refused permission to sit, after the preliminary test. He was by now well known as a composer of works which rank high amongst his output, as they always must do, such as the *Habanera* (later to become a part of the *Spanish Rhapsody*), the popular piano piece, *Pavane for a Dead Infanta* (which first, perhaps, won him a wide public), the brilliant and original piano piece, *Fountains (Jeux d'eau)*, and, above all, the fine String Quartet.

The incident provoked a real storm of indignation. The *Matin* published an interview with the victim; the *Mercure de France* followed with a stirring article ('is this prize always to be given as the reward of intrigue or bestowed by imbeciles?'), and all that was lacking to the completeness and force of the journalistic campaign that now opened was the survival of Berlioz who, himself a Rome Prizeman, had in his day written some very sarcastic pages on the almost incredible stupidity of the conditions under which the awards were made (probably nobody more regretted Berlioz's absence than Berlioz himself; one can imagine him 'leaning over the bar of heaven' with dissatisfaction; it was a lost opportunity!). The fuss over this rejection led to the resignation of Dubois from the direction of the Conservatoire and the appointment of Fauré in his place. Anyhow, Ravel's disappointment brought 'publicity'—in abundance!

The piano Sonatina followed, with various Songs, the *Mirrors* for Piano, the curious *Natural Histories* for Voice and Piano, the orchestral *Spanish Rhapsody*, the witty Comic Opera *L'Heure Espagnole*,[1] the three Piano Pieces constituting the set, *Gaspard of the Night* (upon strange poems of Bertrand), the five Piano Pieces *Mother Goose* (*Ma Mère l'Oye*—later orchestrated and turned into a Ballet), and, above all, the Ballet usually considered the composer's masterpiece, *Daphnis and Chloe* (on the stocks from 1906 to 1911, and performed in 1912, with decorations by Bakst, and with Karsavina and Nijinsky amongst the protagonists).

Later works were a good many Songs, the Piano pieces collectively called *The Tomb of Couperin*, the very daring sonata for Violin and 'Cello alone, and a number of other things.

Ravel died in 1937.

[1] It is difficult to translate this title, 'Heure' constituting a slight play upon a word which can mean either 'hour' or 'time'—the plot being about clocks.

PERIOD VII
The Neo-Romantics

XX

THE NEO-ROMANTICS

As the nineteenth century wore on there came into view a new succession of romantic composers. We might call them the Post-Lisztian Romantics, for all were continuators of the work of Liszt. Or we might call them the Post-Wagnerian Romantics, for none of them would have written as they did but for the example of Wagner, and some of them are direct continuators of his work.

Franck

Franck and Strauss are two of these. The nature and artistic aims of Franck are as different as possible from those of Strauss. Strauss's heart was in the theatre, and from it he emerged into the concert room to give us music of an almost always dramatic kind. Franck's heart was in the church, and from it he emerged into the concert room to give us music fraught with all the spirituality of the atmosphere of the place he had left. Occasionally, too, he reached the theatre, but there he was utterly *dépaysé* and, after a rapid failure, quickly returned. He was, indeed, in a sense, an enemy of the theatre, for he helped to show a nation to whom music had usually meant the stage, that, like other nations, they had, if they would only recognize it, a talent, too, for 'absolute music'. France had, up to this time, been too much devoted to Italian and quasi-Italian Opera. This composer showed it that the Symphony and the String Quartet also could offer worthy entertainment.

Franck revived and remodelled the classic forms. He was soaked in Bach's polyphony and in Beethoven's symphonic style, and he eagerly accepted the warm humanity of both these composers. And from Liszt and Wagner (respectively eleven and nine years older than he) he learnt the new methods of flexible construction, and from the latter the ease of modulation that comes with the adroit use of chromatic harmonies. He used generative phrases, out of which a composition grew organically. He employed a 'cyclical treatment' re-introducing the same themes in the several movements of a composition, and so connecting them by a thread of unity. In his *Symphonic Variations* for Piano and Orchestra he revelled in the Variation form, with its facilities for showing a musical theme in different lights. In orchestration he was distinctive, but perhaps there is some truth in the allegation that he used his instruments as he used the stops of his organ, and produced an effect of well-thought-out organ 'registration' rather than of discriminative orchestration.

Franck was a Romantic, but where Strauss was a Pagan Romantic he was a Christian Romantic—a sort of later Lamartine of music. He could depict struggle, but he could not depict evil, and when, for dramatic purposes, he tried to do the latter he fell into commonplace.

Franck's creed and his art were one with his life. Debussy, whose life and artistic aims were different, said of him, perhaps a little sentimentally, in a newspaper article one Good Friday:

> I could wish to have drawn the picture of Franck more firmly, in order that every reader might have carried away a definite memory of it. It is a good thing, amongst our too pressing preoccupations, to fix our minds on the great musicians. I have made Good Friday the occasion of offering my homage to one of the greatest of these, thinking that this homage would correspond a little with the idea of sacrifice. . . .

Franck and Debussy were the founders of two very distinct schools, Debussy's (as has already been seen) the school of musical impressionism, and Franck's a school of a sort of modification of the older and heavier type of romanticism. It is commonly said that Debussy was much the more definitely and distinctively French; perhaps he was, and not only French but Parisian, whereas Franck (a Belgian born) is little of a Latin and, so far from being in mind a Parisian, is always humanly provincial. There is nothing of the man-about-town or of the salon favourite about Franck. He belongs, indeed, rather to the cloister than to the drawing-room; he is a mystic, the Fra Angelico of music.

There is a peculiar and moving kind of mystical exaltation about Franck; at his climaxes he rises to real sublimity, and it seems as though he were adding his part to a choir of angels, seen and heard by him, though not by us. He is generally lyrical; his music sings.

The melodies of Franck are peculiarly his own. They tend strangely often to circle about one note, e.g. the F sharp in the great tune of his Symphony:

Allegro (Quick).
Trumpets, Upper Ww., Violins, with *8ves.*

(Accompanying harmonies).

etc.

The Italian composer, Casella, has complained that there is some lack of rhythmic variety in Franck. Perhaps there is; it is a part of the lyric or non-dramatic character of his music. He is often long; Debussy said of him, 'Franck had a prodigious carelessness about time because he did not know what it was to be bored.' Probably he did not. He lived his life eagerly and earnestly, and all he did interested him.

Franck was not of a deeply literary turn. So far as his work was based on literature it was the definitely romantic authors to whom he turned for inspiration—Leconte de Lisle

(Symphonic Poem, *The Eolides*), Bürger (Symphonic Poem, *TheAccursed Hunter*), Hugo (Symphonic Poem, *The Djinns*).

Though much of the piano music of Franck (which constitutes an important part of his output) demands a virtuoso to perform it, there is only one work, the *Symphonic Variations* for Piano and Orchestra, in which he indulges in virtuoso display, and even then he does not sacrifice emotional intensity to showiness.

Richard Strauss

Richard Strauss enjoyed a double fame. He was the most able successor of Liszt as a master of the Symphonic Poem, and of Wagner as a composer of Music Drama. It is impossible to imagine his doing what he did had either of these men not preceded him.

The most obvious difference between the scores of a Liszt Symphonic Poem and one by Strauss is not in any divergence as to artistic aim, but in a more 'advanced' harmony and orchestration and in a better standard of workmanship. The subject of Strauss's harmony cannot be discussed in any very technical way in a book intended for the layman-listener. An example may, however, be given, and it is explained in a footnote for the benefit of readers who have at least a little technical knowledge of harmony.[1]

[1] It is a passage from the opening of *Don Quixote*—the Knight's vision of a battle between a hero and a giant. Muted Trumpets play the Hero

&c.
(continuing
in F sharp as an established key.)

theme, which begins and ends with a fanfare-like *motif*. Two Tubas and Double Basses, all muted, play the bass, the Giant theme (Double Bassoons and muted Violins also help a little).

Note first the F sharp held resolutely by the Oboe, regardless of consequences. This clashing inner 'Pedal' is itself typical.

The first bar and a half are quite simple. Thence there would seem to be no definite sense of key at all until the beginning of the fifth bar. We have simply a chord, common enough in itself, rising chromatically over a bass which takes its own independent course. Sometimes the bass and

Strauss's orchestration is very able and very personal—so personal that one could recognize a few phrases of a Strauss Tone Poem by its orchestration alone, as one can recognize an Andrea del Sarto at a glance, by the clothes of the persons pictured.

There remains the question of general workmanship. First it may be said that Strauss at his best, or perhaps on the whole, makes use of better materials than Liszt. His melodic themes and *motifs* are generally stronger and more significant, and he has more rhythmic variety.

Secondly, his use of those themes and *motifs* shows a greater care and judgement. He is a master of the processes of thematic development, and, equally, a master of counterpoint, for he can weave together melodies with the greatest ease and effectiveness. He is, further, a master of form; he can unfold in music a literary idea, and in doing so achieve at the same time a high architectural value. With his enhanced harmonic and orchestral resources he can express in subtler detail an emotional scheme. In one sense the difference between Tone Poems by Liszt and by Strauss resembles that between Symphonies by Mozart and Beethoven; as music has taken on new powers with Beethoven and so can achieve a greater emotional intensity, so again it has done with Strauss. The genuinely romantic opportunities of musical expression are much emphasized when they come into hands such as his. With the sum of all the powers just mentioned he has been able to make a bigger and more complete thing of the Tone Poem than any of his predecessors or any of his contemporaries.

the upper parts combine to form some familiar chord (as dominant seventh or diminished seventh), but though there is method there is apparently no diatonic basis.

Last characteristic of all—at bar 5 we emerge with D major only to plunge immediately into the unrelated F sharp major, and to 'carry on' in that key on the calm assumption that it is accepted and established.

The art of Strauss is a very supple one, and when he fails it is not from want of skill and power, but from want of judgement. To begin with, he is a great realist, and this fairly often leads him astray. In his *Don Quixote* Tone Poem when the windmill is to be tilted at he makes use of a 'Wind Machine', and at once the attention of everyone in the audience is drawn from the character of the hero and centred upon a matter-of-fact material detail: poetry is 'thrown to the winds'. When in the same piece we hear the extremely realistic bleating of sheep we may say that better sheep were never 'penned', but the thought comes that if sheep are made to talk, why not also the Don and Sancho, and we become uneasy here, as we do in the *Alpine Symphony*, when cowbells are heard, for it is clear that a piece of direct imitation has been inserted just because direct imitation happened to be, for the moment, possible, and not to satisfy any musical or poetic need.[1] The bathing of the baby in the *Domestic Symphony*, the battle and the quarrelling of the pedants in the *Hero's Life*, the 'Brook', the 'Waterfall', the 'Glacier', and the 'Losing the Way' in the *Alpine Symphony* are somewhat similar examples of a sort of childishness that grew upon Strauss until in the last-named work he sank to the level of the gentleman who plays 'The Storm' to summer visitors in the church at Lucerne, or his fellow-worker who has embellished the building with iron chancel gates that, flat and a mere inch thick as they are, embody an effect of perspective, and so simulate an extended iron arcading.[2]

[1] In this matter Strauss may be compared with one or two of the early Venetian painters (notably Crivelli, 1430–94), who occasionally took an opportunity to break from representation into realism, attaching an actual jewel to their canvas instead of merely painting it.

[2] 'Properly, perhaps, we ought to discriminate between (*a*) what Strauss actually mentions in his scores; (*b*) what is, though not so mentioned, understood to be approved by him (e.g. the sheep and the windmills); and (*c*) what, so far as I know, is due merely to commentators (e.g. the baby's bath—not at all obvious, really, in the score).' E. W.

These things are not art, they are mere playful puerilities, and the mind absorbed in the production of such is very apt to let the demand for artistic quality drop out of sight. How far Strauss was sometimes led to do this may be realized by playing the *Alpine Symphony* or the *Hero's Life* from the piano score. The glamour of the vivid Straussian orchestration being put aside, one finds there is little left to interest one so far as these particular pieces are concerned; Liszt, one may almost say, would stand the test equally well. *Till Owlglass' Merry Pranks* is the Tone Poem which best stands this test, and it stands it very well. It is written to a very detailed programme, but it is, to begin with, largely a humorous work, which justifies certain things which might otherwise have been felt to be out of place. But the great merit that saves it is the musical quality of the themes themselves.

Another weakness of Strauss was his megalomania. Nearly all his works call for a huge orchestra, and in many places they are complex beyond the point of effectiveness. The composer, Ernest Bloch, who was for a time intimate with both Strauss and Debussy and observed their methods, once said that when Strauss had finished an orchestral score he did not rest until he had added still more contrapuntal devices, piling complication upon complication, whereas Debussy was never satisfied until he had taken out of his score as many notes as possible, and simplified it to the last degree. Strauss's megalomania was more than a mere technical error; he was a victim of a temporary national failing—a worshipper of the 'Superman' and long a great admirer of the ex-Kaiser, and then a supporter of Hitler. Moreover he often succumbed to the German weakness for profundity, as in his Tone Poem, *Thus Spake Zoroaster*, based on Nietzsche.

But his greatest mistake, as an orchestral composer, was in his misunderstanding the nature of programme music. If he had been content to represent the emotions inherent in a dramatic event or a picture all would have been well, and nobody could do this better than he; if he wanted to reproduce the drama or the picture itself he should have been born a dramatist or a painter.

A number of stories have been told to illustrate Strauss's belief in music's power of realistic reproduction. One (told by Guttmann, a Vienna concert manager) relates that, at supper, after a performance of the *Domestic Symphony*, Strauss dropped a knife and fork quietly on the table and said 'To reproduce a little noise like that so that there may be no doubt in the mind of the hearer as to what made it, requires great artistic technique. I'd like to carry it that far.' Another tells how, sitting at lunch in Boston, with the composer Martin Loeffler, he prophesied that the descriptive capacity of music would some day be developed to such a point that it would be possible to delineate a fork (picking one up) so accurately that every listener in the concert room would recognize it. A third (told by Felix Mottl, the great conductor) is as follows: 'Strauss once asked me if I had ever noticed that one of the women in his *Don Juan* Symphonic Poem had red hair. I replied that often as I had conducted the work I had never dreamed that one of the Don's victims was red-headed. "Then I have failed!" said the composer. "I thought everyone would recognize that".'[1]

Yet when all is said, Strauss is a great master. Ernest Newman, in his very thoughtful volume on Strauss, written, it is true, in 1907, before some of the weakest works had appeared, says (with a curious mixture of metaphor): 'Even when he is spoiling a fine picture by inserting in it details that set one's teeth on edge by their inappropriateness, or their inanity, he always weaves the threads together, the cotton with the

---

[1] These three stories are retailed by the late H. E. Krehbiel in *The Musical Digest*, August 29, 1921. There is probably an element of either joking or boastfulness (or both) about all the assertions, but they do, at any rate, indicate a trend of mind—possibly a real obsession with problems of tonal imitation.

silk, in masterly fashion.' The fact is that Strauss would have been a greater musician had he been a greater man. There seems to have been some weakness in his character, some lack of essential nobility of temperament.

This weakness showed itself also in his Operas. The best of them, the brilliantly written *The Knight of the Rose*, opens with a scene in which a young boy of unbroken voice is seen in a position that, as a setting for sentiment and humour, must be repugnant to any spectator with ideals, and this same work ends with an Act devoted largely to farce of a very cheap kind, quite out of keeping with the Acts that have preceded it. The Music Drama, *Salome*, based on Oscar Wilde's play (which in its turn was based on Flaubert), is painful in its realistic representation of eroticism and cruelty, and its music is only too well fitted to its libretto. There is a strong vein of morbidity about the German Neo-romantic school, and it is probably a sign of decadence.[1]

If one were asked to describe Strauss in two or three words one would call him a Realistic-Romantic. He is, in a way, the Zola of Music.

By temperament and manner Zola belongs emphatically to the romanticists; his sweeping pen, his characterizations of types, his profusion, his colour, his mass formation, even his exaggeration stamp him indelibly of the school of Hugo. . . . There was the other Zola of the realist revolt, who broke away with Flaubert from the imaginary into the natural world, and who wedded the 'romantic' style to the realist matter by depicting what he saw and heard and smelt and touched. To this realistic influence is to be added the scientific doctrine of writers like Taine. Zola was ridden by philosophic theories [here follows an allusion to the Rougon-Macquart series]. . . . It is bad Taine and bad Hugo; bad science and bad fiction, because an imperfect amalgam of both; and, almost necessarily, the products of

[1] 'What about *The Woman without a Shadow*, which seems to me to contain some of Strauss's very biggest and finest music?' E. W.

vice occupied him more than those of virtue. . . . The best of Zola is the temperament, a poetic one which carried his readers forward as on a flood. (Magnus, *Dictionary of European Literature*.)

A very slight paraphrase of this would fit Strauss. The development seen in the works of the two men runs about parallel: there are three Strausses as there are three Zolas—the Romanticist, the Realist, and the Philosopher (the last-named Strauss cropping up in a good many works, but being most clearly represented by the Nietzschean Tone Poem, *Thus Spake Zoroaster*).

Elgar

There are senses in which we might call Elgar an English Franck. Like Franck he finds expression for his essentially romantic spirit rather through the symphonic than the dramatic. He never wrote an Opera, and though he wrote a little Programme Music his greatest instrumental work is to be found in his 'Enigma' Variations, his two Symphonies, and his Violin Concerto. But it may be admitted that his Oratorios and Cantatas show in some places a sense of the dramatic.

Like Franck, Elgar was a Christian Romantic; and like him was a Roman Catholic and a mystic. The Oratorios *The Apostles* and *The Kingdom* are expressions of his Christian Romanticism, and the Oratorio *The Dream of Gerontius* (a setting of Cardinal Newman's Poem) is an expression of a deeply poetic type of Roman Catholic religious feeling.

Elgar was a very sensitive and very subjective composer. He felt his music as much as 'composed' it; but he did compose it, too, and with a strong sense of form made use of great gifts of melody, ever-varied chromatic harmony, and richly coloured orchestration. The passage from Beethoven's Fifth Symphony referred to on page 135 of vol. I of this book (the mystical linking passage between the Scherzo and the Finale) is representative of a type of awed mystery that often recurs in Elgar, as for instance in the wonderful accompanied Cadenza of the Violin Concerto. A sort of reflective brooding is very common with him, as is also a totally distinct quality, that of a sonorous, swinging-rhythmical nobility ('nobilmente' is one of his frequent directions to his players).

Elgar, like Franck, has been charged with the inability to depict evil, and perhaps he rarely does so, but in a large part of *Gerontius* he achieves the feat. The snarling of the demons in that work is, by the way, one of the comparatively rare instances in his work of dramatic representation of details in the Straussian vein, another being Judas' flinging down of the thirty pieces of silver in *The Apostles*.

Elgar's most definitely 'programmatic' work is his Symphonic Poem *Falstaff*, a composition full of passages of the most wonderful beauty, yet so far as public appreciation goes a comparative failure, and necessarily so, since the events and passions represented succeed one another so rapidly that even the most conscientious listener, with his eyes riveted on the programme book which details the happenings, must almost inevitably lose his way and find himself struggling to read into some passage a thought or emotion that belongs to a previous or subsequent moment.[1]

Like Franck, in his symphonic works Elgar has tried to weld his Movements into one by the recurrence of themes. The First Symphony is one of the most notable examples in music

[1] In 1906, as Peyton Professor of Music at Birmingham University, Elgar definitely declared himself in favour of abstract, as against 'programme' music. The *Cockaigne* Overture was written in 1900 and *Falstaff* in 1913. The 'Programme' of *Falstaff*, as given by the composer himself, divides the work into four sections: (1) Falstaff and Prince Henry; (2) Eastcheap, Gadshill, the Boar's Head, revelry and sleep; (3) Falstaff's March, the return through Gloucestershire, the new King, the hurried ride to London; (4) King Henry V's progress, the repudiation of Falstaff and his death. This gives but the main lines; there is much greater detail in the dramatic representation than that would indicate.

of the successful use of this device. His Symphonies, however, remain true symphonies—as Bernard Shaw well said, more Symphonies in the Beethovenian sense than any of Schumann, Mendelssohn, or Brahms.

A common jibe amongst young musicians a few years ago was that Elgar was 'the English Brahms'. Both men were seriously disposed and both were Classic Romantics, and that is about as far as the truth goes. In one respect the work of Elgar goes far beyond that of Brahms—he was a much more able orchestral colourist. He learnt far more from Wagner than from Brahms, and doubtless to him owed his ability to carry on for considerable lengths the weaving of a continuous and highly contrapuntal web. To him he also owed the Leading Motif system which forms an effective feature of his oratorio scores, and to him he certainly owed a good deal of his chromatic harmony. There is also something of the *Parsifal* spirit in the Oratorios. To Liszt he necessarily owed something; most composers of the later nineteenth century do! To Strauss also there is an indebtedness; *Falstaff* might not have been written but for *Till Owlglass*. He is rather a contemporary than a follower of Strauss, however. Like Strauss, he has moments of secondrateness; these occur with Strauss when he is trying to be especially clever in a representative way, and with Elgar when he is trying to express a sort of Chamberlain-Kipling British imperialism, or when he was trying to unbend and to talk to the very man in the street, with *Salut d'amour* and the like. But he is never guilty of the vulgar eroticism of Strauss, and the faults just hinted at belong to the earlier part of his career.[1]

[1] This amusing anecdote, which I had from the composer himself, deserves to be recorded. When Strauss's Opera *Salome* was first to be given in New York, Elgar was in the city for some performances of his Oratorios. Good people who were anxious to maintain the time-honoured purity of thought of New York Society organized a monster Prayer Meeting against the Opera. What more natural than that they should count upon the sympathies of the Oratorio composer against the Opera composer, and ask Elgar to lead it ? This invitation was, however, not accepted!

Allusion has been made above to the occasional programme-music excursions of Elgar. In one composition of a sort of 'programme' character he is an innovator. In his *Enigma* Variations for Orchestra each treatment of the theme is designed to suggest the temperamental and occasionally the physical characteristics of one of his friends, and many of the Variations have the initials of the friends in question attached to them.[1]

Elgar's Chamber Music appeared rather late in his career (curiously, since he began life as a violinist). It is competent and attractive, but does not rank with his Orchestral and Choral Music; it is in his personal idiom, but hardly reveals the bigness of his personality.

The recognition of Elgar abroad has been on the whole disappointing. This is alluded to in the short biography on a later page. There is even in England a 'set' that does not care for his music. Professor Edward Dent, in an article on British music in *La Musica Contemporanea in Europa* (Milan, 1925), speaking of Liszt says, 'In England the best musicians have a real horror of him. The only composer who shows traces of his influence is Elgar, and Elgar, despite his brilliant style, is repugnant to many English musicians, by reason precisely of that chevaleresque rhetoric which badly covers up his intrinsic vulgarity.'[2] This is the only reference to Elgar in

---

[1] An amusing revelation was about to be made at the moment when this book first went to press. The composer had prepared for 'The World's Music' Series of 'Pianola' and 'Duo-Art' Rolls a descriptive analysis to appear on the Rolls of the Variations, and some passages to which fixed interpretations had until then been given by most annotated-programme writers were shown to have been wrongly understood. To give one example —a certain rapidly running bass passage in the Variation devoted to the late Dr. G. R. Sinclair, of Hereford Cathedral, had always been spoken of as intended to represent this organist's pedalling. It now turned out to have been suggested by the sight of the organist's dog enjoying a swim in the river. So much for the power of music to tell a story!

[2] Professor Dent is a strong supporter of the 'Neo-Classic' School of Busoni.

a fifteen-page article of which Stanford receives a page and Rutland Boughton receives a page and a quarter.

Although, as elsewhere stated, America has a good deal neglected Elgar, yet some of the most thoughtfully appreciative criticism of his work has come from an American writer, Mr. Daniel Gregory Mason. (Mr. Newman is much the most understanding English critic of Elgar.) As a specimen of Elgar's very distinctive style there may be given here a passage from the 'Nimrod' Variation of the *Enigma* (the one work, by the way, that is pretty well known and appreciated in all countries):

Of this Mr. Mason says, 'It has all the tenderness coupled with aspiration, the noble plainness, that belong to Elgar at his best. And it is a striking fact that the originality of the passage (for no one but Elgar could have written it) is due to subtle, almost unanalysable qualities in the mode of composition rather than to any unusual features of style.'

He then acutely analyses the unanalysable—the 'predominance of simple triads and seventh chords, especially the more rugged sevenths for which Elgar has a noticeable fondness', the 'frequent use of suspensions', the 'restless motion of the bass', the tendency of the melody to 'large leaps, often of a seventh, in alternating directions, giving its line a shapely, serrated profile', and above all 'the rhythmic flexibility . . . the free sweep of the line scorning to rest on the accents, soaring through its long continuous flight like a bird in a favouring gale'. He concludes, 'We have here, then, the vein of expression, at once plain, serious and noble, which makes Elgar at his best both English and universal.' There is peculiar pleasure to a British admirer of Elgar in taking such an analysis of style as this from the writings of an American author.

MacDowell

Edward MacDowell, the most generally recognized composer America has yet produced, was essentially a Romantic —one of something like the Schumann kind, revelling in the expression of emotion of literary origin rather than the attempted reproduction of definite literary thought. Various items in the list of his works show his love of Heine, Goethe, Victor Hugo, Dante, Shakespeare (Symphonic Poem, *Hamlet and Ophelia*), Keats (Symphonic Poem, *Lamia*), Tennyson (Symphonic Poem, *Lancelot and Elaine*, &c.), and others of the romantic poets. The influence of Celtic Legend is also strong (he came, in after life, to realize how strong the power of his Celtic ancestry was within him and to pride himself upon it).[1]

---

[1] 'In all my work there is a Celtic influence. I love its colour and meaning. The development in music of that influence is, I believe, a new field' (quoted by Gilman). In later years, amongst 'home' composers of Great Britain, Celtic influence became more pronounced, more definite, more avowed, notably in Bax.

In innumerable compositions he shows himself a nature-lover, not merely of the kind that shows its love of nature by knocking birds out of the air and dragging fishes out of water (MacDowell's friends, seeing him return with a gun but no bag, used to say he 'only pretended to hunt'), but also of that kind that can be moved by a sunset or by 'the meanest flower that blows' (he wrote, by the way, many little pieces named after flowers).

MacDowell was a great admirer of Wagner and Liszt, of Tchaikovsky and Grieg, but not so much of Strauss (who apparently leaned too much to the realistic side for his taste) or of Brahms (who apparently leaned too much to the classical side). He seems to have known little of the music of Debussy (who was in boyhood a fellow pupil of his in Paris), and probably the 'impressionistic' style could make little appeal to a man whose leanings were all to the warmer German type of romantic expression.

MacDowell's four Piano Sonatas are respectively entitled *Tragica*, *Eroica*, *Norse*, and *Keltic*. The first was inspired by his emotions at the death of his old master, Raff (a composer whose love of nature and of legend must have been very congenial to him); the second was based upon the Arthurian legend in its Tennysonian setting; the third upon the Scandinavian legend of Gudrun and Sigurd; and the fourth upon the Celtic legends of Deidre and Cuchullin. This last he intended to dedicate to Fiona Macleod (William Sharp), and, but for the loss of a letter in the post, he would have done so; the spirit of Fiona Macleod's writings is the spirit of much of Mac-Dowell—the spirit Wordsworth recognized in the song of the Highland Reaper:

> Will no one tell me what she sings ?
> Perhaps the plaintive numbers flow
> For old, unhappy, far-off things,
> And battles long ago.

—a passage that comes to mind when we read of MacDowell's

recollection of 'once hearing in London a song sung in the streets at night' that meant far more to him than 'the glorious magnificence of tonal texture' of Strauss's *Thus Spake Zoroaster*. MacDowell wrote a fair quantity of poetry (not great poetry, but genuinely felt and neatly shaped), and it is full of the suggestion of the dim and impalpable—of 'far-off things' seen through the mist of ages and the haze of evening. Often he prefixed a specially written stanza to one of his compositions, crystallizing in a few lines the feeling of the music much in the way that Sir Walter Scott crystallized the thought of a chapter of a novel by a specially composed quotation from 'Old Ballad'. He also wrote the poems of many of his songs.

MacDowell's Nature inspiration is shown in the titles of innumerable short piano pieces. Take as examples the *Sea Pieces* (with 'To the Sea', 'From a Wandering Iceberg', 'Starlight', 'From the Depths', 'Nautilus', and 'In Mid-Ocean'), and the *New England Idylls* (with 'An Old Garden', 'Midsummer', 'Midwinter', 'In Deep Woods', 'To an Old White Pine', and 'The Joy of Autumn'). He used, in discussing his art, the term 'Suggestive Music' rather than 'Programme Music', and said that music was not meant to be 'an agent for expressing material things; nor to utter pretty sounds to amuse the ear; nor a sensuous excitant to fire the blood; nor a sedative to lull the senses'. Music, he added, is 'a language, but a language of the intangible, a kind of soul language. It appeals directly to the *Seelenzustände*[1] it springs from, for it is the natural expression of them, rather than, like words, a translation of them into set stereotyped symbols which may or may not be accepted for what they were intended to denote by the writer!'

MacDowell had a great gift of melody, of the kind that all can at once appreciate yet is not commonplace. In his rich and often emotionally moving harmony he was no great innovator; he introduced little or nothing new, but made an un-

[1] 'Soul-states.'

conscious amalgam of what had attracted him in the harmony of others—particularly amongst the German Romantics. There is a certain nobility about much of his music, less deep than that of Elgar and more like that of some parts of Schumann's work.

There is some tendency today, perhaps, to underrate Mac-Dowell. We need, however, more composers of his kind—that is, composers who, with all their literary and musical culture, yet retain the power of wide and immediate appeal. He was an able pianist, and his piano compositions are well written for the instrument; the smaller ones are a boon to the amateur.

Scriabin

From his earliest page to his latest, Scriabin is a Romantic. At first he is a follower of Chopin—the closest original follower Chopin has ever had, producing quiet music of rare, romantic beauty, comparable in every way to Chopin's own. Then he begins to imbibe and to re-express philosophical ideas. He is captured by Theosophy, and soon he has developed into a Romantic of the other type—one who, not content with the expression of Romantic beauty and the vaguer Romantic emotions, strives to express a definite 'programme' of romantic 'literary' ideas. He amplifies his manner of expression; he learns from Liszt and from Wagner (especially from *Tristan*), and soon the stream of Nocturnes, Impromptus, Studies, Mazurkas, and Preludes dwindles. To the end he composes Preludes, but they are Preludes of a much more strongly personal kind, and represent a much more vivid kind of emotional expression, whilst with these slighter forms we now find mingled much bigger things (bigger in the sense not only of size but of emotional scope), such as a *Satanic Poem* (for Piano), a *Divine Poem* and a *Poem of Ecstasy* (for Orchestra), a great *Poem of Fire* ('Prometheus'—for Orchestra with Chorus), and *Towards the Flame* (for Piano).

All the time we find the technical resources expanding and the idiom changing. Look at a very early piece and a very late one and you may not see much resemblance of idiom, but go through the whole series, and you will see as logical a process of step-by-step development as any composer has ever shown.

The classical form remains intact throughout. Of course, the Sonata Form he so often used differs greatly in detail from that which we find in a Haydn or even a Beethoven Sonata or Symphony, but all the formal principles of these are retained. In the matter of form, indeed, Scriabin, despite his preoccupation with a 'programme' of philosophic ideas, is almost a classic.

But the harmonies (and consequently the melodies) pass gradually right away from anything of the Classical or the earlier Romantic period. An idiom is being brought into existence that can express a much wider range of emotions, and express them more definitely, than had previously been possible. Had any composer ever expressed sarcasm in music before Scriabin—to take one small example that comes at once to mind ?[1] Had the ecstasy of joy in all its wildest abandon been so powerfully expressed before ? Had the definitely evil things of the dark places of the mind, the very diabolic itself, the spirit of the Black Mass, been so clearly hinted at before (for unlike Franck and Elgar, Scriabin *could* express evil) ?

Gradually Scriabin has forged his own tools. He has a chord of superposed fourths of his very own (e.g. C, F sharp, B flat, E, A, D) which has gradually built itself up in successive compositions, and at last stands complete and more and more dominates his scores—which have now ceased to bear key-signatures, since the music no longer keeps any key.[2] He

---

[1] A younger Russian, Prokofief, later did so.

[2] It has been said that the whole of *Prometheus* consists of the chord just mentioned. If this is true (and it is certainly true of the first few pages),

develops a definite melodic idiom, a feature of which is large upward leaps with a good many leaps of the interval of a sixth.

He develops a great complexity of rhythm which becomes a notable factor in the expression of frenetic passion. He passes through a period when he says, 'The way to everybody else lies through Beethoven'; then he climbs to a point where he can say 'Of Beethoven I can listen only to the Fifth Symphony'; and at last, right up aloft, he has lost touch with all his earlier friends on earth and says that Beethoven is to him 'no longer music'. There is now a great loneliness. His music resembles no other man's. And so excited is he with his own thoughts that sometimes it seems as though his music is on fire.

There is in Scriabin no Russian folk influence and no influence of the Russian 'Five' (see Vol. II, p. 178), except perhaps in orchestration. But in his nervous excitability and his powerful gloom and love of debatable ideas he is Russian, as Tchaikovsky is Russian—with the national temperament expressing itself by means of a purely personal idiom.

As regards his ideas, Scriabin had a knack of picking up a book, grasping its main point and neglecting minor points, and then changing the main point unconsciously into something different, so that in the end the book had served as the merest starting-point for a very personal train of thought. So

it must be understood that Scriabin gains considerable variety by greatly varying the positions of the notes of the chord in relation to each other and by using the chord at varying pitches (e.g. the root note may be C on one beat, F sharp on the next), and also by using many *incidental* notes not belonging to the chord.

it was with his Theosophy. He got hold of a few ideas—the intuitive or ecstatic manner of receiving doctrine, the idea of the brotherhood of humanity, the idea of the laws of nature and their relation to the psychological power of man, the idea of India as the repository of secret and sacred doctrine. All this order of thought appealed to him.

Scriabin believed in a succession of World Messiahs, each ushering in a new dispensation, and thought himself to be in that succession. And gradually there grew up in him the idea of a great world 'Mystery', a solemn ritual that should be performed in a specially-built Temple in India by 3,000 performers, that is, by its whole congregation, a superb and moving liturgical composition expressing the most ideal feelings of humanity, in which should be combined music, colour, perfume, and so on. (If this was not a Romantic composer when was there one?) The performance of this *Mystery* was to be the final event in the life of the present race, who would then pass away and give way to another. Of his 'Mystery' all he wrote before an early death claimed him was the text (or part of it) for the initial ceremony. It is said that he had come to think that the composition and production of the 'Mystery' itself would fall to some later Messiah.

The last completed orchestral work of Scriabin was his great *Prometheus* or *Poem of Fire*, for Orchestra and Piano, with Organ, Chorus, and (when available) Keyboard of Light. It has been many times performed without the last-named accessory, and once or twice with it.

Schönberg

Schönberg also belonged to the Romantic succession. His earlier music was strongly influenced by Liszt, Wagner, and Strauss. His *Songs of Gurra*, a setting of a text by the Danish novelist J. P. Jacobsen, is through and through drenched in the heavy German Romantic feeling. It has, too, all the outward characteristics, e.g. the megalomania—its orchestra is

huge, and the score, running sometimes to sixty staves on a page, demands fine eyesight on the part of its conductor. Six vocal soloists, three four-part male choirs, and one eight-part mixed choir are needed, and the orchestral instruments include 'some large iron chains'.

The later *Pierrot Lunaire* (1912) is a solo setting of twenty-one poems by Albert Giraud, some sentimental, some humorous, some grotesque, but all romantic. The vocal part is to be rendered in a half-song-half-speech voice, novel and curious,[1] the instrumental parts being written for a Quintet of Piano, Flute (sometimes Piccolo), Clarinet (sometimes Bass Clarinet), Violin (sometimes Viola), and 'Cello. The music is so difficult that it is marvellous that it can ever reach performance, and sometimes so crabbed in its contrapuntal complexity that probably no human ear can properly take it in—but that does not nullify the evident romantic intention. Its harmonies are very different from those of the *Songs of Gurra*, Schönberg having by the time he wrote it developed a new idiom, completely 'atonal'; and it is terse where the earlier work is flamboyant. Its moods, often wonderfully achieved, are some of them those of the neurasthenic and the decadent.

An example from *Pierrot Lunaire* may be given (p. 53). It shows the opening bars of what Schönberg calls 'Valse de Chopin'. It will be seen that it is not 'polytonal' (i.e. it is not a combination of melodies in different keys) but completely 'atonal' (i.e. none of its melodies themselves possess any key).

After about 1923, most of Schönberg's works follow his system of the 'Note-row' (*Tonreihe*). As it is this element in his composition that has caused most discussion, and has also influenced strongly many of his brother composers, an attempt must now be made to give a brief account of some characteristics of this 'method of composing with twelve notes'.

---

[1] This is something of a Schönberg speciality. It is indicated also in one number of the *Songs of Gurra*.

All the twelve notes of the octave are employed in every composition, and all the notes are treated in such a way as to enjoy an equal footing, i.e. there are no notes with special qualities such as those which in the major and minor scales, and even in the chromatic scale, lead to their being called 'tonic', 'dominant', and so on; thus the theorists of the Schönberg school prefer to call his method not chromatic but 'Dodecaphonic' (twelve-note).

Every composition is fabricated out of one theme or formula and in this each of these twelve notes occurs in an order pre-decided by the composer. This formula is used both 'horizontally' (i.e. melodically) and 'perpendicularly' (i.e. in chords), and throughout the composition the notes, whether used singly in a melody or combined in an accompaniment, occur in the same order. If used as an ordinary accompaniment ('perpendicularly') they may occur as chords—complete, or possibly as six in one chord and the next six in another, or three in one chord and the remainder in following chords, and so on, the point being that there should be no departure from the order until the series has been entirely exhausted and can begin again. Thus any chords following one another make up, as a whole, the original set of twelve notes in their original order.

For variety, however, the series may occur in four different ways as follows: (1) As first formulated; (2) With this order reversed so that the first note becomes the last and vice versa —i.e. in 'retrograde motion'; (3) Inverted, i.e. with each ascending note now descending by the same interval and vice versa; (4) With this last also reversed, i.e. in retrograde order. Here is an example:

1. The theme:

2. The theme in retrograde order:

3. The theme in inversion:

4. The inversion in retrograde order:

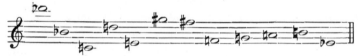

So far as rhythm is concerned there is perfect freedom throughout: this can be varied at any moment according to the composer's desire. Another relaxation from the rigour of the method lies in the fact that any note of the series can appear in any octave; thus a downward leap can be turned into an upward one and vice versa. Moreover the whole note-row in any of its four forms may be used at any pitch-level (or it may be sounded at two or more pitch-levels together in a strange kind of imitative counterpoint), so giving further variety. But it will be seen that the 'egalitarian' principle of no note of the Row having a greater importance than any other is rigorously maintained.

Obvious criticisms of the system might be expressed as follows:

(1) With the disappearance of the Tonic effect, the Dominant effect, &c., there seems to be no means of obtaining

---

* Observe that every note in a Note-row has before it a sign of sharp, flat, or natural, and that double-sharps and double-flats are not needed, since it is understood that so long as the notation used represents the sound to be heard nothing else matters.

Cadences (except so far as mere devices of rhythm can provide the feeling of these); (2) There is, equally, no means of obtaining the variety of *Modulation*: where the pitch-level of the formula is changed this is done without any process other than that of abruptly lifting it or lowering it; (3) The contrast of *Concord and Discord* is practically unobtainable; (4) Inasmuch as the simplest and best-known tune played backwards is practically unrecognizable the use of *Retrograde motion* serves no purpose: indeed it may be said that, so far as the ear is concerned, not one formula is employed, but two (the Palindrome in music never 'comes off').

Composers who have followed the system in greater or lesser degree, and with closer or less close adherence to Schönberg's rules, are led by Schönberg's fellow-Austrians and pupils, Berg and Webern, and include Křenek and Jelinek (both Austrians), the Hungarian Matyás Seiber (now resident in England), the British Humphrey Searle and Elizabeth Lutyens, and the Italian Dallapiccola. The Swiss Frank Martin has adopted the method in certain of his works, and the same is true of the Americans, Wallingford Riegger and Virgil Thomson.

It appears that appreciation of Schönberg's art is more general (or at all events more vocal) in the United States than in Britain.

For further information about Schönberg see the brief biography of him following this chapter, and the explanation of 'Expressionism' in Chapter XXII.

LEADING NEO-ROMANTIC COMPOSERS

(Including brief accounts of some not noticed in the preceding chapter.)

1. GERMAN, AUSTRIAN, AND HUNGARIAN

BRUCKNER

Bruckner, an Austrian, was born in 1824. His father was a village schoolmaster. At ten the boy was a village organist, then at thirteen he became a choir boy in a monastery church, and here he received a good musical training. Various organistships followed, including (at thirty-one) that of the Cathedral at Linz, and (at forty-three) that of the Royal Chapel at Vienna. As an organist Bruckner enjoyed international fame, performing in Paris, London (six recitals at the Albert Hall), and elsewhere. All this time he was studying hard, and was particularly influenced by Wagner's earlier works, at that time becoming known. He held a Lectureship at the University of Vienna and a Professorship at the Conservatoire. Vienna remained his place of residence to the end. He was somewhat involved in controversy, at second-hand, his followers opposing those of Brahms. Nikisch and Hermann Levi believed in him and conducted his works, but the growth of public appreciation was rather slow. He wrote nine Symphonies of a classical-romantic cast, some of them requiring a very large Orchestra.

Bruckner died in Vienna in 1896, aged seventy-two.

STRAUSS

Richard Strauss was a Bavarian. He was born at Munich in 1864. His father was first Horn player in the Court Orchestra, and enjoyed fame for the beauty of his playing. His mother was daughter of a wealthy brewer, and home circumstances were comfortable. Perhaps the boy was a little spoilt.

At four Richard played the piano; at six he had started composing. He went through the usual education in the city schools, but all the time worked at Piano, Violin, and Composition. At sixteen he was locally well known as a musician; at seventeen a String Quartet and a Symphony were publicly performed. He studied for a year at the University, and then went to Berlin for a season, where he met von Bülow, who took to him and put the Serenade for Wind Instruments into his programme for a tour with the famous Meiningen Orchestra, of which he was then conductor. Next year (when Strauss was twenty-one) he succeeded von Bülow in the conductorship of the Meiningen Orchestra, but he soon dropped this to go back to Munich as one of the junior conductors of the Court Orchestra there. Various other conductorships followed.

Strauss.

During the short stay at Meiningen Strauss became intimate with a remarkable man who had a great influence on him— Alexander Ritter, nephew by marriage of Wagner, a violinist in the orchestra, a composer of Symphonic Poems *à la* Liszt, and a devotee of 'The Music of the Future'. Now Strauss's father, fine musician though he was, was no Wagnerite, and no believer in 'Music of the Future', and Strauss had been brought up on the classics. Until he met Ritter he had hardly got so far as an understanding of Mendelssohn, Schumann, or Chopin, but now he went rapidly ahead, began to appreciate Brahms and, at last, to see something in Liszt and Wagner. Henceforward he was himself to be counted amongst those composers whom the conservatives did not appreciate.

The story of Strauss's life after this is the story of many opera conductorships (Weimar, Berlin, Munich, Vienna) succeeding each other rapidly, of many conducting tours, in which his marked ability, especially as an exponent of his own works, won itself universal recognition, of much money earned, and much fame, and a long and ever-growing list of compositions. Some particulars of his Tone Poems and Music Dramas are given below.

He died in 1949.

TONE POEMS, ETC.

1886   (aged 22)   *From Italy* ('Aus Italien'), 'Symphonic Fantasia'.
1886–7 (,,   22–3) *Macbeth*. After Shakespeare.
1888   (,,   24)   *Don Juan*. After Lenau.

1889 (,, 25)   *Death and Transfiguration* ('Tod und Verklä-
                 rung'). A poem by Alexander Ritter is prefixed
                 to the score, but this was written to Strauss's
                 scheme and after the music.

1894 (,, 30)   *Till Owlglass's Merry Tricks* ('Till Eulenspiegels
                 lustige Streiche'), based on the medieval humorous
                 legend.

1894–5 (,, 30–1) *Thus Spake Zoroaster* ('Also sprach Zarathustra'),
                 based on Nietzsche.

1897 (,, 33)   *Don Quixote.* 'Fantastic Variations on a Chevaler-
                 esque Theme.' Based on Cervantes.

1898 (,, 34)   *A Hero's Life* ('Ein Heldenleben').

1903 (,, 39)   *Domestic Symphony.*

1915 (,, 51)   *Alpine Symphony.*

OPERAS, MUSIC DRAMAS, ETC.

1894 (aged 30)   *Guntram.* Libretto by the Composer.

1901 (,, 37)   *The Fire Famine* ('Feuersnot'). Libretto by Ernst von
                 Wolzogen, on a Netherlands legend. 'Perhaps the
                 story does not commend itself to all tastes, and it must
                 be confessed that once or twice . . . the language is of a
                 freedom that has no parallel in opera libretti' (Ernest
                 Newman—but he wrote this in 1907).

1909 (,, 45)   *Salome.* Based on Oscar Wilde (German text by Hedwig
                 Lachmann).

1909 (,, 45)   *Electra.* Libretto by Hofmannsthal, based on Sophocles.

1911 (,, 47)   *The Knight of the Rose* ('Rosenkavalier'). Libretto by
                 Hofmannsthal.

1912, rewritten in 1917 (aged 48 and 53) *Ariadne in Naxos* (originally
                 written as an interlude to Molière's play, *The Bourgeois
                 Nobleman*). Libretto by Hofmannsthal.

1914 (aged 50)   *The Legend of Joseph.* A 'Pantomime'.

1919 (,, 55)   *The Woman without a Shadow* ('Die Frau ohne
                 Schatten'). Libretto by Hofmannsthal.

1924 (,, 60)   *Intermezzo.* Libretto by himself.
                 Whipped Cream ('Schlagobers'). A 'Ballet Pantomime'.

1926 (,, 62)   *The Egyptian Helen* ('Die egyptische Helena').

1933 (,, 69)   *Arabella.* Libretto by Hofmannsthal.

1935 (,, 71)   *The Silent Woman.*

1938 (,, 74)   *Daphne.*

1952 (posthumously produced) *The Love of Danaë.*

REGER

Reger was a Bavarian; he was born in 1873. After early local lessons he studied under Riemann at Sondershausen and Wiesbaden. This was the celebrated Hugo Riemann, the author of more books on musical theory and history than any other three men have ever written—the sort of German scholar who, filled to the brim with both valuable and valueless fact, can pour it out like a widow's cruse. It is not certain that such men make the best teachers; they are too apt to neglect unconscious processes and to make composition a matter of rule and precedent.

At Wiesbaden Reger himself became a teacher in the Conservatoire, but soon he settled in Munich, and then, as University Professor, &c., in Leipzig. Other similar academic positions followed. He was now as prolific in composition as his old master in theory, and, dying at forty-three (1916), he left a list of compositions that ran up to Opus 147 (most of them being multiple works—books of 'Five Humoreskes', 'Fifteen Songs', 'Four Sonatas', 'Three String Quartets', 'Six Intermezzi', and the like). Most of them are decidedly romantic (or 'classical-romantic') in feeling.

In Britain and America Reger has held a certain position of respect amongst organists, but is otherwise comparatively little known. There is a widespread feeling that he is not much more than a Brahms-Wagner amalgam, with an added contrapuntal complexity and a tendency to restless modulation.[1]

MAHLER

Gustav Mahler, a Bohemian, was born in 1860. He was educated at Prague and at Vienna. At the latter place he studied both at the Conservatoire and at the University. From his twentieth year he held, in turn, many conductorships of orchestras and opera houses in Central and Northern Europe, succeeding Seidl at Prague when he was twenty-five and serving as colleague to Nikisch at Leipzig at twenty-six. In 1892 he conducted a London German Opera Season

[1] E. W. says, 'Rather hard on Reger. In spite of everything he can (to me), at his best, give an impression of intellectual nobility, which I find very rare'.

at Drury Lane; in 1897, aged thirty-seven, he began a ten-year period, of great importance, as conductor and reformer of the Vienna Opera. From 1908 he was much in America. In 1911 he returned from that country to Vienna, very ill, and shortly after died—only fifty-one years of age. He left ten symphonies. Like Bruckner, he may be called a 'classical-romantic'.

At the date of writing Mahler is becoming increasingly known to general British concert audiences. This has come late, the Mahler cult of Germany and Austria having exercised comparatively little influence.

SCHÖNBERG

Arnold Schönberg's father was a (Jewish) Vienna merchant, who died when the boy (born 1874) was eight years old, and left the

Schönberg

family in needy circumstances. At about twelve Arnold began to learn the Violin, and his first compositions were little duets for use at his lessons. He soon began to take part in Chamber Music performances with his schoolfellows, and for them he wrote Trios and Quartets. He then taught himself to play the 'Cello, and wrote his own Sonatas for that instrument. One of his biographers points out that his early absorption in Chamber Music influenced the whole of his later musical thought, leading him to consider music very consistently from a contrapuntal standpoint.

Soon the youth decided to make music his life work and, leaving school, studied for some years without help from any teacher. At length a friend persuaded him to ask Zemlinsky to look at his work. This musician was only two years Schönberg's senior, but he held a position of great respect amongst the musical young bloods of Vienna. His compositions are strongly tinged with a Wagnerian-Brahmsian compound. Zemlinsky greatly influenced Schönberg; he dragged him out of his solitude, introducing him to other musicians, got him to make a piano arrangement of his (Zemlinsky's) opera *Sarema*, let him play the 'Cello in his Orchestra, and gave him instruction in Counterpoint. Some years later Schönberg married Zemlinsky's sister.

Tristan was at the early Zemlinsky period the object of Schönberg's closest study.

The first public performance of any work of Schönberg took place in Vienna, when he was about twenty-three; the piece was a String Quartet. The work was appreciated, and gave Schönberg his first local footing as a recognized composer.

Other works followed; some Songs performed at a vocal recital in Vienna in 1898, when the composer was twenty-four, shocked a good many of the audience: 'And since that day', says Schönberg, 'people have never ceased to be shocked at me.'

The next year Schönberg composed the String Sextet, *Resplendent Night* ('Verklärte Nacht'), a work which represents in tone the emotions of a very sombre, even morbid poem of Richard Dehmel (a man and a woman walking together, the woman admitting she has sinned and the man forgiving her because the moonlight is so beautiful—that is what it amounts to in plain English, which blunt language does not, perhaps, treat German romantic thought with all the respect to be desired). This work has been described as the first piece of genuine programme music ever written in Chamber Music form—setting on one side Smetana's *From my Life*, which, whatever its content, is of strictly classical structure.

At twenty-six Schönberg began the composition of his *Songs of Gurra*. He was always a quick worker; the Sextet had been composed in three weeks, and a great part of this new enormous score was completed in a month or two; then came an interruption due to the necessity of pot-boiling work—the scoring of other people's operettas, of which, at this period of his life, Schönberg relates, he accomplished no less than six thousand pages. In little more than a year, however, the great work was (except for part of its orchestration) completed. So big are the forces employed that Schönberg had to get Breitkopf and Härtel to print him a special music paper.

At this time of poverty and struggle Schönberg moved to Berlin, hoping to find some means of living a more successful life. For a time he conducted a theatre orchestra. Still he devoted to pot-boiling orchestration time that he would have liked to give to his composition. The orchestration of his own *Songs of Gurra* remained unfinished.[1] He showed the thing to Strauss, who awarded him the Liszt-Stipend, and gave him a place on the staff of the Stern Conservatoire in Berlin.

In 1903, approaching thirty, Schönberg had returned to Vienna and taken up residence in the same house as Zemlinsky and engaged in teaching and composition. Various works were performed, and the Rosé Quartet became practical supporters of his. (Mahler had previously lent his approval and help.) The Six Songs with Orchestra and the String Quartet in D minor composed at the time show a change of style. Up to this time the Wagner influence had been strong; now it weakened, and what his biographer calls a 'new classical' style gradually took its place, a style of greater reserve and conciseness.

A third period began about 1907, or a little later. Schönberg began to paint, jumping right into the most advanced 'movement' of the day with a growing collection of 'Portraits and Visions' which, from one or two specimens seen, appear to the present writer to exhibit an extreme morbidity and love of real ugliness; they appear to have little similarity to those of Schönberg's friend, the founder of expressionistic painting, Kandinsky, which, however incomprehensible, are always beautiful and never morbid.[2] Amongst his compositions of this period we find the Three Piano Pieces (Op. 11), the famous Five Orchestral Pieces, which have brought tears to the eyes of sensitive audiences all over the world, and the drama with music, *The Happy Hand* ('Die glückliche Hand'). *Pierrot Lunaire* (Op. 21), a cycle of twenty-one poems to be recited to music, came in

[1] Only in 1911, twelve years after the beginning of the work, was the last note of the orchestration in its place. Consequently, as the composer admits, the orchestration of the last pages of the work differs considerably from that of the first pages (one grows somewhat between one's twenty-sixth and thirty-seventh years!). It was two years more before the work enjoyed its first performance, Schreker conducting. It brought Schönberg his first great success in life—but came too late, as he had now to some extent outgrown the style exhibited. Another comparatively early work was performed soon afterwards—the Symphonic Poem upon Maeterlinck's *Pelléas and Mélisande*, already eleven years old.

[2] For reproductions of one of Kandinsky's paintings and two of Schönberg's see Chapter XXII of the present volume.

1912, when the composer was thirty-eight. Amongst the many later works are a String Quartet, a Violin Concerto, a Piano Concerto, &c. The technical device of the *Tonreihe* ('Note-row') is now adopted. (See an account of this on p. 55-7.)

The Nazi régime compelled Schönberg's emigration to the United States. There he died in 1951.

WOLF

Hugo Wolf was born in 1860 at Windischgraz, in Southern Styria (then in Austria, now in Yugoslavia). His life was throughout tragic.

He was intended for the family leather business, but insisted on studying music, and was allowed to enter the Vienna Conservatoire.

After two years he was dismissed, it is said unjustly (the allegation is that some other student wrote, in his name, a threatening letter to the director). He then for a time earned a bare living by giving lessons.

At twenty-two, the post of second conductor in the Salzburg Opera being offered him, he accepted it, but held it for only two months, his heart not being in the routine work demanded.

On returning to Vienna he resumed his life of misery—all the time studying, hearing

Wolf.

the works of the German and French romantic composers and the German romantic poets, and composing musical settings of the works of the latter. At twenty-six he became music critic of a fashionable paper, the Vienna *Salonblatt*. His writing in its pages was very pungent—especially when, as a strong Wagnerian, he discussed the works of Brahms. His critical writings have been collected and published (in German only) and are worth reading, whatever one may think of his violence.

This journalistic post he retained for four years. Then he threw it up, and went to live in a village near Vienna, where he poured out songs in passing spates. In his twenty-eighth year he wrote, between February and May, forty-three settings of poems by the

Swabian pastor-poet, Mörike; between the following October and February he wrote fifty settings of Goethe—and so on. His life became a series of alternations of feverish activity and despondent lethargy.

Gradually the songs were sung and became known.

Then, at thirty-seven, his brain failed, and in 1903, as his forty-fourth year approached, he died in a lunatic asylum in Vienna.

The output of Wolf's twenty years of composing life includes 250 Songs, an Opera, a String Quartet, and two or three Orchestral Pieces.

In the Songs the piano part is very independent, yet voice and accompaniment merge in the effect. Each song has its individuality. The present writer alleges a want of definite musical value in very many of the songs, but those who sing them and many who hear them refuse to agree with him, often describing Wolf as the greatest song-writer who ever lived. Mr. Ernest Newman, in his book *Hugo Wolf*, gives a list of the finest songs of Schubert, composed over a period of fourteen years, and then adds—

> The sober judgement of history must surely be that the work of all this long period can barely compare with the Mörike volume of Wolf—composed in little more than four months in one year— for scope of matter, and certainly cannot compare with it for variety of manner.[1]

DOHNÁNYI

Dohnányi was born in 1877 at Pressburg in Hungary (in the Magyar language, Pozsony; now in Czechoslovakia, and called Bratislava). He early showed talent as a pianist and as a composer. He studied at the Conservatoire of Budapest, and then for some years toured the world with great success as a virtuoso pianist. He first appeared in England at twenty-one and in the United States of America at twenty-two. At thirty-one he became a professor of the pianoforte at the Berlin Royal School for Music, and at forty-two director of the Budapest Conservatoire and conductor of the orchestra

[1] E. W. says, 'Without going so far as Newman I feel that (having been asked my opinion) I must add my aid towards the upholding of the very splendid Wolfian banner against its enemies'.

of the same city, with which he has toured, visiting London in 1928. In 1948 he settled in Argentina.

The Pianoforte music and Chamber music of Dohnányi is the best known, but his chamber and orchestral music is also fairly often heard, and there is a little dramatic music.

Dohnányi may be classed as a younger classical-romantic somewhat of the order of Brahms. He writes effectively and in an individual way, but does not to any extent break virgin soil.

2. FRENCH AND BELGIAN

FRANCK

'On December 10th, 1822, the very day upon which the giant of symphony, Ludwig van Beethoven, put the finishing touches to the manuscript of a work which he justly regarded as his most perfect masterpiece—the sublime Mass in D major—a child was born into the world destined to become the true successor of the Master of Bonn, both in the sphere of sacred music and in that of symphony.' That is how César Franck's most devoted disciple, Vincent d'Indy, opens his classic book upon the master.

Franck.

By birth Franck was a Belgian (as by descent, on one side, was Beethoven also). He was born at Liége in 1822. His father was engaged in banking, but had a love of music and a strong desire that his two sons, Joseph and César, should be musicians. Their early training was received at the local Conservatoire, but when Joseph was sixteen and César fourteen, their father, wishing to give them a larger opportunity, settled in Paris. There César was admitted to the Conservatoire, where he soon established a good reputation, but occasionally irritated the Director, Cherubini (then an old man—approaching eighty), by strange pranks. For instance, competing for the pianoforte prize, and on the point of winning it, he spoilt his chance by a work of supererogation, playing off the sight-reading test with the greatest fluency and accuracy but—transposed a third lower. This was against all law, and yet to refuse the prize to so gifted a performer would be against all justice. How were law and justice to be reconciled ? For perhaps the only occasion in its history the Paris Conservatoire awarded an extra prize, called a 'Grand Prix d'Honneur'. Despite the amusing Berlioz-Cherubini recriminations recorded by Berlioz in his autobiographical writings (Berlioz was at the Conservatoire only about seven years before Franck entered it), it is clear that Cherubini was no fool.

Other prizes followed in succeeding years (twice for fugue), and in 1841, when Franck was nineteen, he competed for the Organ prize. Amongst the tests for this were the extemporization of a Fugue and of a movement in Sonata form, both, naturally, on given subjects. Franck noticed that the two subjects could be effectively treated in combination, and so, by another work of supererogation, lost the first prize. (Cherubini was absent, so there was no one to propose a special award, and only a second prize was given to the wayward genius.)

Next year, just when he was beginning to prepare for competition for the Prix de Rome, his father removed him from the Conservatoire. Why ? Possibly because parental ambitions had always been focused on the rewards of the career of a piano virtuoso. (One is not a banker for nothing!)

Now began a life of patient toil that lasted until death. Joseph and César soon had to take upon them the task of supporting the family. They came before the world, after all, as no virtuosos, but as humdrum music teachers. We will dispose once for all of Joseph. His career was that of an organist and teacher, a minor composer (chiefly of church music), and author (textbooks of harmony and plainsong, and a 'New Pianoforte Method'). César's career, looked at as a business affair, was much the same. Probably to very many of their contemporaries the two brothers were throughout their lives as mere general practitioners of music of equal professional standing.

At twenty-six, César married—an actress, and the family did not like that. He was then organist of the church of Notre Dame de Lorette, occupying his spare time (that is, a part of his nights) in composition. He wrote an opera called *The Farmer's Man*, and failed to secure an opportunity to let the public hear it. At last he was appointed to the newly rebuilt and magnificent church of St. Clothilde, which had a fine new organ by the organ-builder-genius, Cavaillé-Col, and there for nearly forty years (until his death) he remained. His pupil, d'Indy, has given a remarkable account of his organ playing, and particularly of his improvisations (I quote Mrs. Newmarch's translation):

> Here, in the dusk of this organ-loft, of which I can never think without emotion, he spent the best part of his life. Here he came every Sunday and feast-day—and towards the end of his life every Friday morning too—fanning the fire of his genius by pouring out his spirit in wonderful improvisations which were often far more lofty in thought than many skilfully elaborated compositions; and here, too, he assuredly foresaw and conceived the sublime melodies which afterwards formed the groundwork of *The Beatitudes*.
>
> Ah! we know it well, we who were his pupils, the way up to that thrice-blessed organ-loft—a way as steep and difficult as that which the Gospel tells us leads to Paradise. First, having climbed the dark, spiral staircase, lit by an occasional loophole, we came suddenly face to face with a kind of antediluvian monster, a complicated bony structure, breathing heavily and irregularly, which on closer examination proved to be the vital portion of the organ, worked by a vigorous pair of bellows. Next, we had to descend a few narrow steps in pitch-darkness, a fatal ordeal to high hats, and the cause of many a slip to the uninitiated. Opening the narrow *janua cæli*, we found overselves suspended as it were midway between the pavement and the vaulted roof of the church, and the next moment all was forgotten in the contemplation of that rapt profile, and the intellectual brow, from which seemed to flow without any effort a stream of inspired melody and subtle, exquisite harmonies, which lingered a moment among the pillars of the nave before they ascended and died away in the vaulted heights of the roof.
>
> For César Franck had, or rather *was*, the genius of improvisation, and no other modern organist, not even the most renowned executants, would bear the most distant comparison with him in this respect. When, on very rare occasions, one of us was called upon to take the master's place, it was with a kind of superstitious terror that we ventured to let our profane fingers caress this supernatural thing, which was accustomed to vibrate, to sing, and to lament at the will of the superior genius of whom it had become almost an integral part.
>
> Sometimes the master would invite other people, friends,

amateurs, or foreign musicians, to visit him in the organ-loft. Thus it happened that on April 3rd, 1866, Franz Liszt, who had been his sole listener, left the church of Sainte-Clothilde lost in amazement, and evoking the name of J. S. Bach in an inevitable comparison.

But whether he played for some chosen guest, for his pupils, or for the devout worshippers during service, Franck's improvisations were equally thoughtful and careful, for he did not play in order to be heard, but to do his best for God and his conscience' sake. And *his best* was a sane, noble, and sublime art.

To describe these improvisations, the true value of which we only realized when there was no chance of hearing them again, would be an impossible task; I must leave to those who, like myself, were habitual guests at these musical feasts the delight of a memory which will vanish all too soon, even as these inspired and ephemeral creations have already passed away.

No composer has been more fortunate than Franck in the possession of an able, understanding, and sympathetic biographer, and the one or two quotations given in this brief sketch express succinctly the very spirit of Franck.

Official appointments brought him little comfort. At fifty he was appointed Organ Professor at the Conservatoire, but his colleagues did not appreciate him. Occasionally he would arrange (or friends and pupils would arrange for him) private, semi-public, or public performances of his works, but his official superior and colleagues rarely attended them. The honours of Officer of the Academy and, at last, Chevalier of the Legion of Honour came to him, but they came late and then came to him not as composer but as 'Professor of Organ'. His life was not one of public applause but of quiet artistic toil, religious devotion, and comradeship with the band of sincere young spirits who collected around him as pupils. In his sixty-ninth year he was filled with pride for what he felt to be his first success. At a concert of the National Society for Music his String Quartet was heard and there broke out (at last!) a tumult of applause.

The next month, on his way to give a lesson, he was struck by the pole of an omnibus, and six months later (8 Nov. 1890) he died.

THE CHIEF WORKS OF FRANCK

1871   (aged 49), with new edition three years later. *Redemption.* Symphonic Poem for Soprano, Chorus, and Orchestra.

? 1876 (aged 54)	*The Eolides.* Symphonic Poem based on Leconte de Lisle.
1879 (,, 57)	*The Beatitudes.* Solo, eight-part Chorus, and Orchestra.
	Piano Quintet.
1882 (,, 60)	*The Accursed Hunter* (*Le Chasseur Maudit*). Tone Poem based on Bürger.
1883 (,, 61)	*The Djinns.* Tone Poem for Piano and Orchestra based on Hugo. (Like Berlioz's *Harold in Italy*, not a concerto, but a piece in which a solo instrument prominently participates.)
1884 (,, 62)	Prelude, Chorale, and Fugue for Piano.
1885 (,, 63)	Symphonic Variations for Piano and Orchestra.
1886 (,, 64)	Sonata for Violin and Piano.
1886–7 (,, 64–5)	Prelude, Aria, and Finale for Piano.
	Symphony.
1889 (,, 67)	String Quartet.
1890 (,, 68)	Three Chorales for Organ.

Note that the works by which Franck is remembered only began to make their appearance about his fiftieth year. Indeed up to that time, though he wrote, he published very little.

D'INDY

Vincent d'Indy was born in Paris in 1851. He was thus twenty-nine years the junior of Franck, and he was, from the time of his younger manhood to Franck's death, very closely associated with him as pupil, friend, and helper. He was also, as we have already seen, Franck's biographer.

Vincent d'Indy.

A formative influence in d'Indy's life was his attendance in 1876 at the first performance of *The Ring* at Bayreuth. He returned an ardent Wagnerian, and became the right-hand man of the great conductor Lamoureux in his laborious twelve months' preparation for the first Paris performance of *Lohengrin.* Lamoureux was a conductor after d'Indy's own heart; he performed certain Handel and Bach works then little known in Paris, introduced some of Brahms's works, took the leadership of the Wagnerian movement in France, and in 1887 gave the *Lohengrin* performance just alluded to.[1] He also helped the younger French composers, including d'Indy himself, by performing their works.

D'Indy's own social-musical activities were not unlike those of Lamoureux. He gave first performances in Paris (or revivals after long neglect) of works of Monteverdi, Bach, Rameau, and others of the older composers, and offered many younger compatriots their chance. It is worth remembering that, whilst we class d'Indy as a Franckist, and hence look upon him as in the opposite camp to Debussy, he was one of those who defended *Pelléas and Mélisande* at a time when it was laughed at by many. Again, conducting once at Rome, he included in his programme Debussy's *Nuages* (Clouds) and *Fêtes*; at the close the audience shouted and whistled, whereupon d'Indy took up the baton again and repeated both pieces—with the result that they (or he for his boldness ?) now won applause.

With the famous choral conductor Bordes and the equally famous organist Guilmant, d'Indy founded in Paris the Schola Cantorum, a small school of music of definitely religious aim and the highest artistic effort, which bases its teaching upon a close study of plainsong and the classics. Its ideals are, we may say, those of Franck (it was founded six years after his death). D'Indy acted as Principal of this Institution and also as its chief teacher of composition. He has left an important three-volume *Treatise of Composition*, based upon his lessons there.

Amongst d'Indy's works are Operas, Symphonies, Tone Poems, Chamber Music, &c. Everything he wrote is of serious intention and most conscientious workmanship. Opinion as to the value of his music varies, but this much may be said—it is, from the constructive ability displayed, almost always genuinely interesting to the thoughtful musician.

D'Indy was a great nature-lover, and many of his works (*Summer Day in the Mountains*, &c.) testify to this.

He died in 1931.

---

[1] Thus *Lohengrin* had taken just forty years to reach Paris. To reach London it took only twenty-eight. But we are not proud!

FAURÉ

Gabriel Fauré was born at Pamiers, Ariège, in 1845, and died in 1924. For a long period in the later part of his life he was looked up to with veneration by almost the whole body of his juniors amongst French composers, very many of whom were his pupils.

For thirty years Fauré held a series of positions connected with Church Music, culminating with the organistship of the Madeleine at the age of fifty-one. At the time that he took up his work at that church he also became a professor of composition at the Paris Conservatoire. From the age of sixty to that of seventy-five he was Director of this Institution.

Fauré's compositions are very numerous. His Songs are important, and so is his opera, *Penelope*, and Chamber Music. His style is a logical and balanced one; his music flows easily, yet he attains 'finish'. These are usually considered to be 'classical' qualities, and so in themselves they are, but the general bent of Fauré's mind is romantic.

SAINT-SAËNS

Saint-Saëns, of a Normandy family of some importance, was born in Paris in 1835. He studied at the Paris Conservatoire and privately under Gounod. His first successes were as organist. For about twenty years he was organist of the Madeleine. He had composed a symphony at sixteen, and from that age until his death at eighty-six (in 1921) he never ceased composition, in which he had the greatest facility. He was also a considerable author, and delighted in polemic, defending the Romantics, Liszt, Berlioz, and Wagner, and later attacking Wagner on the ground of his Teutonizing influence on French music, and also demolishing 'modernistic' young compatriots.

Saint-Saens.

Yet he himself had been in some sort a pioneer, for his *Omphale's Spinning Wheel* (1871) was the first Symphonic Poem ever written by a French composer.

He was one of the early members of the National Musical Society, and he was also a great defender of the earlier French composers, and especially Rameau. His was a curious temperament, versatility, cosmopolitanism, and narrowness being blended in an unusual way. His reminiscences, as published in several books, are human and entertaining. At Dieppe there is a Saint-Saëns Museum, in which are preserved relics contributed largely by himself—his aunt's pin-cushion and his first copybook (or that kind of thing).

Saint-Saëns was a fine pianist. The bigger world knows him chiefly by his four Symphonic Poems, the one already mentioned, *Phaëton*, *The Youth of Hercules*, and *Danse Macabre*, and by one or two of his Piano Concertos and his very successful Opera, *Samson and Delilah*.

DUPARC

Henri Fouques Duparc was born in Paris in 1848. He was a very favourite pupil of Franck, and, like d'Indy and some other French composers of the period, he was a good deal influenced by visits to Bayreuth in its early days. He was one of the Founders of the National Musical Society. Whilst he was still in his thirties his health broke down and composition ceased. His songs especially, few in number as they are, have made a name for him.[1]

He died in 1933.

MAGNARD

Albéric Magnard was born in Paris in 1865, and killed during the very early days of the First World War.

His father was Editor of *Le Figaro*. The son was educated partly at Ramsgate, England. At the Paris Conservatoire he studied com-position with Dubois and Massenet. He left these teachers, and went to d'Indy, to whom he felt he owed whatever he was afterwards able to do. Roughly speaking, the ideals of Magnard are those of his teacher, d'Indy—in other words, he derives largely from Franck.

In 1892 the Brussels Opera House gave his *Yolande*. Gradually

[1] 'The best four or five of Duparc's songs are surely tremendously fine stuff.' E. W.

his work began to attract moderate attention, but it has never become popular, and perhaps never will.

The manner of Magnard's death was perverse, yet noble. When the War broke out, Magnard, who was wealthy, living on his estate twenty-five miles from Paris a life of devotion to art, literature, and nature, tried to enlist, but was refused. He sent his wife and other women-folk away, and with his step-son remained, swearing, if attacked, to offer resistance to the last. His house was surrounded, his step-son captured, and he fired upon. He returned the fire, killing one German and wounding another. He himself was then shot (or shot himself—accounts vary), and the most valuable contents of his house were carried off, after which the house was set on fire. (It may be recalled that the Germans put the mayor of Senlis to death as a reprisal for resistance offered by the civilian population, and afterwards burnt the town.)

Magnard's lifelong friend was Ropartz, who ever did his best to win recognition for his music. Magnard was still developing when the end came, and had that end been deferred for some years he might have won through to a style of equal dignity and perfection, yet somewhat less severe. But he was already approaching fifty.

ROPARTZ

Guy Ropartz, born 1864, in Brittany, was a fellow pupil of Magnard at the Paris Conservatoire, and when Magnard left to study with d'Indy, Ropartz left to study with Franck. At thirty he became Director of the Conservatoire of Nancy, and when Alsace became French again, he was appointed to a similar position at Strasbourg. He did much conducting, and, as mentioned above, made great efforts to secure recognition for his friend Magnard. In his composition he made much use of the tunes of his native Brittany. He died in 1955, aged ninety-one.

CHAUSSON

Ernest Chausson was born in Paris in 1855, and died in 1899. He qualified in law, and took to music late in life. He studied at the Conservatoire under Massenet, but then, like Ropartz, transferred himself to the teaching of Franck. He was for a time Secretary of the National Musical Society and, in this capacity and privately, did a great deal for the assistance of contemporary French composers.

Like Magnard, Chausson was a wealthy man, and a great lover of all the arts. He was killed by a bicycle accident on his own estate.

Chausson's music shows the influence of his master, Franck, and also that of Wagner, and perhaps sometimes that of Brahms.

LEKEU

Lekeu was a Belgian. He was born in 1870. He came under the influence of Franck, and became first his pupil, and then (on Franck's death) d'Indy's. His Sonata for Piano and Violin, dedicated to and played by Ysaÿe, is the work of his best known to many people. Unfortunately he died of typhoid—the day after his twenty-fourth birthday. In all probability the world lost in him a very great composer.

DUKAS

Dukas was born in Paris in 1865. Like practically every French composer mentioned in this volume, he studied at the Paris Conservatoire. The work of Lalo had some influence on him, as on others of his age. His vivid descriptive Symphonic Scherzo, *The Prentice Sorcerer*, is known everywhere, but his Opera, *Ariadne and Bluebeard*, is considered his *chef d'œuvre*. He was a great friend and adviser of Albéniz, and thus the modern Spanish School owes something to him. He was also a conscientious editor of the works of Scarlatti and Rameau, and wrote a good deal of musical criticism.

He died in 1935.

3. RUSSIAN

SCRIABIN

Scriabin was born in Moscow in 1872. His father was a lawyer; his mother had been one of the best piano pupils of the Petrograd Conservatoire. The mother died when her child was only about a year old, and the father then entered the diplomatic service and went to Turkey. The boy was brought up by his grandmother, and was considerably coddled and spoilt, which possibly influenced his whole life.

At a very early age Scriabin showed a great musical gift. From six onwards he could play a composition of fair length after one hearing.

At ten he was placed in the School for future military officers, but two years before leaving it (i.e. at sixteen) he entered the Moscow Conservatoire, and studied in the two places simultaneously. He had

Safonof as piano teacher, and under him developed very remarkable powers. For counterpoint he was under Taneief, and for composition under Arensky—who thought little of him. At the conclusion of his course Scriabin abandoned his intended military career, and gave himself entirely to music.

He was quickly received into the circle of Belaief, the patron-publisher of Russian music, who planned recital tours for him, and printed his compositions as they were finished.

Scriabin.

For a time Scriabin held a professorship at the Moscow Conservatoire. But he was much occupied with concert giving and composition. It is said that in one year he composed the Fourth Sonata, the *Tragic Poem* for Piano, the *Satanic Poem* for Piano, his third Symphony or *Divine Poem*, and forty smaller works. If this be true, it proves the existence of remarkable productive powers.

In his thirties Scriabin travelled much in Europe and also in America. Brussels was for a time a place of residence.

The support of the great conductor, Koussevitzky, was of high value to Scriabin, as it brought about many performances of his increasingly complex and difficult orchestral works. On one occasion Koussevitzky chartered a vessel and took his Orchestra, with Scriabin, for a concert tour of the Volga.

In early 1914 Scriabin paid a visit to London, during which, at a series of piano recitals, he awakened a great deal of interest. He was then suffering from a tumour of the lip, which unfortunately developed, and about a year later (April 1915) he died in Moscow.

His last thoughts were of the War, which he believed would bring a great cleansing of the World's thought. He suffered extreme pain, and, doing so, paid the country he had recently visited the great compliment of exclaiming, 'I must be self-possessed like Englishmen'.

His was a strange temperament, Russian and fluctuating, carrying him into fits of religious ecstasy and leading him to the abandonment of many once-strong friendships and the desertion of a wife and family he had once adored.

The following anecdote of Scriabin has probably not previously appeared in print. It was told to the author by Mr. T. H. Preston, at that time His Britannic Majesty's Official Agent in Petrograd. He had it from a friend who was present on the occasion alluded to:

A Scriabin concert had been arranged by the Assembly of the Nobility. Scriabin came on and said, 'To-day genius has left me'. He then left the platform, and the money was returned to the audience. The recital was given next day.

GLAZUNOF

Glazunof was born in St. Petersburg (Leningrad) in 1865. As a youth he was recognized by the national pioneers, winning the favour of Balakiref and Rimsky-Korsakof, the latter of whom gave him formal lessons. His First Symphony was performed when he was only sixteen—under Balakiref's conductorship.

Glazunof won the admiration of the wealthy amateur, Belaief (see Vol. II, p. 181), and it is said that Belaief's determination to found a publishing firm to bring before the world the works of Russian composers was prompted originally by the desire to help Glazunof.

World fame came to the young composer. His compositions were quickly taken up.

In 1900, when he was thirty-five, he joined the staff of the Petrograd Conservatory as Professor of Orchestration, and five years after that he succeeded Rimsky-Korsakof as Director.

Glazunof has left eight Symphonies and a very large number of other works of all kinds except Opera (but he also wrote Ballets and incidental stage music, and it fell to him to complete Borodin's Opera *Prince Igor*).

Glazunof began as a composer of the nationalist-romantic type, but gradually took the position of a writer of music of the more cosmopolitan and 'absolute' character.

He died in 1936.

RACHMANINOF

Rachmaninof was a Russian, born 1873, died 1943. He studied at the Conservatories of both St. Petersburg (Leningrad) and Moscow; his teachers included Taneief and Arensky. For some years he lived in Dresden. As a pianist he toured the world, as a conductor he was much respected, and as a composer he made a mark, though possibly not a lasting one, since his works for the most part are inspired by no very strong national or personal feeling, but whilst very skilfully written, are cosmopolitan and general in their expression. They include three Operas, two Symphonies, three Piano Concertos, pieces for Piano solo, Songs, &c. Probably some of his best work was put into the small Piano Pieces and the Songs, many of both of which are perfect in their kind.

4. FINNISH

SIBELIUS

Sibelius was born in Finland in 1865. He studied at Helsingfors, Berlin, and Vienna. When he was thirty-two the State made him an annual grant for life, so that he might be free for composition. He found in his strong national feeling the inspiration of practically all his work. The austerity of a land of a long hard winter, the charm of a land of a short but brilliant summer, are both found there. The influence of national beauty and national legend are equally evident; the mere names of his pieces show the latter, the list of them being largely made up of titles such as *A Saga*, *The Swan of Tuonela*, *Finlandia*, *Karelia*, and so forth. His works include seven Symphonies, eight or nine Tone-Poems, and other orchestral pieces, a Violin Concerto,

Sibelius.

Songs, &c. They are usually very individual in style and feeling, with a deep-seated, rather than a superficial, romanticism. His latest works make no concessions to popular taste. They are very downright, terse, personal documents. He died in 1957.

5. BRITISH

ELGAR

Elgar (born 1857) was brought up in an atmosphere of music, for his father was both an organist and the owner of a music shop. As he

Elgar.

put it, 'A stream of music flowed through our house and the shop, and I was all the time bathing in it'. Until comparatively lately you could still see that shop, in the High Street of Worcester, and the name 'Elgar' over the window.

The real awakening to the possibilities of music, as related by him to the present writer, came in this wise. One day there came into the young musician's hands a copy of Beethoven's First Symphony. He turned over the closely printed pages of the old Wolfenbüttel Edition. The first movement made no particular impression. The slow movement was already familiar as an organ voluntary. The last movement seemed perfunctory. But the Scherzo—he glanced through this, and rushed to a place of solitude. With six active children in the house there was little opportunity for the quiet enjoyment of the treasure. Out he went! and once by himself, he examined it. Here was a revelation—a revelation of romance, fire, poetry. He looked at the page before him:

> . . . like stout Cortez when with eagle eyes
> He star'd at the Pacific—and all his men
> Look'd at each other with a wild surmise,
> Silent, upon a peak in Darien.

A new ocean was in view, and he longed to sail it. An ocean on which you might set forth from the safe harbour of Natural Quay, touch rapidly and momentarily at such adjacent ports as the Quays of One Sharp and Two Sharps, and then, with a sudden favouring breeze, find yourself making for the Coast of Flats—passing quickly from port to port, resting nowhere, and almost before you realized the distance you had travelled from home, find yourself casting anchor for a time and swaying gently on the tide in the Harbour of Five Flats.

Get out your volume of Beethoven's Symphonies and look at the chart—as Beethoven drew it and little eleven-year-old Elgar conned it. It meant as much to him as did Salvation Yeo's much vaunted map to Amayas Leigh—with its 'Cities and harbours, dragons and elephants, whales which fought with sharks, plate ships from Spain, islands with apes and palm trees, each with its name over-written, and here and there, "Here is gold", and again, "Much gold and silver".'

How Elgar learnt to play he hardly knew. He played the Piano, and in later years gained a reputation as an accompanist. He played the Organ, and was able to help his father, and later, to take an organist's post of his own. He played the Violin, and that proved his main entrance into the practical world of music, and was for long years of early struggle his main source of income. He played the 'Cello and the Double-bass well enough to take his part in the Haydn and easier Mozart Symphonies that were then the staple fare of amateur orchestral societies. The Bassoon he played in a wind quintet, and in later years he played the Trombone. So Keyboard, Strings, Wood-wind, and Brass all claimed his attention at one time or another—and if one had only probed a little deeper with one's questions one would doubtless have dug up memories of percussion.

For five years (1879–84) Elgar was Bandmaster of the Worcestershire County Lunatic Asylum, and this gave him his first steady experience of instrumental conducting. He was also Conductor of the Worcester Amateur Instrumental Society, and member of a Birmingham orchestra.

At thirty-two Elgar, still unknown to the larger world, tried to effect a lodgement in London musical life, but, failing in this, settled in Malvern and then in Hereford, doing the ordinary jog-trot tasks of the provincial professional. Gradually he established a footing as a composer, chiefly of those choral-orchestral works which formed the staple fare of provincial musical festivals. He was forty-two before he 'struck oil'—with the *Enigma* Variations for Orchestra, which remained everywhere his most-played work. A year later, and at the Birmingham Festival, was heard his oratorio-setting of Cardinal Newman's great poem, *The Dream of Gerontius*, which to a Catholic composer of strongly mystical vein naturally made a great appeal. Two years later this was repeated at the Lower Rhine Festival, and with great success. Strauss was present, and the public kiss and public words with which he testified his admiration gave Elgar's countrymen, with whom in those days foreign endorsement counted for a great deal, the courage to believe that at last they could claim to possess a great composer of their own; the effect upon British opinion was, indeed, comparable with that of the Parisian applause when Constable's *The Hay Wain* was suddenly hailed as a masterpiece at the Paris Salon eighty years earlier.

The position of Elgar was now assured, so far as his own countrymen were concerned, but, curiously, foreign appreciation went little further. In Germany Elgar was not much heard; in France hardly at all. Beyond 'Enigma' probably hardly anything of his became known in Italy; and in America, where one would expect to find appreciation for him, he has been too little performed to become known to any very large public. It is difficult to account for all this. Why should the French be able to accept the Catholic-romantic mysticism of Franck and not that of Elgar? Why should the Germans be able to accept the romantic-classic Brahms and not the romantic-classic Elgar? There may be something more purely national in his idiom and feeling than a British critic can recognize—or he may simply be 'up against' the obstinately held foreign notion, 'British musician no musician'.

The works of Elgar include, in addition to the orchestral Variations mentioned, two Symphonies and a very difficult and beautiful Violin Concerto, a Violoncello Concerto, the Oratorios, *The Dream of Gerontius*, *The Apostles*, and *The Kingdom*, many fine part songs, &c., the Concert Overture *Cockaigne*, a Symphonic Poem *Falstaff*, Songs, a Violin and Piano Sonata, a String Quartet, and a Piano Quintet. He wrote no Piano solo music of importance.

He died in 1934.

DELIUS

Delius was on his father's side of Dutch descent and on his mother's of German. His parents settled in Bradford and became naturalized; there Frederick was born in 1862. The father was a musical enthusiast, the mother a literary romantic by disposition, who, so goes the anecdote related by the composer, confiscated her boys' 'penny-dreadfuls' (*Sweeney Todd, The Demon Barber of Fleet Street*, and the like) to become absorbed in them herself.

Delius.

Frederick showed musical precocity, and had good local piano and violin lessons. At ten, hearing a Valse of Chopin's twice played, he was able to repeat it from memory. Bradford has always been a musical centre, partly from the Yorkshire love of music and partly from the presence there of a considerable German colony engaged in the wool trade. Thus a good deal of music came the boy's way, including String Quartet parties invited to the house. The comparative austerity of the classics of Chamber Music awakened little appreciation in Frederick Delius, whose bent was then always towards the Romantics.

As a youth Frederick was sent to Germany to learn business methods; he preferred to learn something about Drama, Opera, and Orchestral Music, and more about violin playing (from Hans Sitt). Then, also on business, he went to Sweden and Norway, and established those Scandinavian relationships which remained one of the pleasures of his life. Other business wanderings followed.

But business was not attractive, and at last, as the musical profession was prohibited, the youth succeeded in getting permission to settle in Florida as an orange grower. There he lived in solitude, sometimes for months together seeing no fellow human being. Occasionally a hunting expedition would be undertaken; there are, as a result of Delius's residence there, fewer alligators in Florida to-day, but it is not certain that there are more oranges.

Soon Delius met a fellow musical enthusiast, one Ward, an organist of Brooklyn, who had been sent to the South for his health. This man became his companion and teacher, and to him, apparently, he owed much in the widening of his musical sympathies and the developing of his technique, and especially of his grasp of counterpoint. Then he left the estate and, entirely lost to sight by his parents in England, became for a short time 'Professor Delius', teacher of pianoforte to young ladies in a small remote town, and an admired violinist. A family reconciliation followed, and provided means for a Leipzig education, a certain discreetly organized dinner to Grieg and his (Delius's) father at the Hotel Metropole in London, at which the former expressed himself tactfully to the latter, confirming the new and better family understanding.

Delius's first public appearance as a composer was with the Suite *Florida*, performed in Leipzig in 1888 (when the composer was twenty-five), by an orchestra of sixty, which was conducted by Hans Sitt and paid for with a large barrel of beer, the rates of payment to fiddlers and trombonists not being in those days quite what they are at present.

The introduction of the composer to London was effected at the Concert of his own works which he gave in 1889, at the old St. James's Hall under the conductorship of his friend Alfred Hertz, an event which helped to gain the Conductor his appointment at the Metropolitan Opera House at New York, and hence his later position as Conductor of the San Francisco Symphony Orchestra, but had little immediate result upon the fortunes of the composer, inasmuch as no further note of his was publicly heard in this country during the following eight years. J. F. Runciman later summed up as follows the critical expressions called forth by this Concert: 'The truth was that we didn't know what the devil to make of this music, and most of us were frank enough to say so. That there was intention, real mastery of notes; that every sound proceeding from the orchestra was meant by the composer; that there was no bungling, nor from beginning to end an unanticipated effect—all this every competent critic knew. But the strains sounded unpleasant in our ears.'

The eventual recognition of the genius of Delius in his native country was due to Beecham more than to any one else. German appreciation came more readily.

Delius always favoured France as a place of residence, though France showed him little favour as a composer. From his middle thirties he possessed a small estate near Fontainebleau, and there he spent much time. And there he long lay, crippled by disease that had too early seized him, but lovingly tended by his wife, and visited by many musical friends, British and other. With a good radio apparatus he heard much music, including performances of his own works—for whose fuller understanding he longed with the longing of a man who loves his fellows and wishes to feel in spiritual touch with them.

Amongst Delius's chief works are the Operas, *Irmelin, Koanga, A Village Romeo and Juliet*, and *Fennimore and Gerda*; the Orchestral Works, *Paris, Brigg Fair, Dance Rhapsody, In a Summer Garden, On hearing the First Cuckoo in Spring*; Concertos for Piano, for Violin, for 'Cello, and for Violin and 'Cello, and the Choral-Orchestral works *Appalachia, Sea Drift, A Mass of Life, A Song of the High Hills*, a so-called *Requiem*, and some Chamber Music.

He was a decided Romantic, with (e.g. in the Cuckoo piece above mentioned) some occasional Impressionist leanings. In the expression of such moods as those of dreaminess, or of rich, quiet, but emotional beauty, Delius has never been surpassed, if indeed equalled. Apart from such moods he seems limited. His themes were seldom very strong, he had no great melodic gift (*vide* his Songs), his form was often ineffective, and if ever a composer could be charged with rhythmic weakness, it was surely he (*vide* his *Mass of Life*). He had a subtle harmonic style all his own—a supple, shifting chromaticism.

He died in 1934.

IRELAND

John Ireland was born at Bowdon, Cheshire, in 1879. His father, Alexander Ireland the author, was of Scottish descent, his mother, also an author, of Northern English.

Ireland.

Ireland's musical training was received at the Royal College of Music, under Stanford as teacher of Composition. He went there early, at fourteen, and remained there eight years, i.e. until he was twenty-two.

Since then he has lived a somewhat retired life in London, long exercising on Sundays the duties of an organist, and being seen by most people only at the (far too infrequent) performances of his works. His Piano Works include a very fine Sonata, a remarkable Sonatina (1928), and some romantic pieces of an impressionistic tendency such as *The Island Spell*. His Chamber Music and Songs are notable. Of Orchestral Music the world knows a Symphonic Rhapsody *Mai-Dun*, *The Forgotten Rite*, and a Pianoforte Concerto.

He is an Hon. D.Mus. of Durham University.

HOLST

Gustav Holst was born at Cheltenham in 1874. His father was a professional musician there, as was his grandfather also. The paternal great-grandfather was of Swedish origin, but was born at Riga; he, also, was a professional musician, and as such settled in England. With Holst's daughter, who has appeared in some degree as a composer, we have five generations of musical Holsts, which numerically approaches the record of the Bachs, equals that of the Couperins, and beats that of the Purcells and Scarlattis (see Vol. I, page 94).

Holst was composing as soon as he could hold a pen, and was early a performer on several instruments. When he was eighteen he was playing a village organ and conducting village choral societies. From his nineteenth to his twenty-fourth years he was a student at the Royal College of Music, Stanford being his composition teacher.

He then earned his living as a trombonist, and was for some time a member of the Scottish Orchestra. At twenty-nine he laid down his trombone, and took several music-masterships in schools in and about London. From 1906 the music of the St. Paul's Girls' School was directed by him, and he gave it great importance.

Holst.

From about the same time he was very closely associated with Morley College, on the south side of the river, an institute for working-class education that engaged his fullest sympathies. From 1919 he was a composition teacher at the Royal College of Music, and also Lecturer in Music at Reading College (now Reading University).

During the latter part of the First World War Holst was (under Y.M.C.A. auspices) promoting music in the British Army. The family name up to then had been 'von Holst', but the 'von' having proved an impediment to his going to Holland to work amongst the British soldiers interned there, it was dropped, and this having been done it became possible to smuggle him out to Salonica and then to Constantinople, despite the presence of a presumed one-eighth portion of foreign blood in his veins. At Constantinople he carried on wonderful soldiers' performances, and gave much serious tuition.

Amongst Holst's later and more important works are the great *The Planets* Suite for Orchestra, in which the astrological attributes of various planets are characterized in a very vivid way, *The Hymn of Jesus*, the *Ode to Death*, and a Choral Symphony for Chorus and Orchestra, and the humorous Opera, *The Perfect Fool*. Some of the later works, such as the *Fugal Overture* and the *Fugal Concerto*, resemble in formal aim the Neo-Classic works of Stravinsky (see pp. 115–17), which they slightly anticipated, and the change-over from the use of a big-size Orchestra in such a work as *The Planets* to a small body of instruments minutely contrasted, in such a work as the *Fugal Concerto* (for Flute, Oboe, and Strings), resembles the change in Stravinsky's instrumental method, seen when his *Rite of Spring* is compared with, say, his Piano Concerto.

Like many other composers, Holst does not quite decidedly take his place in any particular chapter of this book. He may be placed amongst the Nationalists on the grounds of the very large use he made of native folk-song (the score of his Opera, *At the Boar's Head*, is practically entirely woven out of traditional tunes), and of the strong sympathy he showed with such movements as that which aims at bringing into use again the national folk-dances; or be placed amongst the Neo-Romantics on the grounds of the mystic-romantic feeling he often expressed (comparable, in its way, with that of Franck, Elgar, and Vaughan Williams), which characteristic is very well exemplified in certain of the movements in *The Planets* Suite, and also in *The Hymn of Jesus*.

He died in 1934.

BAX

Arnold Bax was born in London in 1883 and trained at the Royal Academy of Music under Frederick Corder for Composition

and Matthay for Piano. At twenty he made his first public appearance as a composer. He was already under the 'Celtic' influence that he never attempted to shake off. There is a mystic feeling and a wistfulness about all his work that has often been compared with the similar qualities in the poetry of W. B. Yeats.

Bax's Orchestral Works include seven Symphonies and several Tone-Poems. He wrote much fine Choral Music (accompanied and unaccompanied). His Chamber Music and Piano Music are notable. For

Bax.

the introduction and popularization of his piano works Bax, himself a fine pianist, was much indebted to fellow members of the Matthay Group and, in particular, to Harriet Cohen, who interprets them perfectly. He was knighted in 1937 and became Master of the King's Musick in 1942. He died in 1953.

VAUGHAN WILLIAMS

Ralph Vaughan Williams was born in Gloucestershire in 1872. He was educated at Charterhouse and Trinity College, Cambridge, with two years at the Royal College of Music interpolated. After taking his degree at Cambridge he returned to the Royal College, studying composition with Parry and Stanford. Then he went to Berlin and worked with Max Bruch.

For a time he occupied a position as organist in London, and gave a good deal of time to University Extension lecturing. In 1908, aged thirty-six, he was in Paris studying with Ravel. When the First World War broke out he enlisted as a private in the Medical Corps; towards its very end he

Vaughan Williams.

took a commission in an artillery regiment. He then joined the staff of the Royal College of Music, and was until 1928 Conductor of the London Bach Choir.

Vaughan Williams was a great collector of Folk Songs, and his study both of these and of the contrapuntal English Tudor Music greatly influenced his style. He wrote much fine Choral Music, including an unaccompanied Mass which (like some other works) shows his decided leaning to medieval counterpoint (modal and with abundant 'consecutive 5ths', and the like). His *A London Symphony*, *Pastoral Symphony*, and Symphonies in F minor, D major, and E minor (two), the *Sinfonia Antartica* (1953; based on his music for a film) and the Symphony in D minor are notable, and so are the Violin Concerto, the Piano Concerto, and other works for orchestra. The *Fantasia on a Theme of Thomas Tallis* has become well known not only in his own country but elsewhere.

His Songs and Chamber Music exhibit a remarkable delicacy. The Opera, *Hugh the Drover*, is thoroughly English and very folklike in subject and musical treatment. So is the Ballet, *Old King Cole*. Other stage works are the Operas *Sir John in Love*, *The Poisoned Kiss*, and *Riders to the Sea*, and the 'Masque for dancing', *Job*. In texture Vaughan Williams often shows a tendency to

Impressionism, especially in his earlier works. In his later, more developed, certainly markedly individual style he is very rarely chromatic and is nearly always contrapuntal, but his counterpoint is very free, and often consists of a kind of counterpoint of chords, instead of single lines. There is about his music a strength of solidity, perhaps at times an excessive thickness, but it has always a notable sincerity and depth. Many of his works, as for instance the Violin Concerto, show an economy in instrumental resource that assimilates them in that respect to the work of the composers described in this book as 'the Anti-Romantics', but nearly all his work has a mystical tinge that entitles the author to place this notice in the position where it is found. Obviously this composer could have found a suitable place in several different sections of this volume; he has already been mentioned in the chapter concerned with Nationalism in Music. He died in 1958.

BRITTEN

Benjamin Britten was born at Lowestoft in 1913. He won a

Britten.

scholarship at the Royal College of Music. Amongst his early publications were many choral works and solo songs. The string *Variations on a Theme by Frank Bridge* (who had been one of his teachers) first brought him into serious notice (1937), and from the same period he began a considerable activity as a composer for films. In 1940 there appeared his *Sinfonia da Requiem* and his *Seven Sonnets from Michelangelo* (tenor and piano). From 1945 he became prominent as an opera composer—*Peter Grimes* (1945), *The Rape of Lucretia* (1946), *Albert Herring* (1948), a very freely treated version of *The Beggar's Opera* (1948), *Let's Make an Opera* (for children, 1949), *Billy Budd* (1951), *Gloriana* (1953), *The Turn of the Screw* (1954), and *A Midsummer Night's Dream* (1960).

6. AMERICAN

MACDOWELL

Edward MacDowell was born in New York in 1861. He early showed a love of music and a talent for it, yet was no remarkable boy prodigy. Local teaching made him a reasonably good pianist, and occasionally he had advice and help from the great South American pianist, Teresa Carreño.

At fourteen his talent was sufficiently declared for his parents to send him to the Paris Conservatoire, where he had Debussy for a fellow pupil. At this period a gift for draughtsmanship seemed to be as pronounced as the gift for music, and a member of the staff of the School of Fine Arts, seeing one of his drawings, offered to give

MacDowell.

him a three years' course without fee. Is it far-fetched to see the inspiration of an artist's eye in the large number of pieces he later wrote to titles suggesting natural objects ?

It is usual for European observers to hold the opinion that American youth has its own way to an extent unknown in older countries. MacDowell's mother, who accompanied him to Europe, may have been one of the American parents who established this tradition, for, on the boy, now sixteen, expressing discontent with his teaching at the Conservatoire, she willingly discussed with him a transfer to the Conservatoire of Moscow, Leipzig, or Stuttgart. The last was decided upon, but when tested proved to be unsatisfactory. Then a move was made to Frankfort, in order to profit by the piano teaching of Heymann, a short course of composition study at Wiesbaden under Ehlert, to fill up time, preceding this. At Frankfort the Conservatoire was then under the direction of Raff, and he undertook MacDowell's instruction in composition.

When MacDowell was twenty, Heymann's mind began to show signs of disorder. He left the Conservatoire, recommending MacDowell as his successor. Youth was considered an impediment, and the appointment was not made. MacDowell took private pupils, however, and amongst them was Marian Nevins, an American musician who later became his wife.

Then came the appointment to the Darmstadt Conservatoire as chief Piano Teacher. During the whole of this period MacDowell was soaking in the romantic poetry of Germany and England—Goethe, Heine, Byron, Shelley, and Tennyson. He was also actively exercising himself in composition, and when he took his first Piano Concerto to Liszt at Weimar, in 1882, it received approval. Better still, his *First Modern Suite* for Piano was given a place in the programme of the next festival of the General Society of German Musicians, then largely under Liszt's direction. Up to this time Mac-Dowell had considered himself a pianist who composed, but henceforth he began to consider himself a composer who played the piano. The Suite in question and the *Second Modern Suite* were both published by Breitkopf and Härtel on the recommendation of Liszt, and constituted the composer's first appearance in print. There followed a happy period of early marriage, spent largely in a cottage in the country near Wiesbaden: much composition was accomplished and a fairly wide recognition resulted, in Germany, America, and elsewhere.

At last, in his twenty-seventh year, MacDowell returned to America. He settled in Boston and quickly took an important place as composer, pianist, and teacher. In 1896, when he was thirty-five, he made the false move of his life, in accepting the professorship of music at Columbia University, New York. The chair was a new one; the structure of the organization had to be built from the ground up. There was much necessary drudgery, and into this, with the more interesting work of exposition, he threw himself with conscientious ardour. MacDowell may have been the right man for the position, but the position was not the right one for him. During the eight years spent in time-consuming and vitality-exhausting academic work he composed incessantly, and the double labour was too much. Much of the composition was, however, done in vacation periods on a small estate he had bought near Peterboro, New Hampshire.

He resigned his University position in 1904, and next year there came signs of brain trouble. In 1908, aged forty-seven, he died. He is buried on a hill-top near Peterboro, and the estate he owned there under the direction of his devoted and accomplished wife and of a

MacDowell Association she formed, came into use as a place of quiet work for American musicians and other creative artists.

There is, perhaps, room here for an observation of slight importance on the curious parallels between the lives of the two Edwards, Grieg and MacDowell. Both were, on one side, of Scottish ancestry, and bore Scottish names; both received early encouragement from Liszt. Both were happily married to understanding wives possessing musical talents and able to help them in their creative work; neither of them wrote Symphonies, Operas, or Oratorios, but both excelled in the composition of short pieces of what one of them, MacDowell, called 'suggestive music' (i.e. not definite and detailed 'programme music', but music inspired by outside images which it re-evokes); both of them loved the country and composed in log cabins they had built in places of solitary beauty. MacDowell's last intellectual pleasure was the reading of Finck's *Grieg*, and when Finck called on Grieg, in Norway in 1901, the Norwegian nature-composer made many inquiries as to the American nature-composer. Both were buried amidst the scenes of natural beauty they loved. MacDowell dedicated his Norse and Celtic Sonatas to Grieg. Perhaps, after all, these observations are not of such slight importance as was a moment since suggested. At all events they set in motion a train of thought.

SOME OTHER AMERICAN COMPOSERS MORE OR LESS CLASSIFIABLE AMONGST THE 'MODERN ROMANTICS'

ARTHUR WILLIAM FOOTE, a Massachusetts man, was born in 1853. He was educated at Harvard, and was one of the many older American musicians who admitted indebtedness to the teaching and example of J. K. Paine there. He was for a time an organist. His compositions were very varied and did much to give America faith in its musical self. He died in 1937.

GEORGE WHITEFIELD CHADWICK was born in Massachusetts, in 1854, into a musical family. He studied at the New England Conservatory at Boston, at the Leipzig Conservatoire, and at Munich under Rheinberger. He then took an organ position at Boston and a position on the staff of his old school there, of which in 1897 he became the Principal. He did much conducting. His compositions had a like influence with those of Foote, and as an educator his services were of great value. He died in 1931.

ARTHUR B. WHITING was still another member of what we may surely call the 'New England School'. He was born at Cambridge, Mass., in 1861, and studied across the river, in Boston, at the New England Conservatory, under Chadwick and others, as also in Munich under Rheinberger and others. On emerging from the student period, he lived first in Boston and then in New York. His orchestral music has been a good deal played by the Boston Symphony Orchestra. He cultivated harpsichord-playing, and revived much old music for various instrumental combinations.[1] He died in 1936.

HORATIO WILLIAM PARKER was also a New Englander. He was born near Boston, Mass., in 1863, and died in 1919. In composition he was, like so many other leading American composers, a pupil of G. W. Chadwick, but he also studied with Rheinberger at Munich. Church Music was a main interest of his musical life, and he held a number of important positions as organist and choirmaster. He was also, for a time, a teacher of counterpoint in the National Conservatory of Music, under Dvořák.

The first composition to make Parker widely known outside his native land was the oratorio, *Hora Novissima*, which six years after its first performance in America was heard at the Three Choirs Festival at Worcester, England, in 1899 (the first prominent appearance of an American composer in British festival circles). Thenceforward for a few years Parker was a principal figure at English festivals, and he received the recognition of an Hon. Mus.D. from Cambridge University. In 1894 he became Professor of Music at Yale. The list of his compositions is extended, and includes almost all forms. He had considerable success as an opera composer.

MRS. H. H. A. BEACH, also a New Englander, was born in 1867. She made an early reputation as a pianist, playing widely with the best American orchestras. At eighteen she married, and henceforward gave most of her attention to composition. She wrote much worthy music in many forms. She died in 1944.

[1] W. H. H. says 'Is it not advisable to add that Arthur Whiting has been the chief pioneer of Brahms's music in America ?'

HENRY F. GILBERT, still another Massachusetts man, was born in 1868 and became a pupil of MacDowell and other American teachers. He studied and used American, Indian, and Negro themes, and his compositions, in their very titles, as well as in their thematic content and general style, indicate strong nationalistic leanings. He died in 1928.

FREDERICK S. CONVERSE, another New Englander, was born in 1871, and was, like Foote, a student under Paine at Harvard. He also worked under Chadwick in Boston and under Rheinberger at Munich. Later he occupied positions on the staff of Harvard University and the New England Conservatory. His many works have had wide performance in America. He died in 1940.

HENRY K. HADLEY, also a Massachusetts man, was born in the same year as Converse and was a student of the New England Conservatory under Chadwick and others, and also worked in Vienna. He had much early success as an operatic and orchestral conductor. For seven years he lived in Garden City, Long Island, as organist and teacher, and did much composition there. For five years (from thirty-three to thirty-eight) he lived in Germany, performing and conducting his own works and latterly conducting the opera at Mainz. He composed many Operas, Tone Poems, &c. He died in 1937.

(Except MacDowell the above are all New England composers; it will be seen that they constitute a somewhat remarkable group, and the thought occurs that the oldest-settled and least racially mixed part of the country made the first great contribution to a national repertory.)

CHARLES M. T. LOEFFLER is always considered an American composer, though he was an Alsatian by birth, and, born in 1861, did not enter America until he was twenty, when he joined the famous Boston Symphony Orchestra as a violinist. He lived later in or near Boston. He was very active in composition, and much respected by American music-lovers.
He died in 1935.

For the many more recent American composers see the article *United States* in the *Oxford Companion to Music* and then the numerous articles devoted to the individuals therein mentioned.

7. ITALIAN

PIZZETTI

Ildebrando Pizzetti was born at Parma in 1880. He was trained at the Conservatory there, and later taught composition in it. He also conducted opera in his native city. At twenty-nine he was appointed teacher of composition in the Conservatory of Florence, and at thirty-seven became its Director; at forty-four he became Director of the Conservatory of Milan, and later he joined the staff of the St. Cecilia Conservatory at Rome. He associated a good deal with d'Annunzio, and won fame by his incidental music for two of this writer's plays. He is a very prolific composer of Operas, Orchestral Music, Chamber Music, &c., and an almost equally prolific critical writer. In composition and authorship he shows himself possessed of the highest ideals, but his music looks backward rather than forward, i.e. he is hardly to be associated with the most advanced Italian group. He has written a good deal under the name 'Ildebrando da Parma'.

RESPIGHI

Respighi was born in Bologna in 1879. After studying at the conservatory there he went to St. Petersburg (now Leningrad) to become a pupil of Rimsky-Korsakof, and then to Berlin to become a pupil of Max Bruch. He was afterwards head of the St. Cecilia Conservatory at Rome.

Respighi wrote six or seven Operas (including one delightful, simple work for Marionettes), a little Chamber Music, and some effective Orchestral Music, e.g. the Symphonic Poems, *Fountains of Rome* and *The Pines of Rome*, and the Suite, *Stained Glass Windows* ('Vetrate da Chiesa'), also an 'arranged' Suite, *Old Airs and Dances*. The score of the Diaghilef Ballet, *The Eccentric Toyshop* ('La Boutique Fantasque'), was an arrangement by him of works of Rossini.

Respighi's orchestration was very clear and purposeful.

He died in 1936.

8. JEWISH

BLOCH

Ernest Bloch is a Jew, born in Switzerland, trained there and in Belgium, Germany, and France, and for some years settled in the United States. He was born in 1880.

When his varied musical education was completed he returned to his native place, Geneva, and entered the family business, composing in his spare time. When he was thirty his Opera, *Macbeth*, written many years before, was performed in Paris, where it made a stir as the work of an overturner of the good old musical customs. About the same time he directed in Switzerland concerts of some of his orchestral works, and so began to come further into notice.

Five years later he went to the United States as the conductor for the dancer, Maud Allan, and there he has remained, occupying in turn various educational positions. Most of his later works have been first performed in the United States, and he began almost to count as an American composer. But he desires to express his racial mind in music, often choosing Jewish themes, and shows in much of his work an Oriental rhapsodic exuberance.

Yet there are certain pieces of Bloch in a more atmospheric, evocative, or impressionistic style, and his *Concerto Grosso* (1925) for String Orchestra and Piano showed decided Neo-Classic tendencies. His Violin Concerto, Symphonic Poems, Symphonies, and Chamber-Music have many admirers.

PERIOD VIII
The Anti-Romantics

XXI

THE ANTI-ROMANTICS

I T is unusual that an author should begin a chapter with a confession that he does not fully understand the subject of which he is treating, but perhaps honour may be saved if he asserts that nobody as yet does fully understand the present-day movement and, apparently, least of all its composers themselves.

In considering the music of the twentieth century one thing is, however, clear enough—there has occurred a decided reaction against Romanticism, including that form of it called Impressionism. There have been tendencies

1. To reduce or abolish all strong emotions[1] and literary associations and implications in instrumental works (such as those so often seen in the scores of Weber, Schumann, and Strauss, for instance), and likewise what we may call pictorial or Nature suggestions (such as those of the widely diverse Debussy and MacDowell).

2. To abolish 'Romantic' harmony even when free from such associations (harmonic styles such as those of the composers mentioned and also those of the less 'literary' Romantic composers, such as Chopin, Brahms, Elgar, and Franck).

3. To adopt a pungent rhythmic style, having little in common with the old style of phrases answered by balancing phrases and building themselves up into regular 'Subjects' —and so on.

4. To drop the old stereotyped forms (those of the eighteenth- and nineteenth-century Sonatas, Symphonies, &c.), as being too indirect and long-winded.

5. To discard old methods of orchestration, such as those of Wagner, Strauss, and Elgar, in which a balance and

[1] Cf. some of the modernist poets, e.g. Edith Sitwell, 'Poetry is primarily an art, and not a dumping-ground for emotions' (*Poetry and Criticism*).

merging of tints is sought, and to install in place of them a method of orchestral colours in juxtaposition, sharply standing off from one another.

What the Anti-Romantics say and what they do.

All this makes the new music sound, at first hearing, as different as possible from the old, and it would appear that music has now come nearer 'a fresh start' than at any time since 1600. That much seems clear. Music in the Anti-Romantic period is like Mr. Reginald Wilfer, in *Our Mutual Friend*, whose life's ambition was 'to wear a complete new suit of clothes, hat and boots included, at one time'. Mr. Wilfer never attained this ambition, and music may never attain it either. But it has occasionally come so near it that some of its own best old friends have passed it by, not recognizing it as music at all.

When we bring ourselves down to details, and begin to study the new music in the light of what the composers themselves and their followers and associates say about it, we at once find the further truths we are seeking concealed in a mass of strange and often self-contradictory statements. The general position seems to be this. A number of the composers of the day are, like a number of the painters, sculptors, and writers, strongly influenced in an anti-romantic direction. So influenced they produce a body of music, some of which is undoubted rubbish, and other of which by its force, directness, and certainty of craftsmanship persuades, or almost persuades, one that it is of the level of at least the lesser masterpieces of old. Naturally a good deal of the process of creation is subconscious. Then, driven to self-defence by their opponents, the composers bring their full conscious mind to bear upon the explanation of their production, and their ardent followers do likewise.[1] But the conscious which explains is not half so clever as the sub-conscious which creates, and at once there

[1] But see also page 114.

is brought into existence, for the discomfiture of the simple-minded fellow who 'wants to know', a state of confusion that reduces him to the state of 'either the author's mad or I am—perhaps both!'

A few Examples of the Contradictions

As an example of the confusion. The first volume of the third edition of *Grove's Dictionary of Music* appeared just before this chapter was first written. It included letter 'B'. Bartók is one of the Anti-Romantics referred to in the heading of the chapter, and I turned eagerly to see whether the critic who had made a special study of that composer's work in order to write this important article could give me any real guidance on a subject that admittedly at that moment somewhat puzzled most of us. I read at the end of the article an allusion to the opera *Bluebeard's Castle*, 'a grim and enigmatic work, full of atmosphere and dramatic tenseness, and entirely free from operatic formulas'.

Then follows this passage, contradictory with what has just been said and also, surely, to most readers, self-contradictory in its implications:

> Bartók might be reproached with a singular and systematic lack of emotion. The absence or presence of this quality, however, depends upon the outlook of each individual hearer. In order to appreciate his work it is necessary to expect nothing in the nature of subjective expression on the composer's part. Bartók never sets out to convey his personal feelings to his audience; his art is concerned solely with the delivery of its message in the most lucid possible way; but precisely because of its restraint it is capable of evoking in the listener, provided that he is sufficiently receptive, deeply human feelings of his own.

From this passage one clear general impression, at least, remains. In conscious desire Bartók is an Anti-Romantic. But is he entirely one in achievement ? The description of his work seems to represent it as a muddle. What is this talk of a work 'full of atmosphere and dramatic tenseness' coming from a composer who 'might be reproached with a singular and systematic lack of emotion' ? What is this about a composer from whom we are 'to expect nothing in the way of subjective expression', and who 'never sets out to convey his personal feelings to his audience', yet who can awaken in the hearer 'deeply human feelings of his own' ?

The frequent attempt to make us believe that the music of the Anti-Romantics is scrupulously devoid both of emotion and of 'programme' constantly produces these very curious statements. Thus the well-known conductor, Ansermet ('Great is Stravinsky, and Ansermet is his prophet!'), in discussing the Three Pieces for String Quartet, says 'Stravinsky has affixed no programmes or titles to his pieces, and he wishes them to be listened to abstractedly'. He then goes on to describe the pieces in terms which boldly defy that statement, though apparently he is totally unconscious of their so doing:

> The first represents a group of peasants singing and dancing against the monotonous setting of the steppes. In it one hears the droning piping and the dull drumming of the peasants, and the heavy beat of their feet as the sounds drift for a moment out of the distance.
> The second represents priests chanting in a church, now in plainsong, now with a hint of the *Dies Irae*. More than once the chanting is discordant, and now and again the organ has to support them in their uncertain tones.
> The third is an unhappy juggler who is distraught with a grief that he must hide while he does his little feats before the watching crowd. One hears in certain glinting tones the flash of his tricks, and as a piercing contrast the sorrow that tortures him while he is at his seeming play.
>
> E. Ansermet (translated by F. M. H.).

So, too, the modernist-minded critic, Mr. Edwin Evans, speaking of the Ballet, *The Rite of Spring*, which, its stage setting and action discarded, had come to be performed as a

concert piece, said that it 'is in all but name a modern symphony, and is therefore to be regarded as abstract music,
despite its original purpose'. He added that 'the suggestion of
a programme has done more harm than good', yet goes on to
describe the Prelude of Part II as 'gloomy with the oppression
of the vast forces of Nature, pitiful with the helplessness of
living creatures in their presence'.

It is fair to this writer and the other just quoted to say that
there is warrant for believing that the composer himself has
thought, and sometimes expressed himself, just as confusedly
as they upon the nature of his work. He has written pieces
as Operas, then removed the words and changed them to
Ballets, then removed the action and changed them to instrumental works, and when they have reached this last stage has
claimed that they were always pieces of purely 'abstract'
music. He has been a great rearranger, and as each new
arrangement of a work has been made has defended it as the
true original at last revealed. His *The Nightingale* (founded
on Hans Andersen) began as an Opera, became a Ballet, and
was later (its score re-edited for the purpose) sometimes performed as a Symphonic Poem. His *Renard* followed a similar course of reincarnation. So, too, his *The Wedding*. He
sanctions or instigates concert performances of all his Ballets,
and then, despite the fact that they were originally written
to a very detailed scenario, they are boldly described as
'abstract' music. See, however, E. E.'s statement at end of
Appendix III.

The Anti-Romantic's hatred of Blend

There is, it seems, a definite theory underlying such statements, but it is a difficult one. It may be exemplified by giving
Mr. Ansermet's description of *The Soldier's Story* ('a read,
played, and danced story'):

The work in its general conception combines three elements, the verbal, the musical, and the plastic, without ever

mixing them, realizing thus an idea which is diametrically opposed to the Wagnerian theory of blending the various forms of art. The cohesion of these elements consists merely in the continuous close agreement in their mutual understanding of the subject and the similarity of the 'tones' chosen by them.

In other words, there are three or four rivers flowing along in the same channel at the same pace, always companioning one another and never merging or mingling—like the Rhône and the Arve at Geneva. It is a strange conception, and surely unrealizable[1], but, as an intellectual conception, it is typical of its composer and of his followers and many of his younger contemporaries. For, as already hinted, this school has a horror of mixing and mingling. Its words and their setting must assert their mutual independence. If melodies are contrapuntally combined they must be in different keys—when in any keys at all.[2] If instrumental tone colours are combined each must stand clear of every other (we may have

---

[1] In fairness to Stravinsky the reader should turn to Appendix III and try to grasp his own exposition of this difficult question, as there set out.

[2] Here, from Stravinsky's *Rite of Spring* is an example of combination of melodies in different keys (i.e. an example of 'Polytonality')—

Molto allegro (*Very quick*). ♩ = 166.

The top tune (Woodwind and Strings) is in F major, or something like it. The bottom tune (4 Tubas) is in A flat or D flat. (Details omitted are a Woodwind trill (A–B flat) and a Bass Drum punctuation in triple time.) In playing this extract on the piano put the right-hand part an octave higher, and so allow the two parts to stand off from one another as great differences of orchestral colour cause them to do.

a red and a blue, but they must not blend into a purple). If notes are combined into chords they must refuse to encourage Browning's boast:

And I know not if, save in this, such gift be allowed to man,
That out of three sounds he frame, not a fourth sound but a
    star.

Discord and Concord

To the ear accustomed to eighteenth- or nineteenth-century music, Stravinsky's or Bartók's seems to be all 'discord' (in the popular sense of the word) and no 'harmony' (again in the popular sense). You may search through pages of one of the scores before you meet with a 'common chord'—a simple C—E—G, or anything like that. The notes of all the chords are, indeed, 'standing off' rather than merging. They remain notes and produce no 'star'.

This, however, may be a temporary condition in the listener's experience. 'Discord' and 'concord' are after all relative terms. It is probable that, as in the past, the discords of one age will prove to be the concords of the next. The combination of C E G B flat was once a harsh discord. If used at all it was not to be allowed to remain or to pass heedlessly into some other chord. It had to be 'resolved' in a very particular way, on the chord F A C—the E rising to an F and the B flat falling to an A. Nowadays if a composition ended on the chord C E G B flat with no resolution at all, probably few of us would be in the slightest degree worried and many would not notice the incident.[1] Those four notes have come to merge into what Browning calls a 'star', and some of the later combinations may in time do the same. If any of these Anti-Romantics think that the discordancy of their combinations of notes will always attract the same attention as at present they are probably wrong. As the Irish critic said, 'The greatest

[1] See Chopin's Twenty-third Prelude (in F) for an example of this kind of ending, by the way.

surprise of their life may come to them twenty years after they're dead.' Punch's joke, 'O for the good old days of Debussy!' is already long out of date (as a joke), and should now read, 'O for the good old days of Stravinsky and Schönberg'.

The Anti-Romantic Use of 'Discord'

It is difficult to achieve a satisfactory harmonic analysis of contemporary music, but probably some future theorist will take a piece of Stravinsky's and point out that its discords themselves differ in pungency within as wide a range as that which in our younger days divided the concords of those days from the legitimate and permitted discords. For example, the fluctuation between 'concord' and 'discord' in a piece of Bach's possesses a parallel in the fluctuation between milder and harsher discords in a piece of Stravinsky's. In other words, on this theory, 'discord' and 'concord' are not absolutes but relatives—which seems to be a reasonable enough suggestion, and one which is supported by a study of the history of music during the past four hundred years. Indeed, the only way to consider modern schools of music and still retain one's sanity is to make the fullest use of the doctrine of musical relativity. And if 'discord' and 'concord' are merely relative terms, so are 'romantic' and 'classical', and 'subjective' and 'objective'. There are no absolutes anywhere. The new music is less 'romantic' and less 'subjective' than the old, but if it were as entirely 'abstract' as its protagonists assert it would be the equivalent of a mere geometrical diagram, and would interest nobody at all.

The Abolition of Romance a Vain Dream

The best plan for the man of common sense is to brush on one side all statements such as that the music of Stravinsky is 'pure abstract sound'[1] and that he produces music in which

[1] Edwin Evans, *Musical News*, 4 June 1921.

'every vestige of poetic implication is negated',[1] to recognize that all music is necessarily more or less romantic (the human being cannot live in a vacuum), but to admit frankly that that of the composers in question is of the 'less so' variety. There has certainly never been any good music that was purely intellectual, and never any that was purely emotional; but, naturally, action and reaction occur, and the balance of interest is now on one side and now on the other. At present the intellectual weighs down the scale. Composers are reacting against the excessive romanticism of the age that preceded them. In the eighteenth century the pendulum of music swung to the intellectual side, that of formal beauty; in the nineteenth it swung to the side of emotional expression; in the twentieth it is due to swing again to the intellectual side, and in place of the eighteenth century formal beauty composers are substituting another intellectual element, that of research into the qualities of tone, into the effects of novel combinations of notes, and so forth.

Attempts at a Musical Geometry

The attempt to produce what I have called above 'a mere geometrical diagram' has, it must be admitted, occasionally been made. Stravinsky wrote a piece which he called *Symphonies of Wind Instruments*, which represents advanced progress in the 'abstract' direction. He wrote for wind instruments because they are, on the whole, less 'naturally expressive' than strings, and directed that the music should be played entirely without expression, since its whole charm lay in its exploitation of carefully chosen and contrasted tonal qualities. Koussevitzky conducted this work in London, and the composer, who was present, later charged him in the press with having spoilt it by an attempt to play it expressively. To this the rejoinder was that so far from any attempt being made to play expressively the performers had been fully

[1] Leigh Henry on the Three Pieces for String Quartet, 1922.

occupied with the attempt to play the mere notes, the orchestral parts having arrived too late to allow of any rehearsal. In no former period of history has a composer complained of the importing of 'expression' into his music and a performer defended himself by a denial of having attempted any such thing, and the incident is significant of the new aims and tendencies.

It may also be recalled that Stravinsky wrote certain pieces for the 'Pianola' in which he took advantage of that quite expressive instrument's ability to play inexpressively and mechanically when this is desired: he wanted, he said, to achieve 'timbre independent of sentimental inflections'.

In such pieces as these and the 'Symphonies' just mentioned is seen the revolutionary aim in its most extreme manifestation. But no revolutionary aim is ever completely attained. Wagner set out to merge the arts, and so to do away with the dominance of music in Opera; he succeeded in this so partially that a very large part of his work is capable of performance on a concert platform, i.e. simply as music.

A New Classicism

Amongst the aims imputed to the Anti-Romantics at the beginning of this chapter was (No. 4) that of dropping the old forms as being too indirect and long-winded. They were for 'directness'; they opposed not only the emotional in music, but also the elaborately formal.

In a Beethoven Sonata, for example, they disliked not merely the suggestions of awe and mysticism and courage and love, but also what we may call the technical rhetoric, such as, for instance, the procedure of 'Sonata Form', the building up, from some initial musical thought or *motif*, of a definite statement, or 'Subject', the building up, from some other musical thought or *motif* of another and contrasted musical statement or 'Subject', the treatment (in what is called the 'Development' portion of a Sonata Form movement) of portions of these statements or 'Subjects' in a way closely resembling a preacher's treatment of a text or texts, the re-statement of the 'subjects' and the oratorical peroration which we call 'Coda'.[1]

Similarly, in a Bach Fugue, they disliked the closely argued discussion of the 'Subject' propounded in the opening measures. They were anarchical not only in wishing to destroy the old sentiments of society, but also in wishing to destroy the old constitutional procedure. They would do away not only with the Church and its outlook upon infinity, but also with the State with its codified regulations for men's behaviour. They were not only Anti-Romantics, but also Anti-Classics.

As it happens, however, the 'Anti' capacities of humanity are ridiculously limited by Nature, and are very difficult to sustain over any long period. And so Stravinsky, in a later phase, whilst still opposing Romanticism, made his peace with Classicism to the extent of adopting classic forms. He wrote a Piano Sonata and a Piano Concerto that, so far as general procedure goes, might be looked upon as the work of a twentieth-century Bach. He said (interview in the *Christian Science Monitor*, January 1925):

> I'm an altogether different composer from the Stravinsky of *Fireworks*, *Song of the Nightingale*, and *The Rite of Spring*. You do not know me unless you have heard the music which I have written in the last two years. . . . I have gone back in the centuries and have begun over again, on a historic foundation. What I write to-day has its roots in the style and methods of Palestrina and Bach.

This change dates from 1923–4. The works in question have much counterpoint, and are sometimes very Bach-like in texture, and even fugal. Much of the harmony is 'extreme', but there are passages in which the older harmonies are not

[1] Cf. Chekov to an author friend, 'Cut out all those pages about the moonlight, and give us what you really feel about it—the reflection in a piece of broken bottle', quoted in Murry, *The Problem of Style* (Oxford University Press).

disdained; we even sometimes find two voices running in parallel thirds, and movements, however discordant some of their passages, 'make a good end' on ordinary 'common chords'.

Of this Neo-Classic development the third (and last) Movement of his Piano Sonata (1925) may be cited.

Much of this fugal Movement might, as far as idiom goes, have been written by Bach himself, e.g. the very 'Subject', and some of its treatment—canon, augmentation, tonic pedal, &c. Much of the harmony, too (though not in the following example), is little if any more 'modern' than Bach.

In this extract we find the left hand 'developing' the first bar and a half of the Subject; an interesting feature is that whereas the Subject was originally an unbroken flow of semiquavers, the last four notes, but not the rest (of what is used here), are 'augmented' into quavers.

In the right-hand 'counterpoint' we find still in use what has always been a strongly individual characteristic of Stravinsky—his sharp irregular rhythmic accents—(cf. the second example on page 9 of Volume I), here perhaps suggesting some slight debt to contemporary dance-music.

This neo-classic phase was in one thing not inconsistent with the previous phase, being still in reaction against the nineteenth-century Romantic school—perhaps one should say 'in intended reaction', as some of the movements in these works promote a pretty definite romantic emotion when listened to sufficiently often for their strangeness to cease to trouble.

In Germany, Busoni, at the time of his death in 1924, was engaged upon an attempt at Neo-Classicism, which, looked at in its broad outlines, was very similar in aim to Stravinsky's, and in Britain such works as Holst's *Fugal Overture* (for Orchestra) and *Fugal Concerto* (for Flute, Oboe, and Strings) and Vaughan Williams's *Concerto Accademico* exemplify the same desire to make use of classical forms and styles whilst not abandoning a modern harmonic outlook. Younger French, Italian, and German composers have made similar experiments. A re-reading of what was said about Bach's orchestration in Chapter X of the first volume of this work will show that the modern desire to keep lines of orchestral primary colour distinct, rather than let them merge into blended effects, is quite in keeping with one early phase of classical musical thought.

The Creed of a Moderate Man

As it has been necessary to allude rather plainly to some of the excesses of the protagonists of the new Anti-Romantic school, it seems desirable that the author should state clearly his own attitude towards the new movement. He believes that art 'progresses' not in a straight line, but by alternate divergences to first one side of the line and then the other; he thinks that an excursion to the Anti-Romantic side of the line was due, and perhaps overdue, and welcomes the sight of a group of composers engaged in making that excursion. Looking through history he sees few or no reforms that have not been the work of one-sided minds (fanatical minds, if you like, in many cases), and he believes that the composers now in question, and still more, perhaps, their journalistic supporters, have shown a considerable degree of onesidedness (and occasionally of fanaticism). He thinks that some of them have been more moved, perhaps, by the impulse to destroy than by that to create. He thinks that a good deal of the work produced, however novel in idiom, is not merely experimental but also commonplace, so that it gives the same unhappy combination of pain and boredom as one might get from a dentist drilling one's teeth and talking weather the while. But amongst the huge mass of stuff already produced is to be found some that has high value, and is likely to live. His sympathies are, on the whole, very much more on the side of the Anti-Romantics and Neo-Classics than on the side of the later Romantics, because, temperamentally, he prefers immaturity to over-ripeness. He is convinced of the basic sincerity of the leading composers of the mid-twentieth century. But he thinks that these men and their lesser followers have suffered from an overdose of their own theories, which has driven them in many cases to a too great dependence upon their reason and a slighting of those sub-conscious instincts out of which, in the main, has in the past proceeded the impulse to the production of the world's masterpieces. He looks forward to the coming thirty years as quite possibly a period of return to a better mental balance on the part of a public at present largely antagonistic to any novelty, and a consequent return to better mental balance on the part of composers and writers who are now driven to extreme expressions by the goad of self-defence. There is sometimes an academicism in avoiding academicism, and perhaps these people are at present occasionally guilty of that. Finally, let it be emphasized that the Anti-Romantic movement in music is only a phase of the activities of the Spirit of the Age. In all the arts there are similar manifestations—all the arts but one:

'I asked if in cookery there were no signs of that revolt against suavity which shows in the other arts. He said that, in fact, one of his literary friends was going to write a cubistic cookery book, in reaction against the sameness of food. "Why should rice always be soft ?" "I advised him to put gravel in it!" said Mr. Montagné. But the truth is that though a fashion may induce people to buy dadaist or vorticist pictures and hang them on the walls, they will not risk their stomachs with anything that departs from sound tradition. Criticism of cookery has a certain sincerity.'— Mr. Stephen Gwynne's interview with M. Prosper Montagné, a famous Paris chef, in the *Observer*, 16th January 1927.

LEADING ANTI-ROMANTIC COMPOSERS

STRAVINSKY

Igor Stravinsky was born near St. Petersburg (Leningrad) in 1882. His father was an opera singer of repute.

Stravinsky's education was directed to preparation for the legal profession, but at twenty, travelling in Germany, he met Rimsky-Korsakof, and the impression made on him decided him to take up music, and shortly after this he put himself under that master's direction. The relationship between Stravinsky and his teacher and teacher's family was happy. Some of his piano music is dedicated to Rimsky-Korsakof's sons, and the popular *Fireworks* (for Orchestra) was written to celebrate the marriage of Rimsky-Korsakof's

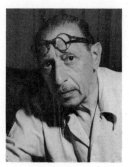

Stravinsky.

daughter. In 1908 he undertook the sad duty of composing a *Dirge in Memory of Rimsky-Korsakof*.

Stravinsky's meeting, about his twenty-fifth year, with Diaghilef, of the famous Russian Ballet, was of great importance. It turned his talent into a channel which, as it has since appeared, gave it free course. The *Fire Bird* was the first Ballet commissioned (1910); then followed *Petrushka* (1912); the Opera *The Nightingale* (later turned into a ballet); and the Ballet, *The Rite of Spring* (1913).

The Fire Bird and *Petrushka*, quaint and tuneful (some folk-tune influence) and gaily coloured orchestrally, despite much that is novel, particularly in the harmony, won easy acceptance. *The Rite of Spring* (1913) was another matter. It appeared to be strongly revolutionary and aroused great argument, especially when the ballet scenario for which it had been written was put aside and acceptance asked for it as a 'Symphony' and as a piece of 'absolute' music. *The Nightingale* (which was first heard later than *The Rite of Spring*) was similarly discussed, and succeeding works re-awakened the discussion—the opera *Renard* (1915), *The Soldier's Story* (1917), the so-called *Symphonies of Wind Instruments, in Memory of Debussy* (1920), and the operas *Mavra* (1921), *The Wedding* ('Noces'), composed in 1917 and first heard in 1923, and the ballet *Apollo Musagetes*, first heard in 1928.

Debate took a new turn in the early 1920's when a Piano Sonata and a Piano Concerto appeared which were said by the Composer to mark his determination to adopt the classical style. (See page 110.) Later works have been the choral-orchestral *Symphony of Psalms* (1930), the Violin Concerto (1933), the opera-ballet, *Persephone* (1934), the ballet, *The Game of Cards* (1937), the Concerto in E flat for 16 instruments (1938), the Symphony in C (1940), the Symphony in Three Movements (1945), and the opera, *The Rake's Progress* (1951).

Paris was long the centre of Stravinsky's activities, partly owing to its being Diaghilef's headquarters. Stravinsky has lived there and in Switzerland, and also in the French Riviera, and at last in the U.S.A.

Note the Oriental influence in the work of Stravinsky's middle period: the rhythms and the oft-repeated tiny snatches of melody of Tibetan musicians heard in London in 1922 strongly reminded many listeners of *The Rite of Spring*.

No account of Stravinsky would be complete that neglected to take account of his sense of humour—sometimes a biting irony. There is no doubt that his choice of humorous, exotic, and magical Ballet subjects has much helped the acceptance of his music; their touch of the grotesque has seemed to many people a justification of harmonies and orchestral touches to which they would normally have shown little tolerance. It may be observed that the subjects, in themselves, are romantic, and the composer's treatment of the earlier ones might also be considered as coming under that description. Gradually, however, a drier wit and a less emotional attitude of mind marked his work, until at last, as already indicated (page 109), he reached a point where he claimed to have utterly discarded all (extra-musical) emotions whatever.

BUSONI

Ferruccio Benvenuto Busoni was born near Florence in 1866. His father and mother were fine musicians; the latter was of German descent. As a child he made a stir, both as composer and pianist, but chiefly as the latter. His first public appearance was in Vienna when he was nine, and it at once established him as a personality in the musical world. He lived comparatively little in Italy, finding Germany his spiritual home. For two or three periods of a few years each he lived in America. Busoni died in 1924, aged only fifty-eight.

Busoni.

No pianist, perhaps, has ever played like Busoni; his subtlety of phrasing was magnificently true, and his variety of tone-colour amazing. This has perhaps led the general public to overlook his activities as a composer, which were almost incessant throughout his career, except for a gap of nine or ten years in his later twenties and earlier thirties. The best way of concisely stating the facts of his later manner is to say that in the attempt to employ the devices and forms of the older contrapuntal period and to apply them to the expression of modern feeling it somewhat resembles the later phase of Stravinsky. Like Schönberg, he theorized a good deal about his methods, and his writings on the subject have been collected and published in book form.

Amongst Busoni's large output are to be found three Operas and a large portion of another, *Doctor Faust* (finished after his death by his pupil Jarnach), a considerable number of larger or smaller Orchestral works, Chamber works, and Piano pieces—the last including an elaborate *Fantasia Contrappuntistica* on themes from Bach's *Art of Fugue* (in two versions, the earlier for one piano, the later for two).

CASELLA

Alfredo Casella was born at Turin in 1883. His mother was his first teacher, but at thirteen he was sent to the Paris Conservatory,

Casella.

where he had a highly successful student career, as pianist and composer. Fauré was his teacher of composition. He had many triumphs in different countries as pianist and orchestral conductor, and, like some other Italian composers of to-day, wrote a great deal of criticism. For a time he taught Piano at the Paris Conservatory, and he was also on the staff of the St. Cecilia Conservatory in Rome. He founded in that city the National Society of Music, later to become the Corporation of New Music, and then the Italian branch of the International Society for Contemporary Music. His national outlook was indicated in the following: he 'was convinced that Italy, now become a great modern nation, ought to regain one of the first positions in the European family'; and he believed that 'through the more developed means of the world's music (a technique towards the formation of which Italy has contributed nothing for about a century) there will at length be reintegrated in Italian music those ancient and eternal characteristics of the Italian genius—grandeur, severity, classic purity, sobriety, robustness, elasticity, equilibrium, and boldness, and virtuosity of means employed'. He condemned the 'fatal confusion that has lasted so long, a confusion of the predominance of vocal melodramatic monody with *true music*, the sense of which, unfortunately, the Italians have for a hundred years lost'. (Quoted here from de Angelis' *L'Italia Musicale d'Oggi—Dizionario dei Musicisti*.)

Casella's own compositions, which in the latest period showed great harmonic freedom, were intended to exemplify his views. He was, in particular, an admirer of the musical France in which he was brought up. He enjoyed special fame as an interpreter of Debussy, and wrote much about him. But in the programme of the performance of his *Heroic Elegy* (1917), a Symphonic Poem in memory of the 'Sons of Italy fallen whilst fighting for her greatness', a work which had a poor reception as 'ultra-modern' and 'un-Italian', he wished (but was forbidden) to say that he 'had been inspired by the criteria of the most recent art, of that art which tries to oppose to Impressionism a preoccupation with dynamic energy, sober robustness, and linear firmness'. With these quotations the position of Casella is perhaps sufficiently defined.

Casella's works include a great deal of Piano music and Orchestral music, and some songs and Chamber music.

He died in Rome in 1947.

MALIPIERO

Francesco Malipiero was born in Venice in 1882, and studied at the Conservatory of Bologna. In 1921 he took up a position as Professor of Composition at the Conservatory of Parma, later becoming director of the Conservatory of Venice and Professor of Music in the University of Padua. He is one of the fiery advance guard of Italian music, and has written a good deal in a polemic way. He is 'modern' in the sense that he scorns tradition of all kinds, harmonic, formal, orchestral, &c. Yet he is intensely Italian in spirit. His stage works are decidedly revolutionary in conception.

BARTÓK

Béla Bartók was born in 1881 at a small place in Hungary (now in Yugoslavia) and died in New York in 1945. At six he began to learn the Piano, under his mother's instruction. At eight the father died, and the mother had to support the family as a school teacher.

At ten the boy had come before the local public as a composer, and the mother wanted to secure the advantages of a large town, so moved to Pressburg (now Bratislava), a very active musical centre. Here good lessons could be taken and concerts and opera performances attended, and there were also opportunities of taking part in the practice of Chamber Music. 'At eighteen', said Bartók, 'I had

Bartók.

a tolerable knowledge of musical literature from Bach to Brahms, and of Wagner as far as *Tannhäuser.*'

The young composer's style was at this time greatly influenced by the music of Brahms and of the somewhat similar-minded Dohnányi, four years his own senior. On Dohnányi's advice the Budapest Conservatory was chosen as the place for further training, and there Bartók stayed until he was twenty-two. He threw himself very ardently at this period into the study of the later Wagner and of Liszt, and for two years did no composition of his own, being regarded by his masters and fellow students as merely a brilliant pianist.

In 1902, when Bartók was twenty-one, he first heard Strauss's Tone-Poem, *Thus spake Zoroaster*: it then horrified older musicians but entranced him. He hastened to study Strauss's works and to begin composition in the new style here suggested. Also, influenced by the strong political-artistic national feeling of the place and time, he began to collect Hungarian folk songs, and wrote a Tone Poem inspired by the life of the national hero, Kossuth, which Hans Richter and the Hallé Orchestra at once performed at Manchester. Other Orchestral and Chamber Music compositions quickly followed, and had fairly wide performance considering the fact that the composer was hitherto unknown.

The Strauss enthusiasm quickly waned, and a renewed period of Liszt study followed. The folk music interest continued, but with a change—Bartók came to realize that the songs usually known as Hungarian folk songs were of but superficial value, whilst all the time, quite unknown to musicians, amongst the genuine peasantry there existed a repertory of much finer and more significant music.

In the collection of this music he had a devoted collaborator in the person of a newly made friend, Zoltán Kodály (see page 122). To the study of Magyar tune was added that of Slovak and Rumanian tune. Few of the melodies collected were in the conventional major and minor scales. The ancient scales, in their variety, though abandoned in serious composition, were still alive. Bartók resolved to use them. Naturally in doing so he found himself bringing into existence new harmonies, and this, in time, led to his gradual abandonment of the existing diatonic system and of the chromatic system based upon it, and to the gradual taking up of a new style in which the twelve notes of the chromatic scale were considered as independent entities, ready to submit to all sorts of unheard-of combinations.

At twenty-six, Bartók was appointed a professor at the Budapest Conservatory. But his compositions met with great opposition in that city. He persevered in the task he had set himself, however, and continued the energetic collection of the peasant material that had inspired him. Straitened financial resources and the circumstance of the First World War were an impediment to the wider travels he had in mind, but he got as far as Biskra and made some study of Arab music.

Towards the end of the First World War the public of Budapest became less hostile to the national composer in their midst. The Pantomime Ballet, *The Wooden Prince*, was heard, and so was the earlier one-act Opera, *Bluebeard's Castle*.

The present notice is closely based on a brief autobiography the composer wrote for a Russian musical paper in (I think) 1924.[1] This concludes:

> Unfortunately this gratifying turn in my affairs was followed by the disturbances of 1918, which lasted for eighteen months and made peaceful devotion to serious work all but impossible. The present state of things does not permit me even to think of continuing to work at musical folklore. My personal means no longer permit this 'luxury'; moreover the scientific investigation of districts separated from the former Hungary has become impossible on political grounds and on account of mutual animosity. And visits to distant countries are beyond our reach. As for the

[1] Kindly translated from the Russian for me by my friend, S. W. Pring.

rest, nowhere in the world does one encounter a genuine interest in this branch of musical science—perhaps as a matter of fact it has not the importance ascribed to it by some who are fanatically devoted to it.

Bartók's compositions are fairly numerous. They comprise, in addition to the two stage works already mentioned, Orchestral Suites, two Piano Concertos, and other orchestral music, six String Quartets, Violin Sonatas, a large number of solo Piano compositions (including the extensive series called *Mikrokosmos*), and a good many volumes of arrangements of Folk Songs. There are also a great number of collections of Folk-Music scientifically displayed (altogether Bartók collected about 7,000 tunes), a Piano School, and editions of classical works prepared for students.

KODÁLY

Zoltán Kodály was born the year after his friend and colleague, Bartók, i.e. in 1882. The place was Kecskemét, in Hungary. He studied at the Budapest Conservatory, and at twenty-four was appointed to its staff as a professor of composition. He has been a very great collector of Hungarian folk-tunes (see under Bartók). He has written a great deal of musical criticism, especially in Budapest papers.

As a composer Kodály is every bit as 'national' as Bartók and perhaps as 'modern'—in other words as little bound by the old ideas as to what constitutes 'concord'. He has not been attracted by the Orchestra, but has written a not very great amount of Chamber Music, Piano Music, Songs, an Opera *Háry János*, &c. A Sonata for 'Cello alone, which exploits perhaps the utmost possibilities of the instrument and of the human hand, has aroused a good deal of interest.

Bartók expressed the highest opinions of the work of Kodály, which he would, indeed, appear to have put before his own.

HONEGGER

Arthur Honegger (1892–1955) was one of the most important of a loosely bound Parisian group, which from 1918 onward existed for a few years under the name of 'The Six' (Milhaud, Honegger, Poulenc, Germaine Tailleferre, Auric, Durey). He was of Swiss descent and nationality, though born and mainly resident in France, and trained at the Paris Conservatory. He composed Chamber Music, Orchestral Music, Songs, Piano Music, &c. Some of his best-known works are the *Summer Pastoral* for small orchestra, the *Pacific No. 231* for large orchestra (a musical treatment of the spirit of the locomotive), and *Rugby* (a football tone-poem), the 'mimed symphony' (generally heard as a purely orchestral work) *Horatius Victorious*, and the dramatic works, *King David* and *Judith* (composed for the folk-theatre at Mézières in Switzerland, 1921 and 1925), *Antigone* (Brussels, 1927), *Les Aventures du Roi Pausole*, and *L'Aiglon*. A choral-orchestral work, *Cries of the World* (1931), awakened much interest. *King David* had a remarkable success, being performed in a concert version in Rome, New York, London, and elsewhere. The harmonic style of Honegger usually inclines towards atonality. His texture is usually very contrapuntal. His orchestration is of that 'modern' style in which the orchestral colours 'stand off' rather than merge. In *King David* he alternates movements or passages of harshest dissonance with movements or passages of old-time harmonic flavour and of old-time formality of construction. Honegger had vitality and the power to achieve the vivid, and therein, probably, lies the justification for the feelings of his admirers.

MILHAUD

Darius Milhaud, a composer of French-Jewish parentage, was born at Aix-en-Provence in 1892. He was educated at the Paris Conservatory. When, after the First World War, Europe saw the phenomenon of six Paris composers momentarily banded together for mutual support (cf. Honegger), he was found amongst them. His art was then already taking an extreme 'modernist' direction, and he has since worked on polytonal lines. His works are numerous and varied, including chamber and orchestral music to Greek plays, a 'satiric drama', *Poèmes Juifs*, a 'musical novel', and so on.

He has collaborated several times with the mystical poet and dramatist, Claudel, as in the remarkable *Christophe Colomb*, wherein all manner of original stage artifices are employed and the spoken voice is used by certain characters, with accompaniment either of orchestra or of mere percussion instruments.

From 1922 he spent much time in the United States (from 1940 on the staff of Mills College, California).

HINDEMITH

Paul Hindemith was born at Hanau, near Frankfort-on-the-Main, in 1895. After studying at Frankfort he came before the public as a violin player and then as leader of the orchestra of the opera-house at Frankfort. In 1923 he became for a time a member (viola) of the newly founded Amar String Quartet. Later he was attached, as teacher of composition, to the Berlin State Conservatory. Under the Nazi régime performance of his works was forbidden and he emigrated to the United States, becoming in 1942 head of the Music Department of Yale University.

As a composer, Hindemith early came to stand in the public mind for the extremest 'modernism'. He is a convinced 'atonalist' with a strong tendency to neo-classicism. Much of his work has taken chamber-music form. Other has been written for chamber orchestra (including a Piano Concerto, a Violin Concerto, Viola Concertos, a 'Cello Concerto). There are also some songs and a few piano compositions including *Ludus Tonalis* (12 fugues), some stage music, including several operas, and an oratorio, *Das Unaufhörliche* ('The Unceasing'). His opera, *Mathis der Maler* ('Mathis the Painter', i.e. Matthias Grünewald of Colmar), has supplied also the material for a three-movement symphony (1934) of the same name. His output has been particularly large and strikingly varied in the resources employed; a buoyant spirit of adventure is everywhere in evidence. In 1954 he received the Hon. D.Mus. of Oxford University.

WALTON

William Turner Walton was born at Oldham in 1902. He was a chorister at Christ Church Cathedral, Oxford, and then much associated with Sacheverell, Osbert, and Edith Sitwell in their skittish youth; writing accompanying music for the recitation, through a mask with a megaphone, of some of Edith Sitwell's poems (*Façade*, 1923).

Walton.

The overture *Portsmouth Point* (1925) was the first work to win the suffrages of any wide body of music-lovers. Amongst his most important works to date are a Viola Concerto (1929), a Sinfonia Concertante for piano and orchestra, an oratorio, *Belshazzar's Feast* (1931), a Symphony (1935), a Violin Concerto (1939), a String Quartet, and successful film music. His opera *Troilus and Cressida* (after Chaucer) was produced in London in 1954. He is an Hon. D.Mus. of the universities of Durham (1937), Oxford (1942), and Manchester (1952). In 1951 he was knighted.

NOTE

For many other contemporary composers, British, American, French, Russian, &c., see the author's *Oxford Companion to Music* under the headings of the various countries and then of the recent composers therein mentioned.)

A FINAL CONSIDERATION

XXII

LIFE AND ART IN THE TWENTIETH CENTURY

(*With a further note on 'Expressionism'*)

The critic should be a quick-change artist, an indiarubber man, a serpent always slipping out of its own skin into that of every other creature, so as to give information from within. (Hermann Bahr.)

> I. There is no Art without Life.
> II. There is no Life without Growth.
> III. There is no Growth without Change.
> IV. There is no Change without Controversy.
>
> (Frank Rutter, *Evolution in Modern Art*.)

MUSIC is not an Art to itself, governed entirely by its own self-made laws. It is one of several arts which, though each of them does have its own laws, are all at every moment sensitively responding to the influences of the social life from which they spring.

From this it follows that if we wish fully to understand the art of a period we should know something of the life of that period, and that if we wish to understand the way in which one art is responding to the influence of the life of its period we may be greatly helped by observing the phenomena of development at the same period in another art.

To this proposition may be added another one—that (in the present age, at all events) there is, further, a direct influence of the arts upon one another. The composer Schönberg was greatly influenced by his close association with the painter Kandinsky and the German Expressionist school generally, and himself painted Expressionist pictures; and the composer Stravinsky has been greatly influenced by living and working in the same city as the painter Picasso and his Cubist companions, and by his close connexion with the ballet-motion art of Nijinsky, Massine, and others, and with the ballet-decorative art of Bakst and others.

Development seems now to have come (temporarily or permanently) to a stage at which no one art can live to itself, and whatever may have been the case in the days of Bach or Mozart it would now be very unintelligent to study the work of the two great modern schools of composition, which may be roughly described as the School of Schönberg and the School of Stravinsky, without at the same time giving a little clear thought to the schools of painting with which they are allied.

Properly, we should study schools of contemporary poetry in the same way, but one cannot do everything—and this is, after all, only a small text-book.

Life in the Twentieth Century

The first thing is to realize that life in the twentieth century is not at all the same thing as life in the nineteenth. We all know that a great change has come about, and yet many of us, when we see artistic phenomena that reflect this change, express astonishment.

This is an age of spreading Education. Take England as an example; at the end of the nineteenth century it had four Universities, now it has more than a dozen, and secondary school education has, of course, expanded proportionately.

This is an age of scientific discovery and the wide diffusion of scientific knowledge. It is an age of Machinery; the nineteenth century's great conquest of space has been enormously extended; we can rush along the roads at a speed that in the eighteen-nineties would have alarmed us; we can travel under the sea and in the air; speakers and musical performers can be heard a thousand miles away before their words or tones have even reached the back of the room in which they are uttered. It is an age of the conquest of time; speech and musical performances can be preserved, so that the speaker or performer is addressing not merely his immediate hearers, but also hearers in all parts of the world, and probably many as yet

ECONOMY

Dress in 1926 and in 1905

unborn; similarly the performance of the actor can be repeated after it is over, and can quickly be seen on the screen in cities and villages everywhere.

In Manufactures we have adopted mass production; in War mass destruction—by submarines, bombing from the air, atomic bombs, poison gas, tanks, and the rest of the efficient modern apparatus.

In Politics a great upheaval has taken place; frontiers have been adjusted to lines undreamed of; we have for some years talked of the self-determination of small nationalities, which implies freedom, and at the same time have had to observe in one country a Fascist or Nazi system and in another a Bolshevist, both of which have meant the control of huge bodies of people in response to the pressing of a button at headquarters; this is only one of the contradictions of modern life, which is full of such contradictions, another being the extension of the franchise in certain countries combined with the direction of the newly freed masses of public opinion by the gathering of the Press into the hands of a few proprietors.

New experiments in government are being tried; two have just been mentioned, and it may be added that Britain in 1924 had its first Labour Government and in 1926 attempted its first General Strike. Lawlessness in some countries increased. 'Gangster' methods were for some time a menace, and in some countries there was a large increase in the traffic in dangerous drugs.

Women in many countries are largely freed. Half a century ago they were housewives, or the playthings of their fathers, husbands, and brothers; now they earn their living, vote at elections, and—smoke, and drink cocktails. They go where they want, read what they want, and think and say what they want.[1]

[1] In the 1880's a silk dress used 18 yards of material where in the nineteen-twenties it used $2\frac{7}{8}$ yards. The author dare not assume that the cost of such a dress diminished in proportion, but, at all events, the

In Religion there are big changes; large bodies of people now go to the extremes of believing all they are told, or of believing nothing at all; there is a decline in church-going, yet an increased activity on the part of Christian Scientists, British Israelites, High Anglicans, and Spiritualists (throughout this list I am merely registering facts).

Philosophy and psychology are overturned. It seems but a few years since Herbert Spencer's was a great name, and now nobody mentions him; the old ideas as to the workings of the human mind have gone, and we hear of, on the one hand, Jung and Freud and Psycho-Analysis and, on the other, Coué and Auto-Suggestion—two different applications of the new psychology of the subconscious, which psychology has also a very important application to Art.

Glancing over this very partial list of activities of the day we find that nearly all of them can be classed either as over-turnings of well-established mental conceptions or as expressions of a new violence and worship of force or speed, some of them with (this has its bearing on some of the music of the day) a new tolerance of noise. Perhaps the altered mental conceptions represent a new attempt at self-preservation on the part of the spirit of Romance—a new study of emotions, and a new outlet for them; perhaps the increased mechanicalizing of modern life indicates a turning from romance, and a hardening and tightening of the human mind. But it is all very involved, and the historian of the future will have his work cut out to classify the trends of thought and life in the first half of the twentieth century.

Art expresses Life

One thing is certain; that historian will understand, if we (or some of us) cannot, that these changes necessarily involved

figures were significant of Woman's casting off of all that cumbered her, and a symbol of the movement towards simplification in painting and music. Architecture and furniture offered other symbols.

a new Art. All Art, to live, must be a revelation; it must throw some new light upon humanity, and when the mind of humanity takes a sudden new direction, Art must become revolutionary. A moment's thought should convince any reader that the artistic conventions of the nineteenth century (and Art is inevitably a matter of conventions, whatever the young artists of any period may think) could not possibly respond to the needs of the twentieth.

The Analogy between Painting and Music

Studying the changes that have, since the late eighteen-sixties or early eighteen-seventies, come about in the pictorial art (which, as already claimed, will help us to understand those that have come about in the musical art), we find them to be, very briefly stated, somewhat as follows:

1. Romantic painting, often, up till then, story-telling in paint, took a new turn—IMPRESSIONISM (Manet, Monet, Pissaro, and others mostly French). As to subject this was now much less often a form of story-telling and much more a representation of phases of nature, and it had much less solidity of appearance, being concerned with colour more than with line, and with light upon objects than with objects them-selves.

In music (see pages 11–14) this has a rather close parallel in the work of Debussy.

2. There followed a group of NEO-IMPRESSIONISTS who, whilst still extremely interested in colours, began to seek clearer line drawing, to surround their figures, for instance, with a black line (Gauguin, Van Gogh, Matisse, and others), and to attempt more solidity of representation (Cézanne). The effort to attain the representation of solidity led to a frequent tendency to an early Cubism. We can either call this group Neo-Impressionists or early Post-Impressionists.

In music the outline drawing has, perhaps, a parallel in the work of Ravel, which tends to a greater distinctness of outline than that of Debussy. Gauguin worked in the South Seas, and set a fashion for exotic subjects, which has some parallel in the influence of barbaric rhythm upon Debussy (to some extent), and (much more strongly) upon the early and middle-period Stravinsky.

3. Matisse, and still more Picasso, began to adopt much more definitely the CUBIST method of attaining an effect of solidity (a three-dimensional effect). There was a departure from all previous conventions here that to many appeared startling and violent. Curves were at a discount, for curves were too soft and graceful and straight lines were 'stronger'.

A kind of parallel is perhaps the (at first hearing equally startling and violent) use of forceful rhythms, heavy chords much repeated, and orchestral colours made to 'stand off' rather than to merge, in Stravinsky and Prokofief, and also some of the younger Frenchmen. The old idea of grace, blend, and smooth shaping has now gone entirely, from much of both music and painting (i.e. so far as the composers and painters were following the line of progress here laid down—there are, of course, always plenty of followers of the old ways, but with them we are not for the moment concerned).

4. Picasso, Braque, and their followers now cast to the winds the very last shreds of old convention. They often painted what seem to many of us mere 'puzzle pictures', in which bits of the front, sides, and back of an object were strewn about the canvas. This has been called an 'orchestration of vision'— a combination in simultaneity of different aspects of what we may call the tune or theme. Picasso seems to have considered this a new form of realism. 'It was not realism', he argued, 'to show merely one aspect of an object from one point of view. The reality included all possible aspects from all possible points of view' (conversation quoted by Rutter in *The Evolution of Modern Art*, page 88) but it soon tended to a form

of non-realism or definitely ABSTRACT PAINTING,[1] and some of the younger painters were quickly declaiming against all kinds of illusionism.[2]

The first impression one receives of their work is similar to the first impression one gets of a composition based on the principle of Atonality. One has lost touch with all previous standards.

5. At this point the painters in question approached very near the German EXPRESSIONIST school, which paints not what it sees with eyes turned outwards, but what it sees with eyes turned inwards.

Most of this Expressionist painting tends to the production of a pattern: it is a sort of new Classicism, the emphasis being again on design. This suggests a parallel with Stravinsky's late phase (see page 110).

Other of it conveys a mental state (e.g. one or two of Kandinsky's 'Compositions', based on *motifs* of cannon and bursting shells, which vividly express the war-emotion); this presumably is supposed to have a parallel in the musical work of Kandinsky's friend Schönberg.

There are other designs of a more formal kind, too, but Kandinsky generally manages to convey (or fails to avoid conveying) some touch of romantic feeling, and in this he resembles Schönberg.

Undoubtedly both Painters and Composers are suffering from an overdose of theory, and the result is, in many cases, the production of a 'puzzle picture' or a 'puzzle quartet', that wins the approval of no big public, but of only a small

---

[1] 'Abstract' sculpture also exists—in fact has become common.

[2] A somewhat different explanation of these 'puzzle pictures' is: 'Starting from a single natural object, Picasso and the Cubists produce lines and project angles till their canvases are covered with intricate and often very beautiful series of balanced lines and curves. They persist, however, in giving them picture titles which recall the natural object from which their minds first took flight' (Michael Sadleir, in the Introduction to Kandinsky's *The Art of Spiritual Harmony*).

group of people who dare to maintain they see what the painter or composer is 'driving at', and when they do maintain this often carry little conviction.

One idea that opponents of their art should put resolutely out of mind is that the advanced 'modernist' painter is a charlatan who would draw and paint if he could, and since he cannot, makes 'puzzle pictures' to bluff the public. There are charlatans in every art, of course, but a glance through any volume of Picasso's work will be sufficient to throw doubt upon that theory so far as it concerns one of the leaders of the movement. Not only will he be seen to have produced a large amount of accomplished work in what most of my readers probably still think of as the normal style, but he will be seen to have produced examples both of this style and of the extreme modernist style in the same year. Evidently he knows perfectly well what he is doing—whether he be thought by us to be right or wrong in doing it.

Probably the same thing is true of the Picassos of music. In early days Stravinsky wrote a quite effective Symphony of the old type, and much in the old harmonic idiom, so presumably he could do so still; and Schönberg's early works showed, to say the least, the full possession of the regulation German Romantic technique.

Expressionism

Some special treatment of the subject of Expressionism seems called for in view of the declared intention of the Schönberg school to serve as its musical representatives.

A good brief German definition (and Expressionism is German in origin) is that of the familiar Brockhaus *Lexikon*, which can be freely translated as follows:

> Expressionism is that direction in present-day art (since about 1912) which strives to express the inner experience instead of impressions of the outer world, being now inspired

ROMANTICISM
Géricault's Wreck of the Medusa

IMPRESSIONISM
Whistler's Battersea Bridge

EARLY CUBISM
Cézanne's Landscape in Provence

LATER CUBISM
Picasso's Lady in Mantilla

'ORCHESTRATION OF VISION'
Picasso's Three Musicians

EXPRESSIONISM
Kandinsky's Improvisation No. 29

EXPRESSIONISM
Schönberg's Visions

by a melancholy temperament, now by religious mysticism, now by the wish for abstract construction.

Expressionism is found as much in the plastic arts as in music and poetry; it is influenced always by the material of the art (colour, line, surfaces, sounds, rhythms), and always works by means of them, awakening or increasing feelings but not imitating Nature. Expressionism develops itself as the contrary of Impressionism [in view of the usual specialized use of this last word it would be better to say 'as the contrary of every form of realism' or 'of representation'], with a recognized revolutionary character and as a European movement. Yet, even in the art of primitive folk, near to Nature, as in the Gothic, Baroque, and other epochs of artistic creation, various examples are found.

Leaders of Expressionism in the plastic arts are the Germans Pechstein, Nolde, and Marc, the Frenchmen Henry Rousseau and Matisse, the Norwegian Munch, and the Russians Kandinsky, Chagall, and Archipenko (Sculptor) [a list of Expressionist poets follows].

In music Expressionism is especially led by A. Schönberg, who in his composition and manner of instrumentation casts off all rules, thereby to win a complete freedom for his musical expression. Schreker and his school also follow this direction.

It is impossible here to discuss everything that is stated or implied in this description. The main point, obviously, is that the Expressionist artist paints not what he outwardly sees, but what he sees in his mind's eye and what he feels. As Hermann Bahr, the great apologist for Expressionism, puts it (ignoring those alleged early instances referred to in the dictionary description just quoted), 'All that has hitherto been the aim of painting, since painting first began, is now denied, and something is striven for that has never yet been attempted.'[1]

That last claim may be true of painting, but it is not true of music. That the painter should attempt a direct expression of his emotions, or a direct reproduction of forms that have

[1] Bahr, *Expressionism*, translated by R. T. Gribble.

shaped themselves within his mind,[1] may be new, but this is, surely, exactly what the composer has always done. The composer has had no model in nature for his symphony or fugue; he has always directly expressed his own emotions and his own tone-shapes, only rarely, in a few crude passages (like that of Strauss's sheep; see page 37), imitating Nature. Thus we must willingly admit that Schönberg is an Expressionist, but add—surely so are all other composers!

We may even quote Bahr himself in support of this contention:

> On what does the whole effect of music rest ? The tones do not reach the composer from without. He does not hear the world, he hears himself, his soul sounds within him. . . . The sound which the ear produces as soon as it receives the inner movement is stored up by the artist, so that later he may conduct it outwardly to our ear, and through it to our soul. From within the artist to his ear, then the tone here produced fixed in a symbol, this symbol again translated by instruments into vibrations, these, sounding in the ears of listeners, the tones seizing the listener's soul—this is the path of music from soul to soul.

And Bahr pertinently sums up the whole attempt of the Expressionist painters in the words—'What the painters of the newest tendency strive after is, so to say, music for the eyes' (which reminds one of Pater's saying about all the arts ever striving to attain the condition of music, in other words, to attain what Bahr calls a direct path 'from soul to soul').

---

[1] Critics writing of plays (but it applies all round) have spoken of Expressionism as 'the objectivization of the subjective', e.g. Mr. A. D. Peters in the *Daily Telegraph*: 'The scene in *Macbeth* where the ghost of Banquo appears and is visible to Macbeth and to no one else, is Expressionism. Here you have the objectivization of the subjective made intensely dramatic, and its power lies mainly in the appearance of Macbeth's embodied thought amongst a group of ordinary people who cannot see it and do not understand. Shakespeare might have shown Macbeth grappling alone with his thought. But, being Shakespeare, he did not.'

It may be asked then, what do the German Painter-Expressionists (like Kandinsky[1]) mean by claiming their friend Schönberg as a Composer-Expressionist, and one of their number ?

The answer is that they probably sense in him (or think they do) an attempt to express more of the real inner man than did previous Romantic composers, the expression of whose Romanticism had tended to base itself upon a group of accepted melodic and harmonic formulae. In that case they would probably claim Scriabin as equally an Expressionist, and indeed he has been so claimed.

They probably admire in Schönberg the readiness to cast aside previously existing melodic and harmonic clichés and orchestral flavours, and, at times, previously existing musical forms, and (ignoring the fact that some composers whom they do not claim as Expressionists have been just as iconoclastic) to see in this an evidence of the direct expression of the soul.

Perhaps, too, there is sometimes in Schönberg's work a hint of the revelation of feelings usually hidden unless brought to light in the clinic of the psycho-analyst—of an unashamed uncovering of the darker deeds of the sub-conscious. Expressionistic plays much resemble dreams, and perhaps there is a dream quality about some of Schönberg's music. Probably the 'Vision' paintings of Schönberg (of which two are here reproduced) have done something to qualify him for enrolment in the ranks of the Expressionists, and still more probably certain of his dramatic texts written by himself.

That is as far as the present writer can, at the present moment, go in the exposition of Schönberg and the Schönbergians and their Expressionism in music. To him (taking a rather narrower definition than Hermann Bahr and some of the other German writers) Expressionism, being an attempt

[1] Kandinsky is Russian by birth, but a great part of his artistic life was spent in Germany, and Expressionism was originally a Munich movement. (Later he settled in France.)

at the direct revelation in art of the 'happenings of the soul', is thus a present-day off-shoot of the old Romantic Movement. That is one reason why he has included Schönberg in the chapter upon the Neo-Romantics, whilst he has placed Stravinsky in the chapter on the Anti-Romantics. But, of course, classification is always very relative.

If there are errors in his attempt first to understand and then to expound Expressionism he apologizes. He has done his best to grasp the arguments of its protagonists, but one of the very leaders of these, Bahr himself, says, 'I cannot deny that I never feel quite comfortable when Expressionists begin to theorize. They are fond of speaking in a fog.'

APPENDIXES

APPENDIX I

A LIST OF RELEVANT BOOKS IN THE ENGLISH LANGUAGE

MOST of the books in the list can, of course, be found in the larger public libraries.

BARTÓK

Haraszti, *Béla Bartók* (In English; Lyre Bird Press, Paris, 1938).

Bartók, Béla, *Hungarian Folk Music.* Transl. Calvocoressi (300 pp., Oxford, 1931).

Stevens, Halsey, *The Life and Music of Béla Bartók* O.U.P., (New York, 1953).

BAX

Bax, Arnold, *Farewell, my Youth* (112 pp., Longmans, 1943).

Hull, Robert H., *A Handbook on Arnold Bax's Symphonies* (51 pp., Chappell, 1933).

BRITTEN

Mitchell and Keller (Editors), *Benjamin Britten: a Commentary on his Works from a Group of Specialists* (400 pp., Rockcliff, 1952).

BRUCKNER

Engel, Gabriel, *Life of Anton Bruckner* (Roerich Museum Press, New York, 1931).

Tovey, Donald, *Essays in Musical Analysis* (Oxford; vol. ii has analyses of the *Romantic Symphony*, in E flat, No. 4; and of the Symphony in A, No. 6).

BUSONI

Dent, Edward J., *Ferruccio Busoni: a Biography* (380 pp., Oxford, 1933).

Busoni, Ferruccio, *Letters to his Wife* (319 pp., Arnold, 1938).

—— *Sketch of a New Esthetic of Music* (45 pp., Schirmer, New York, 1911).

DEBUSSY

Vallas, Léon, *Claude Debussy: his Life and Works* (350 pp., Oxford, 1933).

—— *The Theories of Claude Debussy* (189 pp., Oxford, 1929).

Lockspeiser, Edward, *Debussy* (292 pp., Dent, 1936).

Thompson, Oscar, *Debussy, Man and Artist* (395 pp., Tudor Publishing Co., New York, 1940).

Liebich, Mrs. Franz, *Claude-Achille Debussy* (92 pp., Lane, 1907).

Debussy, Claude, *Monsieur Croche, the Dilettante Hater* (171 pp., Douglas, 1927).

Shera, Frank, *Debussy and Ravel* (58 pp., Oxford, 1925).

Gilman, Lawrence, *Debussy's 'Pelléas et Mélisande': a Guide to the Opera* (84 pp., Schirmer, New York, 1907).

Cooper, Martin, *French Music* (240 pp., Oxford, 1951).

DELIUS

Heseltine, Philip, *Frederick Delius* (184 pp., Lane, 1923).

Delius, Clare, *Frederick Delius: Memories of my Brother* (277 pp., Nicholson & Watson, 1935).

Fenby, Eric, *Delius as I knew him* (240 pp., Bell, 1936).

Hull, Robert H., *Delius* (45 pp., Hogarth Press, 1928).

Tovey, Donald, *Essays in Musical Analysis* (Oxford; vol. iii has an analysis of the Violin Concerto).

D'INDY

Rolland, Romain, *Musicians of Today* (a twenty-five-page sketch in this book of 324 pp., Kegan Paul, 1915).

Mason, Daniel Gregory, *Contemporary Composers* (a seventy-page sketch in this book of 290 pp., Macmillan, 1918).

Hill, Edward Burlinghame, *Modern French Music* (a chapter in this book of 406 pp., Houghton Mifflin, New York, 1924).

Cooper, Martin, *French Music* (240 pp., Oxford, 1951).

ELGAR

Maine, Basil, *Elgar: his Life and Work* (2 vols., 485 pp., Bell, 1933).

Dunhill, Thos., *Sir Edward Elgar* (210 pp., Blackie, 1938).

Reed, William H., *Elgar as I knew him* (200 pp., Gollancz, 1936).

McVeagh, Diana, *Edward Elgar: his Life and Music* (260 pp., Dent,

Young, Percy, *Elgar, O.M.* (Collins 1955). [1955].

Newman, Ernest, *Elgar* (the earliest book on the composer, 187 pp., Lane, 1906).

Powell, Mrs. Richard, *Edward Elgar: Memories of a Variation* (98 pp., Oxford, 1937).

Birthplace of Elgar (Pictures, 12 pp., Bulletin Press, Hereford, and Novello, 1947).

My Friends Pictured Within: the Subjects of the Enigma Variations as portrayed in Contemporary Photographs and Elgar's Manuscript (35 pp., Novello, 1947).

Dyer, Louise B. M., *Sir Edward Elgar* (List of Works, 19 pp., Oxford, 1931).

Shera, Frank H., *Elgar: Instrumental Works* (75 pp., Oxford, 1931).

Tovey, Donald, *Essays in Musical Analysis* (Oxford; vol. ii has the Symphony in E flat, vol. iii the Violin and 'Cello Concertos, vol. iv *Falstaff*, the *Enigma* Variations, and the *Cockaigne* Overture, vol. vi *In the South* and the *Introduction and Allegro*. All of these are repeated in the same author's *Some English Symphonists*, Oxford).

Jaeger, A. J., Analytical Notes and Book of Words to *The Apostles* (63 pp., Novello).

—— Analytical Notes and Book of Words to *The Kingdom* (48 pp., Novello).

—— Analytical Notes and Book of Words to *The Dream of Gerontius* (50 pp., Novello).

FALLA

Trend, J. B., *Manuel de Falla and Spanish Music* (190 pp., Knopf, New York, 1929).

FRANCK

D'Indy, Vincent, *César Franck* (286 pp., Lane, 1910).

Mason, Daniel Gregory, *From Grieg to Brahms* (a forty-page sketch in this book of 225 pp., Macmillan, 1924).

Tovey, Donald, *Essays in Musical Analysis* (Oxford; vol. ii has an analysis of the Symphony and vol. iii one of the Variations for Piano and Orchestra).

Grace, Harvey, *Franck's Organ Music* (articles in *Musical Times*, Feb.–April, 1923).

Cooper, Martin, *French Music* (240 pp., Oxford, 1951).

GLAZUNOF

Montagu-Nathan, M., *A Short History of Russian Music* (chapter in this book of 346 pp., W. Reeves, 1914).

Tovey, Donald, *Essays in Musical Analysis* (Oxford; vol. iii has an analysis of the Piano Concerto in F minor).

HINDEMITH

Hindemith, P., *A Composer's World: Horizons and Limitations* (220 pp., Harvard & Oxford, 1952).

HOLST

Holst, Imogen, *Gustav Holst* (200 pp., Oxford, 1938).

—— *The Music of Gustav Holst* (164 pp., Oxford, 1951).

Dyer, Louise B. M., *Holst: Complete List of Works* (12 pp., Oxford, 1931).

Tovey, Donald, *Essays in Musical Analysis* (Oxford; vol. v includes the *Hymn of Jesus*).

MACDOWELL

Gilman, Lawrence, *Edward MacDowell: a Study* (190 pp., Lane, 1909).

Page, Elizabeth F., *Edward MacDowell: his Work and Ideals* (85 pp., Dodge, New York, 1910).

Brown, Abbie F., *The Boyhood of Edward MacDowell* (251 pp., Stokes, New York, 1927).

MacDowell, Edward, *Critical and Historical Essays* (293 pp., Schmidt, Boston, 1912).

—— *Verses* (58 pp., Schmidt, Boston, and Elkin, London, 1915).

MAHLER

Walter, Bruno, *Gustav Mahler* (160 pp., Kegan Paul, 1936).

Stefan, Paul, *Gustav Mahler: a Study of his Personality and Work* (132 pp., Schirmer, New York, 1913).

Mahler, Alma, *Gustav Mahler: Memories and Letters* (234 pp., Murray, 1946).

Engel, Gabriel, *Gustav Mahler, Song-Symphonist* (Bruckner Soc. of America, 1932).

Tovey, Donald, *Essays in Musical Analysis* (187 pp., Oxford, 1939; an analysis of the Fourth Symphony in vol. vi).

MEDTNER

Sabaneyeff, L., *Modern Russian Composers* (chapter in this book of 253 pp., International Publishing Co., New York, 1927).

Montagu-Nathan, M., *Contemporary Russian Composers* (chapter in this book of 328 pp., Cecil Palmer & Hayward, 1917).

NIELSEN

Simpson, *Carl Nielsen, Symphonist, 1865–1931* (236 pp., Dent, 1952).

RACHMANINOF

Lyle, Watson, *Rachmaninof: a Biography* (Reeves, 1939).

Sabaneyeff, L., *Modern Russian Composers* (chapter in this book of 253 pp., International Publishing Co., New York, 1927).

Rachmaninof, Serge, *Recollections told to O. von Riesemann* (not accepted by the Composer as entirely correct; Allen & Unwin, 1934).

Further Reading 145

RAVEL

Demuth, Norman, *Ravel* (214 pp., Dent, 1947).

Goss, Madeleine, *Bolero: the Life of Ravel* (303 pp., Tudor Publishing Co., New York, 1940).

Shera, Frank, *Debussy and Ravel* (58 pp., Oxford, 1925).

Cooper, Martin, *French Music* (240 pp., Oxford, 1951).

SAINT-SAËNS

Hervey, Arthur, *Saint-Saëns* (159 pp., Lane, 1921).

Lyle, Watson, *Camille Saint-Saëns: his Life and Art* (210 pp., Kegan Paul, Dutton, 1923).

Saint-Saëns, Camille, *Musical Memories* (282 pp., Murray, 1921).

—— *Outspoken Essays on Music* (186 pp., Kegan Paul, Dutton, 1922).

Cooper, Martin, *French Music* (240 pp., Oxford, 1951).

SCHÖNBERG

Wellesz, Egon, *Arnold Schönberg* (159 pp., Dent, 1925).

Armitage, Merle (Editor), *Schönberg* (essays by 20 writers; 325 pp., Schirmer, New York, 1937).

Schönberg, *Style and Idea* (224 pp., Williams & Norgate, 1951).

SCOTT

Hull, A. Eaglefield, *Cyril Scott, Composer, Poet, and Philosopher* (196 pp., Kegan Paul, 1918).

Scott, Cyril, *My Years of Indiscretion* (282 pp., Mills & Boon, 1924).

—— *The Philosophy of Modernism in its Connection with Music* (135 pp., Kegan Paul, 1917).

Also many volumes of the Composer's poems—original and translations of Baudelaire and Stefan George.

SCRIABIN

Montagu-Nathan, M., *A Short History of Russian Music* (chapter in this book of 346 pp., W. Reeves, 1914).

—— *Contemporary Russian Composers* (chapter in this book of 328 pp., Cecil Palmer & Hayward, 1917).

Calvocoressi, M. D., and Abraham, Gerald, *Masters of Russian Music* (chapter in this book of 510 pp., Duckworth, 1936).

Sabaneyeff, L., *Modern Russian Composers* (chapter in this book of 253 pp., International Publishing Co., New York, 1927).

SIBELIUS

Abraham, Gerald (Editor), *Sibelius: a Symposium* (essays on different aspects of his work by Ralph Hill, Gerald Abraham, Ralph W. Wood, Scott Goddard, Eric Blom, Astra Desmond, and David Cherniavsky, 200 pp., Drummond, 1947, now Oxford).

Ekman, Karl, *Jean Sibelius: his Life and Personality* (270 pp., Wilmer, 1936).

Törne, Bengt de, *Sibelius: a Close-up* (Faber, 1937).

Newmarch, Rosa, *Jean Sibelius: a Short Story of a Long Friendship* (Birchard, Boston, Goodwin & Tabb, London, 1944).

Gray, Cecil, *Sibelius* (224 pp., Oxford, 1931).

—— *Sibelius: the Symphonies* (77 pp., Oxford, 1935).

Tovey, Donald, *Essays in Musical Analysis*, vols. ii, iii, and vi (Oxford; in vol. ii the Third and Fifth Symphonies; in vol. iii the Violin Concerto; in vol. vi the Seventh Symphony and *Tapiola*).

STRAUSS

Newman, Ernest, *Richard Strauss* (144 pp., Lane, 1908).

Mason, Daniel Gregory, *Contemporary Composers* (a twenty-seven-page essay in this book of 290 pp., Macmillan, 1918).

Rolland, Romain, *Musicians of To-day* (a chapter in this book of 324 pp., Kegan Paul, 1915).

Finck, Henry T., *Richard Strauss: the Man and his Works* (Little, Brown, New York, 1917).

Correspondence between Richard Strauss and Hugo von Hofmannsthal, 1907–18 (355 pp., Secker, 1927).

Strauss, Richard, *Recollections and Reflections* (174 pp., Boosey & Hawkes, 1953).

Gilman, Lawrence, *Strauss' 'Salome': a Guide to the Opera* (85 pp., Lane, 1907).

Hutcheson, Ernest, *Elektra: a Guide to the Opera* (61 pp., Schirmer, 1910).

Schattmann, Alfred, *Richard Strauss—'Der Rosenkavalier': a Guide to the Work*; transl. Kalisch (90 pp., Schirmer, 1913).

Blom, Eric, *Strauss: the Rose Cavalier* (62 pp., Oxford, 1930).

Armstrong, Thos., *Strauss's Tone Poems* (56 pp., Oxford, 1931).

STRAVINSKY

Stravinsky, Igor, *Chronicles of my Life* (indifferent translation from the French, 286 pp., Gollancz, 1936).

—— *Poetics of Music in the Form of Six Lessons* (142 pp., Oxford and Harvard, 1947).

White, Eric W., *Stravinsky's Sacrifice to Apollo* (150 pp., Hogarth Press, 1930).

—— *Stravinsky: a Critical Survey* (192 pp., Lehmann, 1947).

Armitage, Merle, *Igor Stravinsky: a Collection of Articles* (Schirmer, New York, 1936).

Sabaneyeff, L., *Modern Russian Composers* (chapter in this book of 253 pp., International Publishing Co., New York, 1927).

Belaiev, Victor, *Igor Stravinsky's 'Les Noces', an Outline* (45 pp., Oxford, 1928).

Evans, Edwin, *Stravinsky, 'The Fire Bird' and 'Petrouchka'* (44 pp., Oxford, 1933).

Ramuz, C. F., *'The Soldier's Tale'* (libretto in English by Rosa Newmarch, 32 pp., Chester, 1924).

VAUGHAN WILLIAMS

Dickinson, A. E. F., *An Introduction to the Music of R. Vaughan Williams* (83 pp., Oxford, 1928).

Howes, Frank, *The Music of Ralph Vaughan Williams* (366 pp., Oxford, 1954).

Vaughan Williams, Ralph, *National Music* (146 pp., Oxford, 1934).

—— *Beethoven's Choral Symphony, with Writings on other Musical Subjects* (172 pp., Oxford, 1953).

Tovey, Donald, *Essays in Musical Analysis* (Oxford; vol. ii has analyses of the *Pastoral Symphony* and the *Concerto Accademico for Violin*, and vol. iii one of the *Wasps* Overture; all these are also included in the same author's *Some English Symphonists*, Oxford).

WALTON

William Walton: a Short Account of his Life and Works (14 pp., Oxford, 1932).

Howes, Frank, *The Music of William Walton* (2 vols., 151 pp., Oxford, 1942).

Tovey, Donald, *Essays in Musical Analysis* (Oxford; vol. iii includes the Violin Concerto; this analysis is repeated in the same author's *Some English Symphonists*).

WOLF

Newman, Ernest, *Hugo Wolf* (280 pp., Methuen, 1907).

Walker, *Hugo Wolf* (Dent, 1952).

APPENDIX II

THE TWO FRANCES IN MUSIC

M. Rolland in his *Musicians of To-day*, concluding an essay on Debussy's *Pelléas and Mélisande*, said that foreigners who wished to penetrate France's genius would have to study this Opera 'as they would study Racine's *Bérénice*'. Then he continued:

Not that Debussy's art, any more than Racine's, suffices to represent the French genius. There is quite another side to this genius, which is in no wise represented here: it is heroic action, mental intoxication [*l'ivresse de la raison*], laughter, the passion for the light, the France of Rabelais, of Molière, of Diderot, and, in music, shall we say (for want of better), the France of Berlioz and Bizet. To tell the truth, it is this that I prefer. But God forbid that I should disavow the other! It is the equilibrium of these two Frances that makes the French genius. In our contemporary music, *Pelléas and Mélisande* is at the one pole of our art, *Carmen* at the other pole. *Carmen*, all external, all light, all life, without shadows, without mystery [*sans dessous*]. The other, all occult [*intérieure*], all bathed in twilight, all shrouded in silence. It is this dual ideal, it is these alternations of pure sunshine and light cloud, that make the sweet, luminous, yet veiled sky of the Ile de France.

APPENDIX III

STRAVINSKY ON 'MUSIC ITSELF'

The following is a note of a conversation of the Author with Stravinsky in July, 1921. It was written out at the time and checked and revised by Stravinsky and has now acquired an historical interest.

As the question of the connexion between the ballet action and the music of the various stage works has often been raised in the British Press, I asked Stravinsky to explain the nature of that connexion. He put it like this—'I have never tried, in my stage works, to make the music illustrate the action, or the action the music; I have always endeavoured to find an architectural basis of connexion. I produce "music itself". Whenever "music itself" is not the aim, music suffers.

'This brings us to the question of extra-musical emotion. For instance, Beethoven's works are never purely musical in their construction; his form is always dialectic, influenced by the philosophical constructions of Hegel. Wagner commits the same sin, influenced for his part by Schopenhauer, and so with all the Germans!'

'And what of Mozart?'

'Ah, Mozart was not a German! We are talking of Bonn, and Berlin, and Hamburg—not of Vienna.'

'And Bach?'

'Well, he stands apart, doesn't he? Bach belongs to the earlier half of the eighteenth century, and, moreover, properly speaking, he is not a representative of secular music.'

'Understand', added Stravinsky, 'that this idea which I have just expressed is not one which underlies merely my most recent music. I have always felt the same. I have never made "applied music" of any kind. Even in the early days, in the *Fire Bird*, I was concerned with a purely *musical* construction. The only forms which are worth anything are those which flow [*découlent*] from the musical *material* itself. We have wind instruments, stringed instruments, percussion instruments, and the human voice—there is our material. From the actual use of these materials the form should arise.'

'Will you explain in a little more detail what you mean by "pure music"? Some people seem to be puzzled at the music you so describe having subjects, such as *The Rite of Spring*, or *The Nightingale*, or *Renard*.'

'Well, suppose I am a painter. I paint, say, a portrait of a lady in *toilette de bal*, with her jewels. My portrait resembles the person painted. None the less, it is painted for the pleasure of painting, despite its subject. Or I paint a picture of a street fight. The fight is my pretext for the picture, but the painting of it may be pure painting. The same thing applies to all my works. In *The Rite of Spring*, for instance, the pretext of the pre-historic birth of spring has suggested to me the construction of the work that I have called *The Rite of Spring*. The "pretext" I choose is but a pretext, like the painter's pretext for painting. If any one objects, and prefers anecdote to a simple musical monument, they are surely in their mental infancy.'

'The *Rite* exists as a piece of music, first and last. Two different choreographies have been adapted to it, the earlier by Nijinsky, the later by Massine. The choreographic construction of Nijinsky, being of great plastic beauty, was, however, subjected to the tyranny of the bar; that of Massine is based on phrases each composed of several bars. This is the sense in which is conceived the free connexion of the choreographic construction with the musical construction.'[1]

APPENDIX IV

POLYTONALITY AND ATONALITY

The following explanation of these harmonic phases, which originally appeared in the *Observer*, is here reprinted from the Author's *Crotchets—a Few Short Musical Notes* (1924), by kind permission of Messrs. John Lane. It may be found still to possess interest as representing a phase of musical thought in the mid-nineteen-twenties.

I. POLYTONALITY

There must be a good many people who are still asking themselves 'Whence and Whither?' They are aware of the need for patience with 'modern music'. They know they cannot at once hope to

[1] E. E., dissenting from some of my remarks in Chapter XXI, commented as follows:—

'The conversation you append to your history seems to me so clear and so logical that anybody not hampered with preconceived notions will understand it. It is a matter, not of opinion, but of recorded fact, that the second tableau of *Petroushka* was originally a concert piece, unnamed, for piano and orchestra. The title came later. There is unfortunately no similar record concerning the *Sacre*, but I was in close touch with Stravinsky in those days and I *know* that, but for the accident of Diaghilef requiring a ballet, it would have been a symphony. The oldest portion of it (the *Danse Sacrale* at the end) was written before *Petroushka*, and conceived as the finale to a symphonic work.

'Stravinsky has always been obsessed with construction. And construction must inevitably tend to abstract music. Despite his great skill in harmony, in instrumentation and in rhythm, he was always at heart a contrapuntist, and contrapuntists always care more for their construction than their material. That is the reason why, many years ago, before there were any signs of his present tendency, I wrote in an American paper something to the effect that: "Just as a certain type of intellect seems inevitably destined to find an ultimate haven in the Roman Catholic Church, Stravinsky is fated in the long run to seek a refuge with Bach." I leave it to you to decide whether I was a true prophet.'

grasp the whole purport of music fashioned upon a new system (and for many the *Rite* is still that), but, as every new style recorded in the history of music has grown out of an earlier one, and led to a later one, they would like some convinced modernist to relate to them his ancestry and forecast his posterity, for the experience of apparently unrelated phenomena is always disturbing. After their failure to make themselves clear on the aesthetic side, on which I have sometimes commented, can the modernists at least make themselves clear on the technical ?

Well, Milhaud, in an article, 'Polytonalité et Atonalité', in the *Revue Musicale*, succeeded in giving a pretty plain exposition of two phases of the 'modernist' harmony, showing how they have evolved by perfectly logical processes out of the previously accepted system, and hinting, at the end of his article, at the nature of the further growth which is inevitable. He classes modernist harmony under two heads, 'Polytonality', or simultaneous use of different keys, and 'Atonality', or entire absence of key. I here summarize briefly his treatment of the one phase, and will do the same later for his treatment of the other.

The harmony in which we were brought up was for the most part diatonic, that is to say, the notes making up a chord, or the 'parts' woven together into a contrapuntal fabric, all belonged to a definite (major or minor) key, and of keys there were twenty-four (twelve major and twelve minor). Necessarily, however, the music passed, from time to time, from one key into another. The admission that succession of key, or 'modulation', was acceptable inevitably implied, says Milhaud, that, at some later stage, superposition of key ('Polytonality') would also be found equally acceptable. This hardly seems to follow, but the writer has omitted a stage in the argument, of a hint as to which I will make him a present. For thousands of years only unisonous (and octave) singing was tolerated, i.e. only succession of notes; then, at last, the practice of harmonic singing grew up, i.e. superposition of notes. Apply this, by analogy, and the missing link in the argument is, I think, supplied. Since, a thousand years ago, we began to pass from Homophony to Polyphony and accomplished the process successfully, there seems no reason why we should not similarly pass from Homotonality to Polytonality.

An astute suggestion is made by Milhaud to the effect that the device of 'canon' sometimes pointed to a polytonal future for music. Here, for instance, is the opening of a Bach strict canon, at the interval of the fourth:

Read the upper part of this without reference to the lower; it is in the key of D minor—modulating to G minor and A minor (its Subdominant and Dominant). Read the lower part without reference to the upper; it is in A minor, modulating to D minor and E minor (*its* Subdominant and Dominant). There, then (when the piece is *contrapuntally considered*), is a specimen of Polytonality—with Bach appearing as an eighteenth-century Milhaud-modernist. Now read the two parts together and see how Bach has, as a matter of fact (the piece being *harmonically considered*), skilfully evaded Polytonality, his lower part supplying harmonies to the upper, somewhat different from what one, at first sight of the former, felt to be the natural ones, harmonies in which both parts can share, in a reasonable spirit of give and take, without parting company into different keys. This, then, is in one sense Polytonality avoided rather than accepted: or, as one may say, listened to strictly horizontally, the piece is polytonal; listened to perpendicularly, it is monotonal.

What are called appoggiaturas, accented passing notes and suspensions, supply Milhaud with another argument, pretty obvious and by no means unfamiliar. At one period in history ears would stand only unison-singing, or, as an Irishman might say, one-note chords; next they tolerated two- and three-note chords, consisting of the simplest and most natural intervals (the third and the fifth); then they began to tolerate certain four-note chords (such, for instance, as the dominant seventh or certain 'suspensions'). So far, all the notes of a chord had been in the one key, but soon it became common to insert in a chord a note borrowed from another key, provided it quickly merged into its 'resolution'. Cut out the resolution and you have Stravinskyism, Satieism, Milhaudism—all of which, a purist might say, enforces the Sunday-school lesson of the danger of small steps in the wrong direction. Our dilemma is that if we decide to follow this purist we shall, to be logical, have to make an effort to thrust ourselves back into fifth-century unisonous singing, or, indeed, into (literally) monotonous chant; whilst, on the other hand, if we elect to act upon the Milhaud theory, we must, equally logically, in time pass into a condition where anything is possible, almost the position, by the way, where he wishes us to be, as illustrated by this example of his own writing:

Other arguments I can only briefly mention. They are drawn from (*a*) the device of pedal, with modulations above it, as found commonly in the classics; (*b*) chords such as that of the ninth, eleventh, and thirteenth (here Milhaud, without knowing it, adopts the old 'Day theory', in which some of us who used Macfarren's Harmony were brought up—i.e. he considers such chords as being combinations of two different chords). And so on. It is all very alarming, as strict logic often is. But dare we say 'Down with logic'? Up to the present there is seen to have been a very strict logic governing the development of music, and it is probable that we cannot escape it.

II. ATONALITY

In the preceding pages I briefly discussed Milhaud's argument, based upon historical precedent, as to the propriety of Polytonality (or simultaneity of key), a principle which governs the harmonic structure of a good deal of music to-day. I need hardly say that no argument, however logical, can justify a piece of music; the music has to justify itself, but if the argument is sound it should have the effect of inducing us to exercise greater patience than we might otherwise have done, and so to give the music a chance of making its own appeal. To a musician who has several times heard Ravel's Sonata for Violin and 'Cello, the Sonata probably becomes, in itself, an argument in favour of Polytonality, but until he has heard it several times it is quite possible that he may need to apply some logical argument about Polytonality in favour of the Sonata. History shows that composers do not as a rule first theorize as to harmonic systems, and then carry out their theories; rather they subconsciously feel their way towards new harmonic systems and then go on to discovery of the principles of these. That is precisely what is now occurring in the case of Polytonality and Atonality; they are systems already in active being, and the process of explanation and theoretical justification, which began some years since, is now working itself out pretty clearly. There will be written reams of thoroughly bad Polytonic and Atonic music, as there have been written reams of thoroughly bad Diatonic music. What we are interested in for the moment is not the value of the music but the soundness of the system. But in listening to the music, to-morrow or next day, it should be the other way about.

Having shown how Polytonality grew out of Homotonality by a perfectly natural evolution (canon, accented passing notes, pedals, &c.), Milhaud proceeds to show us how Atonality is already growing out of Polytonality. The argument is, briefly, this. Two or more perfectly regular diatonic melodies superposed, each going its way regardless of the other, produce a harmonic effect of Polytonality; horizontally considered, the music is diatonic, perpendicularly considered, it is rarely so. Some few of the chords produced by the coincidence of the notes of these diatonic melodies may also, by accident, be normal diatonic chords, assignable to one key or another, and when this happens the effect is momentarily diatonic, otherwise the result is chromatic. The diatonic is the accident, the chromatic the rule, and Polytonality is thus harmonically a chromatic system. Presumably, if our ears were sufficiently trained to the appreciation of the effects, we should feel the two systems in use at one time, the one in each separate part, the other in their combination, and this is probably what happens with a genuine polytonic composer; indeed, to him the pleasure of his music probably consists largely in the agreeable conflict thus introduced. Obviously the kind of listening required is an extension of the kind of listening required for the appreciation of a Byrd madrigal or a Bach fugue—the perception, so to speak, of warp and woof at one glance. Now, chromaticism knows no key. The series D, D sharp, E, F, F sharp, for instance, is no more in any one key than in any other, whether it be used melodically or harmonically, and a good deal of Polytonality being harmonically chromatic, it is a small step deliberately to make the separate parts or voices or strands also chromatic, taking our separate melodies or parts from the keyless system. This done, we have something like a complete Atonality, or absence of key, the only reservation being that even now, by pure accident (or the merciful hand of Providence) a combination here or there may be a recognizable 'chord' of the old system, though even in this case, two such chords, assignable to the same key, are little likely to occur in sequence, so that no key effect is set up, and we have complete Atonality.

For the practice of Polytonality, Milhaud gives simple but ingenious tables showing the combinations possible. Superposing all other possible major chords upon that of C major, we have obviously eleven combinations. Superposing all possible minor chords on it we have eleven more. Superposing all the major chords on the chord of C minor we have another set of eleven, and superposing all the minor chords upon it still another set. This makes forty-four Polytonic chords upon the one note C. As the same process can be repeated over C sharp, D, &c., the forty-four can be multiplied by eleven = 484. Then come in the 'inversions' of all these chords, but already I tire of arithmetic, whilst when it comes to the combinations possible by juxtaposition of three chords, or four (and these not necessarily simple 'common chords', but also chords of the seventh, ninth, eleventh, thirteenth, &c.), I 'reel to and fro, and stagger like a drunken man and am at my wit's end'. And if all this is done in the green wood of Polytonality, what shall be done in the dry of Atonality ? Presumably a senior wrangler would make short work of the little sum called for, but its prospect leaves me staring wild-eyed into infinity.

Then comes the troubling question (and Milhaud never really faces it)—Will all this variety of resource give us, in practice, greater variety of effect ? For the ear, to enjoy, has to classify; classification is, with the ordinary listener, subconscious, of course, but none the less it goes on. Then, of course, one not only classifies single chords, feeling them as major, minor, diminished, &c., but 'progressions' of two chords as dominant to tonic, tonic to subdominant, major to minor, and minor to major, and so forth. Is any such classification possible to our ears under the limitless new dispensation, and if not, shall we not simply experience a vague nondescript effect, one 'chord' being very like another, and one progression like another ? What will be the composer's own method of selection of his effects ?

Then how, in the wonderful days that are coming, will students in composition be trained ? It is all very well for Milhaud to talk airily of 'complementary studies':

> Polytonality and Atonality are not arbitrary systems. They are, the one a development from diatonic harmony and counterpoint, the other a development from chromatic harmony and counterpoint, and ought to be made the object of complementary technical studies.

How are these studies to be carried out ? All that he proposes is obviously lawful. But when, from precedent to precedent, the bounds of freedom have been broadened down to this extent, any one can do anything, and nobody can say him nay. Which is all very right and proper, but art necessarily implying selection, a principle for the selection will have to be first felt and next discovered. Milhaud seems to imply a safeguard in a sort of *canto fermo* system:

> The factor which will determine the Polytonic or Atonic character of a work will be much less the process of its composition ['le procédé d'écriture'—I don't quite follow] than the essential melody which will come from the 'heart' alone of the musician. It is the absolute and organic necessity of the initial melody which will prevent the progressions ['procédés'] from congealing into a system otherwise still-born. The whole life of a work will depend upon nothing else than the melodic invention of its composer, and Polytonality and Atonality will do nothing more than furnish him with a vaster field, richer means of composition, a more expressive and complex scale, wherewith to employ his sensibility, his imagination, and his fancy.

All very fine and large—especially the latter! And, after this, what next? Why, of course, a quarter-tone system, composition in which has already begun. And, after that—well, let us hope the resources here laid out for use will last our lifetimes. Posterity must look out for itself!

APPENDIX V

COMPOSITION IN QUARTER-TONES AND OTHER MICROTONES

There is at the present moment a limited movement going on towards a use in composition of intervals smaller than the semitone (down to the sixteenth of a tone—theoretically at any rate!). The following composers are some of those known to the present author as having engaged in experiments in this direction.[1]

ALOIS HÁBA, a Moravian, born in 1893. Trained in Vienna and Berlin, now resident in Prague. He has written quarter-tone works for String Quartet and small Orchestra and also for a Quarter-Tone Harmonium, and a Quarter-Tone Piano, and has

[1] See also *The Oxford Companion to Music*, s.v. 'Microtones'.

also composed in sixth-tones. He has published a book on the subject of microtonal composition,[1] and many articles.

R. H. STEIN. A German, born in 1882; an author on philosophical and musical subjects, and the composer of quarter-tone music and magazine articles on the subject. He had prepared a Quarter-Tone Piano and a Quarter-Tone Clarinet, and wrote for both. He died in 1942.

CARRILLO (or Carillo—variously spelt), a Mexican composer, born in 1875. Mr. Leopold Stokowski, formerly conductor of the Philadelphia Orchestra, writes, 'One of the most mature experiments in this direction is the music of Carrillo, the Mexican composer. He has composed music based on quarter, eighth, and sixteenth of tones, he has constructed instruments to play this music; a new system of notation was necessary to write it, this he has invented—a notation simple, brief, and of mathematical precision. I have studied this music with Mr. Carrillo, and find that its inner construction is true to itself: beneath an apparent complexity lie simplicity and a fabric of well-balanced tonal relations. Personally I must make a great effort of mental and oral concentration in listening to it, or I overlook much of its subtlety of tone-combination. Mr. Carrillo claims no more for it than that it is an experiment and an attempt at a new departure, and it is in that sense that we present it to the public. It is a voyage to an unknown land of infinitely rich new possibilities which so far have been very little developed.' (Philadelphia Orchestra Programme, March 1927.)

J. H. FOULDS. Born at Manchester in 1880. Used quarter-tones and also third-tones in orchestral music. (See reference later to his wife.) He died in 1939.

A Quarter-Tone Piano was exhibited at the Frankfort Music Exhibition in 1927. Microtonic keyboard instruments have, however, often been constructed in the past, the difficulty being not to make them but to play them—with only ten fingers. Instruments of the 'Pianola' type would seem to offer the proper means of producing quarter-tone music.[2]

---

[1] *Neue Harmonielehre des Diatonischen, Chromatischen, Viertel-, Drittel-, Sechstel-, und Zwölftel-Tonsystem* (Kistner & Siegel, Leipzig).

[2] Previous to the introduction of Equal Temperament, keyboard instruments were sometimes constructed with optional notes to allow of a greater variety of modulation without bad effect, e.g. Smith's organ in the

Logically, one would imagine that the use of intervals smaller than a semitone must in time come into music, and the logic of the matter was recognized long ago. Christopher Simpson, in his *Compendium of Practical Musick* (1667), says:

'Some do fancy that, as the Diatonick scale is made more elegant by a mixture of the Chromatick; so likewise it might be bettered by help of the Enharmonic Scale.'

He is sceptical about the vocal use of microtones, however:

'As to their use in Practical Musick, I am yet to seek. For I do not conceive how a natural voice can Ascend or Descend by such minute Degrees, and hit them right in tune.'

To this we can now reply that the thing has been done. In 1926 Maud McCarthy (Mrs. J. H. Foulds—see above) broadcast a lecture on the Music of India, and in its course sang up and down the Hindu scale of twenty-two notes. The present writer tested her by his piano as she started, as she reached the top, and as she returned to her first note, and can testify that she was exactly in tune. The Hindu system does not employ all these notes in any one tune, but makes a selection from them. For an explanation see A. H. Fox-Strangway's excellent article on *Indian Music*, in the later editions of *Grove's Dictionary*.

The problem is, however, not merely the performance of Quarter-Tones (many vocalists and string players are even clever enough habitually to produce such without ever knowing they are doing it!), but the recognition of them by the listener. Mr. Stokowski alludes to his own difficulty above, and there are few Stokowski ears in an average audience.

Perhaps by the time a later edition of this volume appears the Microtone experiments of Hába and others may have come into the field of practical politics, and in that case they shall receive a fuller treatment.[1] The object of this book, as stated in the Introduction

Temple Church, London, built in 1684, had notes both for E flat and D sharp and A flat and G sharp. Zarlino had more than a century earlier invented a keyboard of nineteen notes to the octave.

[1] The first movement of Hába's *Duo in Sixth-tones for Violins alone* will be found in Album 5 of the present author's *Columbia History of Music* and is also separately obtainable (Col. DB. 1791).

to the first volume, is to help the music lover to a historical understanding of what he is likely to meet in the concert room, &c., and very little intentional microtonic music is yet to be heard.

Most people at present are probably in the position of Christopher Simpson centuries since:

> 'I am slow to believe that any good musick (especially in many parts) can be composed by Quarter-Tones, although I hear much talk of it.'[1]

APPENDIX VI

ON THE TWO EXTREMES IN THE ATTITUDE TO MODERN ART

The following extracts from Hermann Bahr[2] surely show an admirable impartiality. In them the two attitudes that hinder the acceptance of new styles and ideals in Art are equally condemned. The titles I have attached to the passages are my own:

I. THE OLD PHILISTINE

People who for the last twenty years have been accustomed to trust my opinion of Artists are now furious with me, because I endeavour to understand Expressionism. To them this seems anathema! It is amusing, though in rather a sardonic way, to watch them fling about the same arguments which twenty years ago, when they were still young, their elders used against them. They do not notice that they are the old folk now. I, however, mean to remain young, at least in this, that I cannot yet get myself to believe that the world must suddenly come to a standstill. It is curious how every one will allow history to develop only as far as his own arrival on the scene; it may grow and develop only up to his birth. Its whole aim from the beginning seems to have been only to produce him, and once this object is attained history is to progress no more. That it should still dare to proceed, and to advance even beyond him, seems scandalous. And here we are wrangling as to which of us is really the traitor. I accuse them of having been unfaithful to their youthful tradition, which emphatically demanded its own individual expression: a new age is to-day

[1] See a short article by Gerald Hayes in *The Musical Times*, January, 1924.

[2] Mr. R. T. Gribble's Translation of *Expressionism*.

making identical demands. And they accuse me of attaching myself to the adversaries of Impressionism which until lately I had championed. But I still champion it. Its Art still represents for me the highest expression of the spirit of my generation. Yes, even more, it signifies to me the completion, the climax of all classic Art. We only differ in this, that I cannot imagine that mine is the last generation of humanity. But if another generation follows mine, surely it will be a different one. As long as humanity does not die it renews itself, and no son will ever remain satisfied with the work of his father. Friday has a different task from Thursday, says Lagarde. To attain this we had to strive formerly against our elders. Do you remember this no longer? And now a new younger generation has come, and again demands the same right for its own task. You, however, just as those others did in the old days, want to have Thursday lasting for ever. And now you take up the same attitude towards the youth of to-day that those of yesterday held towards you, and you accuse them of the same follies that once so enraged your predecessors against you.

II. THE YOUNG PHILISTINE

That which gives him pleasure he considers inartistic, just because it pleases him. If he is to acknowledge that something pleases him, it must above all really displease him. From the fact that it displeases him, he surmises that it is a work of Art, and so he feels bound to assert his pleasure in it. Art is that which disquiets him, that which offends him, even horrifies him. He says, 'This reacts on me just as Wagner and Ibsen and Manet did on my parents, therefore in thirty years' time its greatness will be acknowledged, and I don't want to be called a fool!' For this reason the present age has a prejudice in favour of everything new; in this lies its contrast with the past. The Philistine of culture has turned completely round and faces in the opposite direction: formerly he stood facing towards yesterday, now he stands facing to-morrow; his chief characteristic used to be resistance, to-day it is defencelessness. One used to be able to recognize him by the fact that he could not be made to advance; to-day he is characterized by his belief that the advance is not rapid enough. He now prides himself on his endeavour to do justice to every new appearance. This is how he would put it; but the question remains whether justice can be done by one who estimates a thing according to its novelty. And this is the only landmark left by which he can take his bearings when dealing with a work of Art. He has been brought up to classify as a work of Art only that which reminds him of the samples shown him while at School; fear has taught him to overcome this tendency, and so he can henceforth only believe that to be a true work of Art which reminds him of nothing he has ever yet seen. It must be something which has never existed before, and the horror he feels will immediately reveal this to him. For this reason too he will be enthusiastic over one *Work of Art* at one moment and unfaithful to it the next, because it can only raise his enthusiasm as long as it remains the newest form of Art, and because he is always haunted by the fear that in the meantime an even newer form of Art will crowd out his *newest*. Hence his irritation, because he has always the feeling of being cheated; he is always searching for the last word, and none ever remains the last; by to-morrow he may already have to renounce his love of to-day. Hence, too, the jealousy of these Philistines of culture amongst each other in their race after novelty, and this is enhanced by the fact that none of them believes that the other is *really* pleased with his latest discovery, for each privately considers every other creature of his kind a deceiver and a cheat—though to his own conscience he excuses himself by the dictum that no one dare lag behind the times, one must be in the swim. It has never before been so difficult, so strenuous, to be a Philistine of culture.

APPENDIX VII

FUTURISM

Futurism was an Italian movement initiated by Marinetti about 1907, and carried on under his direction. As its name implied, its interests looked forward, not backward—so much so that Marinetti, objecting to Italy being considered a museum-country, would have liked to destroy those relics which brought foreigners to her with their eyes turned on her past.

Associated with the musical activities of Marinetti was Russolo, a great inventor of new noises. Some of Marinetti's performances in Italy resulted in a great waste of garden produce on the part of audiences, and police protection had to be provided for him after the performance. Some idea of the nature of Marinetti's musical entertainments will be gathered from the following apologia of Russolo:

The art of music sought first for limpid purity and sweetness of sound. Next, it blended different sounds in an effort to caress the ear with pleasant harmonies. To-day, the art of music seeks to blend sounds that are most dissonant, most strange and strident. We thus approach noise-sounds. This evolution in music is parallel to the growing multiplication of machines which share in human labour. In the resounding atmosphere of our great towns, as in country districts heretofore silent, the machine has to-day created so great a number of varied noises that pure sound, through its smallness and monotony, no longer arouses any emotion. To excite our sensibilities music has developed in seeking a more complex polyphony and greater variety of timbres and of instrumental colour. It strives to obtain successions of the most complicated dissonant chords, and has thus prepared the way for musical noise. This evolution towards noise-sound is only possible to-day. The ear of man in the eighteenth century could never have borne the discordant intensity of certain chords produced by our orchestras (tripled as to the number of performers); our ear, on the contrary, rejoices in it, used as we are to it through our modern life, rich in noises of all sorts. In fact, our ear, far from being satisfied, incessantly demands acoustical sensations still more vast. On the other hand, musical sound is too restricted as to the variety and quality of its timbres. Until now, the number of timbres has not been amplified because of a lack of exact knowledge of the difference which separates sound and noise. We believed it to be enormous and profound. It is minute. In reality it is only a difference of quantity in the number of harmonics (overtones) which accompany the fundamental tone. These harmonics are more numerous in noise than in sound. It was therefore necessary to create instruments constructed in such a way as to give each one the timbre of a noise with the possibility of modifying the pitch of the tone with all the diatonic and chromatic variations. That is what I have realized with my '*bruiteurs*', constructed in collaboration with Ugo Piatti. These instruments are absolutely new, with new timbre and with tone which can be modified at will. With my '*bruiteurs*', diatonic and chromatic melodies may be performed in all possible tones of the scale and in all rhythms. To play the '*bruiteurs futuristes*' one turns a crank with the right hand, and with the left operates a lever which slides on a plane on which the notes of the scale are marked. Some of the '*Bruiteurs*' have, instead of a crank, an electric button which the musician presses in order to give the vibrations which produce the sound noise. Up to the present I have perfected the following twenty-nine '*Bruiteurs*': three *Hululeurs* (low, medium, high), three *Grondeurs* (low, medium, high), three *Crépiteurs* (low, medium, high), three *Strideurs* (low, medium, high), three *Bourdonneurs* (low, medium, high), three *Glouglouteurs* (low, medium, high), two *Eclateurs* (low, high), one *Sibileur* (low), four *Croasseurs* (low, medium, high, very high), four *Froufrouteurs* (low, medium, high, very high).

The low, medium, and high '*bruiteurs*' correspond in a certain manner to the different ranges of the double bass, violoncello and violin, as well as to the different ranges of bass, contralto, and soprano.

The name '*bruitier*' (noise-maker) has led superficial minds to consider my instruments as shocking and cacophonous. But I firmly declare that my '*bruiteurs*' in general and my *glouglouteurs* and *froufrouteurs* in particular are more agreeable to the ear than the sweetest instruments of the orchestra. In my opinion the invention of the '*bruiteurs*' should enrich the orchestra which during two hundred years has hardly been altered in its essential instruments. For this reason I have deemed it appropriate to let my twenty-nine '*bruiteurs*' be heard with the seventeen essential instruments of the orchestra. The six musical compositions which my brother has created, employing an orchestra more varied than any other, will give a variety of harmonic pleasures as surprising as they are delicate.[1]

There were, of course, futurist poets and painters and sculptors connected with the movement (Severini is the best known of the painters, and Boccioni of the sculptors). Marinetti also invented a new art, an art of touch—'Tactilism', a branch of sculpture, apparently, to be felt instead of looked at.

Here is an extract from a report by the Rome correspondent of *The Times* of a performance in Rome of a new Marinetti drama. All reports of his performances, dramatic or musical, resemble this.

Small wonder that the audience grew so furious that towards the end the actors could hardly be persuaded to come on the stage at all. Marinetti himself, who fought well for Italy during the war, supported the bombardment almost without flinching, although he was hit on the head several times by apples and tomatoes and his dress-shirt was spotted with tomato juice, but the company was not quite so brave. When Futurist artists came on the stage carrying paintings they had achieved, they used their masterpieces quite frankly as shields.

[1] Quoted in the New York *Freeman*, 5 July 1922.

At one time when the curtain was down a member of the audience dashed on to the stage to fill his pockets with ammunition that was lying there, but one of the younger Futurists saw him and pursued him, giving him a mighty kick as he jumped into the nearest box, and thereafter the audience was definitely hostile. A vase, several saucers, and five and ten centesimi pieces were hurled at the actors, and the leading lady received a severe blow over the eye from an unripe tomato. The occupants of the orchestra stalls suffered considerably from tomato juice and beans. And the performance came to a premature end when the actors themselves began to hurl vegetables and fruit back at the audience.

After the theatre had closed, Marinetti was badly handled by the mob in the street because he refused to return their money, and he had to be rescued by troops. He had certainly succeeded in rousing the crowd, but it is doubtful if anybody drew any profit from the performance except Marinetti himself, who obviously understands the art of advertising.

There would appear to be little future for Futurism, and readers may sleep quietly in their beds.[1]

[1] After this book, in its first edition, was published Mussolini made Marinetti a Senator and put him in charge of the cultural side of Fascism. Presumably the collapse of the Fascist movement entailed that of the Futurist movement also.

INDEX